Dictionary of
INDOLOGY

Dr. Vishnulok Bihari Srivastava

Published by

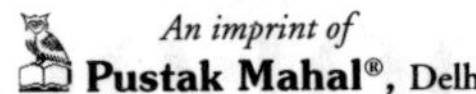

An imprint of
Pustak Mahal®, Delhi
J-3/16, Daryaganj, New Delhi-110002
☎ 23276539, 23272783, 23272784 • *Fax:* 011-23260518
E-mail: info@pustakmahal.com • *Website:* www.pustakmahal.com

Sales Centre
10-B, Netaji Subhash Marg, Daryaganj, New Delhi-110002
☎ 23268292, 23268293, 23279900 • *Fax:* 011-23280567
E-mail: rapidexdelhi@indiatimes.com

• Hind Pustak Bhawan
6686, Khari Baoli, Delhi-110006
☎ 23944314, 23911979

Branch Offices
Bengaluru: ☎ 22234025 • *Telefax:* 22240209
E-mail: pustak@airtelmail.in • pustak@sancharnet.in
Mumbai: ☎ 22010941
E-mail: rapidex@bom5.vsnl.net.in
Patna: ☎ 3294193 • *Telefax:* 0612-2302719
E-mail: rapidexptn@rediffmail.com
Hyderabad: *Telefax:* 040-24737290
E-mail: pustakmahalhyd@yahoo.co.in

ISBN 978-81-223-1084-9
Edition : September 2009

Printed at : Param Offsetters, Okhla, New Delhi-110020

Dedication

To my respected father,
late Dr. Raj Bansh Sahay Hira,
Ph.D. D.Litt., former professor of Hindi, M.U.,
Bodh Gaya, Whose Momery has been a fountain
of inspiration for me at every step.

Publisher's Note

Scriptural Transliteration has not been used in this book **"Dictionary of Indology"**, instead only **'ā'** has been taken from it for long 'a' sound, which is otherwise very difficult to write in Roman Script. Rest of everything is as written in government papers, educational and other institutions, general books, newspapers and magazines etc. It will help the general reader to read and understand easily: numerous Indian words and names. It is difficult to write Shlokas and Indian words in Scriptural Transliteration but more difficult to read. The reason is simple, the writers know about it but most of the readers know almost nothing about the signs used in Scriptural Transliteration.

Names of persons have not been given in Italics to avoid confusion. All the entries have once been given in non-Italicized for the sake of general readers; though, initially they are given in bold-Italics.

Several Samskrit words coined together have been separated for clarity.

Since, the Indians never attached importance to date of birth, death and personal life, so a lot of precious time and energy is regularly wasted in proving or disproving the dates. As far as practicable, we have refrained from them.

Efforts have been taken to reduce the repetition of similar matters, yet repetitions are bound to occur because at their different places they are an integral part of the term being explained. Take for example, the play Abhigyānashākuntalam, which is there as a drama, as the work of the author Kālidāsa as well as mentioned in the Nātyashātra.

The whole book is packed with information, and each reader will get a lot.

Publisher's Note

Abhidhā-vritti-mātrikā: Abhidhā-vritti-mātrikā is a minor work that contains mature ideas on poetics. The authorship is attributed to Mukul Bhatta who became famous in the 9th century. The work justifies *Abhidhā* as the only *Shabda-shakti*, and the other two *Vyanjanā* and *Lakshanā* as its offshoots. The text consists of 15 *kārikās*. The author has written a *vritti* on it. He opposed *vyanjanā* taking it to be an inferior mode of expression. He has discussed ten kinds of *Abhidhās*, and was lenient enough to permeate six kinds of *lakshanā* into it. Mammata was deeply influenced by his formulations. The influence is evident in his *Kāvya Prakāsh*.

Abhigyāna-Shākuntala: Abhigyāna Shākuntala is a drama by Kālidāsa in seven acts. It is based on the love, separation and re-union of Shakuntalā and Dushyanta that comes from the *Ādi Parva* of the *Mahābhārat*. With minor changes the writer has created dramatic effect and given grandeur. It has acquired a new dimension, as the characters are given more liberty to evoke *rasa*. The amorous king of the Mahābhārat is refashioned as a character that is more daring, agile and firm.

Kālidāsa has deliberately introduced the episode of the curse by Durvāsā and the loss of ring to wash away the stains from the character of Dushyanta. For Shakuntalā of Kālidāsa, love is no contract. It defies all considerations.

1st Act: Dushyanta arrives at the hermitage of Kanva in his absence and fascinated by her beauty falls in love with Shakuntalā who readily gives consent to his proposal.

2nd Act: A messenger urges Dushyant to return to the kingdom to partake in the rituals being performed by the queen. He confides in his friend Mādhava who backed out and did not proceed to the capital.

3rd Act: Shakuntalā is shown writing letters to Dushyant to lessen the pain of the agonising separation.

4th Act: Dushyant returns to the kingdom and gives a ring to Shakuntalā for identification. Maharishi Durvāsā comes to the hermitage but finds none to greet him. Shakuntalā is lost in the memory of her lover. Out of anger Durvāsā curses her that, he would forget her in whose memory she is so deeply engrossed. She awakens and prostrates before the Rishi begging for forgiveness. He calms down and shows a way that a mark of identity will give his memory back and her friend can identify her husband. Grief gripped the hermitage when Shakuntalā departs for her husband's palace.

5th Act: Shakuntalā arrives at the court but Dushyanta fails to recognise her, as she had lost the ring en route. She is abandoned and gets shelter from seer Marichi.

6th Act: The courtiers take the ring from a fisherman and give it to the king who regains the memory and realises his mistake. He launches a search operation to find Shakuntalā.

7th Act: Dushyant reaches the cottage of Marichi and is astonished to see a boy playing with a lion. He catches hold of a magical gem falling from the hand of the boy. It remains unchanged though it would have changed into a stone if touched by a person other than the boy's father. The surprised maid informs Shakuntalā and the identity of Dushyanta is revealed. She is handed over to her husband. The play ends on a pleasant note.

Abhinava: Abhinava was a 10th century poet of Kashmir. He wrote an epic *Kādambari-sāra*. He has narrated the story of Kādambari in *Anushtupa Chhanda*. He was the son of Jayant I, an eminent critic of *Nyāya Darshan*.

Abhinava Gupta: Abhinava Gupta was an eminent critic and philosopher. He wrote *Abhinava Bhārati* and *Dhvanyāloka-lochana*. These commentaries are of immense importance. Other than these two he wrote 39 more books on criticism, meditation and grammar. While his critical formulations contribute to his philosophical ideology, his philosophy has a direct bearing on his criticism. He has tried to resolve the problem of *Rasa* with the help of *Shaivāgam* theory. His theory of *rasa-nispati* is called *Abhyukti-vāda*. He says that *rasa* is generated through *vyanjanā*. He has conceived *dhvani* as the soul of poetry, which survives because of its ability to generate *rasa*. For him, pleasure is the ultimate end of poetry.

Abhinava Gupta is in accord with modern psychological approach. He overshadows the interpretations given by the critics like Bhatta Lollata, Shri Sankuka and Bhatta Nāyaka, with his interpretations of the terms *samyoga* and *rasa nispati*. He termed it as *prakāshya-prakāshaka* relationship

The dormant emotions preserved in the heart as *vāsanā* flow out as *rasa* through *vibhāvanā vyāpāra* of *vyanjana vritti* with the help of *vibhāva, anubhāva* and *sanchāri- bhāva*. Smell already lies in a pitcher, which comes out when water is poured in it. Likewise, the dormant emotion preserved in the heart of the reader or spectator comes out in the form of *rasa* after reading *kāvya* or watching a play performed on the stage.

Abhinava Kālidāsa: Abhinava Kālidāsa was a court poet of Rāja Shekhara, the king of Vijaya Nagar Empire. He wrote *Bhāgavata Champu* in six stavakas based on the 10th Skanda of Shrimad Bhāgavata, and Abhinava's Champu deals with the amorous life of the court. His description passes all moral boundaries.

Abhisheka: Abhisheka by is a drama by Bhāsa, based on the coronation of Sugriva by Rāma. The title reflects the coronation. Moved by the plight and suffering of his friend Sugriva, the deposed king of *Kishkindhā*, Rāma promises to win back his kingdom. He eliminates Bāli while the two, Bāli and Sugriva were locked in pitched battle and restores him his kingdom.

Bhāsa has tried his level best to give his drama originality and a distinct look. He has described several incidents from the *Rāmāyana* in his way to give an added colour and flavour to *Abhisheka*. He gives plausible arguments to justify the killing of Bāli. Rāma is made to cross over the ocean without a bridge. In his Bāla Charita, a drama based on Bhāgavata, Vasudeva is forced to cross over Yamunā without a bridge. He has used simple and evocative language to bring home the ideas. At places, the character of Bāli seems to have an edge over that of Rāma, as Rāma is shown only as an archer.

Ādi Purāna: Ādi Purāna is the oldest among the 24 *Purānas* and is attributed to Jains. It deals with the story of the first Jain Tirthankara Rishabha Deva. It consists of 12 thousand *shlokas*, divided into 47 *parvas*. Jinasena, the successor of Shankarāchārya, has written it. Rishabha Deva was the 8th of the 24 incarnations of Vishnu described in the Purānas. He was a Yogi and propogated *Parama-hansa* Religion. He was *digambar* and partially abnormal. He finished his life by self-immolation. Marudevi was his mother. He opposed Monism and tried to formulate independent ideas about the creation of the universe including the living and non-living beings.

Agni Purāna: Agni Purāna, chronologically, is the 8th *Purāna*, the encyclopedia of Indology presenting the entire gamut of knowledge coming down the ages. It covers subjects like grammar, medical science, dictionary, poetics and astrology, and different kinds of *riti, vritti* and *abhinaya*, forms of epic, five forms of *gadya kāvya* along with *akhyāyikā, kathā, khanda kathā, pari-kathā* and *kathānikā*. Seven forms of *padya* have been referred to: *Mahākāvya, kalp, prabandha, visheshaka, kulaka, muktaka* and *kosha*. Different *rupakas*, forms of *rasa*, classes of *Nāyikā* and figures of speech are the added attraction. It consists of 383 chapters and 11,457 *shlokas*.

Akāla-Jalada: Akāla Jalada was the grand father of the eminent critic Rāja Shekhara who belonged to 8th century. No written work of Akāla Jalada is available. His *sukties* are found in the collections like *Sārangadhara*.

Alankāra Sarvasva: Alankāra Sarvasva is a celebrated work on *alankāra* by Rājānaka Ruyyaka. It has three sections: *sutra, vritti* and illustrations. Illustrations have been quoted from other works. His commentator Jayaratha put a curtain on all speculations and controversies by accepting Ruyyaka as the author of both the *sutras* and *vritti*. Ruyyaka's credit lies in a scientific division of *Alankāras*.

Amar Chandra Suri: Amar Chandra Suri is a famous Jain poet and is placed between 1241 and 1260 AD. His epic *Bāla Mahābhārata* comprises of 44 cantos and 6,950 *shlokas*. He has presented a brief account of *Mahābhārat* in a simple and in ornate language. His other works are *Kavi-kalpa-latā* and *Padma-nanda*. A disciple of Jinadatta Suri, he was the court poet of king Vishāla Deva.

Amar Kosha: Amar Kosha is an authentic dictionary of Samskrit by Amar Singh. He has done a stupendous work by compiling this monumental dictionary written in a unique style of synonyms. It shows his in-depth study as a scholar, which is reflected throughout the work. The amazing fact is that it is still accepted as an authority. He has spun out the roots or genesis from which a particular word is coined. Succeeding dictionary writers have borrowed immensely from him.

Amaru Shataka: Amaru Shataka is erotic poetry, which has never been reckoned as poetic creation, and has survived in the laps of folk songs and *Prākrit*. Many poets and scholars have tried to revive it but the mass sentiment could not digest it. In the middle ages it took shelter in courts as the amorous descriptions suited its milieu.

In *Amaru Shataka*, the stanzas are not tied like the flowers of a garland. The thread has been loosened allowing each stanza to retain its independence and be a part of the whole. Life in its multiple facets, have been appropriately expressed with the depiction of both the brighter and darker sides of life.

Ambikā Datta Vyāsa: Ambikā Datta Vyāsa was an eminent poet, prose writer and dramatist of the 19th century. His popularity rests on his prose work *Shiva-rāja-vijaya* written on the pattern of *Kādambari*.

Ānanda Rāmāyana: Ānanda Rāmāyana is the principal work of Rasika sect of Rāma bhakti. Several examples from Ādhyātma Rāmāyana have been given in it. It has 9 chapters and 12,352 shlokas. **The 1st, Sāra Kānda** has 13 sargas and deals with the story from birth till the abduction of Sitā. **The 2nd, Yātrā Kānda** has 9 sargas and deals with Rāma's journey to various pilgrimage centers. **The 3rd Yagya Kānda**, has 9 sargas and deals with Ashwamegha Yagya performed by Rāma. **The 4th, Vilāsa Kānda**, describes the beauty of Sitā in all its grandeur. **The 5th, Janma Kānda**, deals with the birth of Luva and Kusha. **The 6th, Vivāha Kānda**, highlights the marriages of eight sons of the four brothers. **The 7th, Rājya Kānda** has 9 sargas and describes the victories of Rāma. **The 8th, Manohar Kānda**, depicts the methods of worshipping Lord Rāma. **The last one** has 9 sargas and describes the coronation of Kusha and the departure of Rāma and Sitā to heaven.

Ānand Varman: Ānand Varman was an eminent critic and the exponent of the school of *dhvani*. He accepted *dhvani* as the kernel or essence of poetry, rejected *avidhā* and relegated *alankāra, riti, vritti* and *guna* to lower pedestal with his famous work *Dhvanyā-loka*, which is written in *kārikā* and *vritti*. He divided *dhvani* in three broad divisions: *vastu dhvani* (content suggestion); *alankāra dhvani* (figurative suggestion); and *rasa dhvani* (emotional or aesthetic suggestion). Only *rasa dhvani* is appreciated and relished. It is held that *rasa* gets revealed only in *vyanjana*.

Later on, Māhima Bhatta overshadowed him and in *Vyakti-viveka* pointed out many shortcomings in Ānand Varman's theory of *dhvani*.

According to *Rāja-tarangani* Ānand Varman was a contemporary of Avanti Varman, a 9th century king of Kashmir. Besides *Dhvanyāloka* he has also written *Arjuna-charit, Devi-shataka, Tatva-loka* and *Visham-vana-lilā*.

Anant Deva: Anant Deva, the grand son of Ekanāth, was a political commentator of 17th century, associated with the court of king Rāja Bahādura Chandra. He wrote a political treatise *Rāja-dharma-kaustubha* at the behest of the king. It is divided in four sections called *Dadhiti* and consists of 88 chapters dealing with the royal duty. In place of formulating novel theories and ideology, he has discussed the accepted principles related to royal duty and state religion. His other works are: *Sainika-shāstra*, *Trivirnaka Dharma* and a drama *Krishna Bhakti Chandrkā*.

Anargha Rāghava: Anargha Rāghava is a drama in seven acts by Murāri. It lacks artistic grandeur, structural harmony and dramatic skill. Some acts run in 200 verses and some contain only 50 verses. Some dialogues are very long and some are cut short, and some descriptions are redundant which destroy the intensity and beauty of the drama.

It deals with the story of Rāma from the arrival of Vishwāmitra to the court of Dasharatha onwards.

Summary

1st Act: Vishwāmitra seeks the permission of Dasharatha to take away Rāma and Lakshamana to thwart the designs of the demons to enable the Rishis to perform *yagyas* peacefully.

2st Act: Rāma displays his ability as a seasoned warrior killing several demons including the most dreaded Tārakā.

3st Act: Deals with the svayamavara of Sitā. Rāma breaks the bow of Shiva.

4st Act: Rāvana approaches his sister Shurpanakhā who changes herself into a maidservant of Kaikeyi and suggests her to send Rāma into exile to clear the way for Bharata using the promises by Dasharatha.

5st Act: Rāma along with Sitā and Lakshamana leaves for the forest and kills many demons. With the help of Mārich Rāvana abducts Sitā, faces a stiff opposition from Jatāyu, kills him and comes to Lankā with Sitā. Rāma meets Sugriva, kills Bāli and Sugriva gets the throne again.

6st Act: Rāma, with Sugriva and his army of monkeys, invades Lankā, kills Rāvana.

7st Act: Rāma and Sitā are reunited, return to *Ayodhyā* with associates.

Angirā Smriti: Angirā Smriti is a work on moral codes of conduct composed by the renowned ancient Rishi Angirā. The prose extracts of this text are available in *Smriti Chandikā*. Only 72 *shlokas* of *Angirā Smriti* are available in *Jivānanda Samhitā*. It deals with receiving edible and potable materials from the

Shudras, the atonement for causing physical injury to cow, and on the method of putting blue garments by women.

Annan Bhatta: Annan Bhatta was a prominent scholar of *Nyāya* School of philosophy. His reputation rests on his seminal work *Tarka Samgraha*, the *Dipikā* (commjentary) on *Tarka Samgraha* and commentaries like *Rankojjvāni,* (on *Nyāya Sutra*); *Brahman Sutra Vyākhyā; Ashtādhyāyi-tikā; Udyotana; Siddhānjana* (on Jaideva's *Chandra-loka*). Among the 25 commentaries on *Tarka Samgraha, Nyāya Bodhini* by Govardhana Mishra and *Nila-kanthi-tikā* by Nila Kantha Dikshit are important.

Anukramani: Anukramani is an index of Vedic gods, ascetics and *Chhandas*. Each Veda has a separate *Anukramani*. These are designed to preserve Vedas from the rust of time. Shaunaka has written ten *Anukramani* texts; five of them present detailed account of gods, Rishis and *Chhandas* in ten *mandals* with *anuvākas* and *sutras*. They are metrical compositions in *Anushtupa Chhanda*. His *Brihad-devatā* presents elaborate description of Rig Vedic gods in 12,000 *shlokas*.

Kātyāyana's *Sarva-anukramani*, another popular work, contains the *richās* of Rig Veda, name and *gotra* of Rishis and gods of each *mantra* and *chhanda*. The number of *Anukramani* on Sāma Veda exceeds the other Vedas. Kātyāyana has compiled another work, *Shukla-yaju-sarva-anukrama-sutra* in five chapters.

Āpastamba Dharma Sutra: The 28th and the 29th questions of *Āpastamba-kalpa-sutra* is called Āpastamba Dharma Sutra. Its language is more primitive than that of *Baudāyana Dharma sutra*. Its several findings resemble those of Jaimini, and many words from *Mimāmsā* School are incorporated in its texture. It may have been written in 600 BC, and Āpastamba's place of living may have been *Matasya Desha*.

Apishali: Apishali was a predecessor of Pānini. His sutras have been frequently quoted in *Ashtādhyāyi, Mahābhāsya Nyāsa* and *Mahābhāsya Pradip*. Besides grammar he has written four other books: *Dhātu-pātha, Ganapātha, Shikshā* and *Unādi Sutra*.

Appaya Dikshit: Appaya Dikshit was an eminent grammarian, philosopher and critic. He has written more than hundred books on wide ranging subjects. He was the most revered scholar in the court of Shāhji, the king of Tanjore. His works on poetics gave him popularity. They are: *Vritti Vartikā; Kuvalayānand* and *Chitra-mimāmsā*. *Kuvalayānand*, based on Jaideva's *Chandra-loka* is the most successful work in which he has added 24 other *alankāras*. His merit lies in pointing out the shortcomings of *Lakshanās* and in an appropriate description and analysis of *alankāras*.

Āranyaka: Āranyakas are part of Vedas and include the books by people retiring to forests after successfully completing their worldly responsibilities and duties. *Āranyakas* are entirely different from *Brāhmanas*, and are called *parshishta* (appendix) of *Brāhamanas*.

Āryabhatta II: Āryabhatta II was a scholar of astrology. He has written a significant book *Mahā-Ārya-Siddhānta*. It is divided in 18 chapters. The entire text is written in *Ārya Chhanda*. They are 625 in number. Besides discussing various aspects of Jyotisha, he has included Mathematics and thus widened its scope. The details of his life are not known.

Ārya Saptashati: Ārya Saptashati is a *Muktaka Kāvya* by Govardhāchārya in 700 *Ārya Chhandas* on the pattern used by famous *Pāli* poet Hala's *Gāthā-saptashati*. He had the patronage of Lakshamana Sena, the king of Bengāl. He flourished around 1116 AD. *Ārya Saptshati* is a work of *Shringār-rasa* in its twin form: *Samyoga* and *Viyoga* (union and separation). It depicts the gesticulations of both countrywomen and women living in posh-areas. The poet has taken the recourse of *Anyokti alankāra* for expressing *shringāra*.

Āryodaya Mahākāvya: Āryodaya Mahākāvya is a poetic history of Indian civilization. It brings out its merits that have made it the most pioneering and promising of all the ancient civilizations. Pt. Gangā Prasād Upādhyāya wrote it in 21 chapters and 1,166 *shlokas* in two sections: **the 1st** aimed at describing the grandeur of Indian culture while **the 2nd** deals with Swāmi Dayānand Sarswati. The epic begins with the description of the universe that culminates in the plot hatched for the assassination of Swāmi Dayānand Saraswati.

Āshcharya Chudāmani: Āshcharya Chudāmani is the only extant book of Shaktibhadra available. The other *Unmāda-vāsava-datta* is only referred to, but is not available. *Āshcharya Chudāmani* is a dramatic version of Rāma's story. Its specialty lies in the *nispati* of *Āshcharya rasa*, which is a rare phenomenon in poetry. He has written two books on drama: *Tāpti Svyambara* and *Subhadrā-Dhananjaya*.

Ashtādhyāyi: Ashtādhyāyi is an excellent book on grammar. It is the oldest work on the structure of words. It is divided in 8 chapters: each chapter consists of 4 *padas*. With the addition of 14 *Pratyāhāra Sutras* the number of *Sutras* in it goes up to 3,995. **The first two chapters** deal with *Subanta pada*, division of *tinganta* and their relationship in a sentence. **The third chapter** discusses *Shabda-shakti*, (the power of words) where as **the 4th** and **the 5th chapters** are devoted to *Pratipadikā* and *shabda-siddhi*. **The 6th and the 7th chapters** revolve round the *siddhi* of *pratyayātmaka* of *tinganta* words and *swars*. **The 8th chapter** deals with the impact of *swars* and *varnas*.

The topics falling under the compass of Ashtādhyāyi include: noun and its definition; distinction between *swars* and *vyanjanas; dhātu-siddhi-kriyā-pada; kāraka; vibhakti; samāsa; kridanta; subanta; taddhita; āgam; ādesha; swar-vichāra*; and *sandhi*.

Ashwaghosha: Ashwaghosha was a renowned Buddhist poet and philosopher. Buddhist scriptures testify that he was contemporary of Kanishka, the *Kushāna* king who ascended the throne in 78 AD. He participated in the 4th Buddhist *Sangati* convened by Kanishka at *Kundala-vana* in Kashmir. His name has also been mentioned in the *Sārnātha* inscription of Kanishka.

The poetic skill of Ashwaghosha is evident in *Buddha-Charita* in 28 cantos and in *Saunderānand*. *Buddha Charita* deals with the causes leading to the foundation of Kapilvastu; the birth of Buddha and Nanda; Nanda falling in love with Sundari and the conflict and grief of the couple. The rest of the book is marred by philosophical ideology leaving him more as a preacher than a poet.

A drama named *Sāri-puta-prakarana* has also been assigned to him. It deals with Maudalyāyana and Sāriputra being initiated in

Buddhist cult by Lord Buddha. It has all the dramatic elements: *nandi*; preface; *sutra-dhāra*; synthesis of prose and poetry and use of words both from Samskrit and *Prākrit*. In his works he has profusely discussed the doctrines of Buddhism in simple and general language. There is a confluence of *shringāra, karunā* and *shānta rasa* in his works.

Atharva Veda: Atharva signifies magic, sorcery and witchcraft. It is concerned with the activities related to *mārana, mohan* and *uchchātana*. It is a collection of hymns and mantras of several sacred rites. Atharva Rishi perceived them. Previously it was called *Atharva-āngirasa*, which included two Rishis Atharva and Āngirasa. Its words have been taken from local dialects. The *ritvija* of Atharva Veda is *Adhvaryu* who recites the hymns at the time of *yagya*. It consists of 20 *kāndas*, 731 *suktas* and 5,987 hymns. In each *kānda* there are *prapāthakas, anuvāka, sukta* and *mantra*. There are 34 *pratipāthakas*, 111 *anuvāka*, 731 *suktas* and 5,849 *mantras*. About 1,200 hymns have been taken from Rig Veda. The first 13 chapters deal with *mārana, mohan* and *uchchātan* and the rest with the ritual of marriage. Out of its nine branches, only *Pippalāda* and *Shaunakiya* are available. The subjects are physical, (king, statecraft, battle, enemy, vehicle); spiritual (Brahma, *Parmātmā* and the four stages of life); and celestial (God, *Yagya* and Time). Indra, Varuna and Maitreya have been described as manifestations of the same Almighty. Some of the *suktas* are related to diseases and remedy.

Atharva Veda Pratisākhya Sutra: Atharva Veda Pratisākhya Sutra is aimed at unveiling the mystery associated with the study of Atharva Veda. It helps us understand it.

Āyurveda: Āyurveda is the branch of Vedas that teaches how to achieve longevity by leading a disciplined life and using herbal medicines. It has eight organs: *shalya chikitsā* (surgery); *salkya* (diseases related to ears, eyes, *ghrāna* and throat); *kāya chikitsā; Bhuta Vidyā; Kaumārya Bhartya* (diseases related to children); *agada tantra* (treatment of poison); *rasāyana tantra* (treatment with chemicals); and *vājikarana tantra* (rejuvenating a man).

The chief exponent of Āyurveda is Dhanvantari who emerged out from the churning of the ocean with *Amrita Kalash* (Nectar). Aitareya, Kashyapa, Harita, Agnivesha, Bheda, Charak, Sushruta, Jivaka and Vāga Bhatta are associated with. *Āyurveda, Vaidyaka Shāstra*. They were great *Vaidyas* and have written treatises on it, called *Samhitā*. ■■

Bāla-Rāmāyana: Bāla Rāmāyana is a mega-drama by Rājashekhara consisting of 10 acts. The plot of this drama is based on the story of Rāma from the *svayamavara* of Sitā to Rāma's return to *Ayodhyā* after killing Rāvana. The **first act** is called *pratigya-paulastya*. It deals with Rāvana's participation in the *svayamvara* of Sitā, and his resolve to marry her. He expresses his desire before Janaka to marry Sitā and leaves the palace in wrath on Janaka's refusing to accede to his proposal. The **second act** is called *Rāma-Rāvaniya*. Parsrurāma bursts into anger after listening to the proposal of Rāvana, and prepares to settle scores with him. The war between the two is averted. The **third act** is called *Lankesvara* act. In this act, the scene of the *svayamvara* of Sitā is shown on the stage to flatter Rāvana but the latter is infuriated losing his temper while watching the scene of Rāma breaking the bow and Sitā garlanding him. His anger soon goes down and he reconciles himself to the situation. The **fourth act** is called *Bhārgava* act, which depicts the battle between Rāma and Parasurāma. The **fifth act** is called *Unamatta Dasānana*. It shows Rāvana gripped with panic for failing in his attempt to win Sitā, and gets consolation with the wooden idol of Sitā. The **sixth act** is called *Nirdosa Dasharatha*. It deals with the incident of Rāma's leaving for exiled life in forest. The **seventh act** is called *Asama-parākrama*. It describes the scintillating and sparkling dialogue between Rāma and Samudra on the issue of erecting a bridge on the sea. The **eighth act** has been referred to as *Vira Vilāsa*, which depicts the battle between Rāma and Rāvana and the killing of Meghanāda and Kumbhakarana. Rāvana tries to create panic in the heart of Sitā by showing her the illusory head of Rāma. In the **ninth act**, Rāvana is killed. The **last act** is called *Sānanda Raghunātha*. It deals with the fire-test of Sitā and the latter emerging victorious out of it. Rāma leaves for *Ayodhyā* along with Sitā and Lakshmana boarding the *Puspaka Vimāna*.

The drama lacks in dramatic skill and the dramatist has unnecessarily stretched the story causing vexation to the readers. Instead of depicting the incidents associated with Rāma, the poet has taken more care in depicting the incidents occurring in the life of Rāvana. He has also drifted from the original story of Rāma as depicted in *Vālmikiya Rāmāyana* and has tried to make major changes in the original text using his imagination to give his text a distinct look. The staging of the *svayamvara* of Sitā and Rāvana's consoling himself by erecting a wooden statue of Sitā are the episodes deliberately introduced to the framework of the drama to create dramatic effect. Rājashekhara has failed to create effect by stretching it to funny length. The drama lacks movement and flow.

Bālacharita: Bāla Charita is a drama by Bhāsa in five acts based on the story of childhood days of Shri Krishna as narrated in *Harivansa Purāna*. It incorporates the story from the birth of Krishna till the killing of Kansa. The **first act** depicts the story of the birth of Krishna and Vāsudeva shifting him to *Gokula*. The **second act** deals with the killing of Yashoda's daughter who was substituted for Krishna but she miraculously survived. The **third act** deals with the *lilās* of Krishna including the killing of Putanā, Keshi, Sakata and Dhenuka. The **fourth act** deals with the story of Krishna giving a fitting reply to the arrogant snake Kāliya-nāga forcing it to abandon the river Yamunā along with his family. The **fifth** and final act deals with the exploits of Krishna and Balarāma at the court of Kansa, the wrestling with Mushtika and Chānura culminating into the killing of the dreaded wrestlers and Kansa too. *Vira-rasa* is the dominant *rasa* of this drama.

The dramatist has violated the established rules of classical drama by depicting the execution of Arista, Chānura and Kansa on the stage.

He seems to be at the loggerheads with accepted dramatic conventions and is more concerned with creating dramatic effects at the cost of flouting well-established rules and regulations.

Bānabhatta: Bāna Bhatta is the most celebrated prose-writer of Samskrit Literature. His popularity rests on his prose works *Kādambari* and *Harsha-charita*. Besides this, he has also compiled *Chandi-shataka* in *Shragdhara Chhanda,* which consists of 100 *shloka*s expressing his devotion to Chandi. The text is not available, its reference is found in *Sukti-granthas*. The ornamental style of Subandhu's prose writing is mirrored in the writings of Bānabhatta. He laid emphasis on the external embellishment of his prose and used almost all the weapons available in his armoury to give a new tint and colour to Samskrit prose. From Bāna onwards a new trend emerged, which preferred figurative expression to plain expression. He gave vent to terse and high-flown style avoiding the simple one. In this respect he differs from Kālidāsa who seldom tries to play on words. His command over description often falters and a series of sub-plots intrude into the framework of the main-plot. In the introduction to *Harsha-charita*, Bāna has pinned up faith in a style or diction marked by an expression coupled with puns and decorated with poetic figures aimed at creating miraculous meaning. The beauty of Bāna's prose work lies in his amazing descriptive acumen.

Three distinct forms of Bāna's prose style are evident: *Dirgha-samāsa-vati, Alpa-samāsa-vati* and *Samāsa-rahita*. They are called *Utkalikā*, *Churnaka* and *Abhiddhā* respectively. He has taken recourse to *Utkalikā* in long statements. He has cultivated beauty, refinement, sophistication and balance during the description of his prose work in order to revive fantastic flavour and colour. Except a few passages, Bāna's style has been more or less comprehensible. He has also introduced small dialogues according to the requirement of the situation. His prose works maintain the pace and rhythm of poetry and his muse has come out with varied facets and colours to make an artistic portrayal of the natural beauty and thus has added warmth and vigour to his prose. Moved by his amazing and miraculous narrative tecnique, scholars have rightly observed '*Bānochchhistam Jagat Sarvam'* (The rest of the works are merely imitation of Bāna). Bāna invited the ire of some critics for his terseness, excessive love for poetic figures, unfamiliar diction and long statements coupled with exaggerated expressions. He will continue to rule the roost of the readers for the artistic grandeur which he cultivated in his prose using unique narrative technique, verbal music, terse diction and rhythmical combination of words.

Baudhāyana Dharmasutra: Baudhāyana Dharma Sutra is a text of *Dharmashāstra* written by Baudhānyana. It is not available in complete form. It consists of eight chapters and most of them have been written in *shloka*s.

The list of subjects which it consists includes customs practised in the north and the south, atonement, duties of *Brahmācharin*, significance of celibacy, rules regarding significance of *yagya* and the duties of a king, five severe offences and punishments accorded for committing grave offences, punishment for killing birds, rules for purgation from *Brahmahatyā* and other evil deeds, kinds of will, right of elder son, atonement by man and woman for adultery, methods of *Niyoga* and rules of *Samyāsa*.

Bhāguri: Bhāguri was a grammarian of the pre-Pānini period. The reference to his grammatical text is available in Jagadisha Tarkālankāra's *Shabda-shakti-prakāshikā*. His works include *Bhāguri Vyākarana*, *Sāmavediya-shākhā*, *Trikānda-kosha*, *Sāmkhyabhāsya* and *Daivata-granthi*. Somesvara has quoted him in *Sāhitya-kalpa-druma* and Abhinavagupta in *Dhvanyā-loka-lochana*.

Bhāmah: Bhāmah was a prominent rhetorician and author of the text *Kāvyālankāra*. It is the earliest work on *Alankāra*. Bhāmah is supposed to be the exponent of *Alankāra Sampradāya* and has accepted *alankāra* as the most significant element of *kāvya*. He flourished in the middle of the sixth century. It has been established from the reference to *Dinga-nāga* found in *Kāvyālankāra*. Many critics have acknowledged Bhāmah as the successor of Dandin but now it has been proved that Bhāmah was the predecessor of Dandin.

Bhāmah enjoyed an independent stature among rhetoricians. He brought *alankāra* to a new height. He strictly made it clear that as a young lady loses her charm without ornaments so, the poetry loses its efficacy without *alankāra*.

Kāvyālankāra is divided into 6 chapters and contains 398 verses. The **first chapter** containing sixty verses describes the making of a poet and difference between prose and poetry. This chapter also covers *vaidarbhi* and *gaudi* styles and literary blemishes. The **second chapter** is devoted to the discussion of *madhura, prasāda*, and *Oaj gunas* and the description of as many as 39 *alankāras*. The description of *alankāras* continues unabated to the **third chapter** also. He does not admit the status of *hetu, sukshma, lesha* and *vritta* amid *alankāras*, since they are badly wanting in *vakrokti*. The **fourth chapter** deals with 11 kinds to poetic blemishes and the **fifth chapter** is devoted to the causes of poetic blemishes. The **sixth chapter** is a modest suggestion to the poet to maintain grammatical accuracy to make their work readable.

Bhana: Bhana is a kind of *Rupaka* describing the wicked. Several texts on *Bhana* have been written in Samskrit. A text entitled *Chaturbhani* has been published from Kerala in four volumes. The authors of this text are Vararuchi, Ishvaradatta, Shyāmalika, and Shudraka. *Vararuchi* has written another *Bhana* named *Ubhaya-abhisārikā*. It has a very lucid and enriched style. One more *Bhana* entitled *Padma-parābhritaka* has been attributed to Shudraka. One of its *shlokas* is quoted in Hemachandra's *Kāvyānushāsana*. It deals with the story of Muladeva, an ancient artist. Ishvaradatta's *Bhana* is known as *Dhurta-vita-samvāda*, which passes a scathing remark on harlots through the dialogue between Dhurta and Vita. Among other *bhanas* in Samskrit, Bāmanabhatta's *Shringāra bhushana*, Rāmabhadra Dikshita's *Shringāra Tilaka*, Vardāchārya's *Vasanta Tilaka*, Shankara Kavi's *Sharadā-tilaka*, Nallakavi's *Shringāra-sarvasva* and Yuvarāja's *Rasa-sadana Bhana* are worth noting.

Bhangaduta: Bhagna-duta is a form of *Duta-kāvya* written by the 8th century poet Shrikrishna Deva. No exact evidence is available about the writer. It is based on Kālidāsa's *Meghaduta*. It consists of 126 *mandākrāntā chhandas*. Agonised by the separation of Krishna, a *gopi* sends her message to him through the black bee. Towards the end of the message, Krishna appears before the *gopi* blessing her with divine grace.

Bhanga Sandesha: Bhanga Sandesha embodies the message to beloved by Vasudeva, a 15th or 16th century poet. He was the court poet of the king of Calicut. He had also written a *kāvya* entitled *Vasudeva-vijaya* by way of an analysis of the sutras of Pānini. It is incomplete. His other works include *kāvya*s such as *Devi-charita, Shivodaya* and *Achyuta-lilā*. The story of *Bhanga Sandesha* is imaginary. The structural pattern is based on the *Meghaduta*. The services of the black bee is sought to send the message by the lover to his ladylove. Like *Meghaduta* it has been divided into *Purva* and *Uttara* sections and the poet has used *mandākrāntā chhanda* as well. *Purva* section consists of 95 *shloka*s and *Uttara* section consists of 80 *shloka*s.

Bhānudatta: Bhānudatta was a renowned critic belonging to the later half of the 13th century. His popularity basically rests on his twin treatises *Rasa Manjari* and *Rasa Tarangini*. Besides them four other works: *Alankāra-tilaka*, *Chitra-chandrikā*, *Gitagaurisha* and *Kumār Bhārgaviya* have also been attributed to him. *Rasamanjari* is a mature work dealing with *Nāyaka-Nāyikā bheda*. It has been written in the form of sutras. Achārya Gopal had written a commentary entitled *Viveka* on it. *Rasatarangini* presents a scientific analysis of *Rasa* particularly the various components of *Rasa* including *Bhāva, Vibhāva*, *Anubhāva* and *Sanchāri-bhāva*. Bhānudatta has borrowed substantially from *Dasha-rupaka*. It consists of 8 *tarangas*. *Alankāra-tilaka* is based on *Sarasvati-kantha-bharana*, which deals with several forms of *kāvya* such as *Alankāra*, *guna, riti, dosha*, and *Kāvya-bheda*. The style of Gitagovinda has been followed in the lyrical poetry *Gita-gaurisha*.

Bhānudatta has accepted *shringāra* as the dominant *rasa* and merged rest of the *rasas* into it. He has accepted *Rasa* as the soul of poetry. He has made three categories of *Kāvya*: *uttama, madhyama* and *adhama*. He has also accepted two types of *rasas*: earthly (*laukika*) and unearthly (*alaukika*). All the *rasas* including *shringāra* are placed in the category of *laukika*. *Alaukika rasa* has been divided into *Svapnika, Manorathika* and *Aupnayika*.

Bharata: Bharata was an eminent scholar of poetics and the author of *Nātya Shāstra,* which is an encyclopaedic dictionary.

He was a versatile genius. His muse finds expression in *Nātya Shāstra* (dramaturgy), *Sangeeta* (music), *Kāvya-shāstra* (poetics) and *Nritya* (dance). He has made a minute and scientific analysis of these topics. His analysis of *Rasa* is based on dramas available during his period. He recognised only 8 *Rasas*. He codified one *sutra* for the manifestation of *Rasa*. This sutra is that Rasa is manifested by the co-ordination and crystallisation of *Bhāva, Vibhāva, Anubhāva* and *Sanchāribhāva*: (*Bhāva-vibhāva-anubhāva-sanchāri-bhāvasam-yogatra-sa-nispattih*). The sutra was later variously interpreted by four Samskrit critics Sri Shankuka, Bhatta Lollata, Bhatta Nāyaka and Abhinava Gupta. Bharata's analysis of *Rasas* is very authentic. His opinion on music is equally important. He, for the first time, made the analysis of four poetic figures, *Upamā, Rupaka, deepaka* and *Yamaka*.

Bharata's contributions to the enrichment of Samskrit poetics cannot be ignored. There are certain practical difficulties in bringing together *Bhāva* like comic (*Hāsya*) and the pathetic (*Karuna*) or erotic (*Shringāra*) and gruesome (*Vibhatsa*). Mere experience of Bhāva is not Rasa. Rasa is the state that follows such an experience. The recollection (*smarana*) and the relish (*āsvāda*) of that experience is *Rasa*. *Rasa* emerges when the Bhāvas are properly combined. *Rasa*, supported by inadequate *Bhāva*, is what he calls fugitive *Rasa (Rasa-bhāsa).*

Bhāravi: Bhāravi was a great Samskrit poet who achieved the distinction of making a new way out of the tender and delicate poetry of Kālidāsa. He is credited with introducing ornamental style of poetry, which reigned supreme during post Kālidāsa period. His fame chiefly rests on his epic poetry *Kirāt-Arjuniya*.

The plot of *Kirāt-Arjuniya* is based on the story described in the *Vana parva* of the *Mahābhārata*. It depicts the fight, which Arjuna had to wage against *Shiva* who disguised himself in the form of a Kirāt. Arjuna was deputed on a mission to secure *Pashupatāstra* from Shiva in order to ensure victory in the ensuing battle of *Mahābhārata*. But the poet seems to have travelled a long distance in introducing situations and episodes, which have no connection with the main story. Bhāravi is also said to have fallen prey to the existing norms of poetry, which gave way to rhetorical expression and use of hackneyed vocabulary. The plot of the epic is not fit enough to be considered as an epic. It also lacks the flow and rhythm, which is urgently required in an epic. The poet has tried to bridge the gulf by natural descriptions.

Bhartrihari: Bhartrihari was an eminent poet of the three *shatakas*: *Shringāra Shataka, Niti Shataka* and *Vairāgya Shataka*. No clear account of his life is available. The works of Bhartrihari contain his deep resentment over the harsh treatment meted out to him by his disloyal wife who deserted him. All his works are real masterpieces. Every *shloka* in his *shatakas* is complete, and communicates messages with regard to *Shringāra*, morality and renunciation. Most of the *shloka*s are the outcome of his personal experience.

When he was fully in love with his wife, he wrote *shringāra shataka*, when he ruled over his kingdom as a judicious king, he wrote *Niti shataka* and when he renounced the world and became a Yogi, he wrote *Vairāgya Shataka*. Bhartrihari was the disciple of Matsyendra Nāth who was himself the *guru* of Gorakha Nāth. It is said that it was under the influence of his guru that he renounced this world and became a *samyāsi* and took religious order. There is also a hearsay that his guru created confusion in his mind that his wife Pingalā was unchaste and this also added to his sense of frustration. *Sutra kāvya* matured with the poetic efforts of Bhartrihari. His every *shloka* contained in these *shatakas* is aphoristic.

Bhartrihari: Bhartrihari was a renowned grammarian and author of the popular grammatical text *Vākya-padiya*. Although he is entirely different from the poet Bhartrhari, some of the critics have taken both of them as the same person. *Vākya-padiya* is a book in which Bhartrihari has shown the relationship between word and meaning. Word is like a flower and meaning is its fruit: *Shabda Pushpāni Artham Phalamavaha*. Meaning may be myriad and multi-dimensional, and it may transcend the literal meaning of the word. That is what he meant by the word as fruit. According to Bhartrihari wisdom depends upon word. He says that without words, knowledge is unattainable. It is only from their integrated form that the entire knowledge is brought to light. Word is the cause of object because object is born of word. So word may be regarded as the cause of object.

***Bhāsa*:** Bhāsa was a dramatist of the pre-Kālidāsa era. He wrote 13 dramas in all. Unfortunately, nothing substantial about the life of Bhāsa has yet emerged. For the first time, Ganapati Shāstri brought the dramas of Bhāsa to limelight. He collected the manuscripts of his dramas from various places and published them in 1912. Scholars are not unanimous about the authenticity of the dramas of Bhāsa. One set of scholars has assigned the authorship of these dramas to Bhāsa. On the basis of the mode of plot-construction, style and diction, these dramas are supposed to be the composition of a single person writing prior to Kālidāsa. Another set of scholars has declined to accept Bhāsa as the author of these dramas and have instead accepted the author of *Matta-vilāsa-prahasana* as the author of these dramas. The third set of scholars though, accepting Bhāsa as the author of these dramas have declined to accept the validity of the texts available.

On the basis of the subject matter the dramas of Bhāsa's plays can be put into four categories (i) Dramas based on the story of the *Rāmāyana*: *Pratibhā, Abhisheka,* (ii) Dramas based on the *Mahābhārata: Bāla charita*, *Pancharātra, Madhyama Vyāyoga, Duta-vākaya, Urubhanga, Karnabhāra* and *Duta Ghatotkacha* (iii) Dramas based on the story of Udayana, *Svapna-Vāsava-dattā* and *Pratigyā-Yaugandharāyana* (iv) Dramas based on imaginary plots - *Avimāraka* and *Daridra-Chārudatta*.

His dramas based on folk tales are more successful. *Svapna-vāsava-dattā* and *Pratigyā-Yaugandharāyana* are thus, placed among the most successful dramas of Bhāsa. He did not retain the plot of the original sources as usual rather he broke away from the beaten track and made necessary changes in the plot and even added new episodes to serve at least two-fold purposes, first, to mitigate monotony and to make the plot compact and wholesome and secondly, to elevate his characters to a novel height purging out their blemishes.

Bhāsa's diction is very simple. There is no craving for poetic figures in his writings. His verses do not appear to have been added to the text rather they are neatly associated with the incidents.

Bhāsarvagya: Bhāsarvagya was a 9th century philosopher. He has the credit to compose the famous text on *Nyāya shāstra* entitled *Nyāya sāra*. In this text, he has referred to only a single proof of *Nyāya*, and rest of the 15 objects has been assimilated into it. As opposed to the other *Naiyāyikas*, Bhāsarvagya has signaled out four kinds of *Pramāns: Pratyaksha, Anumāna, Āgama* and *Upamāna*. His ideals do not conform to those of other scholars.

Bhatta Nāyaka: Bhatta Nāyaka was an aesthetician and scholar of Indian poetics. He had compiled an anthology *Hridaya darpana*, which is not available. This text was intended to contradict the theory of *Dhvani*. His ideas are contained in *Abhinava-bhārti, Vyakti-viveka*, *Kāvya-prakāsha* and *Kāvyānushāsana*. He had also written a commentary on Bharata's *Nātya Shāstra*. He held the view that *Rasa* is something to relish or *bhoga*, and is called *Bhuktivāda;* that Rasa is neither generated nor inferred, it can only be relished or experienced. According to Bhatta Nāyaka there are three word powers (*Shabda Shakti*) *Abhidhā, Bhāvakatva* and *Bhojakatva*. *Abhidhā* means surface meaning or the literal meaning. It is limited in range. In drama, it is relished by the hero and the heroine and the persons associated with them. But *Bhāvakatva* is superior to it. The spectators or *sāmājikas* relish it that witness the drama and interpret it in their own manner. By *sāmājika*, he meant competent recipient. The stage of *Bhojakatva* is the final stage. At this stage, the meaning of a dramatic performance is relished by *sāmājika*, not only as it is presented on the stage but also as it is received by the recipient. At the stage of *Bhojakatva* the characters on the stage lose their personal identity and become the characters they are playing. Dushyanta and Shakuntalā no more remain Dushyanta and Shakuntalā, rather they symbolize lover and beloved in general. It is a matter of common experience that nobody wants to enter the purely personal life of any man. But here the situation is different. The characters are depersonalized. This depersonalization of Characters makes them universal in nature. This is the secret of *sādhāranikarana*. During the state of *Bhojaktva, raj* and *tamas gunas* vanish from the heart of the audience and they enjoy perfect bliss (*satva*).

Bhatta Nāyaka opposed *Dhvani* tooth and nail and he tried to reveal the worthlessness of the school of *Dhvani* through his work *Hridayadarpana*.

***Bhattatauta*:** Bhatta Tauta was the author of *Kāvya-kautuka*, a text of poetics. He was the teacher of Abhinava Gupta who has written a commentary on *Kāvya-kautuka* entitled *Vivarana.* A reference to this has been given in *Abhinava-bhārati*. The original text of *Kāvya-kautuka* is not available. The views expressed in this book are embodied in *Abhinava-bhārati*, *Auchitya-vichāra-charchā*, and *Kāvyānushāsana*. Bhattatauta's popularity rests on elevating *Shānta Rasa* to the position of the most dominant *Rasa*.

***Bhatti*:** Bhatti was the author of *Bhatti Kāvya* or *Rāvana Badha*. He was basically a grammarian and critic whose purpose was to give sufficient teaching of grammar and *alankāra* to the princes. No reliable information regarding his life is available. Although towards the end of his *kāvya*, he has given reference to his personal life. He enjoyed the privilege of Shridhara Sena, the king of *Vallabhi*. In the inscription of the king, the account of donation of land to a poet called Bhatti has been mentioned. In this way, Bhatti seems to be his contemporary who ruled around 650 A.D.

***Bhattikāvya*:** Bhatti-kāvya is an epic written by Bhatti, which is intended to unveil the complexity imbued in the study of grammar through the story of the *Rāmāyana*. It is variously called *Rāvana badha*. It consists of 22 cantos and 3624 *shlokas*. The epic deals with the incidents occurring in the life of Rāma. It has been divided into four *khandas: Prakirna khanda, Adhikāra Khanda*, *Prasanna khanda* and *Tinganta khanda*. The first five cantos in the **first** *khanda* present the account of Rāma's life from his birth till his departure to forest. The talent of Bhatti as a poet is manifested in this *khanda*. The **second**, Adhikāra khanda is basically concerned with grammatical facts which is spread up to the 9th canto. The **third** *khand*, which is confined to the 13th canto, deals with different kinds of *Shabdālankāras* and *Arthālankāras*, and *shlokas* using these *alankāras* have been introduced in this section. The **fourth**

khanda from the 14th to the 22nd canto, 9 *lakshanās* of Samskrit grammar have been introduced. Actually Bhatti's intention is to provide the derivatives of words and their relative usage in proper context. That is why besides narrating the story of the *Rāmāyana* he inserted grammatical teaching as well. Bhatti has mentioned in a *shloka* that it serves as a lamp, which brings light removing darkness to those inclined to study grammar. But the same lamp ceases to be a source of light for those who are least interested in grammar. For them it is as good as a lamp in the hand of the blind.

There is an amazing manifestation of Bhatti's poetic talent in 10th to the 14th canto. Bhatti seems unparalleled in outpouring his feelings and emotions in a language embellished with all sorts of poetic excellence and grandeur. He has excelled others in the use of puns and hyperboles. He is equally at ease with the depiction of natural scenery.

Bhatti has also made an innovation in the original story of the Rāmāyana. Dasharatha is portrayed here as an ardent disciple of Lord Shiva. In the same way, no deity emerges from the site of the *yagya* to offer the *prasāda* to the queens of Dasharatha to enable them to conceive. Bhatta has mentioned only the marriage of Rāma and Sitā. These changes do not affect the pace of the epic rather they add substantially to its perfection.

In the opinion of the poet, it is a festivity for an inspired man but it is a toxic for a defunct person. The selection of verses in Bhatti *Kāvya* is not independent it is shut up in duress. Bhatti is a torchbearer and harbinger. He represents that tradition of Samskrit poets who crave for a blend of scholarship and poetic sensibility. His characterisation suits the accepted tradition of epic writing.

Bhatti failed miserably in giving the details of the object and streamlining the vital and touching episodes of the story. His growing apathy for the episodes of the marriage of Sitā and thereafter Rāma leaving for forest raises doubt about his ability to handle an epic theme coherently and systematically. The story of the marriage of Rāma has been told in one *shloka*. The incident of abduction of Sitā by Rāvan has also figured prominently in this epic.

***Bhattalollata*:** Bhatta Lollata was an eminent critic who propounded the theory of *Utpatti-vāda* to substantiate his *Rasa siddhānta*. He has also written a commentary on *Nātya Shāstra,* which was very popular. No independent work of Bhattalollata is available, though his critical formulations are preserved in several texts on poetics including *Abhinava-bhārati*, *Kāvya-prakāsha*, *Kāvyānaushāsana*, *Dhvanyā-loka-lochana* and *Kāvya-pradeep*. He was the successor of Udbhata. He contended that the original characters and heroes and heroines playing the role also share the enjoyment of *Rasa*.

Bhatta Nārāyana: Bhatta Nārāyana is the author of the drama *Veni-samhāra*. He was the adherent of the *Vaishnava* sect. Reference to Bhattanārāyana has been given in Vāmana's *kāvyalankāra sutra*. In this way, his timing is fixed around the 1st half of the 8th century.

The plot of Venisamahāra is based on the *Mahābhārata* War. The story revolves round the promise of Draupadi to wash her hair with the blood of Duryodahana. Her promise was fulfilled when Bhima kills Duryodhana in the *gadā-yuddha* and combs the hair of Draupadi with his own hands soaked in the blood of Duryodhana. This incident served as the title of the drama *Veni-samhāra*.

Bhatta Nārāyana's talent as poet has been successfully cultivated through his dramas, though the dramas failed miserably to cope with the demands of dramatic art. The influence of Kālidāsa, Māgha and Bāna cannot be overlooked on his poetry. Since *vira rasa* is the dominant *rasa* in his dramas, he has resorted to *gaudi riti* to voice the anger and resentment of the characters particularly Bhima and Draupadi. He is successful in generating a situation suited to poetry dominated by *Vira Rasa* using terse, and long sentences and difficult words which carry the weight of anguish of the characters successfully. Such a style is bound to hamper the movement of the drama. Therefore, it has been acknowledged inappropriate from the dramatic standpoint. The poet's leaning towards the use of *alnkāra* is also worth-noting. He has used *Anuprāsha, Yamaka, Rupaka, Upamā* and *Parikara alnkāras.* In the dialogues between the monsters, he has used twin languages *Magadhi* and *Saurseni*.

Bhattoji Dikshita: Bhattoji Dikshita was an eminent grammarian who gave a new orientation to Samskrit grammar by the composition of *Siddhānta Kaumudi*. He belongs to the 16th century. He has written several works, which include *Shabda-kaustubha, Siddhānta Kaumudi, Praudha Manorama* and *Veda-bhāsya-sāra*. *Shabda-kaustubha* is the interpretation of *Ashtādhyāyi* and *Praudha-Manorama* is the interpretation of *Siddhānta Kaumudi*. His grandson Hari Dikshita has written two commentaries on *Praudha-Manorama* entitled *Brihad-shabda-ratna* and *Laghu-shabda-ranta*. The second one is very popular. Seven commentaries on *Shabda-kaustubha* are available. Of them *Visamapadi* of Nāgesvara and *Bhāvapradeep* of Krishna Mishra are prominent. The other commentaries on *Siddhānta Kaumudi* include *Tatvadipikā* by Rāmānanda and *Bālamanoramā* by Vāsudeva Vājpayee. Pandit Rāja Jagannātha has written a rebuttal on *Praudha-manorama* entitled *Manorama kuchamardini*.

Bhavabhuti: Bhavabhuti was an eminent dramatist who composed a significant drama *Uttara Rāmacharita*. He is placed only next to Kālidāsa. His muse successfully found expression in his dramas and has even excelled Kālidāsa in many respects. He was a man of philosophical bent of mind. He was well versed in philosophical speculations and was an authority on various philosophical ideologies.

Bhavabhuti has given sufficient information about his life in the preface to his dramas particularly *Mahāvira charita*. He was the inhabitant of Padmapura falling under Vidarbha region. He did not mention his period in his works, information to this effect can be obtained from Vākpatirāja's *Gaudabaho* in which the poetry of Bhavabhuti has been applauded. Bhavabhuti enjoyed the patronage of Yosho Vermā towards the later part of his life and the fact to this effect has been established in *Rājatarangini*. Bhavabhuti's *shlokas* have also been quoted in Vāmana's *kāvya-alankāra-sutra-vritti*.

Bhavabhuti has written three dramas: *Mālati-Mādhava, Mahavira charita* and *Uttara Rāmacharita*. *Mālati-Mādhava* is a *prakarana* consisting of 10 acts. It is based on the imaginative love story of Mālati and Mādhava. In *Mahavira-charita*, the story of the *Rāmāyana* has been recast in 7 acts. The *Uttara Rāmacharita*, the most successful of all his dramas, is also based on the *Rāmāyana* depicting the plight of Sitā after her banishment from the palace. His dramas were meant for staging on the occasion of the festival of Mahakāla.

In Bhavabhuti's works, his poetry often overweighs his drama. His dramas are placed in the category of lyrical drama. His style is not uniform throughout. Often he skates from delicacy to toughness. Critics have questioned Bhavabhuti's ability as a dramatist by pointing out numerous shortcomings in his writing. His failure to abide by the principles of three unities, exaggerated expression, lack of humour, obscurity and terseness of language and long dialogues have hampered the smooth flow. He has also violated the accepted norms of classical drama. These combined together earned the ire of critics. They conspired to underrate the achievements of Bhavabhuti whose poetry despite all drawbacks was charming enough. He is by far the most successful dramatist of Samskrit literature after Kālidāsa. Expressing his utter dismay and grief over the distaste shown by the readers and critics for his works he has remorsefully uttered the heart-rending words in the preface to *Mālati-Mādhava* that he would eagerly await the birth of the able reader of his drama who will possess literary sensibility similar to his own. He is sanguine that such a reader will do justice to his work. Such reader may not be available at present, but there is no doubt that he will be born in future because time is endless and the earth is vast: *utpatsyatehi-mam-kopi-samāna-dharmā, kālohiyam-nirvadhir-vipulā-cha-prithavi.*

Bhāva-prakāsha: Bhāva Prakāsha is a famous work of *Āyurveda*. It is placed among three important texts, i.e., *laghutrayi*, of *Āyurveda*. Bhāva Mishra has written it. Scholars have fixed 15th century as the period of its composition following the description of phiranga disease, which is connected with Portuguese. It is divided into three *khandas*: *Purva, Madhya* and *Uttara*. The first *khanda* deals with the origin of *Āyurveda*. The second *khanda* deals with the treatment of fever and the last *khanda* is confined to *vājikarana*. The author has introduced almost all the methods of treatment in vogue during that period which shows his authority over *Āyurveda*.

***Bhavishya Purāna*:** Chronologically, Bhavishya Purāna is the ninth *Purāna*. The texts contained in the *Purāna* have been undergoing constant changes at regular intervals. Scholars have added incidents of different ages within the framework of this Pauranic text. This has laid to a vital change in the original text. According to *Nārada Purāna*, it consists of five *Parvas: Brahma Parva*, *Vishnu Parva, Shiva Parva, Surya Parva* and *Pratisarga Parva*. It comprises of 14,000 *shlokas*. This *Purāna* basically deals with *Brahma Dharma*, moral codes and *Varnāshrama dharma*. Al-Biruni has also referred to this *Purāna* in his travel account. This *Purāna* also presents the dynastic history of several kings of *Kaliyuga* up to queen Victoria.

***Bhela-samhitā*:** Bhela Samhitā is a text of *Āyurveda* composed by Bhela, a disciple of *Punarvasu Aitreya*. The existing form of *Bhela samhitā* is incomplete and is deeply influenced by *Charaka samhitā*. The titles of its chapters have been mostly borrowed from this book. Its description of heart does have a similarity with that given in *Sushruta samhitā*.

Bhoja: Bhoja was the king of Dhārā who displayed his scholarship by writing on different forms of literature including *Vyākarana, Jyotisha* and *Āyurveda*. He flourished in the 1st half of the 11th century, which is established by an inscription of his successor Jaya Singh who flourished in 1055. The number of texts ascribed to Bhoja has risen to 84, which include texts on *Dharma-shāstra*, *Jyotisha*, *Yoga-shāstra*, *Vaidyaka-shāstra*, *Vyākarana* and *Kāvyashāstra*. He wrote an excellent work on architecture entitled *Samarāngana-sutradhāra* consisting of 7000 *shlokas*. He wrote two books on *Dharma-shāstra: Yukti-prakāsha* and *Tatva-prakāsha* and one on medicine named *Rāja-māratanda* in 418 *shlokas*. He also wrote a *Kāvya Shringāra-manjari* and a *champu Mandāra-maranda-champu*. He has written two books on poetics *Shringāra-prakāsha* and *Sarasvati-kantha-bharana* in which there is an elaborate discussion on the nature and function of *Kāvya*, its kinds, *rasa*, poetic figures, drama, style, *vritti, Sāhitya*, *Nāyaka-*

Nāyikā bheda, *Shabda-shakti* and *dhvani*. He defined *kāvya* in three ways: *Vakrokti, Rasokti* and *Svabhāvokti*. Of the three *Rasokti* has been termed as the best form of *kāvya*. Streamlining the significance of *rasa* in *Kāvya*, he has presented a philosophical and psychological analysis of *Rasa* in *Shringāra-prakāsha* and has merged all the *rasas* in *shringāra rasa*, treating it the most dominant of all *rasas*. He has categorised poetic figures under *Shabdālankāra*, *Arthālankāra* and *Ubhayālankāra* and has in all discussed 72 *alankāras*. He has developed egalitarian ideology by making a thorough analysis of all the theories of poetics, which is of great significance.

***Bhojaprabandha*:** Bhoja Prabandha is a peculiar *kāvya* in prose and verse: Ballāla Sena wrote it. It presents eulogy of Bhoja, king of Dhārā by several poets. The popularity of *Bhoja-prabandha* rests on its verses whereas its prose is very commonplace. Several renowned poets including Kālidāsa, Bhavabhuti, Māgha and Dandin were introduced to the court of king Bhoja. Although this text does not have historical significance, its importance from literary standpoint is still growing.

***Bhushundi Rāmāyana* :** Bhushundi Rāmāyana is the primary work of the *Rasika* branch of Rāma bhakti segment. It consists of 36,000 *shlokas*. The entire story has been narrated in the dialogue form exchanged between Brahma and Bhusundi. It consists of four *khandas: - Purva, Pashchima, Uttara, Dakshina*. **Purva Khanda**, consisting of 146 chapters, deals with the questions pertaining to the story of Rāma as narrated by the saints and the pilgrimages made by Dasharatha. **Pashchima khanda** deals with the story of the birth of Sitā till her *svayamavara* during the dialogue exchanged between Bharata and Rāma in 72 chapters. **Dakshina khanda** deals with the coronation of Rāma, his banishment and his leaving for forest, abduction of Sitā by Rāvana, killing of Rāvana and meeting Rāma with Bharat in the hermitage of the Rishi Bharadwāj on his way back to *Ayodhyā* from Lanka in 242 chapters. **Uttara khanda**, consisting of 53 chapters, deals with the significance of the story of Rāma by deities.

Bilhana: Bilhana was a Kashmiri poet who wrote a historical epic entitled *Vikramānka-deva-charita* dealing with the gallantry of the predecessors of his patron king Vikramāditya VI, the Clālukya king belonging to the 11th century. The epic is equipped with plenty of historical facts and thus throws ample light on ancient Indian society. The first 7 out of 18 cantos possess numerous historical materials. The love affair between the hero and the heroine has been depicted between 8th and 11th cantos. The 12th, the 13tht and the 16th cantos are confined to water gamble and hunting and the 14th and the 15th cantos are restricted to family feud. The 17th canto deals with the defeat of *coli* and the genealogy of the poet.

There is a unique blend of history and poetry in the writing of Bilhana. He has achieved a remarkable success as a poet as well as a historian. His *Vikramānka-deva charita* along with Kalhana's *Rājatarangini* give a composite picture of the early medieval Indian society. The facts contained in the text are still very relevant and have helped historians reach an understanding on various issues related to Indian life and culture during the early medieval period. Bilhana has also succeeded in reviving artistic excellence by maintaining a blend of fact and fiction. His imaginative faculty is also at work particularly in the depiction of the beauty of the heroine and in the interaction between the hero and the heroine. But at the same time, he has tried to maintain the originality of his narrative and poetic skill.

Brahmagupta: Brahma Gupta was an eminent scholar of astrological mathematics. He wrote two astrological texts *Brahma-sphota Siddhānta* and *Khanda Khādyaka*. The first consists of 24 and the second consists of 10 chapters. He is considered a great scholar of astrology and exponent of Algebra. These two books have been translated into Arabic under the title *Asinda Hinda* and *Alarkanda* respectively. He has contradicted the findings of Aryabhatta, Shrisena and Vishnu Chandra and at several places in his texts maintained that the method of calculation adopted by these scholars do not establish the real position of the planets (*grahas*). He also challenged Aryabhatta's theory of movements of the earth and ruled that the earth is static. For the first time, Brahamagupta separated mathematics from Astrology and expressed the need to study them as separate disciplines. Voicing his strong opposition with Aryabhatta, he advanced his arguments in the first eight chapters of *Khadna Khādyaka*. Besides throwing light on the facts concerning astrology, he laid down cogent theories in other disciplines like Algebra, Arithmetic and Mensuration. The findings of Brahmagupta are still relevant and his theories are treated valid.

Brihaspati smriti: A law book dealing with Hindu code and conduct compiled by Brihaspati, an eminent economist of ancient India. About 700 *shloka*s of *Brihaspati Smriti* are available in *Mitākshara* and other *bhāsya*s. In *Mahābhārata*'s *Shānti Parva*, Brahmā has referred Brihaspati as one who compiled in 3000 chapters the abridged forms of his texts pertaining to *Dharma, Artha* and *Kāma*.

The entire text of *Brihaspati Smriti* is not available. Dr. Jolly had published a book contaning 711 *shloka*s, which consists of various definitions and theories relating to practical knowledge. The influence of *Manusmriti* on *Brihaspati smriti* cannot be denied. References to this text can be obtained from *Smriti chandrikā, Mitākshara*, *Parāshara Mādhaviya*, *Nirnaya Sindhu* and *Samskāra kaustubha*.

Brihat kathā: Brihat Kathā contains stories in prose written by Gunādhya. He was the court poet of Hala. Actually Gunādhya had compiled this text in Paisāchi language bearing the title *Baddakahā*, but the original text is missing. Its references are found in the writings of Subandhu, Dandin and Bāna, which confirm the authenticity of the text. Proofs with regard to the existence of *Brihat kathā* can be had from *Dasha rupaka*, Trvikrama Bhatta's *Nala-champu* and Somadeva's *Yashas-tilaka,* and in an inscription found from Combodia engraved in 875.

At present, three Samskrit translations of Gunādya's text are available. Of the three translations that of Kshemendra (11th century) entitled *Brihatkathāmanjari* is authentic. It consists of 7500 *shloka*s. The other two are *Brihat-kathā-shloka*s-*Samgraha* by the 9th century poet Buddha Swāmi and *Kathā-saritasāgar* by Somedava, a contemporary to Anant, king of Kashmir. It consists of 24,000 *shloka*s.

Brāhmana: Brāhmana Texts form part of Vedic literature portraying numerous policies and codes of conduct concerning Hindu religious approach including *yagyas*. These texts are basically concerned with religious rites. *Sabar-bhāsya* has streamlined the subjects figuring prominently within the area of *Brāhmana* texts. Four of them are more significant *Vidhi* (law), *Arthavāda*, *Upanishada* and *Ākhyāna* (story). *Vidhi* includes rules for performing rituals and *yagyas*. Use of different kinds of mantras have been suggested to achieve different objectives. Arthavāda includes stories to interpret the significance of *yagyas*. The reference given in these books on linguistics are also significant. The stories in Brāhmana texts are also significant from historical point of view. They throw ample light on the social and political life of the *Āryans,* and their conflict with *Anāryas*. The story of Pururvā and Urvasi and Sunahsesha is also significant from literary standard. They have rich literary flavour.

The *Brāhmana* texts have been written in prose. They present embellished and refined form of prose. The language of Brāhmana texts is difficult and agile.

Brahmānda Purāna: Chronologically, Brahmānda Purāna is the 18th and last in the series of *Purānas*. It consists of 109 chapters and 12,000 *shlokas*. This *purāna* is aimed at highlighting the significance of *Brahmānda*. According to *Nārada Purāna*, Vāyu provided Vyās with the concept of *Brahmānda*. It is divided into four *kāndas: Prakriya, Anusanga, Upoddhātta* and *Upasamhāra*.

In the first kānda, elaborate geographical description of Brahmānda has been given. The description includes Jambudweepa, mountains, rivers, Planets, stars, constellations and yugas. The description of the dynasties of Kshatriyas is also very significant from historical point of view. The reference to *Adhyātma purāna* has been given in the content of *Brahmānda Purāna*, although it is not available as text. It also incorporates the story of Parasurāma and the arrival of the Gangā on the earth by the efforts of Bhagiratha. *Chandra-vansi* and *Surya-vansi* kings also figure in the description.

Brahma Purāna: Chronologically, Brahma Purāna is the first *Purāna*. It deals with the facts leading to the creation of the universe by Brahmā. It consists of 245 chapters and 14,000 *shlokas*. *Brahma Purāna* has been divided into two sections: *Purva* and *Uttara*. It is a *Vaishnava Purāna*. It includes all subjects concerning *Purāna* and displays special inclination for ancient pilgrimages. It begins with the description of the creation of the universe, which is followed by the description of the *Surya* and the *Chandra* dynasties. The first five chapters are designed to give an account of *Sarga, Pratisarga* and *Manavantara.* The next hundred chapters deal with *vansa* (dynasty). *Brahma purāna* also gives a detailed account of the life of Shri Krishna. Towards the end of this text *shrāddha*, codes leading to religious life, *Varnāshrama Dharma, Svarga, Naraka* and advantages of the worship of Lord Vishnu have been laid down. It also presents a detailed account of the philosophical hypothesis of the school of *Sāmkhya*.

Brahma purāna also contains numerous citations from the *Mahābhārata* and other *Purānas* like *Vāyu, Vishnu* and *Markandeya Purānas*.

Scholars are of the opinion that original text comprises just 175 chapters and the rest 75 chapters are interpolations. There is no unanimity of opinion about the period of composition of *Brahama Purāna*.

Brahma Vaivarta Purāna: Chronologically, Brahma Vaivarta Purāna is the 10th *Purāna*. According to *Matsya Purāna* it consists of 18,000 *shlokas*. Its objective is to prove the majesty of Lord Krishna and Vaishnavite worship. It comprises four *Khandas: Brahama Khanda, Prakriti Khanda, Ganesha Khanda* and *Krishna-janma khanda*. Rādhā has been portrayed as the power of Krishna. The amorous sport of Rādhā and Krishna has been presented in a fantastic manner. The basic form of the spiritual mystery of the *Gaudiya Vaishnava* sect, *Vallabha* sect and Rādhāvallabha sect is preserved in this *Purāna*. Rādhā has been acknowledged as the fundamental force behind the creation and Krishna has been treated as the seed out of which universe shot forth.

Brahma khand deals with the creation of the universe by Lord Krishna. It consists of 30 chapters. **Prakriti khanda** narrates the dignity of goddesses including Durgā, Lakshmi, Sarasvati and Rādhā. **Ganesha Khanda** deals with the birth and gallantry of Lord Ganesha. He is portrayed as the incarnation of Krishna. **Shri Krishna Janma-khanda** deals with the story of childhood days of Krishna and his marriage with Rādhā. In *Brahma-vaivarata Purāna* Krishna has been conceived as *Purna Brahma* or the universal law. Etymologically 'Krish' means devotion to God and 'na' means total surrender. Since Krishna gives *Bhakti* or devotion and the spirit to surrender to his devotees, he is called Krishna. At the time of creation, Krishna manifests himself in two forms - *Prakriti* and *Purusha*.

His right organ is called Purusha and the left is called Prakriti. Prakriti is none but Rādhā who is eternal and without attributes and is an integral part of Krishna. Krishna appears in manifold forms like Mahā Vishnu, Shiva, Ganesha and Nārāyana. Likewise Rādhā appears in many forms like Durgā, Sarasvati and Mahā Lakshmi.

Buddha-charita: Buddha Charita is an epic narrating various aspects of the life of Lord Buddha written by eminent Buddhist scholar and poet Ashvaghosha. Only 14 cantos of this epic are available now. It consists of 28 contos, which are still available in its Chinese and Tibetese translations. The **first canto** is incomplete which deals with the story of king Suddodhana and his wife Mayādevi and the birth of Siddhārtha. Mayādevi dreamt of an elephant entering her womb, which presages the birth of a strange child. The **second canto** deals with the king's efforts to provide his son with all sorts of worldly luxuries so that he might be lost in them smacking his detachment from the world. In the **third canto**, the scenes of a weird man, an ailing man and a corpse infused in him, an impulse to renounce the world, which is full of miseries.

In the **fourth canto**, king's efforts to cast a spell on his son including sending him to the company of young and beautiful damsels proved futile. In the **fifth canto**, Siddhārtha meets a *shramana* while he was on his way to the forest and he decides to lead the life of a recluse on his way back. In the **sixth** and the **seventh cantos**, Siddhārtha reiterates his determination to live the life of a recluse putting off regal robe. He commits to perform rigorous penance. In the **eighth canto**, Siddhārtha leaves for the forest accompanied by Chandaka. When Chandaka returns off hand, the faces of Siddhārtha's wife Yashodharā and others turn pale. In the **ninth canto**, the king makes a fruitless attempt to bring Siddhārtha back to his kingdom. In the **tenth canto** Bimbisāra, the king of Magadha, urges upon Siddhārtha to return to the kingdom. In the **11th canto** Siddhārtha refuses to come to the town expressing his apathy over worldly objects including state and wealth. In the **12th canto** Arada Satisfies Siddhārtha with his sermons. In the **13th canto** Māra (cupid, Kāmadeva) tries to disrupt the penance of Buddha, but he fails miserably. In the **14th canto**, Siddhārtha achieves *Nirvāna* or *Buddhatava*. From the **15th canto** onwards Buddha disseminates the teachings of Buddhist philosophy and gives weight to the desire to attain *moksha*. *Buddha-charita* is basically aimed at spreading the ideologies of Lord Buddha making it more relevant in the changing scenario.

Buddhaghosha: Buddha Ghosha was an eminent Buddhist scholar belonging to 400 B.C. He compiled an epic *Padma-chudāmani* in 10 cantos. He has occupied a respectable place among the *Pāli* writers as the interpreter of Buddhism. He has also compiled a philosophical text entitled *Vishuddhi-māgga* aimed at disseminating the philosophical ideas contained in Buddhist scriptures. Popular Buddhist texts *Mahāvansa* and *Attha-kathāyen* have also been attributed to him. One of his books was translated into Chinese language. He has left an indelible mark on Buddhist literature by his significant contributions. He broke new grounds by giving new twist and turn to his writings. His writings are still of paramount importance showing his in depth study of Buddhist philosophy.

Buddhism: Buddhism is one of the schools of Indian philosophy that Lord Buddha founded. Slowly it took a form of religion. It spread over to many countries and since many millenniums it is a global religion.

He belonged to the 6th century B.C. The teachings of Buddha are preserved in three books: *Sutta-pitaka, Vinaya-pitaka* and *Abhidhamma-pitaka. Sutta-pitaka* consists of the sermons of Buddha, *Vinaya-pitaka* consists of Buddha's teachings on moral code and conduct, and *Abhidhamma-pitaka* presents the philosophical ideas of Lord Buddha. These three texts are called *Tripitaka. Pitaka* means caskets. It contains codes for leading a moral and ethical life.

In the course of time, Buddhism was divided into two different sects *Mahāyāna* and *Hinayāna. Mahāyāna* texts have been written in Samskrit and *Hinayāna* texts are available in *Pāli*. The prominent texts of Mahāyāna include: *Saddharama-pundarika, Pragyā-Pāramitā-sutra, Dashabhumika-sutra, Ratnakuta, Sukhavati-vyuha, Suvarna-prabhā-sutra* and *Lankā-vatāra-sutra*.

Buddha did not try to solve recondite and intricate spiritual problems, rather he was concerned with the cessation of misery facing common man. Therefore, he worked out measures to set man free from the bondage of life and death and to enable him to enjoy the state of eternal bliss. Buddha' philosophy founded on four pillars which are called four noble truths (*ārya satya*) i. There is suffering in life, ii. There is cause of suffering, iii. Cessation from suffering is possible, iv. There is a device for cessation from suffering.

Buddha has suggested eight right paths through which suffering of man can be shunned. These eight ways are called eight fold paths. They include: *Samyaka Dristi-* to concentrate on the original nature of the object; *samyaka samkalpa-* to be committed to one's stand; *samyaka vāk-* to speak the truth and avoid telling a lie; *samyaka karmānta-* to shun violence, stealing and to put a restrain on senses; *samyaka ājiva-* to earn the livelihood through proper means; *samyaka vyāyāma-* to make efforts to perform rightful action; *samyaka smriti-* to avoid avarice and to remain calm and quiet; and *samyaka samādhi-* be aloof from love and hatred and concentrate on one's mind.

Buddha's sermons are based on three philosophical hypotheses- *Pratitya-samutpāda, Karma-kshanika-vāda,* and *Anastitva.* Lord

Buddha has tried to understand the cause of suffering on the basis of the theory of *pratitya-samutpāda*. It is also called theory of causation. *Pratitya-smutpāda* signifies the existence of other object. This theory indicates that there is a reason behind every action. Therefore, there must be a cause of sorrow. Once the cause of suffering is over it can be easily eradicated. It is a theory of middle path (*madhyama mārg*). It also observes that present action of man will determine his future course of action, and the present life is the outcome of his actions in previous life.

Another leading principle of Buddhism is *Kshanikavāda*, according to which we live in a state of flux. Buddhism believes in incessant change. The world is fleeting. Every object of this world is changing fast. Nothing is static. What we were a moment ago, we are not now and we will not be in that position or posture after a moment. The world moves in a cyclic order.

There are four prominent schools or sects of Buddhism - *Vaibhāsika*, *Mādhyamika, Sautāntrika* and *Yogāchāra*. All of them accept the existence of objects falling within or outside the world. They can be visualised. This belief is also called *Sarvastivāda*. The texts of this school are *Abhidhamma-gyāna-prasthāna-kosha* by Kātyāyani-putra, and *Abhidhamma kosha* by Vasubandhu. *Sautāntrika* sect also confirms the existence of both external and internal objects with a difference that external objects are not visualised rather their existence can be felt through inference. Kumāratala, Shritala, Vasumitra and Yashomitra are four prominent interpreters of this school.

Mādhyamika is also called *Shunya-vāda*. This sect emphasises that the entire universe is a void. The objects of universe; whether external or internal, are unreal. Nāgārjuna was the exponent of this sect who wrote *Mādhyamika-shāstra* to substantiate his philosophical speculations.

Yogāchāra is also called *Vigyānavāda*. The exponent of this sect is Maitreya who wrote *Madhyāntara Vibhāga, Sutrālankāra* and *Mahāyāna Uttaratantra*. Dinganāga, Dharmakirti and Dharmapāla are other important exponents of this sect. This sect observes that external elements are not real. They are merely reflection of mind.

It only accepts the existence of mind or *Vigyāna*. Therefore, it is called *vigyānavāda*.

While tracing the source of misery, Buddha went step-by-step to trace the root of suffering and he came to the conclusion that *Avidyā* or ignorance is the root cause of suffering. He speaks of twelve spokes of wheel, which is called *Dvā-dasha-chakrāni* in Buddhist philosophy. These twelve chakras or wheels are *Dukha, (Jarā-Marana): Jati, Bhāva, Upādāna, Trishnā, Vedanā, Sparsha, Sadayatna, nām, rupa, vigyāna, samskāra* and *avidyā*.

As the whole philosophy of Buddhism is based on the philosophy of misery, Buddha didn't consider it desirable to solve any other question save the question concerning misery. When somebody went to Buddha to put questions relating to God and soul, he maintained reticence; meaning thereby that he didn't give any answer to such question's because he knew that his answer will be accepted as truth, this will lead to infinite hierarchy or *Anavastha Dosha*. Actually these questions cannot be answered. This is what is called *Avyaktāni* in Buddhist literature. Whenever such questions were put to Buddha he kept quiet. Ānanda and Maudgalāyana later explained that Buddha's silence did not show his inability to answer these questions but it simply meant the inexplicability of these questions. So it is wrong to hold that Buddha denied the existence of God or soul.

Buddha further suggested that *Nirvāna* or salvation might be attained during lifetime. This is called *Jivanamukti*. When a man attains the stage of dispassion and detachment and rises above worldly passions and his sense organs are shunned, and are fully under his control or subjugated to his higher knowledge, he may be said to have attained *mukti*, although he lives in this world. As the flame of a candle lamp goes out and nothing remains behind it, so after attaining *Jivanamukti* no base passion is left behind, it is complete extinction of worldly desires and passions.

The stories of the several births of Buddha are given in *Jātaka* stories. It is said that Buddha took many births: came in the form of goose, tiger and so on. In each of his birth, he gave some valuable sermons. He spent such a life, which set an example of high morality and religiosity for others to follow. Among the *Jātaka* stories, *Kunāla Jātaka* and *Dasharatha Jātaka* are worth mentioning.

Buddhism pays equal emphasis on Buddha, *Dhamma* and *Sangha*. Man can achieve *nirvāna* by way of constant effort. The people of India, China, Jāpān, Korea, Bhutān, Nepāl, Tibet, Cambodia, Lankā and Indonesiā etc follow Buddhism.

***Brihadāranyaka Upanishada*:** Brihad-Aranyaka-Upanishada is related to the last two branches of *Shatapatha Brāhmana*. It consists of three *kāndas*. Each of them consists of two chapters. These three *kāndas* are called *Madhu-kānda, Yāgyavalkaya-kānda* and *Khila-kānda*. The first chapter deals with the theories with regard to the creation, *srishti* (universe) through stories. The second chapter deals with Yāgyavalkya deciding to go to the forest dividing his property equally between his two wives Maitreyi and Kātyāyani. The third and the fourth chapters deal with the story of Janaka and Yāgyavalkya. It also narrates the story of Janaka's effort to get *Brahma-gyāna* from Yāgyavalkya. The fifth chapter deals with the story of Kātyāyani and Maitreyi. It also describes various subjects including ethics, universe and *paraloka*. The sixth chapter deals with various kinds of symbolic worship. This *Upanishada* aims at propagating the philosophical ideas of Yāgyavalkya. It has been written in prose. ■■

Chaitanyamata: Chaitanya Mata is an important school of *Vaishanava Darshana* sponsored by Mahāprabhu Chaitanya. His name was Vishvambhara Mishra who was born at Navadweep in Bengāl in 1485. He was deeply influenced by the songs of Jayadeva and Vidyāpati. No independent work of Chaitanya Mahāprabhu is available. His disciples have accepted *Dashmula shlokas* as his work. The ideas of this sect are brought on the firm footing by his two disciples: Roopa Goswāmi and Jiva Goswāmi. Roopa Goswāmi wrote *Ujjwala Nilamani* and *Bhakti-rasa-amaritha-sindhu*. His elder brother Shri Sanātana's *Hari-bhakti-vilāsa* is considered the most prominent literature of *Gaudiya Vaishanavamata*. *Chaitanya* sect accepts the world as real because it is the reflection of the Māyā of God. The devotee gets the union of God through devotion. He has successfully delineated the theory of this school. Jiva Goswāmi's *Bhāgavata Sandarbha* is also a monumental work dealing with Chaitanya's philosophy of the *Achintya-bheda-abheda* sect. Other important follower of this sect, Vishvanātha Chakravarti has written a commentary on *Shrimad Bhāgavata* named *Sārārtha-darshani*.

Chaitanya sect is also popularly known as Gaudiya Vaishanava sect, which lays emphasis on the prayer of Rādhā and Krishna. Rādhā has been depicted as the beloved of Krishna. *Shrimad Bhāgvata* is considered the most important book of this sect. The *Lilās* undertaken by Krishna: Vrindāvana Lilā, Mathurā Lilā and Dwarkā Lilā have been prominently covered in this sect. Chaitanya has added one more '*prema*' to the four purusārthas: *dharma, artha, kāma* and *moksha*. He has termed *prema* as the most desired mission of human beings. Chaitanya sect considers God as the storehouse of numerous qualities. Like Shankarāchārya, Chaitanya has accepted Brahman as *Akhanda* who is blessed with four powers, *Swarupa, Shakti, Tatastha-Shakti* and Māyāshakti.

Champukāvaya: Champu Kāvya is a form of *kāvya* (poetry) accommodating both prose and poetry. Dandi defined it for the first time. Vishvanātha has also accepted a work comprising of *gadya* and *padya* as the example of champu. Like *mahā kāvya*, it can have more than 8 cantos, whereas number of cantos can be less than 8 like *khanda kāvya*. It is divided into *stavaka* or *ullāsa*. It borrows its raw material from the *Purānas,* but the author is at liberty to include subjects falling outside the area of *Purānas*. The *Champu kāvya*s have shown their inclination towards the expansion of their narration, whereas less emphasis has been laid on subject matter. The hero of *Champu kāvya* can be either a god, *gandharva*, man, bird or an animal. It can have more than one hero. The presence of the heroine is not necessary. There is no specific rule regarding the ŋumber of characters to be introduced in it, and the poet is more concerned with depicting the personality of the central figure. *Shringāra*, *vira* or *shānta rasas* can be treated as prominent *rasas,* and rest of the *rasas* can be included as subsidiary *rasas*. There is a deliberate attempt to beautify both the versions of prose, and poetry whereas the prose section is modelled on the pattern of *samāsa*. Both *Vartikā* and *Mātrikā chhanda*s are used and songs too are used at regular intervals. Like *Mahā kāvya*, it also begins with *Mangalā-charana* or invocation. Detestation for villains and reverence for saints are its other features. The provision of *Phala-shruti* or conclusion with suggestion is also made in it.

Seeds of *Champu kāvaya* can be discerned in the Vedic texts itself. A style assimilating prose and poetry is available in the Krishna Yajurveda and the Atharvaveda. The *Brāhmana* and the *Upanishada*s also contain fair amount of writing comprising of prose and poetry.

The most outstanding work of *Champu kāvya* is *Nalachampu* by Trivikrama Bhatta dealing with the story of Nala and Damayanti. After it as many as 245 *champu kāvya*s have been written. Of them 74 have been published.

Besides *Rāmāyana* and *Mahābhārata*, *champu*s have borrowed the raw materials from *Purānas*, *Jaina Puranas, Charita Kāvya*s and *Yātrās*. *Champus* dealing with local deities, fictitious stories and philosophical speculations have also been surfaced.

Jain saints Harishchandra and Yashastilaka wrote *Jivan-dhārā Champu* and *Yashastilaka Champu* respectively in the 10th century. In the 11th century, Bhoja Rāja, Abhinava Kālidāsa and Someshvara wrote *Rāmāyana Champu*, *Udaya Sundari kathā* and *Kirti-kaumudi* respectively. In the fifteenth century, Vasu-deva-ratha and Ananta Bhatta wrote *Gangā vanshānucharita* and *Bharata Champu* respectively. Among the *Champus* written in the 16th century, Raja-chudāmani Dikshita's *Bharata Champu*, Jiva Goswāmi's *Gopāla Champu*, and Sheshakrishna's *Bhāgavata Champu* can be mentioned. Chakrakavi's *Draupadi Parinaya Champu* is a work of the 17th century whereas Bāneshvara's *Chitra Champu* and Ananta's *Champu Bharata* are included as the writings of the 18th century. Between the 10th and the 16th century all trends of *Champu kāvyas* had emerged.

Chandrakirti: Chandra Kirti is one of the celebrated scholars of *Mādhyamika* School of Buddhism. He lived between 600-500 A.D. He is a great scholar of *Mahāyāna* Sect and has learnt about *Shunya vāda* from his teacher Kamalabuddhi. He has written three books: *Mādhyamikāvatāra*, the original text is missing, however its Tibetan translation is available; *Prasanna-pāda*, a commentary on Nāgārjuna's *Mādhyamika-kārikā;* and *Chatuh-shataka tikā*, a commentary on Āryadeva's *Chatuha-shataka*. *Mādyamikāvatāra* presents a detailed analysis of the philosophy of *Shunyavāda*.

Chandraloka: Chandraloka is a mature book on *Samskrit* poetics written by Jayadeva. He is a critic of *Alankāra* School. (It is worth mentioning that the rhetorician Jayadeva is different from the poet Jayadeva, the author of *Gita-Govinda).* He considers Alankāra as imperative for poetry and as its necessary ingredient.

***Chhanda*:** It is the fifth of the six *Vedāngas*. Knowledge of *Chhanda* is badly needed for the recitation of the Vedic hymns. A proper recitation of the mantras is not possible without the knowledge of *Chhanda*. Kātyāyana has ruled that thorough study of the mantras is not possible without the knowledge of *Chhanda*, Rishi and Devatā; the three important organs of the Vedic literature.

Pingalāchārya has written an outstanding book on *Chhanda* entitled *Chhanda-sutra*. It consists of 8 chapters. The *lakshana* (characteristics) of Vedic *sutras* is traceable up to the seventh sutra of the fourth Chapter. Halayudha Bhatta has written *Mritasanjivani*, a commetary on *Chhanda-sutra*.

Chhanda has been called as the legs of the Vedas. Among the prominent Vedic *Chhanda*s: *Gāyatri* (24 letters), *Ushnika* (28 letters), *Anushtupa* (32 letters), *Trishtupa* (44 letters) and *Jagati* (48 *aksharas*) are important. There is no accent on syllables like *laghu* and *guru* in Vedic *Chhanda*s. They consist of 1, 2 or 3 *padas*.

***Chhāndogya Upanishada*:** Chhāndogya Upanishada is the last section of *Chhāndogya Brāhmana*. It has been written in prose, and complex philosophical discussions have been expressed under the garb of stories. The first five sections are concerned with various facets of the Almighty while the last three are devoted to Metaphysics. The mystery of *Sāma* and *Omkār* has been revealed in the first **two** chapters. The **third** chapter deals with the prayer to *Surya* and *Gāyatri* and the origin of *Surya*. The story of Satyakāma Jabālā forms the stuff of the **fourth** chapter. The **fifth** chapter deals with the facts related to creation. In the **sixth** Āruni's son Svetaketu has been sermonized. Brahmacharya and the analysis of Brahma-tatva have been given through the analogy of *Vata briksha*. The **seventh** chapter deals with the nature of '*Bhuma-darshana*'. In the **eighth**, practical approach leading to attainment of *Ātma-tatva* through the story of Indra and Virochana is narrated.

***Chitra Champu*:** The authorship of *Chitra Champu kāvya* is attributed to Vāneshvara Vidyalankāra. It was written in the year 1744 at the behest of Chitra Sena, the king of Vardamāna. It presents a peculiar blend of travel account and devotion. It is a unique combination of 294 verses and 131 prose segments.

***Cholā Champu*:** A 17th century poet Virupāksha wrote *Cholā Chmpu kāvya*. This work is basically confined to the prayer of Lord Shiva. He has written another *Champu kāvya* named *Shiva-vilāsa-champu*.

Charaka Samhitā: Charak wrote Charaka Samhitā, the most accomplished and outstanding work on *Āyurveda*. He is considered the royal *Vaidya* of Kanishka, although scholars are not unanimous on this fact. The word "Charaka" has been used in its plural form in *Upanishadas*. Charaka *Samhitā* basically deals with *kāyā-chikitsā*. The subjects discussed in it are: *rasāyana, vājikarana*, fever, *pitta, prameha, kusta, rājayakshmā, unmād, sothe, udān, pāndu, svāsa, atisāra, vāta-vyādhi* etc. Subjects falling within the range of philosophy and economics have also been included. It has been accepted as the milestone in Indian medicinal science and has been translated into almost all the prominent Languages of the world.

Chārudatta: Chāru Datta is the last drama written by Bhāsa. Shudraka had derived extensively from this work for his drama, *Mrichchhakatika*. *Chāru Datta* has been divided into four acts. The entire story revolves round the love intrigue between Chārudatta and Vasantasenā. They have to subdue the conspiracy hatched by Shakāra, the villain. They undergo a good deal of mental agony and finally romp home successfully thwarting the nefarious designs of the enemies. The drama comes to an abrupt ending with Vasantasenā opting to move to Chārudatta's house amidst heavy rain. Perhaps the premature death of Bhāsa might have caused the sudden end.

Chārvāka Darshana: Chārvāka Darshana is the materialistic school of Indian philosophy, which considers matter the primary element. Every object including idea is originated from it. Its another name is *Lokāyata*. It is also considered an atheistic philosophy since it does not have faith in God nor does it accept the authority of the Vedas. This school of philosophy does not have an independent book. References pertaining to the ideology of materialistic school figure, in other philosophical treatises in course of opposing the fundamentals of materialistic philosophy.

Brihastpati is tipped to be the exponent of Chārvāka doctrine. He is supposed to have spread this doctrine among the demons to restore the lost glory of gods. They were virtually subdued following the emergence of ardent admirers of Vishnu among the demons like Prahalād and Bāli, who spread the message of peace and non-violence.

Some scholars are of the opinion that the school of Chārvāka philosophy originated from saint Chārvāka. In *kārikā-vritti*, a saint named Chārvi has been referred to who spread the materialistic ideology and his disciples were referred to as *Chārvāka*. Yet another group of scholars have argued that the name Chārvāka was given to a group of people who spread their messages in a palatable manner. Their theory of eat, drink and be merry: *Yāvat Jivet Sukham Jiveta, Rinam Kritvā Ghritam Pivet*; pleased all and sundry.

The knowledge obtained only through senses has been accepted as credible by the Chārvākas. Therefore, apparent knowledge is considered the only authority whereas knowledge obtained through other sources like inference, *shabda*, statement of revered people and others are incredible. The world, which is perceived through senses, is real and that which stands beyond its reach is unreal. They do not have faith in the Vedas and have considered the authors of the Vedas as shrewd, frivolous and incredible: *chaturvedasya kartarau dhurta bhānda nisācharah*.

The Chārvākas have ruled out the existence of sky (*Ākasha*) and have maintained that human body is constituted out of four elements earth, water, fire and air, and these elements return to their respective elements after final dissolution of body. Chārvākas have outright rejected the existence of soul or *ātman* within a living being. Chaitanya or life is the feature of body, not *ātman*. Life also ends with body. Therefore rebirth, heaven, hell and continuation of previous *karma* do not carry any meaning. ■■

Dandi: Dandi is the most revered prose writer and mahākavi of Samskrit literature. He is supposed to have written three books: *Dasha-kumāra-charita*, *Kāvyādarsha* and *Avanti-sundari-kathā*. *Dasha-kumāra-charita* and *Avanti-sundari-kathā* are placed in the category of fiction. The third book *Kāvyādarsha* is an excellent work of poetics. Scholars are not unanimous in attributing the authorship of these books to Dandi on this or that ground. It has been maintained that the theories regarding the fictional writing, which Dandi had put forward in *Kāvyādarsha*, he has seriously violated in *Dasha-kumāra-charita*.

The fact available in his works and his narrative technique have helped arrive at a consensus about the timing of Dandi. These fact further strengthen the speculation that Dandi may have flourished around 600 A.D. and thus he is proved to be the predecessor of Bāna which some scholars concur. Had Dandi been the successor of Bāna, his prose would have been marked by ornamentation, which was the specialty of the writings of Samskrit prose writers from Bāna onwards. Contrary to this, Dandi's work is less embellished and is marked by simplicity and sonorousness. Secondly, the society, which Dandi has portrayed is of pre-Harsha era. Actually he has depicted the deteriorating condition of Indian society in the decadence of the Gupta empire, which was marked by chaos, disorder and anarchy. In this way, Dandi is proved to be the predecessor of Bāna.

Dashakumāracharita: Dasha-kumāra-charita is a popular prose work attributed to Mahākavi Dandi. It has been divided into two sections, *Purva pithikā* and *uttara pithikā*. Both *pithikā*s have been further divided into *uchchhavāsa*s. The entire work deals with the story of 10 princes but the form of the book, which is available to us is an enlarged edition of the original text. The original text deals with the story of Rājavāhana and his seven friends. It runs into 8 *uchchhavāsa*s and is placed after 5 *uchchhavāsa*s of the *purva pithikā*. The *purva pithikā* deals with the story of king Rājahansa who after being deposed retires to a forest, and the kumāras, receive training under his patronage.

The ten princes in the story include prince Rājvāhana, seven sons of ministers and two princes of Mithilā. All the princes are on a mission to conquer the world after completing their learning. They are separated from each other at Vindhyavana. All ten princes narrate their stories and finally join the company of Rājavāhana, who is supposed to be the main link among the princes. Finally, the princes return to Pushpapura after receiving the message of King Rājahansa. They kill their enemy Manasara and rule over the country pleasantly. Dandi seems to have followed the technique of *Panchatantra* to connect one story to the other and finally attach it to the main web. He however, does not intend to impart a moral teaching through his stories. His only objective is to amuse the readers.

Dasharupaka: Dasha Rupaka is a great work of *Nātya Shāstra* written by Dhananjaya. It is considered to be the most popular work on dramaturgy after Bharata's *Nātya Shāstra*. In this book he has made a detailed discussion of *Rupaka* and its different kinds, taking inspiration from Bharata. It consists of 300 *kārikā*s. It is divided into four *prakāsha*s. The **first** *prakāsha*, consisting of 68 *kārikā*s, deals with *lakshana* of *rupaka, vishkambhaka* and other issues. The **second** *prakāsha*, consiting of 72 *kārikā*s, discusses *Nāyaka-Nāyikā-bheda* and the language of the characters of a drama. The **third** *prakāsha* deals with the ten divisions of *rupaka*. It consists of 76 *kārikā*s. The **fourth** and the final *prakāsha*, consisting of 86 *kārikā*s, deals with the nature of *rasa*, its parts and a detailed discussion of all the nine *rasas*.

The merit of this book lies in presenting all the important aspects of drama in a very simple manner. Of all the commentaries available on *Dasharupaka* that of Dhanika's *Avaloka* is the most prominent.

Dhananjaya seems to have a close affinity with the Bhatta *Mimāmsakas*. Like them, he accepts *abhidhā, lakshanā* and *tātparya* as three facets of *shabda*. He has opined that the real pleasure of *Rasa* is experienced by the spectator and in this way he seems closer to Bhatta Nāyaka. As the boy enjoys the pleasure of the real horse or elephant out of the clay toy, in the same way the spectators enjoy the drama taking the actor playing the role as real.

Deshopadesha: Deshopadesha is a satire by Kshemendra. The poet has satirised the Kashmiri society and the ruling class. His description of various Kashmiri communities is very impressive and suggestive. He has successfully highlighted the weaknesses and shortcomings inherent in their personality in a humorous manner. *Deshopadesha* consists of eight *updeshas* (teachings). The butt of the first *upadesha* has been made Durjana or evil persons, and misers have been targeted in the second. The character of harlot has been highlighted in the fourth. The activities of vita and *Gaudadeshiya* students have been brought to the limelight in the fifth and the sixth. The seventh *upadesha* concentrates on the activities of tender aged spouse of an advanced businessman and a sense of laughter has been created. The last *upadesha* satirises the activities of *Vaidya, Bhatta, Kavi, Baniyā, Guru* and *Kāyastha*.

Devanabhatta: Devana Bhatta was an eminent political essayist. His text on polity, *Smriti chandrikā* is placed in the category of classics and has enriched the repertory of Samskrit literature with its outstanding treatment of the subject matter and analysis of the topics in a new perspective. Devana Bhatta followed a different standpoint and had accepted polity as part of *Dharma Shāstra*. His timing has been fixed around 1260 A.D. *Smriti chandrikā* has been divided into *kānda*s of which five are available. These *kānda*s are called *samskāra, ahnika, vyavahāra, shrāddha* and *shaucha* (purity) respectively. In order to justify the findings of *Dharma Shāstra* he has cited illustrations from *Dharma Shāstras, Rāmāyana* and *Purāna* in his text. His merit lies in bringing polity and *Dharma Shāstra* on parity.

***Devaprabhasuri*:** A 13th century Jain poet, Devaprabha Suri has written the story of the Mahābhārata in his *kāvya Pāndavacharita* in 18 cantos. The entire text has been written in *anushtupa chhanda*. His objective was to highlight the achievements of the *Pāndavas* and to justify the necessity of war in the wake of depriving them of due share. War is imminent in the sense that all avenues leading to truce are virtually closed and hopes of the warring factions reaching an agreement and coming to the negotiating table to settle their dispute are finally thwarted. It is also termed as a means to obliterate the outlaws and to restore harmony, balance, system, order and cohesion in society which is badly disturbed in the wake of the interest of a particular section is largely ignored at the cost of the other.

***Devibhāgavata*:** Devi Bhāgavata is a *purāna,* which has been written in praise of Devi or *shakti*. Both *Shrimad Bhāgavata* and *Devi Bhāgavata* are called *Mahā-purānas* in Samskrit literature. In the *Shrimad Bhāgavata*, the importance of Vishnu has been brought out. In the *Devi Bhāgavata* the significance of *shakti* has been brought out. In the book there are 12 chapters and 18,000 *Shloka*s. In the serial order of the *Purāna*s, *Bhāgavata* stands at the fifth place. *Devi Bhāgavata* has not been enumerated in *sātvika purāna*s. *Purāna*s like *Vāyu purāna*, *Matsyapurāna* and *Aditya up-purāna* admit *Devi Bhāgavata* as *mahā purāna* whereas in *Padma purāna*, *Garuda purāna* and *Kurma purāna* , it has been considered *up-purāna*. In the *Shrimad Bhāgavata*, there is no reference to the *Devi Bhāgavta* but in its eighth section there is the reflection of the *Shrimad Bhāgavata*.

***Dhananjaya*:** Dhananjaya was a critic. He has written a memorable work on dramaturgy entitled *Dasha-rupaka*. He belonged to the 2nd half of the 10th century. The book was written during the reign of Munja (974-944 A.D.), king of *Paramāra* dynasty. *Dasha Rupaka* consists of four *prakāshas* and 300 *kārikā*s. Almost all the questions pertaining to *rupaka* have been answered convincingly in it. Dhananajaya has advanced fresh arguments in support of *rasa*. He was opposed the view that *Dhvani* is the essence of poetry. The relationship between *rasa* and *kāvya* is that of *bhāva* and *bhāvaka*. He has strictly ruled that, *rasa* is experienced by the audience (*sāmājika*). The *anukārya* (hero/ character) does not have any such experience. He has termed *shānta Rasa* as inappropriate to drama. In a state of quietness normal activities are set to naught. Therefore, those activities cannot be staged. Dhananjaya joined hands with Bhatta Nāyaka, Kuntaka and Māhimbhatta to raise a banner of protest aloft against *Dhvani* giving it a serious jolt. Dhnanjaya's brother Dhanika, himself an eminent critic, wrote a commentary on *Dasha Rupaka*.

Dhaneshvara Suri: An eminent Jain scholar of the 7th century, Dhaneshvara Suri, wrote an epic called *Shatrunjaya*. It has been divided into 14 cantos and it deals with the popular mythologies associated with several kings.

Dharāmakirti: A 7th century scholar of Buddhist philosophy, Dharma Kirti has written as many as seven books on *Buddha*-Pramāna *Shāstra* of which Pramānavartikā and Nyāyabindu are prominent. It has been written in 1500 *Shloka*s and has been divided into four *parichchhedas*. There is a lengthy discussion on *Svārthānumāna, Pramānasiddhi, Pratyaksha Pramāna*, and *Parārthānumāna*. *Nyāyabindu* is the most significant work on Buddha *Nyāya*. It has been written in the form of Sutras. It is divided into three *parichchhedas*. The **first** *parichchheda* deals with *Pramāna* and *Pratyaksha*. The **second** *parichchheda* deals with *anumāna* (inference) and its three forms: *svārtha* and *parārthānumāna* and *hetvābhāsa*. The **third** *parichchheda* presents an in depth analysis of *Parārthānumāna*.

Dharmasutra: Dharmasutras are part of *Kalpa*. They deal with various codes of conduct. They are close to *Grhyasutras* in the sense that almost identical subjects have been covered in them. A detailed analysis of marriage, *samskāras*, students, *snātakas, shrāddha* and *madhuparka* has been given in *Dharmasutras*. The *samskāras* related to normal life are sparingly introduced. Among popular *Dharmasutras* the following can be included: Gautama *Dharmasutra*, Baudhāyana *Dharmasutra*, Āpastamba *Dharmasutra*, Hiranyakeshi *Dharmasutra*, Vashistha *Dharmasutra*, Vishnu *Dharmasutra*, Harita *Dharmasutra* and Sankha *Dharmasutra*. Kumarila Bhatta has mentioned the *Dharmasutras* of different Vedas in his *Tantavartikā*. Gautama *Dharmasutra* was utilised by the admirers of Sāmaveda. The followers of the Rigveda used Vashistha *Dharmasutra*, Disciples of Vajasaneyi *Samhitā* used Sankha *Dharmasutra* and the followers of *Taittariya* branch used Āpastamba and Baudhāyana *Dharmasutras*.

Dhvanyāloka: Dhvanyāloka is the most celebrated work on *Dhvani* composed by Ānadavardhana. Dhvanyāloka is the landmark of Indian poetics in which accepting *Dhvani* as a universal theory sufficient light has been thrown on its various aspects. The book has been divided into four *Udyotas;* and *Kārikā*, *Vritti* and illustrations form its three parts. In the **first** *Udyota* the ideas of the predecessors showing their allegiance to *Dhvani* have been highlighted. In the same section, three possible allegations on *Dhvani* triggered by its detractors like Māhimbhatta, Kuntaka and Dhananjaya have been opposed. The writer has taken *Dhvani* as the soul of poetry and has maintained that *Dhvani* cannot be merged into any theory of poetics. On the contrary, other theories can be assimilated within *Dhvani*. The **second** *udyota* deals with the kinds of *Dhvani*. The **third** *udyota* discusses kinds of *Dhvani*. Besides this, *gunibhuta vyanjana* and *Chitrakāvya* have also been interpreted. The **fourth** *udyota* deals with the significance of *Dhvani siddhānta* extensively.

Abhinava Gupta wrote the only commentary on *Dhvanyāloka* entitled *Dhvanyā-loka-lochana* in which he outrightly rejected the rival claims of the detractors of *Dhvani* theory and strongly recommended *Dhvani* as the soul of poetry.

Ānandavardhana maintains that the beauty of poetry doesnot lie in its component parts but in its totality as the beauty of a damsel doesnot lie in her different limbs but in what she is in the sum total of all the excellences which is called *lāvanya* or grace. The beauty of poetic meaning lies in its *pratiyamāna ārtha* or suggestive meaning, which transcends bald or flat meaning: *abhidheyārtha* and metaphorical meaning: *lakshyārtha*. He asks us to be on guard against neglecting *abhidheyārtha*, the basis of all the meanings. He observes that as a man cherishing light must take care of the oil of the lamps similarly a man looking for *dhvanyārtha* or *Pratimānārtha* must take care of *abhidheyārtha* on which the super-structure of meaning is laid. In fact, *abhidheyārtha* is the foundation and *laksyārtha* and *vyanjanārtha* are its scaffoldings.

In order to illustrate *dhvanyārtha*, Anandavardhana gives a very suggestive example. There lived a beautiful young girl in a cottage, which was situated in the midst of a dense forest. A young chap madly loved her. A hermit was in the habit of frequenting the cottage of the girl, which was a great impediment in the way of the union with her lover. The hermit was very much afraid of the dog, which lived outside the cottage. The girl asked the hermit to come to her place fearlessly since the dog, which lived nearby was of late killed by the tiger. The intended meaning is just the opposite of what she says. It means that the hermit must not come to the place because tigers come there. The hermit was afraid of the dog and so quite naturally the name of the tiger would strike a terror in his heart. The meaning is implied and suggestive and is nowhere found in the version of the damsel. It is the outcome of the total sequence. It is suggestive. It has nothing to do with literal meaning or metaphorical meaning.

Anandavardhana divided word-power (*Shabda-Shakti*) into three divisions: denotative meaning (*Abhidhā*), metaphorical meaning (*lakshanā*) and suggestive meaning (*vyanjanā*) and showed the supremacy of *vyanjanā* over first two. He emphatically stated that where *abhidhā* and *lakshanā* become inoperative *vyanjanā* helps to complete the meaning. *Abhidhā* is the description of bare facts. This is a cow - is *abhidhā*; *lakshana* derives its meaning from curved expression. His heart is of stone: is *laksha; vyanjanā* excels the two. It suggests a meaning, which is available neither in *abhidhā* nor in *lakshanā*. The bell is gone suggests several meanings. For a schoolboy it means the classes are now dispersed. For a prostitute it means the time of business has come and so on.

Dinganāga: Dinga Nāga was an exponent of Buddha *Nyāya* and eminent scholar of Buddhist philosophy. 100 books, pertaining to the school of Buddha *Nyāya,* have been attributed to him. But his popularity chiefly rests on his book *Pramāna Samuchya*. The original text is missing. Only the Tibetan translation of this text made by Hema Vermā is available. The entire ideology of

Nyāya Shāstra is packed up within the corpus of this monumental work. It is divided into 6 *parichchhedas* in which pratyaksha, Svārthānumāna, Parāthānumāna, hetu dristānta, and yāvriti have been discussed showing his command on the philosophy of Buddha *Nyāya*. An elaborate analysis of his book, *Pramāna Samuchya* has been made by Dinganāga himself in *Pramāna-Samuchya-vritti.*

Dinganāga: Dinga Nāga is the author of the drama *Kundamālā,* which is based on the story of the *Rāmāyana* with some changes. Unlike the Rāmāyana, Dinganāga has given a comic end to the tragic story of Sitā. Prithvi (earth) comes to the rescue of Sitā declaring her untainted and pious allowing Rāma to have the fold of her wife and children. The influence of Bhavabhuti's Uttara Rāmacharita, which also ends on pleasant note with Sitā joining the company of Rāma after her ordeal, cannot be denied.

The entire drama is divided into 6 acts which deals with the story of the life of Lord Rāma from his coronation onwards. It finally culminates in the reunion of Rāma and Sitā. In the **first act**, Laksmana accompanies Sitā to the bank of the Ganges in the thick forest and comes back to the palace leaving her alone there in order to carry out the errand of Rāma. Rāma had to take deterrent action against Sitā as a reaction to allegations. The **second act** deals with the birth of Lava-Kusha. The **third act** depicts Rāma in a state of utter frustration. Walking on the bank of the Gomati, along with Lakshmana. Rāma bursts into tears after looking at the garland of *kunda* flowing in the Gomati. Sitā, who is also present there along with her sons, watches the entire incident disguising in the bush. In the **fourth act**, an *apsarā* named Tilottamā further aggravates the misery of Rāma assuming the figure of Sitā. The **fifth act** deals with the story of Lava-Kusha reciting the Rāmayana in the court of Rāma. In the **sixth** and final act, Prithvi comes to the rescue of Sitā and sets at rest the speculations leading to the deportation of Sitā and paving the way for Rāma enjoying the company of his wife and sons for the rest of his life.

Divākara: Divākar was a 17th century scholar of astrology. He learnt this science from his uncle Shiva Daivagana. He has shown efficiency in Phalita Jyotisha and has written *Jāka-paddhati*, which is a masterpiece. He has himself written the commentary on another book *Paddhati Prakāsha*.

Draupadi Parinaya Champu: Draupadi Parinaya Champu has been written by Chakra who belonged to the latter half of the 17th century. He was the court poet of the kings of Pāndya and Cherā dynasties. This *champu* has been divided into 6 *asvāsas*. The story has been derived from the *Ādiparva* of the *Mahābhārata*. The poet has retained the original story. The story ends with Dhritarāshtra agreeing to hand over half of the kingdom to Yudhisthira and the latter taking over the charge of his office following the agreement. His other works include: *Rukmini-parinaya, Jānaki-parinaya, Pārvati-parinaya* and *Chitra-ratnākara*.

Dutaghatotkacha: Duta Ghatotkacha is a drama written by Bhāsa. The story of the *Mahābhārata*, from which the subject matter is derived, has been presented in a new perspective. The characters of the Mahābhārata have been assigned a different role, as opposed to the role assigned to them in the original text. Hidimba's son Ghatotkacha, who caused a great havoc in the camp of the *Kauravas* on a fateful day compelling *Kaurava* warriors to bite the dust and turning the tide in favour of the *Pāndavas*, is serving a different cause. He is on a peaceful mission to convince Dhritarāshtra of the impending danger awaiting his doorstep in the wake of Arjuna's vow to avenge the murder of his son Abhimanyu by killing the assassin Jayadratha before dusk. Dhritarāshtra forces Duryodhana to reconsider his decision smacking the result of the war but to no effect, since Shakuni misguides the latter. He fails to respond to the tiding of his father. This leads to a rift between Ghatotkacha and Duryodhana and the former hurls a threat at the latter to take him to task, although Dhritarāshtra intervenes and pacifies the two belligerent generals. Finally, Ghatotkacha departs holding out a threat to avenge the murder of Abhimanyu. The plot of the text is imaginary and it also lacks *Bharatavākya*.

Dutavākya: Duta Vākya is a *vyāyoga* (part of *Rupaka*) written by Bhāsa having only one act. Krishna has been sent to the court of the *Kauravas* by the *Pāndavas* as their messenger to sign a peace treaty in order to evade the devastating war. The drama begins with Duryodhana raising his objection reprimanding Kanchuki for addressing Krishna as *Purushottama*. He also warns his courtiers not to show respect to Krishna on his arrival to the court otherwise they would be severely punished. The courtiers stand from their seats as a mark of respect for Krishna ignoring the alarm of a punitive action by Duryodhana. Krishna gives his proposal of peace and truce and suggested that half of the kingdom should be handed over to the *Pāndavas*. Duryodhana vehemently opposes this proposal and rebukes Krishna for serving the cause of the Pāndavas. Krishna responds in the same manner. Duryodhana issues an arrest warrant against Krishna after hot exchange of words between the two. But nobody dares comply with the order. Duryodhana himself comes forward to execute his order but is flabbergasted to see the gigantic image of Krishna. In a state of sheer wrath, Krishna allows *chakra sudarshana* to chop off the head of Duryodhana. But the *chakra* does not respond. Krishna finally regains his mental poise. Dhritarāshtra surrenders on the feet of Krishna showing his helplessness. The drama concludes with the *Bharatavākya*.

'Dutavākya' is a perfect example of *vyāyoga*. It fully adheres to its norms. The hero of a *vyāyoga* must be aggressive and the story should have a historical background. *Vira Rasa* is the dominating *Rasa* since war is the focal point of *Vyāyoga*. In this sense, Dutavākya fulfills all its requisite conditions. The title also justifies in the sense that Krishna is on a peace mission serving as the messenger of the Pāndavas.

Dvisandhānakāvya: Dhananjaya, a 10th century poet, has written Dvi-sandhāna-kāvya, also known as *Rāghava Pāndviya. Dvisandhāna kāvya* has been divided into 18 cantos, which narrates the story of the *Rāmāyana* and the *Mahābhārata* simultaneously. Being complex in nature this style of writing did not gain ground and except Dhananjaya, no poet of repute did try his muse to handle it. Dhananjaya has also written a dictionary named *Nāmamālā*. Nemichandra has written an elaborate commentary on *Rāghava Pāndaviya*. Rājashekhara, an eminent critic, has also praised Dhanajaya in his *Suktimuktāvali*.

Dwijendranāth Mishra Dwijendra Nāth Mishra is a twentieth century poet. His works include various aspects of Samskrit literature ranging from criticism and *kāvya* to history. Among his prominent works are *Yajurvedabhāsya*, *Rigveda-bhāsya-bhumikā-prakāshāta*, *Vedā-tatva-avlokanam*, *Samskrit Sāhitya Vimarsha* and *Svarājya-vijaya*. *Samskrit Sāhitya-Vimarsha* is an exhaustive study of Samskrit literature. He has thrown sufficient light on the different areas of Samskrit literature. He has been impartial in his treatment and his analysis of the contributions made by various poets is manifested in it. ■■

European Scholars of Samskrit: The first systematic attempt to popularise the study of Samskrit in Europe was made by Sir William Jones. His efforts finally culminated into the establishment of the Asiatic Society of Bengāl which contributed significantly in the translation and publication of several manuscripts. William Jones himself translated *Abhigyāna-shākunatala* in English in 1789, which attracted European scholars towards the study of Samskrit. William Jones also supplied the English translation of *Manusmriti* and *Ritusamhāra*. On the basis of his English translation the German scholar George Forster translated *Shakuntalā* in Germany for which Goethe showered unreserved praise.

The attraction of western scholars for Samskrit, started, way back in the 7th century, with the translation of *Panchtantra.* Besides the translation works, Christian missionaries active in India for propagating Christianity also contributed immensely to spread Samskrit. A Christian priest named Abraham Rouser gave a Portuguese translation of the shloka of Bhartrihari.

The spread of Samskrit continued unabated after the establishment of 'Asiatic Society of Bengāl'. Another important contribution in this regard was from Charles William who translated Gitā' in 1785. He also translated *Shakutalopākhyānam* and '*Hitopadesha'*. Thomas Colebrook achieved a milestone by translating *'Amarkosha'*, '*Kirārtarjuniya'*, '*Hitopadesha'* and '*Ashtādhyāyi'*. He also wrote a book 'A Digest of Hindu Law of Contracts'.

Famous German scholar Schegal translated *Bhāgavadgitā* and '*Ramāyāna'* in 1829. His contemporary Bopp wrote an essay on contemporary philology and provided a Latin translation of the story of '*Nala-Damayanti'*. He has also written a grammar and a *kosha* of Samskrit. *Upnishadas* were translated in German by Shelling. Ferguson James made a thorough inspection of dilapidated buildings and places of worship to present archeological account, which is successfully contained in his work 'Hindu Principle of Beauty in Art'.

German scholar Max Muller's contribution in this respect is most significant. He studied Samskrit literature for 56 years and published an enlarged edition of the 'Rigveda' along with *Sāyana-bhāsya*. He also published 'A History of Ancient Samskrit Literature', which throws sufficient light on various aspects of Samskrit literature. He also provided German translations of '*Meghaduta*' '*Hitopadesha*', '*Dhammpada*' and *Upanishada*. In the sacred book of the east series running into 48 volumes, he translated several Samskrit classics. Wilson wrote a book entitled 'Hindu Theatre' and made an arduous task by translating *Vishnu-purāna* and Rigveda in 6 volumes. The German scholar Ruth's Samskrit-German *Kosha* needs to be given special attention. Around 1870 H. Grassman and Wilson provided English translation of Rigveda on the basis of *Sāyana-bhāsya*. Dr. Pischel's lectures on Samskrit in Berlin University also made an outstanding contribution to the popularity of Samskrit in western countries through his work 'Vedic Studies'. Weber, MacDonnell and Keith's contribution is immense and have become legend in this regard. Weber's 'History of Samskrit Literature' is a systematic analysis of various trends and movements in Samskrit Literature. MacDonnell also enriched Samskrit literature through 'History of Samskrit Literature', 'Vedic Reader', 'Vedic Grammar' and 'Vedic Index'. Keith's 'History of Samskrit Literature' is also an authoritative work in this discipline. His other works include Vedic Index, Religion and philosophy of the Vedas and *Upanishadas*, Buddhist philosophy in India and Ceylon and Samskrit drama. Besides these scholars Winternitz's 'History of Samskrit literature' is another significant contribution in this respect. German scholar Dr. Thobby wrote essays on *Mimāmsā* and *Jyotisha* and published a *bhāsya* on *Vedānta-sutra* along with Shankara and Rāmānuja. The scholar of Jaina literature Dr. Yacobi translated Jain *sutras*. Goldstucker wrote a very authentic work on Pānini in English giving emphasis on his period.

Dr. Aufrecht prepared a voluminous reference book entitled 'Catologous Categorum', which presents the account of Samskrit manuscripts. Moiser made a commendable job by writing Original Samskrit texts in 5 volumes, which presents integral texts basically of Vedic literature and their Samskrit translation. Roman scholar Adfesta provided Roman translation of the Rigveda and *Aitareya Brāhman*.

William White Whitney (1827-94) popularised the study of Samskrit in America. His grammar of Samskrit written in 1879 is a monumental work. He also provided English translation of '*Atharva-pratisākhya*' and '*Surya-siddhānta*' 'A Test of Jyotisha'. Prof. Olderberg translated '*Vinaya-pitaka*'. Prof. Bloomfield's translation of Atharva Veda needs special mention. Hillbant wrote Vedic Mythology in 3 volumes. Bothling, an eminent grammarian edited *Brihdāranyaka* and *Chhāndogya Upanisada* and published *Ashtādhyāyi* and Hemachandara's *Abhidhāna Chintāmani*. Rise Davidson, Morris Hardy and Spare have made significant contribution on Buddhist literature. Monier Williams and T. Borough wrote philological grammar of Samskrit. T. Borough's Samskrit Language has become very popular. Sorenson's *Mahābhārata* index is another milestone in this regard. Wakernegal wrote the most significant philological grammar of Samskrit in German in 4 volumes. The French scholar Luis Reno wrote Vedic India and Vedic Bibliography in French. Griffith made an outstanding contribution by making a verse translation of the Vedas. Several Samskrit texts have been translated in Russian language. The Russian translation of the Mahābhārata has also been published.

■■

Gadādhara Bhattāchārya: Gadādhara Bhattāchārya is one of the exponents of *Navya-nyāya* branch of Nyāya School of philosophy. He hails from Bengāl and is an ardent supporter of Gangesha Upādhyāya. He has laid more emphasis on the interpretation of various *pramānas* (proof) as opposed to the ideologues who accepted *pramān* as the means to achieve liberation or moksha. *Navya-nyāya* takes *pramān* both as means and end. He broke a new ground by according a firm footing to Indian logic. The germs of logic can be traced out in the writings of *Navya Naiyāyikas*. His interpretations are very systematic and coherent and have added a new dimension to the study of *Navya-nyāya*.

Gadanigraha: Gada Nigraha is Āyurvedic text composed by Soddhala. He belonged to the 13th century and was an inhabitant of Gujarāt. The book has been divided into ten sections covering major diseases and their remedies. The first section comprises: six adhikāras: *churna, gutikā, avaleha, āsava, ghrita* and *taila*. It is also a compilation of 585 yoga exercises. The rest of the nine sections deal with: *kāyachikitsā, sālakya, salya, bhuta-tantra, bala-tantra, visha-tantra, vājikarana, rasāyana*, and *pancha-karmādhikāra*. Soddhala has also written a book on medical science entitled *Guna-samgraha*. The scholarly treatment of diseases and their remedial measures put forward by Soddhala are sufficient testimony to his rich knowledge and experience. He elevated Āyurveda to a new height by his scholarly works, which have given new dimension to the study of Āyurveda.

Gangesha Upādhyāya: Gangesha Upādhyāya was an eminent exponent of *Navya-nyāya* branch of the *Nyāya* School of philosophy. He brought about a vital change in the ideology of the *Nyāya* School through his monumental work *'Tatva-chintāmani'*. This book is divided into four sections in which special attention has been given to four *pramāns* including *pratyaksha*. The logic embodied in it, is so thought-provoking that as many as 10 lakh pages have been written on it. Prominent among the commentaries on *Tatva-chintāmani* is that of Pakshadhara Mishra's Āloka. Gangesha Upādhyāya's son Vardhana Upādhyāya was an equally gifted man and wrote a commentary entitled *Prakāsha* on *Tatva-chintāmani*.

'*Navya Nyāya*' is a peculiar theory and has contributed immensely to the enriched repertory of Indian philosophy. Indian logic and argumentative skill has acquired a new dimension by the efforts of Gangesha Upādhyāya who brought philosophical speculation to a high pedestal by his exceptional contemplative acumen. The *Navya Naiyāyikas* have given up the sutra style of writing, which was prevalent in the preceding periods and have reposed faith in independent works. The exponents of *Navya Nyāya* have used part of the 16 *padārths* of *Nyāya* School, and have rejected part of the *pad padārths*.

Garuda Purāna: Chronologically Garuda Purāna is the 17th *Purāna,* which has been named after Garuda, the vehicle of Lord Vishnu. Vishnu has imparted invaluable teachings to Garuda regarding the creation of universe. It is significant in the sense that recitation of *Garuda Purāna* is made compulsory in the last rites. It incorporates almost all useful topics and in this way is considered an encyclopedia like *Agni Purāna*. It is divided into two sections: *Purva-khanda* and *Uttara-khanda*. The former consists of 229 chapters whereas the latter comprises of 35. There are 18,000 *shlokas* in it. Being a *Vaishnava Purāna*, it is basically concerned with the worship of Vishnu, *Vaishnava Vrats*, atonement, and significance of pilgrimages. It also lays emphasis on *pancha-devopāsanā* (offerings to five gods Vishnu, Surya, Durgā, Shiva and Ganesha) alongside the offering to Shakti. Besides incorporating the topics of *Rāmāyana*. *Mahābhārata* and *Haribansha*, it also hinges round *srishti-karma*, astrology, *sakuna-vichāra*, *Sāmudrika-Shāstra*, *Āyurveda*, *Chhanda, vyākarana, ratna-parikshā* and moral teachings.

A major portion of Yāgyavalakaya *Dharma Shāstra* has also been included in *Garuda Purāna*. It has also included veterinary science along with several medicines which are used to cure numerous ailments. It also includes *chhanda Shāstra* and politics. The story of *Gitā* and *Krishna lilā* has been assimilated. The *Uttara-khanda*, which is also called *Preta-kalpa*, deals with various situations a *Jiva* faces after death. The religious significance of Gayā, and the last rituals performed here have been given extensive treatment.

Gāthāsaptashati: Gāthā Saptashati is a collection of 700 verses in *Prākrita* in a metre called *Gāthā*. This collection is attributed to the king of Pratishthānapura named Hāla or Shālivāhana. His queen Malayavati was an erudite scholar at whose behest the king studied *Samskrit*.

Gāthā-saptashati represents a work of that period when regional languages were growing and presenting a graphic picture of the lives, customs, manners, and rituals of the village folks. The portrayals made in the *Gāthā-saptashati* are very lively and they touch upon inner chord of heart. There is a complete negation of the amorous life of court and an urge for homely life led by the mass. Its beauty lies in the picturesque description of the lives of the common people. There is a moving description of a newly wedded girl, whose husband is ready to depart telling him not to leave her soon since the hair, which she used to give a proper shape using oil have yet not been strangled.

Gāthā-saptashati is a precious gem of lyric literature in *Prākrit* language. Its special features are the expression of novel thought, manifestation of esoteric meanings and manipulation of tender and evocative words. It has the credit to be quoted in works of poetics like Dhvanyāloka, Kāvyaprakāsha and Rasagangādhara.

Gautama: Gautama is the pioneer of *Nyāya* School and the writer of *Nyāya-sutra*. There is no unanimity of opinion regarding the authorship of *Nyāya-sutra* by Gautama. His timing is fixed around 4th century *Vikrama Purva*. There are five sections in *Nyāya-sutra* and each section is further divided into two sub-sections called *ahnika*. It deals with 16 *padārtha*. As it is apparent from the ancient procedure of *Nyāya*, they were twofold, first, in which prominence was given to *ādhyātma* and second, in which prominence was given to logic. While Gautama fostered the first, Akshapada fostered the second procedure. The two philosophers in their own way endeavoured to prove the existence of God, soul, rebirth, cycle of life, creation of universe and life after death.

Gautama Dharmasutra: Gautama Dharma-Sutra is the oldest of all the *Dharmasutras*. It is related to the Sāmaveda. Reference to Gautama has been given in Latyāyana *Shrauta-sutra* and Drahyāyana *Shrauta-sutra*. Gautama's *Dharma-sutra* presents a synoptic view of the principles appearing in *Grahya, Shrauta* and *Dharma-sutras*. Haradatta has written a commentary on it. The entire work, running into 28 chapters, is written in prose. Its subjects cover various kinds of *samskārs* including *upnayana. Grihastha*, Marriage, provision of punishment for crimes of different hues and colours, *shrāddha* and atonement.

Gitā: Gitā is the teachings of Lord Krishna to Arjuna, his ardent disciple, to enable him to tide over his cowardice and prepare himself for fighting; and through that to all human beings to perform one's duty irrespective of the outcome. It is a part of the *Bhisma Parva* of the *Mahābhārata*. Veda Vyāsa wrote it. It consists of 719 *shlokas* and has been divided into 18 chapters. The objective of this book is to tackle moral, and spiritual problems facing an individual who is left in a state of dilemma finding it almost impossible to come out of the mess. It has been included among *Prasthāna-trai,* the three prominent works of Indian Classics; and accommodates gist of philosophical ideologies imparted in the *Upanishadas, Sāmkhya, Karma-mimāmsā, Yoga* and *Pancha-rātra*. Thousands of commentaries on the *Gitā* have come out since its composition. Prominent among the writers are: Shankara, Rāmānuja, Tilaka, Gāndhi, Aurobindo, Radhā Krishnan and Vinobā Bhave. The universal acknowledgement of the philosophy of *Gitā* can be gauzed from the fact that it has been translated into almost all the prominent languages of the world. Eminent scholars from all over the world have showered praise on the *Gitā*.

We need to be given proper training about the immortality of soul which can neither be burnt by fire, nor be drenched by water, nor be dried by air or severed by weapon and so on: *nainamchhindanti Shāstrāni, nainam dahati pāvakah, na chainam cledayāntāpina shosayati mārutah*. One need not be afraid of death because death is nothing but a door to new life. As a man puts off his tattered garments and puts on a fresh one, similarly, death simply destroys the body and leaves the soul untouched, which assumes a fresh form in a new body.

Gitā has given equal importance to *Gyāna, Bhakti* and *Karma* by bringing them on equal footing. While *Kāma* (sex), *Krodha* (anger) and *Lobha* (greed) have been treated as means leading to the ultimate downfall or catastrophe, it lays utmost emphasis on *karma yoga,* which is the sum and substance of the philosophy of the *Gitā*. Krishna has insisted that one should crave for that (*karma*) which is well within his reach and that (outcome of the action) falling outside the confine of one's purview should not be taken into consideration. The action should not be aimed at achieving a desired result. It should be *nishkāma karma*, deed performed with complete detachment. *Bhakti* (devotion) is the heart of the *Gitā*. Life without *bhakti* is meaningless and worthless. Krishna has advised to surrender to the Almighty, as he would free one from all sins: *sarvadharmāna parityajyat māmekam sharnam vraja; aham tvā sarva pāpebhyo mokshashyāmi mā shuchah.*

In the sixth chapter of the *Gitā* special treatment has been given to *dhyānayoga*. In order to restore equipoise to the disturbed self and make it concentrate on God, various Yogic devices including *āsana* and *pranāyāma* have been suggested. The *Gitā* does not limit itself to the philosophical plane it imparts teachings descending to the practical surface. Ideals raised in the *Gitā* are as much relevant to the modern man as to the persons belonging to the *Mahābhārata* period.

***Gita Govinda*:** Jayadeva, a devotee of Shri Krishna, wrote Gita Govinda. It is a lyrical poem of high order. Jayadeva was the court poet of Laksmana Sena of Bengāl. His period is fixed around the later half of the 12th century. In Gita Govinda, there is lucid, picturesque and moving description of *lilās* of Rādhā-Krishna.

Jayadeva lived in Kenduli (Bengāl). Jayadeva's *Gita Govinda* describes Rādhā and Krishna as divine beings, and as symbols of crystal and spiritual love. The poet himself is full of applause for the lyrical quality of *Gita Govinda*. It has 10 *sargas* and every *sarga* is packed with mellifluous and musical lines that is a reason that its many extracts are sung during poojā in temples as well as at homes. The first four verses are *mangalā-charana*, introduction with the objective of the poem and the identity of the poet. Thereafter *Dashāvatāra* is described. Then the basic text begins and the poem ends on a note of praise of the poet. From the theme of *Gita Govinda*, it appears that the main aim is to give a description of *Rāsa lilā*. The two kinds of *shringāra: samyoga* and *viyoga* find expression here.

Gopatha Brāhmana: Gopatha Brāhamana is the only *Brāhamana* text of the Atharva Veda. It is divided into *Purva Gopatha* and *Uttara Gopatha*. The first section consists of five chapters and the second consists of 6 chapters. These chapters are divided into *kandikās*, which are 258 in number. The authorship is attributed to Gopatha Rishi. It has been written prior to Nirukta since Yāska quotes its hymns. It enumerates the qualities of the Atharva Veda, which has been accepted as the most accomplished of all the Vedas. In the **first** chapter, the power of *Omkāra* and *Gāyatri* has been highlighted. The **second** chapter is devoted to the rituals of *Brahmacharies* whereas the **third,** and the **fourth** are devoted to the activities of *Ritvijas*. The **fifth** chapter focuses on *Samvatsara*.

Uttarakhanda of *Gopatha Brāhmana* is less organised. It deals with various kinds of *yagyās* and stories related to them. Several facts pertaining to linguistics have also been incorporated into it.

■■

Hammira Kāvya: Hammira Kāvya is an epic written by Nayana Chandrasuri. The poet has presented a lively description of the battle between Rānā Hammira, the famous Rānā of Rānāthambhor, and Alāuddin, the king of Delhi, which culminated in the death of Hammira. It consists of 14 cantos and 1515 *shloka*s. The authenticity of the events described by the poet is further proved through historical dates made available through various sources. The epic begins with Alāuddin getting cross with Hammira who threatens Hammira to teach a lesson in the battlefield for failing to comply with his command. The rivalry between the two intensified when Alāuddin's Muslim forces invaded the fort of Rānāthambhor leading to heavy casualties on both the sides including the death of Nusaratha Khān, one of the most trusted generals of Alāuddin. The news of the killing of Nusaratha Khān spreads like a wild fire and Alāuddin pledges to avenge the death of Nusaratha Khān. He himself goes to the battlefield for a final showdown with the army of Hammira. The battle takes a sudden turn when one of the generals of Hammira, named Ratipāla shifts his fidelity to Alāuddin and betrays his master. This incident proves disastrous. The Rajputa, soldiers fight bravely displaying exemplary courage and gallantry in the battlefield, but this much is not sufficient to romp home and to turn the tide in their favour. Huge casualty is reported from Hammira's side and the fighting persists till the last soldier is killed. Though defeated, Hammira and his soldiers force their enemies to bite the dust. Their women counterparts are also not far behind in protecting their chastity, preferring to perform *jauhara* by throwing themselves into the flame of fire to forbid the invaders to spoil their chastity, leaving behind only a heap of ashes.

This battle was fought in the year 1357. It is said that Nayana Chandrasuri had seen for himself the entire incident through his eyes wide open. The dominant *rasa* of the epic is *Vira rasa*. The poet has accepted his indebtedness to Kālidāsa with humility, particularly his style used in *Raghuvansha.*

Hanumāna Nātaka : Hanumāna Nātaka is a drama written by Damodar Mishra. On the basis of some of its *shloka*s coming in *Dhvanyāloka* he is supposed to have flourished around the beginning of the ninth century. Ānandavardhana's period has been fixed in the middle of the 9th century. The story of this drama has been derived from the *Rāmāyana*. Two versions, old and new, of this drama are available. While Dāmodar Mishra is supposed to have written the old version, the new version has been written by Madhusudana Dāsa. The old version consists of 14 acts while the new one consists of 9 acts. The drama is in verse. Prose has been used in this book by fits and starts. Multiple characters and the absence of clown mark this drama. *Vishkambhaka* is nowhere found. *Sutradhāra* is also missing.

Hansa Sandesha: Hansa Sandesha is a *Sandesha kāvya* intended to communicate a message. Purnasārasvata has written it. He flourished in the beginning of the 13th century. Nothing with regard to his life is available. In this poem a damsel belonging to *Kānchipura* delivers her message to Krishna through a Hansa (swan). The damsel, after narrating the dynasty, habitation and indomitable power of swan, suggests the swan to go to Vrindāvana to find out the whereabouts of Krishna. It has been written in 102 *Mandākrāntā Chhanda*.

***Haracharita Chintāmani*:** Haracharita Chintāmani is an epic written by Jayadratha, an inhabitant of Kashmir. The epic deals with *lilā*s performed by Shiva in *anustupachhanda*. Jayadratha was the court poet of Rājadeva, the king of Kashmir, who ruled over his kingdom between 1204 and 1226 AD. He is the brother of Jayaratha, the commentator of *Alankārasarvasva.* The poet has very skillfully presented various aspects of the life of Lord Shiva in a simple and flexible style.

Haribhadra: Haribhadra is a scholar of Jainism. He belonged to the 8th century. His important works are: *Saddarshana Samuchchya* and *Anekānta Jayapatākā.*

***Harishchandra*:** Harishchandra was a noted Jain poet belonging to the 12th century. Two books *Dharmasarmābhyudaya* and *Jivandhara Champu* have been attributed to him. The former is an epic consisting of 21 contos, which deals with the life of the 15th Jaina *tirthankara* Dharmanāthajee. *Jivandhara Champu* deals with the story of king Satyandhara and Jain prince Jivandhara. It aimed at disseminating the teachings of Jainism through the story of Jivandhara. It presents a unique blend of simple and figurative style. There is complete lack of linguistic uniformity in this poem.

***Harisena*:** Harisena was a scholar of great renown in the court of Samudragupta. He is placed in the category of those poets of *Samskrit* whose works have been engraved on stones in the form of panegyrics. Materials connected with the life and poetic craftsmanship can be collected from his *Prayāga* panegyric. The Gupta king Samudragupta whose Prayāga panegyric, written in 345 A.D., is engraved on an Asokan pillar, patronised him. This panegyric throws ample light on the victories of king Samudra Gupta and his outstanding personality. It has been written in Shragdhara Chhanda. It also incorporates ornamental prose. His poetry achieves the height of Kālidāsa while his prose comes closer to the writings of Bānabhatta.

***Harivansha Purāna*:** Harivansha Purāna is called the supplement to the *Mahābhārata*. It has not been accorded the status of an independent *Purāna* and has always been attached to the *Mahābhārata*. *Harivansha* is divided into three *parvas*. It consists of 16374 *shlokas*. The first *parva* called *Harivansha* consists of 55 chapters. The second parva entitled Vishnu *parva* consists of 81 chapters and the third *parva* entitled *Bhavishya* consists of 135 *parvas.* It deals with the exploits of Lord Vishnu. Besides this, it also presents the story of Lord Krishna and various *lilā*s performed by him in *Braja*. It begins with the description of the genesis of the universe and also narrates the five *laksanas* of the *Purānas*. It deals with *Pralaya*, the genealogy of kings and varied stories of saints in accordance with their dynasties and *Manavantaras*. It also incorporates various philosophical ideologies such as *Sāmkhya* and *Yoga*, Vaishnava, Shākta and Shaiva ideologies have also been included in it.

The *Harivansha Parva* deals with the story of Dhruva, Daksha and his daughters, king Vena who is supposed to have opposed yagya and the Vedas, his son Prithu, Vishvāmitra, Vashistha, king Ikshvāku and Krishna.

Hari Vilāsa: Hari Vilāsa is an epic written by Lolimbarāja consisting of amorous sports of Krishna including his *Bāla lilās* in five cantos. He flourished in the middle of the ninth century and was contemporary of Harihara, the king of Vijayanagar empire. He has also written a book on herbal medicine entitled *Vaidyajivana*.

Harshacharita: Harsha Charita is a prose work by Bānabhatta. It deals with the heroism and valour of king Harshavardhana in eight *Uchchhavāsas*. The epic follows conventional method and the **first** chapter begins with invocation and condemnation of rugged poets. It is followed by the genealogy of Bāna who has tried to establish his links with Sarasvati, the Goddess of learning. Once in heaven the seer Durvāsā pronounced incorrectly the hymns of Sāmaveda while quarrelling with the other saint, which provoked the laughter of Sarasvati. It created the wrath of Durvāsā who cursed Sarasvati to spend her life on the earth for a certain period. Sarasvati was shifted to the bank of the river *Sonanada* from *Brahmaloka*. Her bosom friend Sāvitri accompanied her. One day she saw the son of the seer Chyavana named Dadhicha riding a horse and fell in love with him. Their union finally gave birth to a son named Sārasvata. When the period of curse was over, Sarasvati left for heaven along with Sāvitri and Dadhicha left his son to the service of the wife of a seer named Akshamata. Aksamata's son was Vatsa with which Bāna has linked his lineage. The author has also introduced his friends and has mentioned his nomadic tendency during his childhood days.

The **second** *Uchchhavāsa* begins with an elaborated description of the summer season. The author has described the charity and valour of king Harsha in a sentence running into 140 lines. The **third**

Uchchhavāsa deals with the dynasty of Harsha. His descriptions include those of Pushyabhuti, Shrikantha Janapadavarnana, Sthānavishvara, Bhairavāchārya and his disciple. The **fourth** *Uchchhavāsa* deals with the life of Prabhākaravardhana, the son of Pusyabhuti. It leads to the birth of Rājyavardhana, son of Prabhākaravardhana. The birth of Harsha and his birthday celebrations have also been described in detail. The **fifth** *Uchchhavāsa* deals with the death of king Prabhākarvardhana. Rājyavardhana is deputed for a mission to quell the rebellion of the Hunas. Harsha accompanies him. Harsha returns to the kingdom after receiving the news of the ailment of his father. The latter embraces Harsha on his way back home. The king dies. This incident leads the queen to perform *satīvrata*. In the **sixth** Rājyavardhana also returns to the kingdom and consoles Harsha. In the mean time, the king of Mālavā kills the king of Maukhari Grahavarman, the brother-in-law of Harsha, and his sister is imprisoned. Rajavardhana becomes angry and immediately rushes there to take on the tyrant king to avenge the murder of his relative. Rājavardhana fights bravely and finally collapses. A shock wave grips the entire kingdom with Harsha pledging to bring the whole of the Aryavarta within his sovereignty. In the **seventh** *Uchchhavāsas*, Harsha leaves for the battlefield along with a mammoth army. The departure of armed forces caused immense hardships to the common people. Harsha makes a spot inspection of his army to boost the sagging morale of his soldiers and to ensure that no loophole is left. The king of *prāgjyotisapura* (*Āssām*) offers a celestial umbrella to Harsha. Other gifts are given by Bhāskara Varman. Harsha's sister Rājyashree reaches the Vindhya region along with her relatives. Harsha riding a horse makes a search for her. In the **eighth** Uchchhavāsa, youth of Sabara clan named Nirghata assures Harsha's assistance in making a search for Rājyashree. Harsha reaches the hermitage of Divākar Mishra along with Sabara and narrates the cause of his arrival. A certain monk divulges the pathetic condition of Rājyashree and Harsha finally catches hold of her. Divākar Mishra imparts teachings to Rājyashree. Harsha escorts her to his army camp.

Harshacharita is based on the pattern of *Akhyāyikā*. Bāna has himself called it *Akhyāyikā*, while *Kādambari* has been termed as *Kathā*. The basic difference between *Akhyāyikā* and *Kathā* is that while the former is based on historical incidents, the latter is the product of the poet's imagination.

Harshavardhana: Harshavardhana was great Emperor belonging to the 7th century. He ruled over the northern India between 606 and 648 A.D. He also contributed to the development of *Samskrit* literature. The information about his life can be had from *Harshacharita* and the travel accounts of Huein Tsang. His father's name was Prabhākaravardhana and his mother was Yashomati. His sister Rājyashree was married to Maukhari king, Grahavarma. He ascended to the throne after the premature death of his elder brother Rājyavardhana. He also excelled in fine arts besides showing exceptional military zeal.

Harshavardhana wrote three books: *Priyadarshikā*, *Ratnāvali* and *Nāgānanda*. The first two are *Natikās* (minor dramas) while the third one is a full-length drama. Indian scholars, on the other hand, have unanimously accepted Harsha as the author of *Ratnāvali* besides his two other dramas. *Ratnāvali* is a popular drama. Several scholars have cited quotations from *Ratnāvali* in their dramatic works. It deals with the love story of Vatsarāja and Udayana in four acts. *Priyadarshikā* also hinges around the character of Udayana. *Nāgānanda* deals with the story of Jimutavāhana who rescued the snakes from the clutches of Garuda. In the Nandi of Nāgānanda, invocation to Lord Buddha has been made which further strengthens the speculation of Harsha embracing the Buddhist cult.

Harsha's poetic quality and talent has been reflected in his poems as well as in dramas. He has depicted natural scenery using opposite words. He seems inclined to portray conventional objects like evening, midday, orchard, garden, stream, marriage ceremony, bathing period, Malaya mountain, forest and towering mansions. His language is embellished with all kinds of artistic devices. It is pregnant with ideas. He is cautious in the use of poetic figures, which has further enhanced the flow and momentum of his language. He willfully avoids terseness and complexity in his diction showing his intimacy with commonplace words. His language successfully conveys his ideas besides generating *Rasa*. He has used *Shārdulavikridita chhanda* on several occasions in his dramas. These long drawn *chhanda*s hinder the natural movement of his drama. The characters of Harsha are not mere puppets in the hands of the dramatist rather they enjoy independence.

***Hema Chandra*:** Hema Chandra was an eminent scholar of poetics and Jain philosophy. He occupies honourable place among Jain scholars. He flourished in the 12th century. He got this name after his initiation into Jain cult. He has written books on wide ranging subjects. His popular works are: *Shabdānushāsana*, *Kāvyānushāsana*, *Chhandānushāsana*, *Abhidhāna-chintāmani*, *Trishashti-salākā-purusha-charita* and *Yoga Shāstra*. The first is a grammatical text, the second is a work on poetics and the third and the fourth are dictionaries. *Kāvyānushāsana* has been written in sutras. It has been divided into 8 chapters. Hema Chandra has himself written a commentary entitled *Viveka* on it. The **first** chapter deals with the aim of *kāvya*, the cause of *kāvya*, *kāvya-lakshana* and word power. The **second** chapter deals with *rasa* and its kinds. The **third** chapter deals with poetic blemishes, the **fourth** with *Mādhurya, Oaja* and *Prasāda gunas*. The **fifth** chapter deals with 6 *shabdālankāras* and 29 *Arthālanakāras*. The **seventh** chapter deals with *Nāyaka-Nāyikā-bheda* and the **eighth** chapter concentrates on the kinds of *Drishya* and *Shravya kāvya*. *Shabdānushāsana* is a mature work on grammar.

***Historical Mahākāvya*:** Historical Mahākāvyas are the epics written on the life of kings dealing with historical events. They shower praise on patrons on the occasion of royal donation given to priests, victories and other events of importance. This kind of epic was marked by veneration to the king. It originated and grew during the Middle Ages when poets were dependent on the royal and rich family and had least freedom. In the beginning, it was short in size but in course of time it assumed the proportion of epic. It presents a graphic picture of the life of the king patronising the poets. Besides this, the entire genealogy of the king also figures in the description. The poet is less concerned with introducing historical facts and more with exhibition of delicacy, refinement and balance in his language so that his work may acquire a distinct look. Among these historical epics *Nava-sāhshankā-charita* of Padmagupta Parimal; *Vikramānka-deva-charita* of Bilhana and *Rājatarangini* of Kalhana are excellent pieces of poetry.

Vikramānka-deva-charita deals with the love story of Sindhurāja, father of Bhoja, the king of Dhārā and Shashiprabhā. It was written in 1005 A.D. Kalhana's *Rajatarngini* is the best of all the historical epics written in *Samskrit*. Written in 1050 A.D., this work presents a vivid picture of socio-political, religious and economic condition of Kashmir in a very efficacious manner. *Rājatarnigi* also refers to another historical epic *Bhuvana Abhyudaya* written by Shankuka in the 8th century.

12th century epic *Kumāra Pāla charita*, written by Hema chanda is also an excellent work dealing with the achievements of Kumāra Pāla and his ancestors from Gujarāt. The 13th century epic *Suratotsava*, written by Someshvara, deals with the life and achievements of Vastu Pāla, the king of Gujarāt. The life of king Vastu Pāla has been depicted by Arisingha in his work *Sukrita-sanikirtana* in 11 cantos. The achievements and military zeal of king Hammira finds expression in Nayachandasuri's epic *Hammira Mahakāvya; Prithavirāvijaya*, an epic written by Jayanaka deals with gallantry and courage of king Prithavirāja. *Jaganagacharita* written by Sarvānanda in 7 cantos is an epic written in praise of a Jaina rich man who came to the rescue of the people of Gujarāt during the severe famine between 1256-58. Rudrakavi, a 16th century poet has written an epic *Rāshtraudal-vansha* in praise of the rulers of Mayuragiri. The epic is spread over 20 cantos. Two women including the queen of Tanjore Rāmabhadrambā and Gangādevi have written epics like *Raghunāthābhyudaya* and *Madurā-vijaya* respectively. Gangādevi's *Madurā-vijaya* is aimed at depicting the exploits of her husband.

Rudrakavi has written another epic *Jahangira-shāha-charita* in 8 *ullāsas* dealing with the victories of Jahangira. 16th century poet of Mithilā Vaidyanātha has written an epic entitled *Tārāchandrodaya* containing 20 cantos dealing with the life of the king of Mithilā Tārā Chandra. Chandrashekhara has also written an epic *Rājā-sudarshana-charita*. Viswanātha wrote *Jagatprakāsha* in 16th century depicting the kings of *Rānaka* dynasty: Kāmadeva and Jagata Singh. Vāninãth has dealt with the exploits of the kings of *Jāma* dynasty of Kaccha in his epic *Jāmavijaya* written in the 2nd half of the 16th century. Several poets have taken initiative to narrate the achievements of Muslim kings, consequent upon the restoration of Muslim dynasties in India. The poet Udayarāja has eulogised Sulatān Mohammad in his epic *Rājavinoda*. *Mahamuda-charita* of Rāmarāja is also a prominent work of its kind. Kālidāsa Vidyāvinoda has successfully exploited the life and adventures of Shivāji in his epic *Shivaji-charita*. Lakshmidhara wrote *Abdullāh-charita* dealing with the contribution of a minister named Abdullāh in the first half of the 18th century. During British rule in India several epics came to light incorporating the gallantry of prominent British Viceroys. The 19th century epic *Itihāsa Tapomani* presents a detailed account of the British occupation of India. *Angareja Chandrikā* written by Vināyaka Bhatta in 1801 also depicts the incidents leading to the establishment of British Empire. Among other prominent epics *Rājānglamahodyāna* of Rāmāswami Rājā, *Ānglasāmrājya* of Rājavarmā and *Āngladhirājasvāgata* by Paravastu-rangāchārya can be mentioned. The achievements of queen Victoria finds expression in Ganapati Shāstri's work *Chakravarti-niguna-mālā*. The contributions made by Mahātamā Gāndhi, Tilaka and Motilal Nehru towards India's Freedom has been successfully highlighted in the works of Vijaya-rāghavāchārya (born 1884) entitled *Gāndhi Mahātmā Tilaka Vaidāgdhya* and *Nehru Vijaya*. Shriswāmi Vidyālankāra of Bengāl has written an epic *Vijayinikāvya* in 12 cantos aimed at depicting the life of queen Victoria. *Samrāta-vijayama* by Pt. Harinandana Bhatta deals with the life of king George V and his wife Marry. 19th century poet Shivakumāra Shāstri has made a detailed study of the various dynasties of the kings of Darbhāngā.

Hitopadesha: Hitopadesha is a prose *Kāvya* that has its origin in *Panchatantra*. It is a popular fable written by Nārāyana Pandita. He was the court poet of Dhawal Chandra, the 14th century king of

Bengāl. The poet has himself admitted that *Panchatantra* provided seeds of this text. This book was basically written in prose but *shlokas* are scattered over here and there. The poet through didactical stories has imparted the teachings of ethics, politics and social codes. The poet has written more or less 679 verses aimed at inculcating moral lessons borrowed from the *Mahābhārata* and the *Purāna* to substantiate his stand. The author of *Hitopadesha* seems to be an ardent admirer of Lord Shiva in the sense that at the end of each section statement wishing Shiva's blessings have been made. It contains two-fifth prose and one-third poetry like *Panchatantra*. Since it is aimed at imparting moral teachings its language is very simple which has helped it achieve success in the long run.

In one of the verses, the author says that one who does well to any one, may he be a stranger, and one that harms may be his close associate. The disease is born in the body and does great harm to the man, but the herbal medicine that is found at distant places, is the saviour of man. So it is not the nearness that counts. It is the motive that counts. ■■

Induduta: Induduta is an example of the form of poetry intended to communicate some message through certain medium reminiscent of Kālidāsa '*Meghaduta'*. It has been written by Vinaya-Vijaya-Gani. The entire kāvya has been written in *Mandākrānta chhanda* consisting of 131 verses: The poet has resorted to moon (*Indu*) to serve as a messenger to communicate his message to his teacher. The poet was staying at *Jodhapura* whereas his teacher was enjoying *chaturmāsa* at *Surata*. As per tradition, the poem begins with the felicitations to the moon followed by a detailed description of its family lineage and its achievements. In course of the journey of the moon from *Jodhapura* to *Surata*, a graphic description of the places covered has been given.

Induduta aims primarily at propagating ethical and religious teachings. The poet has expressed his gratitude to his teacher in several *shlokas,* and has given a lively picture of rivers and cities. The poetry is flawless while the language moves with a great gust. The poet of *Induduta* has presented it with a novel flavour to give his poetry a distinct colour.

Ishāvāsya or Isha Upanishada: Ishāvāshya Upanishada is the 40th and the last chapter of Kānva Branch of Shukla 'Yayurveda Samhitā' consisting of 18 *shlokas*. The name has been derived from the 1st word of its first Mantra *Ishāvāsyam idam sarvam*, for the supreme power, the Almighty who is an unknown entity. This *Upanishada* is very important, as it is a part of the *Mantra Samhitā* and hence is treated as the first *Upanishada*. The very first *shloka* of Ishāvāsya Upanishada tells us that God is far and near and everywhere, inside the world and out of the world. The God pervades the entire cosmos. Therefore, it has been suggested that we should not claim out possession over anything and we should not have lust for possession either. The second *shloka* deals with the theory of Karma and preaches selfless service. Third *shloka* deals with the death caused by ignorance. Theories regarding the knowledge of Brahman have been given from 4th to the 7th *shloka*. Emphasis has been laid on leading a life coupled with *gyāna* and *karma* from the 9th to the 12th *shloka*. The last *shloka* expresses the need to surrender completely to the authority of God. Only He can lead the man to a state of perpetual bliss. The *Upanishada* deals with the omnipresence of God, the need to do selfless service and not to work against the wishes of one's conscience and to strive for getting the knowledge of all pervading power of soul. It says that there is a *loka* covered with perpetual darkness from all the sides and a man who commits suicide is consigned to that *loka*. Therefore suicide is a sin, and after suicide the soul is transported to that dark region.

Ishwarakrishna: Ishwara Krishna an eminent exponent of the school of *sāmkhya* wrote a monumental work '*Sāmkhya-kārikā*' which is considered the backbone of this school of philosophy. Since reference to '*Sāmkhya-kārikā*', have been given in '*Shariraka Bhāsya*' by Shankarāchārya, therefore, Ishwara Krishna is considered his predecessor. Several commentaries have been written on it. Prominent among them are: *Matharāvritti* by Āchārya Mathara (1st century A.D.); *Gauda-pāda-bhāsya* of Āchārya Gaudpāda (7th century); and *Jayamangala Chandrikā* by Nārāyanatirtha.

Sāmkhya-kārikā consists of 71 *Kārikās* in which manifold aspects of the school of *sāmkhya* have been discussed. Of all the theories discussed in it that of *Satkārya-vāda* is most important, which strongly suggests the presence of effect in the cause itself. This theory shows strong opposition to the theory of *Ashat-kārya-vāda* as developed by the school of *Nyāya*, which is opposed to the possibility of effect in cause, and rules out the possibility of pitcher in the clay itself; laying emphasis on the fact that both are the same. And asks a question: why different names have been assigned to them? Why the clay does not perform the work done by the pitcher? *Sāmkhya* philosophy on the other hand insists that if effect is not confined to the cause, how can oil be taken from the mustard and not from sand? It has further divided *Satkārya-*

vāda into *Parināma-vāda* and *vivarta-vāda*. The formation of curd out of milk is the example the first, type where milk is latent in the curd. *Vivarta* is not the real transformation of one element to the other. It is merely an illusion and has no real existence. Out of darkness sometimes a cord is confused for a snake. Which is not real, a snake does not exist in the cord. It is seen out of illusion. This theory has been supported by *Vedānta*, which insists that the universe, which seems to be real; is actually illusory or unreal. Brahman is the only reality but out of ignorance the universe, which emanates from Brahman appears as real.

Sāmkhyākārikā has also accepted the existence of three types of *pramāns*: *Pratyaksha* (apparent); *Anumāna* (speculation, inference) and *Āptavachana* (statement of a reliable person) and rest of the *pramāns* have been merged into it. ■■

Jagadisha Bhattāchārya: Jagadisha Bhattāchārya occupies a crucial place among the most accomplished Naiyāyikas of Navadweep (Bengāl). He belonged to the 17th century. He has written two monumental works on Navya Nyāya. He has also written an authentic commentary on Raghunāth Siromani's famous work *Didhiti*. Another book, *Sabdashakti Prakāshikā* is a dependable book on Sabdashakti, the power of a word.

Jaimini: Jaimini was a commentator (*Sutrakāra*) on *Mimāmsā* philosophy. Unquestionably, he did not propound *Mimāmsā* philosophy because he has himself named some āchāryas: past and contemporary who were associated with this school of philosophy; notable among them are Atraya, Vadari, Aitisayana and Alekhana. But no book written by these scholars is traceable. *Mimāmsā* sutra written by Jaimini is divided into 16 sections in which the fundamental theory of this philosophy has been vividly brought out. The total number of *Mimāmsā* sutra is 2,644. In twelve sections of this book subjects like religion, the varieties of religion, the rights of *Yagyakartā, Tantra, Uh, Karma, Prasanga* etc. have been discussed. Several commentaries and vritties have been written on *Mimāmsā sutras*. The oldest commentator on *Mimāmsā* sutra is *Upvarsha,* whose name is referred to in *Mimāmsā Bhāsya* (1/1/5) by Sabaraswāmi, and *Shāririka Bhāsya* by Shankara (2/3/53). Kumārila Bhatta, in *Pratigyasutra* (shloka-63) of *shloka vartikā,* has referred to his name. The knowledge is based on the correspondence of the two cows. Jaimini following the track of *Nyāya* philosophy assesses the existence of *Anumāna* (imputation, induction). But his assumption is somewhat different from that of *Nyāya* philosophy. Jaimini's concept of *anumāna* is ended on *pratigya-hetu* and *dristānṭa.* In order to prove the authenticity of the Vedas, Jaimini gives importance to *Sabda-*

pramāna. He therefore calls the Vedas *apauruseya*, meaning, which has not been written by human being and can't be won over. According to Jaimini, the Vedas and this world are eternal and everlasting which has no beginning and no end.

Jainism: Jainism is another school of Indian philosophy, which was brought to the high water-mark by Mahāvira. The word 'Jain' is coined out of the root 'Jin', meaning conqueror, or Victor. A Jin is called the disciple of Jaina. One who successfully overpowers worldly pleasures or basic senses like anger, greed, lust, avarice etc. is a 'Jin'. This title is accorded to Mahāvira. He was the 24th Tirthankara of the Jains. Those propagating the ideologies of this school are called Tirthankaras. Rishabhadeva was its first Tirthankara. Altogether 24 Tirthankaras are mentioned in Jain philosophy. The last two Tirthankaras named Parsva and Mahāvira are historical figures. Rishabhadeva is the pre-historical figure. Little is known about his birth and there is a popular saying that he was born in Ayodhyā where there is still a magnificent temple of Rishebhadeva. Jainism believes that the Tirthankaras were the conquerors of base passions and anybody who follows the track of Tirthankaras can be a Jaini. Real pleasure lies not in the satisfaction of sensual pleasure but in eschewing it and this alone can pave the way for *Moksha* or *Nirvāna*.

Jainism does not accept the authority of God, repose faith in the power of Tirthankaras. They try to imitate the lifestyle of the Tinthankaras in order to overcome their problems and make their lives worth living. It lays stress on three elements which are necessary for emancipation from worldly bondage: Samyaka darshana, Samyaka gyāna and Samyaka charitra (*Samyak darsan gyāna charitrāni moksha mārigah*). These are called three jewels (*Triratna*). Jainism holds that purity of character is essential for the seeker of truth in behaviour and speech. One should not hurt anybody by words thus, Jainism lends support to Ahimsā in the true sense of the term. By Samyaka darshana, Jainism means that the devotee or *sādhaka* must have unflinching faith in his devotion. By samyaka gyāna, Jainism means that the nature of truth is not alterable and the knowledge to know the ultimate truth is grave. One who knows that physical pleasure is subject to decay and destruction and only by abandoning physical pleasure one can be gyāni. Gyāna means enlightenment.

There are two major sects of Jainism: *Svetāmbara* and *Digambara*. The *Svetāmbaras* put on white cloth while the *Digambaras* keep on stark naked. There is no basic difference between the two sects on philosophical plane. The difference lies only on ethical front. The literature concerning Jain philosophy is vast and varied and full of illuminating illustrations. Jainism is more practical than Buddhism and that is why it still survives in India and its followers are many. As many as 84 *granthas* dealing with the ideals of Jainism are available and most of them are based on ethics. *Prākrita* is the accepted language and most of the literature is available in *Prākrita*. In course of time, Sanskrit was also used for the composition of Jaina literature. Out of 84 granthas, 41 have been written in the form of sutras. The rest are *Prākrita* works. The division of 41 *granthas* has been made into 11 *angas*, 12 *up angas*, 5 *chedas*, 5 *mulas* and 8 miscellaneous works. The contribution of three scholars - Umasvati, Kundakundāchārya and Samanta Bhadra for giving systematic foundation to Jainism cannot be denied. Umasvati belongs to the 1st century and has written *Tatvarthasutra*. Kundakundāchārya's works include *Samayasāra*, *Panchastikāyasāra* and *Pravachanā*. Samantabhadra wrote *Ātma Mimāmsā*, *Svayambhu stotra* (presenting prayer of Tirthankaras in 143 shlokas) and Jainastuti shloka. Siddhāsana Divākara wrote *Nyāyavatār* and *Sanmatitarka* and laid the foundation of Jain Nyāya. The 9th century Scholar Vadirajasuri's *Nyāyavinischaya Nirnaya* is also an eminent work on *Nyāyashāstra*. The 12th century scholar Hemacandasuri also contributed significantly to Jain literature by his work *'Pramāna Mimāmsā'*. Yasovijaya wrote *Jainatarkabhāsa* in the 17th century. Among other important contributions of this period are *Dravyasamgraha* by Nemichandra, *Syadvadamanjari* by Mallasena and *Prameya Kamalmārtanda* by Prabhāchanda.

Jainism is guided by epistemological ideology. It insists on the existence of two fundamental elements- *Jiva* and *Ajiva*. *Jiva* resides in every living being irrespective of his form. Therefore, Jainism pays special emphasis on non-violence. According to

Jainism self-knowledge or *Ātmabodha* is very crucial for man as well as animal. If he has *Ātmabodha*, he is *jiva* one who does not have *Ātmabodha*, is *Ajiva*. Even man, if he lacks *Ātmabodha* is *Ajiva*. Therefore Jainism pays special emphasis on non-violence.

Jiva symbolises surya in Jainism. As surya enlightens it with its rays, in the same way, Ātman enlightens others as well as himself by its light. *Jiva* is considered the repertoire of knowledge but the pure *chaitanya* form is overshadowed due to the veil of *karma*. Jainism has accepted two kinds of knowledge-*Pratyaksha* and *Paroksha*. Knowledge emanating from soul is *Pratyaksha*, whereas one which is inherited from senses is called *Paroksha* knowledge. *Paroksha* knowledge is of two kinds-*Mati* and *Shruti*. *Mati* emanates with the help of Mind and senses. It is also of two kinds- *Indriya-janya* and *Anindriya.*

Jānakiharana: Jānakiharana is an epic by Kumāradās based on the story of the Rāmāyana. Unfortunately this epic was not known till very recently when it was traced out. Evidence of its existence was there in the works like Bhoja's *Sringārprakāsha* and Rajashekhara's *Kāvya Mimāmsā* in which some of its verses were quoted. Kumāradās has also chosen to avoid any description of his life and timing in his works but on the basis of scattered facts in Jānakiharana, it is assumed that he was living around the 1st half of the 7th century during the reign of Pallava king Narsingha Verma.

Jānakiharana is the sole contribution of Kumāradās. It consists of 20 acts or cantos. The **first** canto gives an elaborate discussion of the city of Ayodhyā, king Dasaratha and his three queens. In the **second** canto, Brihaspati narrates the character of Rāvana who seeks assistance from Brahmā. The **third** dilates upon various amorous sports of king Dāsaratha. The **fourth** and **fifth** acts hinge round the birth of Rāma, and his other brothers and concludes with the killing of Tarakā and Subhu by Rāma. In the **sixth** act Vishvāmitra along with Rāma and Laksmana arrives at Mithila. The **seventh** act revolves round the love of Rāma and Sitā and their consequent marriage. The **eighth** act dilates upon the description of the Sringār of Rāma and Sitā. In the **ninth** act,

Rāma along with his brothers returns to Ayodhyā. The **tenth** act deals with the political teaching by Dasaratha. Rāma is also made the heir-apparent. Towards the end, Sitā is abducted by Rāvana. The **eleventh** act narrates the friendship of Rāma and Hanumāna and the killing of Bāli. In the **twelfth** act Lakshmana ṛeprimands Sugriva for failing to keep up his promise of finding out Sitā. In the **thirteenth** act Lankā is set on fire by Hanumāna. In the **fourteenth** act, the monkeys construct a bridge on the ocean. In the **fifteenth** act, Angada is sent to the court of Rāvana as the messenger of Rāma, as a final bid to dissuade Rāvana from war and prevent large scale killings. The **sixteenth** act hinges round the amorous sports of the demons. From the seventeenth act onwards war breaks out causing huge casualty. It finally culminates in the death of Rāvana. Rāma emeriges victorious.

In the description of tender feelings, in creating mellifluous verses and innovating titillating imagination, Kumāradāsa is without a rival. In this connection his description of the birth of Rāma and marriage of Rāma are worth mentioning but in the description of war the style is laboured and it can appeal only the solvent minds. In the description by Kumāradāsa, there is a restraint and balance. He is a great appreciator of the delicate aspect of nature. He has beautifully described twilight, sunset, darkness, sunrise and moonrise with exquisite excellence which shows innate love for nature.

Jātaka: Jātaka is a book written in Pali language. It contains the past birth history of Lord Buddha. Its objective is to show that by taking birth in several animal species and by gathering various kinds of experiences, Buddha attained Buddhatva. The number of Jātaka stories is 550. In it we get a lot of facts of historical, geographical and social interest. It is a collection of variegated tales found in the form of myths, legends and folk tales. Buddha monks collected and collated these stories from various sources but they moulded these stories to suit their religious cult. They also described many anecdotes which did not suit them. The stories of Jātaka are not only popular in India but also in Jāvā, Indo-China and Sumatra. There is basic difference between the style of telling these stories by the Boddha and the Jains. The story related to

Buddha take us back to the past but the stories related to the Jains are confined to the present. The stories contained in the Jātaka give us practical teachings and touch the chords of our heart. They are wrapped in simple and candid language.

Jayadeva: Jayadeva is the celebrated lyricist of Sanskrit literature. His lyrical epic-poetry "Gita Govinda" occupies significant position among Sanskrit classics. He was the court poet of Lakshamana Sena, the king of Bengal. He belonged to the 2nd half of the 12th century. *Gita Govinda* presents a colourful and erotic description of the lilās of Rādhā and Krishna. It consists of 12 cantos. Jayadeva begins his work with four shlokas which contain invocation, introduction, purpose of the composition and introduction of the poet. After that, the main story begins. Rādhā gets irritated when her friend points out that Krishna is dancing with the Gopikās. When this message is brought to the notice of Krishna, he immediately rushes to the bank of Yamunā, leaving the Gopikās behind, to have a meeting with Rādhā and to ask her forigiveness. He also sends a messenger to Rādhā to tell her fidelity and his pathetic condition in her absence. Rādhā's friend also accompanies Krishna telling him Rādhā's anguish and compels him to see her at the earliest. Rādhā waits for Krishna but to no effect. Krishna does not return. Later on Krishna arrives at Rādhā's house but fails to persuade her.

The poet has basically depicted Rāsalilā in *Gita Govinda*. The poet takes assistance from *Srimad Bhāgavata* in painting various aspects of *Rāsalilā*. At several place its impact can be easily felt. There is however, a marked difference between the timing of *Rāsa*. While *Rāsa* is conducted in winter in the Bhāgavata, in *Gita Govinda* it takes place in autumn.

A very touching picture of both forms of sringāra: love in union and separation, has been delicately depicted in it. Jayadeva was well versed with the contemporary literary trends and different aspects of *sringāra*. Therefore, besides *sringāra*, several aspects of poetics have been prominently covered in the poem.

The two famous streams of lyric poetry *sringāra* and *bhakti* get assimilated in *Gita Govinda*. The entire element in this work have been skillfully assimilated and presented in a mellifluous way to achieve the desired end. It has no peer in any language.

Jayadeva (Playwright): Jayadeva is the author of the drama *Prasanna Rāghava*. One of the shlokas from his work was quoted in *Sāhitya Darpana* of Āchārya Visvanāth which has established the fact that he appeared well before the 13th century.

Besides *Prasanna Rāghava*, his popularity rests on his book on poetics entitled *Chandraloka*. The plot of the drama is based on the story of the Rāmāyana and has been written in seven acts. In order to promote dramatic appeal, the poet has made several changes to suit his purpose. The **first** four acts revolve round the story of *Bālakānda*. *Sitā Svayamvara* also falls into the same domain. In the **second** act, Rāma and Sitā meet each other in the orchard of Janaka. In the **third** act, Rāma and Laksmana arrive at the venue of savayamvara along with Maharshi Viswāmitra. Viswāmitra introduces them to Janaka who later regrets for his promise after having a glimpse of these two princes. The bow of Shiva is also broken in this act. The **fourth** act deals with the fight between Rāma and Rāvana. In the **fifth** act, through the dialogue among Gangā, Yamunā and Sarsvati, the forthcoming incidents in Rāma's life, that of his leaving for forest and the death of king Dasaratha has been portrayed. In the **sixth** act, pathetic condition of Rāma, living in a pool of sorrrow, in the wake of the abduction of Sitā from the cottage in his absence, has been depicted. The exploits of Hanumāna, his burning of the entire Lankā are also included in this section. Sitā's mental conflict whether Rāma would accept her or not has been well expressed. The **seventh** act deals with the battle and defeat of Rāvana.

Jayanta Bhatta: Jayanta Bhatta is the author of the famous book on Nyāyashāstra called *Nyāyamanjari*. He has been placed in the second half of the 9th century. He has disapproved the findings of the followers of Chārvāka, Buddha, *Mimāmsā* and Vedānta.

Jimutavāhana: The eminent 12th century writer of Dharmashāstra, Jimutavāhana hailed from Bengal. His works include: *Kālaviveka, Vyavahāramātrikā* and *Dayābhāga*. He has not written about his personal life in his books. *Kālaviveka* deals with the appropriate period for conducting religious rites, festivals to be celebrated during lunar eclipse. Dayābhāga presents a detailed account of Hindu laws and special emphasis has been laid on bifurcation of property pertaining to woman and reunion. In this book, it has been strictly ruled that sons do not have a birth right on their parental property. They cannot inherit the parental property without seeking their prior permission. The property is naturally transferred to the son after father's death. It has also been ruled that after the death of the husband the widow is entitled to the property of her deceased husband.

Jyotisha: Jyotisha helps us understand the movement of different planets as also the crucial times. The tradition of Jyotisha in India is very old. It finds an important place in Vedic literature. Its importance is brought out in the Vedāngas. In the Vedas, some hints are found dedicated to sun, moon and different planets. The form and colour of the planets and the stars, their mysteries and their effect on human life have also been highlighted. The genesis of Jyotisha may be traced back to the Vedas which contain sutras which finally help Jyotisha emerge as an independent Shāstra: *Jyotisham Netram Smritam*. It has also acquired a significant place among the Vedāngas. The Vedas have discussed extensively the impact of the Graha-Nakshatras. In subsequent years, Jyotisha was developed as an independent Shāstra to discuss the methodology of yagyas, and the position of lagnas. It came to be applied in understanding seasons and sun, and good and evil effects while deciding lagna.

In the beginning there were twin branches of Jyotisha: *Ganita* (arithmetic) and *Phalita* (practical). Later on, five new off-shoots originated from it: *Horā, Ganita, Samhitā, Prashna* and *Nimitta. Horā Shāstra* deals with the future course of action of an individual and its outcome on the basis of the position of planets at the time of birth. It also determines the make up of a man. It is also called *Jātaka Shāstra*. It basically interprets the effect of twelve *bhavas* of horoscope on human beings and predicts the joy and despair, triumph and failure of man. Among the practitioners of this branch Vārāhamihira, Narachandra, Dhundhirāja, Keshava and Sridhara are prominent. *Ganita Jyotisha* includes calculation of years, the analysis of the movement of the planets and position of planets and *nakshatras* (constellations). In *Ganita Jyotisha*, one calculates the time sequence, the movement of sun and moon, the position of planets through question and answer method. It is a science in which one analyses the mental state of the subject through his gestures and movement of limbs. In *Shakuna Jyotisha*, the good and bad effect is known beforehand. It is also called *Nimitta Shāstra*. Samhitā deals with subjects like *Griha-pravesha*, *muhurta* of auspicious works and outcome of the rise and fall of the planets. *Prashna Jyotisha* concentrates on *prashnākshara* and *prashnalagna* and the person putting questions is immediately satisfied. The expression on the face of the person putting questions and his mental condition are closely studied to arrive at a decision, and thus Jyotisha Shāstra comes closer to psychology. In *Shakuna Jyotisha*, knowledge of right or wrong is obtained beforehand.

On the basis of the development of Jyotisha through the ages, its classification has been made as follows - Dark ages (unknown time) the period before 10000 B.C., period of inflorescence (10000 B.C.- 500 B.C.), Ādikāla (499 B.C.- 500 A.D.) Pre-middle ages (501-1000 A.D.), Post-middle ages (1001-1600), Modern age (1600-upto date).

The hymns of the Vedas contain many sutras of Jyotisha Shāstra which finally culminate in *Brihad Shāstra*. The reference to a year consisting of 360 days through the calculation of 12 *Rāshis* is given in one of the shlokas of the Rig Veda. The term *yuga* has been used in the Rig Veda which shows that Aryans had the knowledge of time. Instructions have been given in the Rig Veda with regard to the calculation of time with the help of *Kritikā Naksatra*. 12 Rāsis have been accepted in the Rig Veda. A detailed discussion of Jyotisha Shāstra has been made in the Brāhamanas and the Upanishada. A very graphic description of Nakshatras has been given in the Brāhamanas. In Taitariya Brāhamana, Prajāpati has been referred to as the symbol of Nakshatras and Nakshatras like Chitrā, Swāti, Hasta have been taken as his parts. In the same way, elements of Jyotisha can be obtained from Kalpa sutra, Nirukta and Ashtadhyāyi. From Ādi period onwards independent books poured in on various aspects of Jyotisha. A significant contribution in this field was made with the composition of Vedānga Jyotisha by Rishi Lagadha. It is the earliest work on Jyotisha and the period of its composition comes around 580 B.C. Between 100-300 A.D., Jyotisha emerged as an independent Shāstra and as many as 18 Maharishi-scholars of great repute appeared on the forefront. They include Surya, Vyāsa, Vasistha, Atri, Parāshara, Kashyapa, Nārada, Garga, Manu, Angirā, Lomasa, Chyavana, Bhrigu, Shaunaka, Pitāmaha and Paulisa. In Vārāhamihira's work *Panchasiddhāntika*, reference to their theories has been given. These theories are Pitāmaha Siddhānta, Vasistha Siddhānta, Romaka Siddhānta, Paulisa Siddhānta and Surya Siddhānta.

Pitāmaha Siddhānta deals with the Ganita of Surya and Chandra. Vasistha Siddhānta is more accomplished than the previous one. Lātadeva is the interpreter of the Romaka Siddhānta. Surya Siddhānta is attributed to saint Surya. It is the most significant doctrine on Indian astrology. Besides these texts, some other leading works including Nārada samhitā and Gargasamhitā were written during the same period. Āryabhatta I and II are two other celebrities on astrology who wrote *Āryabhattiya Tantragrantha* and *Mahāryabhatta Siddhānta* respectively.

Pre-Middle Ages is the period of enrichment of astrology. This period witnessed the advent of Vārāhamihira who wrote an outstanding work *Brihad Jātaka*. He was one of the nine Jewels in the court of king Vikramāditya. Kalyāna Verma's *Sārāvali*, Varāhamihira's son Prithuyasa's *Satpanchāsika*, Brahmagupta's *Brahma-sphuta-siddhānata* and *Khandakhadyaka*, Munjala's *Laghumānasa*, Mahavira's *Ganita Sārasamgraha* and Sridharā-chārya's Ganitasāra are other important contributions of this period. A significant development was made in the field of Algebra, Arithmetic, Geometry and Phalita Jyotisha in this period.

The pre-middle age marked the abundance of Phalita Jyotisha, Graha Ganita reached its highest point. During the 6th century link of Indian astrology was established with Greece, Arabia and Persia. Books like Brahama-sphuta-Siddhānta were translated in Arabic language.

Several original texts were produced during the post-middle period. Several inventions were made during this period and new possibilities were explored in the study of celestial planets. Several forms of Phalita Jyotisha were also developed during this period. Prominent among them are *Jātaka*, *Muhurta*, *Sāmudrika*, *Tājika*, *Ramala* and *Prashna*. The influence of Greece is discernible on Tājika and Ramala. The greatest astrologer Bhaskarāchārya belonged to this period. He brought Indian astrology on the international map through his theories contained in his books *Siddhānta Siromani* and *Muhurta Chintāmani*. Ballalasena, son of the king of Mithilā, Laksamanasena compiled the theories of all the preceding astrologers in his book *Adbhuta-sāgara* running into 8000 shlokas. Nilakantha Daivāgna wrote *Tajikanilakanthi* based on the books on astrology written in Arabic and Persian. Among other prominent writers of this period are Satānanda, Hematilaka, Anantadaivāgna, Rāma Daivāgna, Haribhadrasuri, Raghunāth Sharmā and Vitthala Dikshita.

Indian astrology has added a new dimension to the western ideology in the modern times. A comparative study of Indian and western astrology was made in several books by western mathematicians which were translated into Sanskrit. Astrologers like Bapudeva Shāstri and Pt. Sudhākara Dwivedi compiled standard works to enrich Ganita Jyotisha. Munishvara, Kamalākara Bhatta, Ubhayakusala, Bāla Gangādhara Tilaka, Dr. Sampurnānanda, and Dr. Gorakha Prasād are other prominent astrologers of the period.

Maharājā Sawāi Jaisingh holds an important place in the history of Indian Astrology who led the foundation of scientific approach in the field of astrology by installing observatories at Jaipur, Ujjain, Delhi, Vārānasi and Mathurā. ■■

Kādambari: Kādambari is the most distinguished work ever written in *Laukika Sanskrit*. The authorship of this epoch-making work goes to Bānabhatta. It has been divided into two sections: *purva bhāga* and *uttara bhāga*. It is said that Bāna has written *purva bhāga* whereas his son Pulinda Bhatta completed the *uttara bhāga*. A parrot named Vaishampāyana who was blessed with a unique quality to speak like humān beings narrates the story.

The story revolves round the life of the crown prince of Ujjaini Chandrapida and his minister Vaishampāyana. Actually the parrot Vaishmpāyana was the minister in his previous life that had fallen a victim to the curse of a *Sādhu* (saint) due to his arrogant behaviour, and so faced severe mental and physical hardships. The Sādhu Jabāli narrated the story of his previous life to him.

Chandrapida is the son of the king of Ujjaini, Tārāpida and his wife Vilāsavati, whereas Vaishampāyana is the son of Tārāpida's minister Shukanāsha. Both are sent to the *gurukul* (hermitage) together to receive formal education. Later Chandrapida is elevated to the position of the crown prince and leaves for his ambitious plan of *digvijaya* (all round victory) accompanying his friend Vaishampāyana. Once he accomplishes his task, he sets out for hunting and there he comes across a girl named Mahāshvetā near Achchhodā pond. She tells him that she had fallen in love with the son of a saint named Pundarika. Mahāshvetā wants to join the company of Pundarika but before she reaches her destination, Pundarika passes away. Mahāshvetā is left in the state of utter dismay and ennui and decides to reduce her to ashes by throwing herself on the funeral pyre of her beloved. In the meanwhile, a miracle takes place. An enlightened person descends from heaven and takes away the body of Pundarika with him consoling Mahāshvetā to do the needful to get back the body of her beloved. Mahāshvetā keeps waiting near the pond for her deceased friend along with her friend Taralikā. After listening to the pathetic story of Mahāshvetā, Chandrapida consoles her and accepts her hospitality. Mahāshvetā later on decides to have a meeting with her friend Kādambari asking Chandrapida to accompany her to the house of Kādambari which he readily accepts. Chandrapida fell in love with Kādambari at the very first meeting. In the meanwhile, Chandrapida returns to his kingdom after receiving a letter from his father asking him to return to the capital immediately in the wake of imminent danger posed from across the border. He becomes restless in absence of Kādambari. Later on a lady named Patralekhā narrates the sad plight of Kādambari and also her message to Chandrapida. At this critical juncture, the *purva bhāga* of Kādambari ends.

The *uttar bhāga* begins with Chandrapida expressing his anxiety to have a meeting with Kādambari after listening to her pathetic plight. A messenger named Keyuraka, sent by Kādambari, apprises him of Kādambari's agony and frustration. Chandrapida decides to leave for Gandharva lake to restore life to the dying veins of Kādambari. His army returns to Dashapura. Therefore, he sends his message to Kādambari through Patralekhā and starts for his expedition to bring Vaishampāyana back taking permission from his father. He does not have a meeting with his friend. He is informed that Vaishampāyana has settled near Achchhodā pond and is not ready to leave the place. Once again he leaves for Achchhodā pond to compel him to reconsider his decision. Failing to catch sight of Vaishampāyana, he reaches the cottage of Mahāshvetā who reveals that her curse metamorphosed Vaishmpāyana into a parrot. Both Vaishampāyana and Chandrapida die. Kādambari mourns over the body of Chandrapida and vows to finish her life. In the meantime, a message is delivered through an oracle that the spirit of Chandrapida has been preserved in heaven and Kādambari must protect his body till the period of his curse is over. Patralekhā jumps into the pond along with Indrayuddha in order to bring a vehicle for Chandrapida.

Pundrika comes out from the river apprising Mahāshvetā of the events he had to face after his death. Kapinjala also took birth as a horse, Indrayuddha and was to regain his original form after taking a dip in the river. Kapinjala was also told that Chandramā would descend to the earth as the son of Tārāpida of Ujjaini. Pundrika would be taking birth as Vaishampāyana and Kapinjala as the horse of Chandrapida.

The parrot takes a flight to meet his beloved Mahāshvetā but is caught by a Chandāla on his way whose daughter brings him to the court of king Shudraka. Chandāla tells Shudraka that his daughter is the mother of Vaishampāyana. Now the danger is averted, and thus she has brought Vaishampāyana to his court. In fact, Shudraka was Chandrapida in his previous life. Shudraka recalls his previous life and ends his life. He becomes Chandrapida. In the meantime, Pundrika (Vaishampāyana) also reaches there and the two jointly leave for the place where their beloved Mahāshvetā and Kādambari were staying.

The story of Kādambari is a fabricated one. It presents the story of three successive lives of Chandrapida and Vaishampāyana. The king of Magadha was Chandramā in his first life, Chandrapida in the second life and Shudraka in his third life whereas Vaishampāyana was Svetaketu's son Pundrika in his first life, Vaishampāyana in his second and parrot in the third life. It has also accepted the trend of *Brihat-kathā* of interweaving several stories within the framework of the main story. Besides relating the story in the first person, Bāna has retained many features of folk-tales including that of a parrot speaking as man, a saint like Jabāli having power to tell past, present and future.

Kaiyyat: Kaiyyat was a grammarian and commentator of *Mahā-bhāsya*. The title of his commentary is *Mahā-bhāsya Pradip*.

Kākusthavijaya Champu: Balli Sahāya wrote Kākustha Vijaya Champu. In this *Champu* the story of Shri Rāma has been narrated on the basis of Vālmiki *Rāmāyana*. It has been written in 8 cantos in a simple style.

Kalhana: Kalhana is the famous author of the prominent historical epic *Rājatarangini* dealing with the history and adventures of the kings of Kashmir from the ancient time up to the 12th century. It is the best historical *mahākāvya* written in *Sanskrit*. In *Rājatarangini*,

Kalhahna has given a fairly good amount of information about his personal life. The name of his father was Champaka who was the Prime Minister of Harsha, the King of Kashmir. He was a *Shaiva Brāhmana* by birth, which has been endorsed by his prayer to *Ardhanārishvara* Shiva in each *taranga* of *Rājatarangini*. His original name was Kalyāna. He compiled this monumental work between 1148 and 1150 during the reign of Jaya Singh.

Rājatarangini has been divided into eight *tarangas*. The book is of unique distinction for being a historical document as well as an excellent piece of literature. In order to make his description authentic Kalhana has taken recourse to several unimpeachable historical incidents. In the beginning of Rajataranagini, he has made it clear that a good poet is one who like a judge is detached and above ill-will in the depiction of the events of past. He has tried his best to remain committed to his stand. Although he depicts historical events in his work, yet he does not use ornamental style which was at its peak during his period fearing that it might affect adversely the relationship between the poet and the reader and obstruct his mission to convey his ideas to a large number of people, and has thus deliberately retained the language of the common people in his work. *Shānta Rasa* reigns supreme throughout the work.

***Kālidāsa*:** Kālidāsa is considered to be the best poet and dramatist in Sanskrit literature. The essence of Indian culture is fully embodied in the works of Kālidāsa. There is complete lack of unanimity of opinion about the facts relating to the life of Kālidāsa. The poet has not left any written record about his personal life in his works, which has further added to the confusion. He was probably born in Ujjaini as we find abundant references to Ujjaini people and their culture. There is a hearsay that during his boyhood days he was stupid, and once he was cutting the branch of a tree on which he was sitting. His fans and friends however managed to get him married to a princess who was an erudite scholar and was at home in Sanskrit language and Indian Philosophy. The marriage was solemnised following a strategy when some pundits declared Kālidāsa a scholar and there was some talk between Kālidāsa, and the princes over the monotheistic nature of God in which the pundits unanimously declared Kālidāsa as victorious. But on the very wedding night Kālidāsa was exposed. The princess taught him and in course of time he became a great scholar and poet. He wrote many lyrical poems and plays. His lyrical poems include *Megahduta*, *Ritusamhāra*, *Raghuvansha* and *Kumārasambhava*; and his plays are *Abhigyāna-shākuntala*, *Vikramorvashiya* and *Mālvikāgnimitra*.

From the literary output of Kālidāsa, it is apparent that he had travelled widely in Bhāratvarsha and had perfect knowledge of Indian seasons and its geographical topography. His lyrical poem *Meghaduta* is a testimony of it. The theme of *Abhigyāna-shākuntala* resembles that of Meghaduta, as here also Shakuntalā and Dushyanta are separated. In *Kumār-sambhava*, the marriage of Shiva and Pārvati has been narrated in highly romantic terms. It is followed by the birth of Kumāra Kartikeya.

Other works of Kālidāsa like Vikramorvashiya and Raghubansha are also poignant with deep thought and spiritual feeling in keeping with the ideas of Hinduism.

Kālidāsa's poetry is highly mellifluous, full of spontaneity and alliterative charm. He is called the master of simile. No *Sanskrit* poet can compete against him in the use of rich similes. He had a perfect command over words and phrases. *Meghaduta* has been written in *Mandākrāntā* metre (*chhanda*), which is noted for rhythmical music, lilt, sonorousness and stately and graceful movements. His description of nature is highly realistic and absorbing. He is primarily a poet of Nature and *Shringāra rasa*.

Kālidāsa as a Playwright: *Sanskrit* drama scaled new heights at the hands of Kālidāsa. His dramas brought *Sanskrit* drama to the high pedestal pushing it close to dramas written in any language of the world and sometimes excelled all. Both Indian as well as western dramatic critics have unanimously reposed faith in his skill as a dramatist elevating him to the position of the greatest dramatists of the world. In all the dramas of Kālidāsa, the three elements: *Vastu* (plot), *Netā* (hero) and *Rasa* (enjoyment, aesthetics) have been properly crystallised. The objective of Indian drama is to generate a fair amount of entertainment. That is why *Sanskrit* drama ends on a note of pleasure and bliss, and with *Bharat-vākya*.

The plot of *Malvikāgnimitra* is based on a historical story which deals with the love story of Mālvikā and Agnimitra. Kālidāsa has carved out a unique technique to enable the heroes to win the affection of his heroines that of assisting her when she is in dire strains facing stiff challenges. The hero not only ensures the safe release of the heroine but also wins her confidence.

In *Vikramorvashiya*, Pururvā protects Urvashi from the clutches of the dreaded monster and thus evades the impending danger posed upon her, which paved the way for Urvashi's affection for him. Dushyanta wins Shakuntalā's love by overpowering the black-bee causing affliction to his ladylove enabling her to tide over her impediments.

The characterisation in his dramas is so perfect that even subsidiary characters, contributing almost nothing to the development of the drama, also leave an indelible impression on our mind. His characters are full of confidence and courage, and show exemplary synchronisation of head and heart. This delicacy has been maintained in the use of language. While minor characters speak *Prākrita,* a local dialect suggesting their lowly status, the cultured and māle characters speak *Sanskrit.*

Kalpa: Kalpa are books that make systematic study of *karmas* approved by the Vedas, which include marriage, upnayana and yagya: *Kalpoveda vinitanām Karmānāmānupurpeva, kalpanā-shāstram. Kalpa sutras* have been designed to present an abridged code of rules relating to the performance of *yagya*. They occupy a significant place among the *Vedāngas*. It has been divided into four parts: *Shrauta Sutra, Grihya Sutra, Dharma Sutra* and *Sulva Sutra*.

Shrauta Sutra presents a systematic study of the *yagyas* approved by *Shruti*. These *yagyas* include those performed for twelve days: *Darsha, Purnamāsa, Chaturmāsya, Somayagya*, those performed for one year- *Gavamayana* and those lasting between 2 and 11 days: *Vājpeya, Rājsuya*, *Sautramani, Ashvamedha* and *Purushamedha*. Each Veda has independent *Shrauta sutra*.

Rigveda has two *Shrauta Sutras*: Āshwalāyana that contains 12 chapters and Sāmkhayāyana consisting of 18 chapters. The *Shrauta sutra* of Yajuraveda is called *Kātyāyana Shrauta sutra,* which comprises of 26 chapters. Krishna Yajurveda has got several srauta sustras-Bodhāyana, Apastamba, Hiranya kesiya. Shrauta sutra of Sāmaveda is called Latāyana whereas 'Vaitana' has been named shrauta sutra of the Atharvaveda. **Grihya Sutra** presents a detailed account of *yagyas* performed in front of the domestic fire. It dilates upon *upanayana*, *vivāha* and *shrāddha* (last rites). Each Veda has a separate Grihya sutra. The *Grihya sutra* of Rigveda includes *Āshwalāyana Grihya sutra* and *Sāmkhayāyana Grihya sutra*. These sutras contain several rituals. In *Sāmkhayāyana Grihya sutra*, the method of construction of building and dwelling time has been described. The third Grihya sutra of Rig Veda deals with the rituals related to marriage, *upanayana*, agricultural work and *shrāddha* (last rites). Yajurveda has got one *Pataskar Grihya sutra*. Several commentaries particularly those of Jairāma, Gadādhara and Vishvanātha are available on it. The *Grihya sutra* of Krishna Yajurveda includes Baudhāyana, Āpastamba, Bharadwāja and *Kathāka Grihya Sutra*, where as the Atharva Veda has lone *Grihya sutra* entitled *Kaushika Grihya Sutra*.

Dharma Sutras deal with the duties of the king and the function of four *Varnas* and *Āshramas*. In the Rigveda a man asserts that he is a *Brāhmin* while one of his brother is *Kshatriya* and the other is *Vaishya*. This suggests that categorisation of persons in different *varnas* was made keeping in mind the profession with which he is associated. During the Middle Ages, *Jāti* replaced profession based on the classification of *varnas*, and the son of *Kshtriya* was initiated into the same *varna* irrespective of the profession he followed. In the same way, the entire life span of an individual, which was supposed to be of 100 years, was divided into four āshrams. A man is supposed to follow the guidelines of different *āshramas* in life.

Sulva Sutra deals with the method of the creation of *Vedikā* for *Yagya*. These sutras also present a detailed study of the knowledge of geometry of the *Āryans*. Sulva means cord. This *shāstra* describes a *vedikā* measured by cord. Baudhāyana, Āapastamba and Kātyayana *sulva sutras* are three important sutras.

Kalyāna Varmā: Kalyāna Vermā is a famous astrologer who wrote *Jātaka-shāstra* entitled *Sharāvali* consisting of 2500 shlokas. This book has been compiled on the basis of Vārāhamihir's *Vrihat-jātaka*. He has summed up the ideas contained in the book.

Kanāda: Kanāda, by universal consent, is considered the pioneer of *Vaisheshika* philosophy. In ancient books several names of Kanāda are found. For instance, Kasabhāksha and Kanabhu, Udaināchārya, a prominent scholar of *Nyāya* philosophy has in his book *Kiranāvali* mentioned that Kanāda was the son of Kashyapa Muni. In the *Vāyu Purān*, Kanāda has been called the incarnation of Shiva. From the aforesaid descriptions Kanāda is proved to be the heir of Kashyapa. His teacher was Soma Sharmā.

Kanāda is the author of *Vaisheshika sutra*. This book is the basis of *Vaisheshika* philosophy. It is divided into 10 sections and contains 370 *sutras*. Its early section is divided into two sub-sections called *āhnikā*. In the **first** and **second** sections of this book there is a description of different *dravyas*. In the **third** section, there is the description of the traits of nine *dravyas* .The **fourth** section hinges round the analysis of *Paramānu Vāds,* in the **fifth** section there is description of feature of *karma* and its varieties. In the **sixth** section, there are reflections on ethical problems and *dharma* and *adharma*. The **seventh** section is devoted to the analysis of the *gunas*. In the **eighth, ninth** and **tenth** sections, there are discussions that hinges around *tarka, abhana*, *gyāna* and pleasure and pain. The sutras of *Vaisheshika* philosophy were written much before those of *Nyāya-sutra*. The oldest commentary on *Vaisheshikasutra* is said to be *Rāvana-bhāsya,* which is not available but a reference to this book is found in *Ratna-Prabhā*, a commentary on *Bhrahma-sutra, Shankara-bhāsya* etc. Bharadwāj is also said to have written a *Vritti* on *Vaisheshika sutra*. That also is not available.

According to Kanāda, the cause of creation may be traced back to the combination collation, systematisation and crystallisation of atoms. Kanāda discusses in detail the nature and structure of different kinds of atoms and the process in which they are synthesised to give birth to the universe. The way in which Kanāda describes the origin of the universe in *Vaisheshika* philosophy is strikingly original. There is a hearsay that Kanāda Rishi lived on the *kans* (scattered grains), so he is called Kanāda.

Theory of atomism is the most significant contribution of Kanāda. Although the genesis of this theory can be traced back to the *Upanishadas*, which propagate the idea that all objects are constituted out of *Prithavi, Jala*, *Vāyu, Ākāsh* and *Agni*.

***Kapila*:** Kapila was the exponent of the *Sāmkhya* School of philosophy. Maharishi Kapila is usually considered one of the incarnations of Vishnu. In the *Mahābhārata* two contradictory opinions about Kapila have been expressed; first that Kapila was the son of Brahmā and the second that he was the incarnation of Agni.

Those who believe in the ancient tradition take Kapila as the first philosopher. Shankarāchārya in his *Shankara-Bhāsya* on *Brahma-sutra* has clearly stated that Kapila was the exponent of the theory of *Sāmkhya*. In the Gitā, Krishna says that amongst the *siddhās* he is Kapila: Siddhānām Kapilamunih. Gitā 10/26)

Kapila wrote two books: *Sāmkhya-sutra* and *Tatva-samāsa*. While the former consists of 537 *sutras*, the latter consists of 22 *sutras*.

According to Maharishi Kapila, *Prākriti* and Purusha have been considered two primal forces. Their union was responsible for creation. Purusha is passive and *Prākriti* is active. It is *Prākriti*, which activates Purusha by infusing energy in him. Kapila has given a detailed description how this creation came into being. The conjugation of *Prākriti* and Purusha resulted in *Tanmātrās*, which further gave birth to nature and ultimately to man and woman. In this way Kapila traces the origin of this creation to union and co-ordination of *Prākriti* and Purusha; this is behind the concept of Ardhanārishwar: Shiva and Shakti. None of the two alone is so powerful as to make creation possible. It is the fusion of the two, which causes disturbance in the quiet state of the cosmos. Kapila has mentioned how and when this imbalance in nature takes place and gives birth to this vast cosmos.

Kapila's another important contribution is the theory of *Satkārya-Vāda*. According to this theory, cause is inherent in effect. The formation of curd from milk and oil from mustard are examples. *Satkārya-Vāda* has been furthe. divided into *Prakrti-parināma-vāda* and *Brahma-parināma-vāda*. While Kapila depends on the first approach Rāmānuja banks on the other. Kapila insists that the cause of creation is imbued in *Prākriti*. Rāmānuja, on the contrary maintains that seeds of creation are inherent in Brahma. Kapila's *Parināma-vāda* is also opposed to Shankara's *Vivarta-vāda*. Kapila mandates that the cause exists in the effect and the transformation of cause into effect does take place in reality. The formation of curd from milk is a reality. Shankara on the other hand rules that the transformation of cause into effect is only an illusion. It is caused by sheer ignorance. The cord appears to be a snake in the dark but once the light dawns upon it, the real difference is made apparent.

Kārtavirya Prabandha: Ashwin Shri Rāma Vermā, the crown prince of Travencore, has written *Kārta-Virya Prabandha*, a *champu kāvya* between 1765 and 1794. It deals with the battle between Rāvana and Kārtikeya ensuring the victory of the latter. Vira Rasa dominates the work since entire action of the book has been shifted to the battlefield. The mode of expression is very mature and the poet has a predilection for the verbiage to produce more effect.

Karnbhāra: Karn Bhāra is a drama written by Bhāsa. *Karn bhāra* signifies the responsibility of a military general, which Karna carries on his shoulder following the death of Dronāchārya. The drama depicts the character of Karna based on the story of the *Mahābhārata*. Karna is elevated to the post of Senāpati, (military general) after the death of Dronāchārya. The additional responsibility laid upon the shoulders of Karna has been referred to as the load on Karna, *Karn-Bhāra*. Karna is eager to take on Arjuna thus asking his charioteer to take his chariot ahead of Arjuna's. On the way, Karna narrates to Shalya, his charioteer, the story of securing the weapons and the events, which happened at the hermitage of Parasurāma. In the meantime, a *Brāhamana* appears on the scene who is none but Indra in disguise. Indra is apprehensive of the imminent danger on the life of Arjuna, his son; and in order to evade the impending danger, he asks Karna to part with, the *kavacha* and *kundala* which the latter rejects though he is known for his charity and suggests the priest to take away the clothes and ornaments in lieu of *kavacha* which the priest rejects. Karna finally hands over his *kavacha* and *kundala* to the priest and secures a weapon called *Vimala* from the priest. The whole drama is steeped in *karuna rasa*.

Kathāsaritsāgar: Kathā-sarit-sāgar is an important contribution to the repertory of *Sanskrit* fictional literature. Pt. Somadeva wrote it. It was designed to entertain the queen of Kashmir. She was the daughter of the king of Trigarta (Kullu-kandala). It was written between 1063 and 1081 A.D. This book is divided into 18 sections and there are altogether 124 *tarangas* in it. The total number of shlokas in this book is 20,688. This is a translation of *Brihat Kathā* and it is very popular among the readers. In the very beginning of this book, Somadeva has very sincerely proclaimed that his intention is to reproduce the original story as it is in all its originality. He would not endeavour to make any alteration and addition in the original work. There is a web of story in this book and these stories have influenced the western fiction. *Kathā-sarit-sāgar* is older than the stories of Alif Lailā, which is a significant work in Arabic literature.

The descriptions given in *Kathā-sarit-sāgar* are relatively larger than those of other writers particularly Kshemendra's *Brihat-Kathā-Manjari,* which has only 1,206 *shlokas*.

Kathopanishada: Kathopanishada is a part of the *Kathā* branch of Krishna Yajurveda. It consists of two chapters with each chapter having 3 ballies. It is the most significant among all the *Upanishadas*. It begins with the story of Nachiketā and Uddālaka. Its aim is to establish the validity of monistic philosophy by citing apt examples. It has been written in prose. The teaching of Monism is imparted to Nachiketā by Yamarāja following the latter's repeated imploring for the same. *Kathopanishada* also conveys the ideas contained in the *Sāmkhya* and Yoga school of philosophy. The first chapter commends renunciation, the plight of man guided by false knowledge, advantages of selfless service, grace of Brahma, importance of name, nature of soul, relationship between soul and Brahma, ways and means to secure unison with Brahma, dragging the senses to the service of God from the wrong path. The second chapter dwells upon universality of God, the movement of *Jivātmā*, nature of God, nature and means of attaining yoga, securing the company of God, showing faith in him, movement of *Jiva* after death, and attainment of *Moksha* through knowledge. *Kathopanishada* strictly maintains that union with God can be achieved through the practice of Yoga. Once a man reaches that stage, he transcends the boundary of pleasure and pain.

Kātyāyana: Kātyāyana was an eminent grammarian who wrote *Vartikā* on Panini's grammar. He has been referred to as *Vartikākāra* in the *Mahābhāsya*. He along with Panini and Patanjali is placed in the category of 'Munitraya' of *Sanskrit* grammar. The *Vartikās* are aimed at giving a new dimension to the study of *Ashtādhyāyi*. Kātyāyana has taken pains to bring it to the level of *Ashtādhyāyi* in originality. His timing is about 2700 years before Vikrama Samvata. The *Vartikās* are an integral part of Panini's grammar. The vitality of Panini's grammar has been redoubled with the introduction of the *Vartikās*. Kātyāyana has been variously referred to as Punarvasu, Medhājita and Vararuchi. He has been referred as Vararuchi Kātyāyana in *Skanda Purāna*.

Kātyāyana was a versatile genius. Besides grammar, he has also written dramas and *kāvyas*. His works on *Dharma shāstra* need to be given special treatment. His work *Svargārohana Kāvya* has been referred to as Vararuchi *kāvya* in *Mahābhāsya*. He has also written a work on criticism which is not available but reference to which is available in *Abhinava Bhārati* and *Shrigāra Prakāsha*. His other works include *Bhraja-sangyaka-shloka* and *Ubhayasarbhana*.

Kātyāyana Smriti: The author of this *Smriti* is Kātyāyana who is different from the author of *Vartikās* on *Ashtādhyāyi*. He has been placed between 3rd and 4th century B.C. Although no specific book of Kātyāyana of *Dharmashāstra* is available, still as many as

200 *Shlokas* assigned to him, are scattered over here and there in several books on *Dharma-shāstra*. *Smriti-Chandrikā* contains almost 600 *Shlokas* of Kātyāyana. A book consisting of 500 *Shlokas* is available in Jivānanda Samgraha, which is divided into 29 sections. The *Shlokas* have been written generally in *Anushtupa chhanda*. This book is known as *Karma Pradip* or *Kātyāyana Smriti*. The subjects which this book deals with include: method of putting on sacred thread, sprinkling of water, prayer to Ganesha and 16 *Matrikā-pujās* before performing any rite, description of last rites, pranāyāma, recitation of the hymns of the Vedas, duties of husband and wife and several kinds of *shrāddha*.

***Kavi Karnapura*:** Kavi Karnapura was a 16th century critic of the school of *Alankāra* who wrote a monumental work *Alankāra-kaustubha*. His father Shivānanda was the disciple of Chaitanya Mahā Prabhu. He was born in the year 1524 in the Nadia district of Bengāl. *Alankāra-kaustubha* has been written in ten *kiranas* (Chapters), incorporating within its ambit subjects like *kāvya-lakshanā*, *shabdārtha*, *dhvani*, *Gunibhuta, Vyanjan*, *Rasa-bhāva-bheda, Guna*, *Shabdālankāra*, *Arthālankāra*, *Riti* and *Dosha*. He also compiled a critical anthology entitled *Kāvya-Chandrikā,* which is not available. He wrote a drama on the life of Chaitanya Mahāprabhu in the year 1572.

***Kavirahasya*:** Kavi Rahasya is *shāstra kāvya*. It has been written on the basis of *Bhatti-kāvya* in praise of Krishna Rāja III, the Rashtrakuta king who ruled over his kingdom between 940 and 953 A.D. It is based on the principles of *Sanskrit* grammar. All illustrations given in the work are aimed at elevating the personality of the poet's patrons.

***Kavirāja Dhoi*:** Kavirāja Dhoi was the author of the *sandesha kāvya Pavana Duta* taking inspiration from Kālidāsa's Meghaduta. He was the court poet of Lakshmana Sena, the king of Bengāl. His period has been fixed between the later half of the 12th century and first half of the 13th century. Nothing substantial about Dhoi's life is available. He was awarded the title of *Kavirāja*.

Pavana Duta deals with the message communicated to king Lakshmana Sena of Gaur Desha by his beloved authorising

Pavana as her messenger to express her anguish and sense of despair, which gripped her in the absence of her lover. The king reaches *Malayāchala* after vanquishing the sourthern regions. He falls in love with an *Apsarā* named Kuvalayāvati. Once the king returns to his kingdom, Kuvalayāvati undergoes intense mental trauma and sends her message to her lover through the wind of spring. The poet has presented a vivid description of the entire route covering Bengāl and Malaya Mountain.

Pavanduta has been written in *Mandākrāntā chhanda* and it consists of 104 *Shlokas*. Like *Meghaduta* it is also divided into *Purva* and *Uttara* parts.

Kāvyādarsha: Kāvyādarsha is a mounmental work on *Sanskrit* poetics by Dandi. It consists of three *parichchhedas*, which comprises 660 *Shlokas*. Subjects falling within the ambit of the first *parichchheda* include *kāvya lakshanā*, *Kāvya bheda: gayda, padya* and *Mishra*, *akhyayikā* and *kathā*, analysis of *guna* and three *gunas*. He has also dealt with two styles: *gaudi* and *vaidarbhi*. The second *parichchheda* is devoted to *alankāra*. Besides the definition of *alankāra*, 35 *alankāras* along with their *lakshanās* and illustrations have been discussed. The third *parichchheda* is circled round *yamaka* and its 315 kinds.

The entire discussion revolves around *dosha*, guna and *alankāra* as Dandi takes these elements vital for *kāvya*. Dandi is of the opinion that literary embellishment, which is needed for successful *kāvya*, can alone not lead to the making of a perfect *kāvya*. Bhāmah has suggested that *alankāra* must be coupled with striking quality or *vakrokti* to give that additional flavour to *kāvya,* which helps making it embellished, Dandi has defined *kāvya* as *'ishtārtha vyavachchhinna padāvali.*' He has emphasised the arrangenent of words to cultivate *ishtārtha*. By *kāvya mārga* Dandi means to suggest *bandh* or arrangement of *shabda* and *artha*. Kuntaka further elaborated this arrangement. He insisted that *shabda* and *artha* should enjoy proper arrangement and this arrangement should be made by a genius.

Kāvyālankāra: Kāvyālankāra is a seminal book on Indian poetics written by Bhāmah. He is the first critic giving a full-length discussion on alankāra. Bhāmah's contribution to *Sanskrit* rhetoric is immense. He is the first rhetorician to mention *dharma*, *artha*, *kāma*, and *moksha* as the objectives of poetry. He has expressed the view that both *preya* and *shreya* meaning give immediate and ulterior pleasure. Permanent pleasure should be the aim and objective of poetry. He also gives a detailed account of poetic blemishes. He considers even the inclusion of one blemish in poetry abominable; and poetry, which contains poetic blemishes, is as contemptible as a spoilt son. In his *Kāvyādarsa*, he has deeply probed into the nature and function of *alankāra* and has extended its scope to include *sandhi* and *Vritti* as its integral parts. He has also renamed *svabhāva-ukti* as *jati* and has proved its dominance in poetry.

The credit to analyse poetics independently goes to Bhāmah who divided his book into 6 *parichchheda*s consiting of about 400 *Shlokas*. Five subjects have been touched upon in this book i.e., *kāvyasharira*, *dosha*, *Nyāya-nirnaya* and *shabda-suddhi*. The **first parichchheda**, consisting of 59 *shlokas*, throws ample light on topics like *kāvya-prayojana*, *kavi-prashansā*, *pratibhā*, subjects known to the poet, nature and forms of *kāvya*, *kāvya dosha* and its removal. The **second parichchheda** deals with *guna*, *shabdālankāra* and *arthālankāra*. The **third parichchheda** also revolves round *arthālankāra* whereas the **fourth parichchheda** is restricted to highlighting eleven kinds of literary defects. The **fifth parichchheda** is associated with *Nyāya-nirnaya*. In the **sixth** and **final parichchheda**, grammatical mistakes have been highlighted and poets have been warned to remain cautious about grammitical impurites. He has ruled out the status of *alankāra* to *hetu*, *sukshama*, *lesha vārttā* showing his stern opposition to his predecessors who included them in their list of *alankāras*. He has discussed thirtynine *alankāras* in all.

Kāvyālankāra: The authorship of Kāvyālankāra, a monumental work on poetics, is attributed to the 10th century critic Rudrata representing *alankāra* school. He has repeatedly given emphasis on poetry, which is free from blemishes and is equipped with *alankāras*. His analysis of *rasa* is equally original and striking. His originality lies in giving a scientific analysis of *nāyaka-nāyikā* *bheda*, which is a part of his *rasa* theory. This work touches upon almost all the topics of poetics. The canvas of his book is wider than that of Bhāmah and Dandi.

Rudrata has laid greater emphasis on poetic figures making a detailed discussion of its each and every aspect, and thus 12 out of 16 chapters have been devoted to bring out the specialities of *alankāras*. The topics which find extensive treatment in his work include objects of *kāvya*, definition of a poet and his qualifications, the five *shabdālankāras*, *Vakrokti, anuprāsha, yamaka*, *shlesha*, and *chitra*, the four *rities* or styles: *Vaidarbhi, Panchāli*, *Lāti* and *Gaudi*, and the six *Bhāsās*: (Languages) *Prākirta, Magadhi, Paishāchi, Saurseni*, and *Apabharnsha* to which a poet takes recourse to give vent to his ideas.

Rudarata has classified 66 *alankāras* in five categories on the basis of certain principles and thus he has extended the number of *alankāras.* These five categories are *Vāstava* consisting of 23 *alankāras*, *Aupameya* consisting of 21 *alankāras*, *Atisaya* consisting of 12 *alankāras* and *shlesha* consisting of 10 *alankāras*. His discussion also includes ten *rasas* and two varieties of *shrigāras*: *Samyoga* and *Vipralambha* (love in unison and love in separation).

Kāvya Mimāmsā: Rāja Shekhara wrote Kāvya Mimāmsā to give proper training to the poets. It consists of 18 chapters. The **first chapter** deals with the origin of *alankārashāstra*. It further depicts the teachings of *kāvya-vidyā* in 18 *Adhikaranas*. The **second chapter** deals with *kāvya-nirdesha*, pin-pointing the distinction between *kāvya* and *shāstra*. The **third chapter** deals with the ways of writing superb poetry, which include *shakti*, *pratibhā*, *vyutpatti, samādhi* and *abhyāsa,* making it mandatory for composing meaningful poetry. He uses the word *shakti* for poetic imagination. The flame of poetry can only be ignited if a person is intended to compose poetry works on these aspects of poetry. It also throws light on two types of *Pratibhā* (talent): *kāryitri* and *bhāvayitri*. A poet is endowed with *kāryitri pratibhā* while a critic is endowed with *bhāvayitri pratibhā*. The former is of three kinds: *sahaja*, *ahārya*, and *aupadeshiki*. The **4th and 5th chapters,** falling under the head *kāvyapaka* concentrates on different kinds of poets including *shāstra-kavi*, *kāvya-kavi* and *ubhaya* (both). *Shāstra-kavi* has been further divided into three kinds while 8 kinds of *kāvya-kavi* have been mentioned. An analysis of pada has been made in the **sixth** while the **seventh chapter** is confined to the analysis of vākya. Sources of *kāvyārtha* figure in the **eighth chapter**. The **ninth chapter** deals with seven kinds of *artha* (meaning) besides a detailed discussion of *Prabandha* and *muktaka-kāvya*. The **tenth chapter** deals with *kavicharyā* emphasising the qualification, which a poet must have. **Chapters 11 to 13** are devoted to the discussion 'to what extent a poet is at liberty to use the words and thoughts of his predecessors.' In **chapters 14 to 16**, there is a discussion on *kavi samaya*. **Chapter 17th** is related to Geography and the **18th** is the conclusion. The wide-ranging subjects treated in *Kāvya Mimāmsā* bring it to the level of an encyclopedia of variegated knowledge and wisdom.

Kāvyaprakāsha: Kāvya Prakāsha is a book on poetics by Mammata that presents a synoptic view of the history of Sanskrit poetics from Bharat to Bhoja Rāja. While defining poetry, Mammata laid stress on three cardinal qualitiies of poetry that (a) poetry should be free from blemishes, (b) it should have guna (prasāda, mādhurya and Oaja) and (c) it should have embellishment or ornamentation *alankāra* (figures of speech). Neither word nor meaning by itself is poetry. Mammata takes both word and meaning as crucial for poetry. When he says that poetry should be free from blemishes, he means that poetry must necessarily be garbed in chaste language and it must be expressive and evocative.

Mammata throws sufficient light on the object of poetry. Poetry is written for fame, for earning money, for wordly dealings, for eradication of ominous signs and for attaining ecstatic pleasure; and convey message, like one given to a *kāntā* (beloved): *kāvyam yashase arthakrite, vyavaharavide, shivetarakshate, kāntāsammita upadesayuje*.

Kāvyālankāra-sāra-samgraha: Kāvya-alankāra-sāra-samgraha by Udabhata is a monumental work on poetics dealing basically with *alankāras*. It consist of 6 *vargas* and 79 *Kārikās* with 95 illustrations and has referred to 41 *alankāras*. Udabhata has borrowed the illustrations for this work from his own *kāvya Kumārasambhava*. He considers all the *alankāras* as scaffoldings on *upamālankāra*. He has also mentioned the name of vakrokti in his book, which gives premonition to *dhvani* theory. By introducing *vakrokti* as a new *alankāra*, he has extended the field of *Kāvyālankāra*.

Udabhata has not only enumerated the figures in the same order as Bhāmah does but has borrowed the definition of most of the poetic figures from him. The four forms of *atisayokti*, which Bhāmah has mentioned, are nowhere found in Udabhata. Later writers held Udabhata in high esteem whose findings have made a deep and potent impact on their writings.

Kāvyālankāra-sutra-vritti: Kāvya-alankāra-sutra-vritti is an epoch-making work of the school of *riti* attributed to Vāman who considers *riti* as the soul of poetry. This is the first work ever written on Indian poetics using sutra style of composition. This book has three broad divisions: *Sutra*, *Vritti* and *Udāharana*. While Vāmana wrote *Sutra* and *Vritti,* he borrowed *udāharanas* from different works. It has been divided into five *Adhikaranas*. Each *adhikarana* has been named on the basis of the subjects taken up in it. The titles are *saria*, *dosha darshana*, *guna vivechanā*, *alankāra* and prāyogikā. These five *adhikaranas* are further divided into 12 *Adhyāyas* and 319 *Kārikās*.

The **first** adhikarana deals with *kāvyalakshanā*, *kāvya* and *alankāra* and relation between poet and critic, poetry, kinds of *riti-vaidharbhi, gaudi* and *panchāli*, forms of *kāvya*: *Gadya kāvya*, *padya kāvya*, *prabandha* and *muktaka,* and kinds of *akhyāyikā*.

The **second** *adhikarana* concentrates on *gunas* and *alankāras*. The **third** *adhikarana* deals with ten *artha-doshas*. The **fourth** *adhikarana* revolves round *alankāras*. He has discussed 33 *alankāras*. The **fifth** *adhikarana* is basically concerened with *vyākarana*. It is directly concerned with poetics. Sahadeva has written a commentary on it although *Kāmdhenu-tikā* written by Gopendra Bhupāla is very popular.

Kāvyashāstra: A *shāstra* making a thorough assessment of the excellence of *kāvya* is called kāvya-shāstra. It generally deals with the theory aimed at evaluating the *kāvya* and on the basis of that theory the assesment of a work of poetic art is made. Several names have been used for *kāvyashāstra*: *alankāra shāstra*, *sāhitya shāstra*, *sāhitya vidyā* and *kriyā kalpa*. Of all the names *'Kriyākalpa'* is the oldest one. This word has been used in Vātsyāyana's *Kāmsutra*. This word has been used for poetics in *Lalita-vistāra*. In the *Rāmāyana* also the same has been used for *kāvyashāstra*. In course of time several critics including Bhatta-lollat, Srisand-kuka, Bhatta-nāyaka and Abhinava Gupta have elaborated this sutra in their own way. Their theories are known as *Utpattivāda*, *Anumitivāda*, *Bhuktivāda* and *Abhivyaktivāda* respectively. Ānandvardhana has taken it as a synonym of *dhvani* taking *Rasa* as *vyanjana*. Bhoja also recognised its importance in his book *Shrigāra*-prakāsha' and has assimilated all the *rasas* within *shrigāra*. *Agni Purāna*, Rājashekhara, Bhanudatta and Visvanātha have also accepted *rasa* as the soul of poetry and have contributed significantly to the development of *rasa* theory as an independent school of criticism.

In *Kāvya-Shāstra* there are the following *Sampradāyas* (Sects)

Alankāra Sampradāya: The elements aimed at embellishing poetry are called *alankāra*. This school of *Sanskrit* poetics was popularised by Bhāmah and was further nourished by Dandi, Udabhata, Rudrata, Pratiharendu Rāja and Jayadeva. According to Bhāmah, poetry loses its grace without *alankāra* in the same way in which a young girl is devoid of beauty without ornaments. Bharata has referred to only four *alankāras* but coming to Appaya Dikshita, the number of *alankāras* went up to 125. The analysis of *alankāra* by Mammata, Ruyyaka, Visvanātha, and Pandit Rāja Jagannātha is more scientific. The importance of *alankāra* was overshadowed with the prominence of *dhvani*.

Riti Sampradāya: Riti Sampradāya was propounded by Vāmana taking style as the essence of poety. His merit lies in bringing *guna* and *shaili* (style) on equal footing showing amazing relationship between the two. Style is the generator of poetry while *alankāra* simply enhances its beauty. This theory failed to arrest the attention of succeeding critics who refused to accept it as the soul of poetry.

Dhvani sampradāya: Dhvani Sampradāya is the most celebrated school of Indian poetics propounded by Ānandavardhana and further nourished by Abhinava Gupta, Ruyyaka, Mammata, Pandita Rāja Jagannāth and Visvanātha. Ānandvardhana elaborated his theory of *Dhvani* in his book *Dhvanyāloka* on which at a later stage Abhinava Gupta wrote a commentary entitled Abhinava Bhārati. Ānandvardhana has made a comparative study of different schools of criticism in his work Dhvanyāloka and has established *dhvani* theory as the most valid theory.

The basic premise of Ānandvardhana is that word has three powers or *shakti* namely *vāchyārtha*, *lakshyārtha* and *vyanjanārtha* or *Dhvnyārtha*. *Vāchyārtha* is the bald or literal meaning; *lakshyārtha* is the metaphorical meaning and *dhvnyārtha* is the suggestive meaning. For example, if someone says, "Bring the book". It suggests nothing but the act of bringing a book. It is literal and bald meaning of the word. But when someone says, " Just see, a lion is coming". It means that a brave man or a dauntless man like a lion is coming. This is metaphorical meaning. Similarly, when referring to some noble man one says "He is pure gold." Here the word gold here is suggestive of the nobility of the man. The last one is suggestive meaning or *dhvanyārtha*.

Vakrokti Siddhānta (Sampradāya): Vakrokti Siddhānta was popularised by Kuntaka in his epoch making work *Vakroktijivita*. By Vakrokti, Kuntaka means strikingness. Bhāmah came to the rescue of *Vakrokti* and had denied the existence of poetic figures without *Vakrokti*. Kuntaka developed it as an independent theory accepting it as the essence of poetry. According to Kuntaka, a curved expression or a tangent expression, is Vakrokti. He defines vakrokti as: *vaidagdhya bhangi bhaniti*, meaning an expression, which is sense-provoking as well as curved. The examples of *Vakrokti* cited by Kuntaka are the same that were cited by Ānandvardhana in support of *dhvani* theory.

Auchitya sampradāya: Auchitya Sampradāya came into being with Kshemendra. In his book *Auchitya-vichāra-charchā*, he has tried to establish Auchitya, propriety, as the soul of poetry.

Sanskrit poetics acquired a new dimension with the help of these *Sampradāyas* of criticism. The critics made a detailed discussion of the nature, cause, aim and kinds of poetry by providing the minutest details Three categories of *kāvya* - *uttama*, *madhyama* and *adhama* were made and *dhvani* was accepted as the most accomplished form of *kāvya*. *Gunibhuta vyanjan* was placed next to it, whereas *Alankāra kāvya* was considered as the inferior one. In this way *dhvani*, *rasa* and *alankāra* were accepted as three milestone in Indian poetics. *Kāvya* was divided into *drishya* and *shravya kāvya*.

Kenopanishada: Kenopanishada is the ninth chapter under the *Tālavākara* branch of the Sāma Veda, which is also called *Tālavākaropanishada* or *Jaiminiya upanishada*. It is divided into four small sections, which are written partly in prose and partly in poetry. It has been written in dialogue form exchanged between the teacher and his disciple. In the first section, a question has been posed "From where do the senses get an inspiration?" Brahma has been considered as the chief entity inspiring the senses. The invincibility of God has also been proved. In order to illustrate the omnipresence and Almighty-ness of God and also to demolish the vanity of Agni, Varuna and Vāyu, *Prajāpati* or Brahma placed a dry hey before them and asked them one-by-one to burn it, to drench it, or to keep it away. Despite their best efforts they failed to do so. *Prajāpati* at last sermonised that gods derive power from the God. The story is symbolic but it proves that God alone is powerful and whatever power gods possess is derived from the God. In the second section, jiva has been considered the part of God and the power of senses is said to derive from God. The distinction has also been made between the Brahma in form and formless Brahma.

Keralabharana: Kerala Bharana is a *Champu kāvya* by Rāma Chandra Dikshita, a 17th century poet. The subjectmatter of this *Champu* is based on the discussion between Vashistha and Viswāmitra in the court of Indra over the issue which country is better and worthlooking. Following the order of Indra, two gandharvas travel on the earth and decide that Kerala is more beautiful.

Keshava Mishra: Keshava Mishra was an eminent critic belonging to the second half of the 16th century who enriched *Sanskrit* poetics by his *Alankāra Shekhara* written at the behest of Mānikya Chandra, the king of Kāngrā. It consists of 8 *Ratnas* or chapters which are further divided into 22 *marichies*. *Kārikā*, *Vritti* and illustrations are its three parts. Whereas *Kārikā* and *Vritti* are the own composition of the author, illustrations have been quoted from different sources. Subjects which figure in this book include *kāvya lakshna, riti* (Style) *shabdashakti*, 8 types of blemishes of *padas*, 18 types of blemishes of sentences, 8 types of blemishes of meaning, 5 types of *shabda gunas*, *alankāra* and *Rupaka*.

Keshava Mishra: Keshava Mishra was the most accomplished writer of the school of *Nyāya* who has written a monumental work *Tarka-bhāsha* in which the objective of Nyāya has been explained in simple language. He was born in 1275 A.D. Govardhana Mishra, a disciple of Keshava Mishra has written a commentary on *Tarka-bhāsha* entitled *Tarka-Bhāsha-Prakāsha* in which he has personal records of the life of Keshava Mishra. His father was Balabhadra. While his two brothers were Vishwanāth and Padmanātha. He had learnt *Tarka-Bhāsha* from Vishwanāth.

Khāndadeva Mishra: Khāndadeva Mishra was a follower of the Bhatta branch of the *Mimāmsā* School of philosophy. Like Kumārila Bhatta, he enjoys a unique distinction of introducing "Navyamata" (New ideology) in *Mimāmsā* School in the manner of *Navya-Nyāya*. He has compiled three outstanding books: *Mimāmsā-Kaustubha, Bhatta Dipikā* and *Bhatta Rahasya*, throwing new light to the study of the theory of Navya-mata. *Mimāmsā-Kaustubha* is a commentary on *Mimāmsā-sutras*. *Bhatta-rahasya* is very complex. The language of this book is tough and clumsy due to the adoption of *naiyāyika* approach. Khāndedeva Mishra's books elaborately discuss the ideology and traits of *Nyāya-mata* in a new perspective elevating it to the level of an enriched philosophical school.

Kirātarjuniya: Kirāt Arjuniya is a *mahākāvya* written by Bhāravi. The subject matter of this epic has been borrowed from the *Vana-Parva* of the *Mahābhārata*. It has been written in 18 cantos.

The story revolves around the offerings made by Arjuna to win the grace of Shiva and to secure *Pashupatāstra.* Moved by his tenacity, Indra suggested him to seek the blessings of Shiva. Shiva descends as Kirāta, indulges in dispute over the killing of a boar and reveals his identity following a pitched battle with Arjuna. Arjuna surrenders himself at his feet and Shiva, pleased with his exceptional courage, agrees to hand over *Pashupatāstra*.

The merit of the poem lies in putting the story of an epical stature in a short compass. The poet having a leaning for artistry has extended the boundary of his epic using dialogues and excellent descriptions. The description of autumn and the Himalayas in the fourth and the fifth cantos and playfulness of the Apsarās in the seventh, the eighth, the ninth and the tenth cantos acquire the status of a *muktaka kāvya*. Actually the relationship of the description made in these cantos has been badly disturbed with the main story and appears as independent episodes bearing no obvious link with the main plot. From the 11th canto onwards, the story is back to its usual form.

***Kokilasandesha*:** Kokil Sandesha (message through a cuckoo bird) by Uddanda, a 16th century poet, is modelled on the pattern of Kālidāsa's *Meghaduta*. He was the court poet of Jamurinā, the king of Kālicut. He has also written a *prakarana* named *Mallikāmāruta* in ten acts, which is inspired by Bhavabhuti's *Mālati-Mādhava*. In *Kokila-sahdesha* the poet has sought the services of Cuckoo to send his meassage to his beloved. It has been divided into two parts: *Purva* and *Uttara*. The story deals with the agony of the lover who is separated from his beloved. He recalls the memory of his beloved after listening to the melody of cuckoo in the spring season.

Krishnānanda: Krishnānda was a poet who composed an epic, Sahridayānanda in 15 cantos dealing with the adventure and exploits of king Nala. He was born in the 14th century and was an inhabitant of Jagannāth Puri. One shloka of *Sahridayānanda* is found in *Sāhitya-darpana* of Āchārya Visvanāth.

Kshemendra: Kshemendra was the exponent of the Auchitya School of Indian poetics. His talent is seen in poetics as well as in *kāvya*. His poetic excellence is reflected in his epic *Dashāvatāra-Charita* dealing with ten incarnations of *Bhagwān* Vishnu. The brief stories of the *Rāmāyana* and the *Mahābhārata* have been presented in his *Rāmāyana Manjari* and *Mahābhārata Manjari*. He has also given the *Sanskrit* translation of the unique book of Gunādhya, *Brihat-Kathā Manjari*. Besides many minor stories, the main plot revolves round the love affair of Udayana and Vāsavadattā. In his another work *Bodhisatva-avadāna-kalpa-latā*, stories relating to the life of Buddha have been narrated. It consists of 108 *pallavas* or stories, the last being completed by his son Somendra after his death. His period dates back to 11th century. His critical treatises include *Auchitya-vichāra-charchā*, *Kavi-kantha-bharana* and *Subrat-tilaka*. Noted critic Ānandavardhan was his teacher.

Kshemendra's popularity chiefly rests on *Auchitya-vichāra-charchā* while rest of the books are minor works. In this book he has established *Auchitya* (propriety) as the soul of poetry, and has insisted that perfect *kāvya* is possible only when its constituent parts remain well within its limitations.

Kshemishwara: Kshemishwara was a contemporary of Rājashekhara. He was a playwright who wrote two dramas *Naishadhānanda* and *Chanda-kaushika*. He composed his dramas under the patronage of Mahipāla, the king of Kannauja. His period has been fixed around 900 A.D. In *Naishadhānanda*, dramatic form has been given to the story of Nal and Damayanti as narrated in the *Mahābhārata*. *Chanda-kaushika* deals with the story of the ordeal of king Harishchandra.

Kumāra Dāsa: Kumāra Dāsa was one of the most celebrated poets of the post-Kālidāsa era whose popularity rests on his epic *Jānaki-harana*. He has borrowed extensively from Kālidāsa modelling the pattern of his poetry on his two epic poems *Raghuvanasa* and *Kumārsambhava*.

Kumāradāsa has also imitated the style of Bhatti and Bhāravi who excelled in writing ornate poetry. His growing attraction for poetic figures has come into his way of acquiring the status of an epic poet. His crave for ornamentation has further crippled his originality. Following the footprints of Bhāravi, Kumāradāsa also composed *Ekākshara* and *Dvayākshara Shlokas*. His intense passion for *yamakas* adversely affected his artistic grandeur.

The complete text of *Janaki-harana* is not available. The first fourteen cantos and part of the fifteenth canto are preserved in the Singhalese literature which narrates the story up to Angada's arrival at the court of Rāvana. Some *Shlokas* of 25th Canto dealing with the coronation of Rāma and mentioning the name of the author are there in Singhalese literature. This further suggests that the text of Janakiharana up to the coronation of Rāma has close affinity with Bhatti's *Rāvana baddha*.

Kumāra Sambhava: Kumāra Sambhava is an epic written by Kālidāsa narrating Pārvati's earnest desire to win Shiva through penance and renunciation. It is placed in the category of Kālidāsa's early works but is in no way inferior to his other poems in content, style and diction. The entire epic, running into 17 cantos, relates the story of their daring son Kartikeya and the killing of the invicible demon Tārakā by him. Kālidāsa has given only needed stress on Shiva and Pārvati but since the epic is about what was *sambhava* (possible) with Kumāra Kārtikeya, so he has narrated his life to the extent of the killing of Tārakā in order to bring out the motive of Kumāra's birth.

The story has been derived from the *Mahābhārata*, particularly from the Shakuntalā legend, and has been reshaped by Kālidāsa using his enriched imaginative faculty. Kālidāsa has successfuly exploited his aesthetic sensibility which finds expression particularly in the delineation of Umā's celestial beauty. He has scaled new heights in the creation of sense of humour and seems to have no peer in this discipline.

The **first** canto begins with Umā resorting to intense meditation to win Shiva as her husband. In the **second**, gods urging lord Brahmā to come to their rescue and bring solace to them from the terror of the dreaded demon Tārakā and Brahmā assuring them to undertake appropriate measure to redress their grievances. In the **third**, Kāmadeva desperately tempting Shiva to deviate him from eternal trance, and the latter out of anger reducing him to ashes opening his third eye. The **fourth** canto depicts the plight of Kāma's wife Rati mourning over the tragic end of her deceased husband, and making tireless efforts to pacify Shiva to bring life back to her husband. In the **fifth**, Umā undergoes rigorous penance to secure Shiva's grace. Shiva finally, joins the company of Umā disguising himself as a young hermit urging upon her to reconsider her decision and in return earning the ire of Umā who retaliated with firm rebuke leading on to the hermit revealing his real identity and keeping Umā flabbergasted. In the **sixth**, Shiva's message is communicated to Himavāna by his disciples. In the **seventh**, Shiva and Pārvati are wedded following Pārvati seeking Shiva's consent. In the **eighth** canto, the post-marital life of Shiva and Pārvati has been depicted with fervour and gusto resulting into the birth of Kumāra. The rest of the book describes the childhood and growth of Kārtikeya up to Tārakā *Baddha*.

***Kumārapāla Charita*:** Kumāra Pāla Charita, written by Hema Chandra, is an epic of profound historical importance. It presents the authentic history of the kings of Chālukya dynasty of Gujarāt. Of all the kings of this dynasty Hemachandra has paid more attention to the portrayal of the life and achievements of Kumāra Pāla, his chief patron. Hemachandra was a staunch admirer of Jain ideology. His prime objective is to spread the teachings of Jainism. Kumāra Pāla himself being a supporter of Jain principles helped Hemachandra in many ways to achieve his objective.

Kumāra Pāla Charita is also called a *dva-yāshraya Kāvya*, as it serves dual purpose. Besides giving a detailed account of *Chālukya* kings, the whole epic has been compiled to give illustrations to various grammatical terms and Hema Chandra's experiments. In this way, it is placed in the category of *shāstra kāvya* along with *Bhatti Kāvya*. This epic has two broad divisions: first 12 cantos deal with the life of the predecessers of Kumāra Pāla including Mularāja, Vallabharāja, Durlabharāja, Karna, Siddharāja and Jaya Singh, and has been written in *Sanskrit* while the last eight cantos written in *Prākrit* provide an elaborate description of the exploits of Kumār Pāla. It is the most significant part of the epic. Kumārapāla succeeded Jaya Singh to the throne of Chālukya Empire. He had to face stiff opposition from Anhayaka whom he finally vanquished. The latter agrees to hand over his daughter to Kumāra Pāla. Hema Chandra initiated him into Jain sect. Kumāra pāla undertook several reformative measures for the enrichment of Jainism. He stopped the practice of the killing of animals to show his reverence for his teacher.

Kumāra Tāla: Kumāra Tāla established *Sautāntrika* School of Buddhist philosophy. He lived at Taxilā. The Buddhist tradition has placed him along with three luminaries, Ashvaghosha, Deva and Nāgārjuna. His period has been allocated in the 2nd century A.D.

Dr. Luders at Turphan discovered a manuscript of his work Kalpanā-amanda-tikā-drishhtānta. In this book the teachings of Buddhism are compiled. These stories are imaginary ones. The original work is available in *gadya* (prose). But *Shlokas* have also been added to the text in the middle. The writer begins with the teaching of Buddhism and illustrates it through a story.

Kuntaka: Kuntaka is the celebrated author of the *Vakrokti Jivita*. He was the contemporary of Abhinava Gupta. In his *Vakrokti-jivita*, he profusely cites illustrations from Kālidāsa, Māgha, Bāna and Bhavabhuti. Kuntaka established that *Vakrokti* is the soul of poetry. Ordinarily, literal or bald expression cannot please a man of literary taste. It is the co-existence of word and sense that constitutes *kāvya*. A work may have manifold meanings, but all the meanings cannot operate at a time. It is only the intended meaning, which should be taken into consideration. While formulating his theory, Kuntaka lays emphasis on arch speech, which is different from an ordinary speech. An ordinary speech simply gives us information about something. It is based on facts. So an ordinary speech is concerned with factual statement. But Kuntaka's *Vakrokti* is different from factual statement. It is a speech, which is curved and can be understood and appreciated by susceptible and sympathetic reader who is capable of understanding the niceties of meaning.

Kurma Purāna: Chronologically, Kurma Purāna is the 15th *Purāna* dealing with the kurma-avatāra, tortoise incarnation of Vishnu. This *Purāna* narrates the story of Vishnu taking the Mandarāchala mountain on his back during the churning of the ocean undertaken by gods and demons. It is mentiond in *Matasya Purāna* that Vishnu, taking the incarnation of a tortoise, narrated the entire story to king Indradyumna in the presence of Indra, which consisted of 18,000 *Shlokas*.

Kurma Purāna consists of 17,000 *Shlokas* having two divisions: *Purva* and *Uttara*. Whereas *Purva* consists of 53 chapters, *Uttara* consists of 46 chapters. Out of four *samhitās*: *Brāhmi*, *Bhāgavati*, *Sauri* and *Vaishnavi*, only *Brāhmi*, consisting of 6,000 *Shlokas*, is available. This *Purāna* includes *Purāna Panchalakshana* depicting several incarnations of Vishnu. It has laid great emphasis on the prayer of *Shakti*.

Kuvalayānanda: Kuvalayānanda is a popular work on *Alankāra* written by Appaya Dikshit in which 123 *arthālankāras* have been discussed in detail. It is based on Jayadeva's *Chandraloka*. He has imitated Jayadeva's style of incorporating the definition and illustrations of *alankāra* within the framework of one shloka. He has borrowed the *lakshanā* of *alankāra* straightway from *Chandraloka* and has given his own analysis for its clarification. Appaya Dikshita has introduced 17 new *alankāras*. Although, Bhoja, Shobhākara Mitra and Yāska have already referred to these alankāras yet the merit of Appaya Dikshit lies in making a perfect arrangement of these *alankāras*. Ten commentaries on *Kuvalayānanda* have been published which are in themselves testimony to its popularity. These *tikās* include *Rasa-ranjini* by Gangādhara Vājpeyee, *Alankāra Chandrikā* by Vaidyanāth Tatsate, *Alankāra-dipikā* by Āshādhara Bhatta, *Alankāra-suddha* by Nagojibhatta, *Kāvya-Manjari* by Nyāyavāgisha Bhattāchārya, *Kuvalayānada Tikā* by Mathurānātha, and *Buddha-ranjini* by Vengalasura. ■■

Linga Purāna: Linga Purāna is the 11th *Purāna* in sequence. Its objective is to reveal the mystery regarding worship of *Linga* and to discuss the ways for the worship of Lord Shiva. It consists of 11,000 *shlokas* and 163 chapters. It has been divided into *Purva* and *Uttara Vibhāgas. Purva bhāga* deals with the origin of the world by Shiva. It also presents a detailed account of the kings right from the period of *Vaivasvata Manvantara* till the age of Krishna. He has been shown as superior to Vishnu at several places. This *Purāna* deals with 28 incarnations of Lord Shiva, Shaiva places of worship and Shaiva *Vratas*. The account of *pashu, pāsha* and *pashupati* has been presented in its *uttara* part. Most of the chapters in *Uttara Vibhāga* have been written in prose. It deals with the Vedic name of the famous eight idols of Shiva. It also mentions Kalki and Buddha incarnations and description of *Yogāntara*..

Lakshmidhara Bhatta: Lakshmidhara Bhatta was a political essayist. He was the minister of the grand father of Jayachanda, king of *Kānyakubja*. His period has been fixed around the beginning of the 12th century. His popularity chiefly rests on his monumental work *Kritya Kalpataru*. It is divided into 14 *kandas*. Of these *kandas*, *Rāja dharma kānda* deals with the facts pertaining to statecraft. It is further divided into 21 chapters. The first 12 chapters deal with seven parts of the state. The 13th and the 14th chapters deal with *khadgunaniti* and in the rest seven chapters festivals and offerings, made specially for the welfare of the state, have been highlighted. ■■

Mādhavanidāna : Mādhavanidāna is a popular text of *Āyurveda* written by Mādhava. He flourished around 7th century. It is considered the most popular work on *nidāna* in modern age. Earlier he named this work as *Rāgavinischaya* that was later named *Mādhavanidāna*, This text has been written especially for those who are least aware of the ideas contained in the scriptures. Vijayarakshita and his disciple jointly wrote a commentary *Mādhukoshtikā* and Vāchaspati Vaidya wrote *Atanka Darpana Tikā*.

Mādhva Doctrine : A sect of Vaisnavism pioneered by Ānandatirtha or Mādhvāchārya. This sect is called Brahman Sampradāya and the theory propounded by Mādhvāchārya is called *Dvaitavāda*. He was born at Udupi in south India in the year 1199. He has written about 37 books out of which 14 are very significant: *Brahmasutra Bhāshya, Bhāshya of Aitareya, Kena, Katha and Brihdāranyaka Upanishadas, Gitā Bhāshya, Mahābhārata Tātparya Nirnaya*, and *Vishnutatvanirnaya*. The authentic history of Madhvāchārya has been presented by Nārāyana Pandita in *Mādhavavijaya* and *Manimanjari*. It is said that this doctrine was first handed over to Hanumāna by Vāyu who later on offered it to Bhima. In course of time, it was accepted by Ānandatirtha. Mādhva has accepted devotion as the only way to liberation. He also accepted the authority of God, *Jiva* and *Jagata*.

Mādhva has accepted the existence of the world. The world which has come out of God can not be considered unreal or illusory. For him *Moksha* is the state of eternal pleasure, which can be achieved by means of devotion (*bhakti*). Of all, *Sāyujja Bhakti* is the most acceptable. *Haituki Bhakti* or devotion for the sake of personal interest is the worst and *Ahaituki Bhakti* is the best form of devotion.

Mādhyamavyāyoga: Mādhyamvyāyoga is a one-act play written by Bhāsha. It deals with the story of the marriage of Bhima and Hidimbā and the rescue of a Brāhmana by Bhima who was tortured by his son Ghatotkacha. Actually the entire conspiracy was hatched by Hidimbā to be in the company of Bihma. She deliberately provoked her son to irritate the innocent Brāhmana expecting that the poor fellow would be filing his petition to Bhima and the latter would automatically rush to Hidimbā to know as to how the matter stands.

The dramatist has made radical change in the plot of the *Mahābhārata* from which the story has been borrowed. Although the entire drama revolves around the personality of Ghatotkacha, Bhima also plays a very significant role here and the term *Mādhyama* in the title of the drama refers to Bhima, who mediates between Hidimbā and the Brāhmin.

This drama is placed in the category of *Vyāyoga*. The hero of *Vyāyoga* is a man having exceptional qualities of head and heart showing unprecedented valour and heroism. *Vira* and *Raudra* are dominant *rasas* in *Vyāyoga*. It deals with the single day story. This drama is successful in every way and fulfils the basic requirements of *Vyāyoga* from classical point of view.

Māgha: Māgha was a great Samskrit poet and author of the epic *Shishupālavadha*. This epic is so popular that it was raised to the second position in *Brihatrai* (three big texts), and except the brief account of his family lineage in the last portion of *Shishupālavadha* nothing substantial about his personal life has surfaced. He was born in Gujarāt and his grandfather was the Prime Minister of a certain king named Vermal. Scholars have failed to reach a consensus on the issue of the period of Māgha.

Mahābhārata: The Mahābhārata is a vast history of Indian life and culture written in 1 lakh *Shlokas*. It has been composed by Veda Vyāsa. Winternitz has observed that it is not only a *Kāvya* but a *Sāhitya* in its entirety. Besides being a *Kāvya* and *Sāhitya*, it has also incorporated the entire cultural milieu within its ambit. It is a cultural treasure and is a witness to the enriched cultural heritage of India presenting the gallantry and chivalry of Indian people who have led the world in scholarship, bravery and statecraft. Under the guise of the story of the Kauravas and the Pāndavas, a complete portrait of the contemporary Indian society has been spun out into the fabric. It presents the story of strife torn or conflict-ridden Indian society projecting two different ways of life and values. A polite and gentle effort has been made to assimilate and coordinate the varied ideologies and the spirit and sensibility of that age interrupted by family feud. It also depicts man's growing desire for worldly pleasure. It presents a deglamourised vision of a society that witnessed a marked change in the approach and attitude where moral values degenerated and human relationship shattered into pieces and personal aggrandisement reigned supreme throwing into fore wind the interest of others. It is also accorded the status of the fifth Veda incorporating the entire characteristics of Hinduism. Several ways and means have been suggested in the *Shānti Parva* to overcome the challenges facing an individual in his life, and has been accredited as the holy book among the followers of Hinduism. The most celebrated work; the Gitā is also a part of this voluminous composition. It forms *pancharātrā* along with *Vishnusahasranāma*, *Anu Gitā*, *Bhishmastayarāja* and *Gajendra Moksa*, which also originate from the Mahābhārata. Since it contains one lakh *Shlokas*, it is called *Satasahashri Samhitā*. It has been confirmed in an inscription of the Gupta period in which the term *Satsahashrisamhitā* has been used. The existing form of the Mahābhārata is the outcome of the development made through the ages. Since ancient times, the story of the heroism and gallantry of the Kauravas and the Pāndavas have been narrated. In the Vedas also, the story of the characters of the Mahābhārata has been introduced. Veda Vyās has assimilated these stories scattered over in various texts in the form of a gigantic Kāvyas Mahābhārata. There are three phases of the development of the Mahābhārata: *Jaya, Bhārata* and *Mahābhārata*. In the invocation to the Mahābhārata, showing his deep reverence for the gods, Vyāsa has expressed his heart felt desire to read the *Jaya Kāvya*. The scholars are of the opinion that *Jaya Kāvya* is the original part of the Mahābhārata. The second section is Bhārata, which incorporates the battles between different clans. This text consists of 24000 Shlokas. Mahābhārata is the final stage of this historical development and including *Harivansa* the number of Shloka goes to 1,00,000. At present two editions of the Mahābhārata are available - *Uttariya* and *Dakshinātya*.

The period of composition of the Mahābhārata is yet in oblivion. An inscription dating 445 A.D. has referred to Mahābhārata, which confirms that the Mahābhārata must have been written before 200 years B.C. Asvaghosha has quoted the *Shloka* of *Harivansa* and Mahābhārata in *Vajrasuchi Upanisada*. On the basis of these evidences the timing of the Mahābhārata has been fixed 600 BC. But it may have been composed during a much earlier day.

The Mahābhārata has been divided into 18 *Parvas* or *Khandas*. These Parvas are -*Ādi, Sabhā, Vana, Virāta, Udyoga, Bhishma, Drona, Karna, Shalya, Sauptika, Stri, Shānti, Anushāsana, Asvamedha, Āshramavāsi, Mausala, Mahāprasthānika* and *Svargārohana Parvas*.

The stories occurring in the ***Ādi Parva*** includes the story of the composition of the Mahābhārata, Lord Ganesh accepting the proposal of writing the Manuscript as narrated by Veda Vyāsa by the grace of Brahman, history of *Chandravansa* and the origin of the Pāndavas and the Kauravas, story of Vaivasvata Manu and his sons, the story of Kacha-Devāyani, marriage of Sāntānu and Gangā and Bhisma's promise to remain unmarried throughout his life. The birth of Chitrāngada and Vichitravirya, birth of Dhritarāshtra, Pāndu and Vidura by Vyāsa, birth of 100 sons of Dhritarāshtra and five sons of Pandu, rivalry between the Pāndavas and the Kauravas, appointing Dronāchārya the teacher of the princes, Duryodhana's plot to kill the Pāndavas in lachouse, Bhima getting married to Hidimbā and birth of Ghatotkacha also figure in it. Draupadi's Svayamvara and Arjuna winning Draupadi through archery. She was finally wedded to five brothers. Yudhisthira establishing his capital in Indraprastha, abduction of Subhadrā and her marriage to Arjuna and breaking out of fire in Khāndava forest have also been given sufficient treatment.

Sabhā Parva deals with the story of the amazing court constructed by Maya Dānava, Yudhisthira's desire to perform Rajsuya Yajna, worship of Krishna, the advice of Krishna, Shishupāla's opposition to the proposal and his killing by Krishna, defeat of Yudhisthira in Dyuta, Duhsasāna's attempt to denude Draupadi and the latter invoking Krishna for rescue and exile of the Pāndavas.

Vana Parva deals with the incidents of the arrival of Vidura and Krishna in *Kāmya* forest, Pāndavas seeking blessings of Indra at Indrakit mountain, Arjuna's penance and obtaining *pashupatāstra* from Lord Shiva, Uravasi's infatuation for Arjuna, Uravasi's curse to Arjuna on the latter's reticence, story of Nala- Damayanti, story of Parasurāma, Agastya, Sagara, Bhagiratha, arrival of Gangā, story of Chyavana and Mandhātā, meeting of Hanumāna and Bhima, liberation of Nahusa, dialogue between Draupadi and Satyabhāmā, Duryodhana's defeat from Gandharvas, his protection by the Pāndavas and his repentance, story of Sāvitri and Satyavāna, Indra accepting *Kavacha* and *Kundala* from Karna and dialogue between Yaksha and Yudhisthira.

Virāta Parva, deals with episodes of the Pāndavas leaving for a different secret place following their defeat in Dyuta and settle at Virātanagara, killing of Kichaka by Bhima following his abortive attempt to spoil the chastity of Draupadi, the Kaurava's invasion on Virāta and victory of Virāta with the help of the Pāndavas, marriage of Abhimanyu with Uttarā, the daughter of Virāta.

Udyoga Parva prepares the background for the ensuing battle between Arjuna and Duryodhana both seeking assistance from Krishna. Duryodhana however agreed to receive the whole *Narāyani Senā* of Karishna, and Arjuna gladly accepted the assistance of Lord Krishna Himself, Sanjaya and Krishna leaving for peace mission to the court of the Kauravas and the peace talks failed miserably without yielding a positive result, meeting of the two army in the field of *Kurukshetra*.

In the ***Bhishma Parva*** the battle begins and Sanjaya, seen with his cosmic eye, narrates the development in the battlefield to Dhritarāshtra, Bhishma creating a panic in the Pāndavas camp before his killing with the help of Shikhandi.

Drona Parva deals with the strategy of *Chakravyuha* and killing of Abhimanyu after breaking the sixth barricade. Assassination of Jayadratha by Arjuna, the killer of his son Abhimanyu, of Ghatotkacha by Karna, and Dronāchārya by Dhristadyumna follow this incident. It also describes the use of *Nārāyanāstra* by Ashvastthāmā and Krishna coming to the rescue of the Pāndavas.

It says that life is transient. Material possession is worth nothing. Worldly pleasure is a passing show. Only the cardinal virtues of man: generosity, spirit of sacrifice, love for justice, and devotion to God, truthfulness, and universal brotherhood will endure. ***Karna Parva*** deals with the juvenescence of Karna and the defeat of Yudhisthira by him, killing of Karna by Arjuna and of Shalya by Yudhisthira and Duryodhana entering a pond.

In ***Gadāparva*** Duryodhana emerges from the pond after being challenged by Bhima and his battle with the latter, Balarāma getting infuriated following Bhima breaking the thigh of Duryodhana, his disciple by violating the norms of *gadāyuddha;* and Ashwastthāmā taking over the stewardship have been described.

Sauptika Parva deals with the killing of five sons of Draupadi by Ashwastthāmā, Arjuna taking away the pearl of Ashwastthāmā.

Stri Parva deals with the lamentation of Gāndhāri and Dhriatarāshtra over the death of his sons and relatives. Gāndhāri got enraged.

In ***Shānti Parva***, Yudhisthira expresses deep shock after listening to the real story of Karna from Nārada, Srikrishna trying to pacify Yudhisthira, teaching of polity to Yudhisthira by Bhisma, description of Sāmakhya-Yoga, story of Janaka and Shukadeva.

Anushāsana Parva deals with the efforts made by Bhishma to console Yudhisthira and death of Bhishma.

In the ***Asvamedhika Parva***, Yudhisthira expresses shock over the death of Bhishma and Krishna consoles him, Krishna gives new life to the dead body of Parikshita.

Āshramavāsi Parva deals with the death of Dhritarāshtra, Gāndhāri and Kunti.

Mausala Parva deals with the destruction of the *Yaduvansis*.

In ***Mahāprasthānika Parva,*** Pāndavas leave for the Himalayas, death of all Pāndavas except Yudhisthira who goes to heaven alive.

In ***Swargārohana Parva***, Yudhisthira departs for heaven, his brief stay in hell and his decision to stay their after noticing his brothers crying violently, consoling of Indra and Dharma to Yudhisthira, Yudhisthira departs for *Divya Loka* where he meets Krishna and Arjuna.

The moral brought out in the Mahābhārta is that one should be submissive, docile and charitable but not timid. One must keep oneself prepared for the worst consequences if justice so demands; then suffering is a boon in disguise; the real victory is moral victory. The message given by Bhishma to Yudishthira embodies the quintessence of Hindu philosophy.

Mahābhāshya: Mahābhāshya is an illuminating treatise on grammar written by Patanjali. It is a commentary on Pānini's *Astādhyāyi.* It consists of 85 *Ahnikas* (Chapters). Bhartrihari has maintained that it is not only a grammatical text rather almost all kinds of knowledge are collected into it. Patanjali has made an in-depth study of all grammatical texts available to him and has dealt with all the issues pertaining to grammar. His style is argumentative and aphoristic. The complexity and abstruseness of *Astādhyāyi* was mitigated to a large extent by Mahābhāshya. Of the 3995 sutras of Pānini grammar including 14 *Pratyāhāra* sutras, Patanjali had written his commentary on 1689 sutras and rest of the sutras have been retained as usual. He has expressed deep reverence for Pānini's theorising. At some places Patanjali has also shown the limitations of Pānini.

Patanjali has propounded an authentic theory of grammar through Mahābhāsya. Mahābhāsya is more than an elucidation of Pānini's *Astādhyāyi.* It is a book on the philosophy of grammar and linguistic. Patanjali conceived shabda as Brahman that knows no limitations. As Brahman is infinite, so the range of word's meaning is infinite. Even the knower and correct user of a single word are entitled to salvation.

He observes that word and its meaning enjoy eternal relation; and words are themselves blessed with the quality to emanate various facets of meaning. He has accepted four forms of *Pada - Guna, Kriyā, Ākriti* and *Dravya*. *Ākrti* is called *Jati* that remains unimpaired even after the destruction of *Dravya*. Patanjali has expressed genuine ideas with regard to the use of words, their position in sentence and their ability. He states that the aim of grammar is to restore order and propriety. He makes necessary changes in lexicography to make it competent enough to be used in sentence. He has elevated grammar to the status of philosophy and has put forward original theories taking inspiration from their use in general life. He has accepted word as the form of Brahman.

Mahāprabhu Vallabhāchārya: Vallabhāchārya is the exponent of *Pushtimārga* and the propagator of *Visuddhādvaitavāda*, a doctrine of *Vaishnavism*. He was born in the year 1535 in Madhya Pradesh. He made a new path of devotion on the basis of *Bhāgavata*. The path is known as *Pushtimārga*. He wrote several books, which include *Anubhāshya*, a *Bhāshya* on 2500 chapters of *Brahmasutra, Purvamimāmsābhāshya* and *Tatvadipanibandh*. *Subodhini* is an interpretation of *Shrimadbhāgavata*. He placed Shrimadbhāgavata in the category of *Prasthānachatustai* with the help of his Subodhini, commentary on it, the other three being *Brahmasutra*, *Gitā* and *Upanishada*. His philosophical hypothesis *Suddhādvaitavāda* is a reaction against the Monistic theory of Shankarāchārya. According to this theory, the world emerged out of Brahman is bereft of *Māyā*. It does not accept the existence of Brahman attached to *Māyā*. Shankarāchārya has accepted two forms of Brahman: *Upādhivishishta Saguna* Brahman and *Upādhirahita Nirguna* Brahman. Of the two, Shankara accepts the second does not have faith in the first, since it is embedded with *Māyā*. Vallabhāchārya on the contrary accepts both the forms of Brahman. Brahman can acquire the status of *Saguna* and *Nirguna* both at the same time. Brahman is one yet He appears varied and remains under the control of His disciples though enjoying an independent status. Vallabha accords the status of Brahman to Shrikrishna and accepts him the creator of the world but he does not seek the assistance of *Māyā* in the creative process. Brahman is equipped with two powers-*Āvirbhāva* and *Tirobhāva*. He manifests Himself into the form of creation by virtue of His *Āvirbhava Shakti*; and causes complete annihilation by assimilating the world forces by His *Tirobhāva Shakti*. Vallabha accepts the existence of both *Jiva* and *Jagata*. Brahman manifests himself into three forms- *Ādhidaivika, Ādhyatmika* and *Ādhibhautika*. *Jagata* is the manifestation of Brahman. He appears as Jagat in the state of *Āvirbhāva* and becomes Brahman in *Tirobhāva* status.

Jagat is merely a sport of Brahman. Shrikrishna has been considered *Sachchidānanda*. He is a combination of *Sat, Chit* and *Ānanda*. *Jiva* consists of *Sat* and *Chit* (life, consciousness). *Jagat* is only blessed with *Sat*. It does not possess either *Chit* or *Ānanda*. *Akshara* Brahman has nothing to do with *Ānanda* too much but *Parabrahman* is blessed with *Ānanda*. Both forms of Brahman can be realised through different means. *Akshara* Brahman can be obtained only through knowledge but devotion is required to secure the blessings of *Parabrahman* or *Purushottama*.

Brahman manifests Himself in *Jiva* shaking off *Ānanda* from His being. This process of creation is the outcome of the desire of God. *Māyā* does not have any role to play in it. As *Sphulinga* or flame originates from fire, in the same way *Jiva* originates from Brahman. Since it is attached to *Avidyā*, it is called *Samsāri* (worldly). In case of liberation, it regains Ānanda and becomes *Sachchidānanda* in unison with God.

The canon of devotion developed by Vallabha is called *Pushtimārga* which signifies the blessings of god. Devotion takes place in the heart of devotee only after the consent of God. It is called *'Pushtimārga'* since blessings of God is considered the only means of obtaining *Moksha*. Vallabhāchārya has suggested three ways to obtain the blessings of god - *Pushtimārga, Pravāhamārga* and *Maryadāmārga*. Of the three, *Pushtimārga* is the best way. The devotee of *Maryadābhakti* craves for outcome while the devotee of *Pushtibhakti* does not cherish any desire. Vallabhāchārya held that Krishna is perfect Brahman. He is the incarnation of 16 *Kalās* whereas Rāma was the incarnation of 10 *Kalās*. Four additional *Kalās* like *Dyuta Kalā, Kāmakalā, Chaurya Kalā* and *Kapata Kalā* were added to the character-tenets of Krishna. It is not easy to understand Krishna. While other Gods are straight in form, Krishna is curved at three places in form: at knee, at waist and at neck. While discussing this cult Vallabhāchārya said that for realisation of Krishna unflinching faith in his supremacy is necessary. No one can have faith in an unknown entity. We can have curiosity for the unknown but no faith. For faith some form is necessary. Krishna is that form. What he calls *Pushti* is unflinching faith, to some extent blind faith (*Pushti tad anugrahāt*).

Mahāvira Charita: Mahāvira Charita is a drama by Bhavabhuti, compiled in seven acts. It deals with the story of the first half of the Rāmāyana that is to say from the marriage of Rāma till his coronation. Rāma has been addressed as a great warrior. That is why he has been referred to as Mahāvira. The aim of the dramatist is to focus the heroic personality of Rāma. The dramatist has made drastic changes in the original story to make the drama more interesting and to accelerate the interest of the audience.

Mahāvira Charita lacks maturity from dramatic point of view. Since it is Bhavabhuti's maiden attempt, these limitations are apt to creep into the texture of his drama. He has given various twists and turns to the story of Rāma to accord it a new taste and flavour. The dialogue between Rāma, Parashurāma, Janaka and Dasaratha stretches to two acts, which hints at the immaturity of Bhavabhuti as a dramatist. These dialogues are attractive but they are inapt from dramatic point of view. The poet has displayed his talent in the art of characterisation.

Mahendrasuri: Mahendra Suri was a scholar of Astrology and flourished in the later half of the 12th century. He was patronised by Phirozshah Tughlaq. He wrote a very important work on the Mathematics of planets entitled *Yantra Rāja*. It is divided into five chapters and each chapter has been named after the subject contained in it such as *Ganit Adhyāya, Yantraghatan Adhyāya, Yantrarachanā Adhyāya, Yantrashodhan Adhyāya* and *Yantravicharn Adhyāya.*

Māhim Bhatta: Māhim Bhatta was an eminent scholar of Samskrit poetics. He wrote a monumental work *Vyaktiviveka* in which he repudiated the theory of *Dhvani* and ramifications and merged it into inference (*anumāna*) He made it a commonplace theory suffering from several defects. He was the inhabitant of Kashmir and was awarded the title of *Rājanaka*. He flourished in the middle of the 11th century. He took recourse to the doctrines of *Nyāya* School to find fault in the theory of *Dhvani* and exhibited its shortcomings enunciated by Ānand Vardhana. He replaced the word *Dhvani* by his term *anumāna*. He found out as many as ten defects in the nature of *Dhvani* showing his scholarship. Had Mammata not come to strengthen the theory of *Dhvani* in his *Kāvyaprakāsh*, Māhimbhatta would have destroyed *Dhvani* theory root and branch. He acknowledged *Avidhā* as the only *Shakti* of word showing its least affinity either with *Lakshanā* or *Vyanjanā*. He has accepted two types of meanings -*Vāchya* and *Anumiti*.

Mālati Mādhava: Mālati Mādhava is a Prakarana consisting of 10 acts written by Bhavabhuti. It deals with the love story of Mālati and Mādhava. The story is wholly imaginative. The **first act** deals with the deal reached between two brāhmina friends to agree on marital alliance. Two Buddhist nuns were witnesses to the contract. In course of time, one of the two friends named Bhurivasu became the minister of the king of Padmāvati, the other named Devavrata became the minister of the king of Vidarbha. Fortunately, Devavrata produced a son named Mādhava and Bhurivasu begot a daughter named Mālati. Devavrata sent his son Madhava to Padmāvati for further studies. One day, he reminded Bhurivasu of his promise made to him. In another major development, one of the close friends of the king of Padmāvati named Nandana, urged upon him to prevail upon his minister to get his daughter married to him. Bhurivasu was in a state of dilemma and finally acceded to the wishes of his king. The Buddhist nun came to the rescue of Mādhava suggesting him to go to the palace of Mālati at regular intervals. This led to Mālati falling in love with Mādhava. They met each other in the garden to ensure that their marriage materialised. In the **second act**, the bid of Bhurivasu to get his daughter married to Nandana was foiled by the nuns who secretly prepare Mālati to marry Mādhava. In the **third act**, according to the preconceived plan Mālati leaves for the garden near the Shiva temple to have a meeting with Mādhava. In the meanwhile, panic is created because a lion in a cage, is set free. Mādhava's friend Makaranda kills the lion. But both the friends receive severe injury. In the **fourth act**, they are made to come back to senses by Mālati and Madayāntika. Makaranda falls in love with Madayāntika. The news of the marriage of Mālati and Nandana is floated by Vishkambhaka.

In the **fifth act**, Mādhava rescues Mālati from the impending danger caused by the Aghora Kāpālika trying to sacrifice Mālati at the altar of Karalā Devi. In the **sixth act**, Mālati is captured by the soldiers and is brought inside the premises of the Shiva temple to be married to Nandana. But Kamandaki, the nun, very skillfully replaces Mālati by Makaranda and Nandana is married to Makaranda. On the other hand, Mālati and Mādhava perform *Gandharva* marriage. In the **sixth and seventh acts**, Makaranda, disguising himself as bride assaults Nandana during their first meeting at night. Madayāntika appears on the scene to pacify her sister- in-law but she is amazed to see Makaranda in the guise of a bride. Her joys knew no bounds. In the **eighth act**, Mālati and Mādhava are waiting for Makaranda and Madayāntika in the garden. In a major development Makaranda is captured for the crime of abducting Madayāntika. Mādhava decides to come to the rescue of his friend leaving Mālati alone. Finding an appropriate opportunity the Kāpālika takes Mālati to Shri Mountain. Makaranda and Mādhava are locked in a pitched battle with the soldiers. The king, pleased with their heroism, sets them free.

In the **ninth act**, Mādhava is seen moving on the Vindhya Mountain along with Makaranda lost in the memory of Mālati. In the meantime, Kamandaki's disciple Saudāmini informs that Mālati is safe and is staying in the cottage. In the **tenth act**, Bhurivasu, Kamandaki and Madayāntika decide to commit suicide as they-fail to identify and save Mālati. Makaranda appears on the scene to tell them the news of the welfare of Mālati. Mālati and Mādhava also arrive at the place and Makaranda is married to Madayāntika. The story ends with *Bharatavākya*.

From classical point of view Mālati Mādhava fulfils the requisite conditions of a *Prakarana*. The plot is based on an imaginary story in *Prakarana*. The hero is very modest and the heroine is either a cultured lady or a prostitute. The hero is either a minister, a Brāhmin or a Vanika. *Shringāra* is the dominant *rasa* in a *Prakarana*.

Mālavikāgnimitra: Mālvikāgnimitra is a comedy written by Kālidāsa. It is the first of his three dramas. It is a historical drama based on the love story of Mālavikā and Agnimitra. It is divided into five acts. In the event of unprecedented onslaught on Mādhavasen by Yajnasen, the panic-ridden sister of Mādhavasena, Mālavikā rushes to Vidisā to seek refuge in the company of Queen Dharini and stays there, as her attendant receiving training in the art of dancing. One day,

Agnimitra catches hold of the portrait of Mālvikā and falls in love with her. Vidushaka arranges the dance of Mālavikā that paves the way for the two coming close to each other. Next day, when Mālavikā prepares the garland for the King Agnimitra and Irāvati, his wife, he separately enjoys the beauty of Mālavikā, disguising himself in the bushes. Agnimitra, not aware of the presence of Irāvati, comes close to Mālavikā and offers his proposal of love to her. This incident infuriates Irāvati and the latter puts Mālavikā behind the bar for causing a breach in their relationship. In a major development, Vidusaka falls a victim to snakebite and Mālavikā is set free in order to provide Vidusaka with the ring on which snake is embossed to cure him. Mālavikā and Agnimitra avail of their company. But this meeting proves short-lived since Agnimitra departs shortly to protect his daughter from the mischief of the monkeys. Meanwhile, Mādhavasena manages to overcome his enemy and the real identity of Mālavikā is also revealed. These developments help Agnimitra once again enjoy the company of his beloved Mālavikā.

Except the five acts, the rest of the qualities of this drama are very akin to a *nātikā* (minor drama). The story takes place in the limited region of the court and *Pramadāvan*. The language is very simple, lucid and flexible and the dialogue is also very impressive and thought provoking.

Mammata: Mammata is known mostly for his 'Kāvyaprakāsh'. His time can be established through inference by the fact that the commentator of Kāvyaprakāsh, Ruyyaka flourished in the 1st half of the 12th century. In this way, Mammata must have produced his work at least 60-70 years before him. Scholars are of the opinion that Mammata had written up to *parikara alankār* in the tenth *parichchheda* and the remaining text was completed by another Kashmiri scholar Allata. Opinion has also been expressed that *Kārika* part was written by Bharata and Mammata simply wrote its *Vritti*. A section of scholars has considered Mammata, the author of both *Kārika* and *Vritti*. The author of *Sāhitya Kaumudi* and commentator of *Kāvyaprakāsh*, Maheshwar, has insisted that Bharata had not composed any text except *Nātyashāstra*. Besides this no other text of Bharata has been indicated in ancient texts. There is a complementary *Shloka* in the beginning of

Kāvyaprakāsh. Had Kārika and Vritti been written by two different persons, there would have been no complementary Shloka (*Mangala Vachan*) in the beginning of both texts. On the basis of these material evidences Mammata is taken as the author of *Kāvyaprakāsh*.

For the first time, Mammata worked out a perfect analysis of different parts of Indian poetics such as *Shabdashakti, Dhvani, Rasa*, defects, merits and *alankāras* and helped accord them importance in the same proportion. Mammata was a stern supporter of *Dhvani* theory of poetry and had virtually rejected the critical formulations of its opponents like Bhāmaha, Dandin, Kuntaka, Shrishankuk and Dhananjaya.

He refused to accept *alankār* as the essence of poetry and passed his verdict in favour of *Dhvani* stating in unequivocal terms that poetry could be possible without an *alankāra* though poetry is not possible without *Dhvani*. Mammata replaced ten *gunas* by three - *Mādhurya*, *Ooj* and *Prasāda* and rejected 6 *Shabdālanakāras*, 60 *Arthālankāras* and *Shankar* and *Sanshriti* as useless.

After Abhinava Gupta, Mammata is the only critic who thoroughly studied the wider implications of *Rasa* and proved without any shadow of doubt that no great poetry can be composed without *Dhvani*. Mammata cited several examples to prove his point. His Kāvyaprakāsh is an encyclopaedia of *Dhvani* School.

Māndukya Upanishad: It is a minor Upanishad consisting of 12 Khandas. It is written in prose. It presents a poignant interpretation of *Omkāra*. It has accepted *Aum* as *Atmā* or *Parmātmā*. Gaudpadāchārya has written a *Bhāshya* on it entitled *Māndukyakārika*.

Mankhaka: Mankhaka was a Kasmiri poet who composed an epic named *Shrikanthacharita*. He was the disciple of Ruyyaka and was the court poet of the 12th century king of Kashmir, Jaya Singh. *Shrikanthacharita* deals with the battle between Lord Shankar and Tripurāsura. It has a very brief plot but the poet has tried his level best to follow the basic rules of an epic. A description of the poets of Kasmir has been given in the 25th Canto of this epic. He has also written a dictionary entitled *Mankhaka-Kosha* which is not yet published. It also includes the words used by the poets of Kashmir. His doctrine with regard to *Kāvya* and poet in his *Shrikanthacharita* is sufficient to show his discerning power. In this way, he seems to be a poet as well as a critic intertwined together.

Manuduta: Manuduta is a poem by Tailanga Vaidyanāth, a fourteen century poet. It is aimed at communicating message to the earnest and dearest. The poet takes inspiration from Kālidāsa's *Meghaduta*. It deals with the message sent by Draupadi to Krishna to come to her assistance and to protect her chastity in the court of the Kauravas. When Duhsāsana at the behest of his brother Duryodhana, was bent upon undressing her. Draupadi sends her inner self (*Mana*) as her messenger to Krishna. The *Kāvya* begins with the poet praising the *Mana* of Draupadi, which is followed by a graphic description of Dwārakāpuri. It also throws ample light on the worship of Lord Krishna and his towering personality who has the capability to save his devotees who were confronted with insoluble problems.

Manoduta: Manoduta is a poem by Vishnudās communicating a message. Vishnudās flourished in the 1st half of the 6th century. In this *Kāvya* the poet has sent his *Mana* (mind or self) to communicate his message to God surrendering himself to His feet. This *Kāvya* is also inspired by Kālidāsa's *Meghaduta*. It consists of 100–101 *Shlokas*. It is a superb work both from the point of view of content and poetic diction.

Manusmriti: Manusmriti is a text of moral and social code written by Manu who is considered the father of human beings. This fact has been substantiated by several hymns of the Rig Veda. *Satapatha Brāhmana* also narrates the story of Manu and *pralaya*. According to the facts available in *Taittariya Samhitā* and *Aitareya Brāhmana* Manu distributed his assets among his sons depriving one of his sons of his due share. Manu has been referred to as Svayambhu and Prachetasa in the *Shānti Parva* of the Mahābhārata. It has been mentioned in the *Manusmrti* that Virāta originated from Brahman that caused the birth of Manu and the saints like Bhrigu and Nārada originated from Manu. Some of the scholars are of the opinion that the authorship of *Manusmriti* was attributed to Manu to establish the antiquity of the text. Some wrongly claim that *Manusmriti* is the revised form of Manavacharana's *Dharmashutra*. In the Mahābhārata, Svayambhu Manu has been considered the author of *Dharmashāstra* and Prachetasa Manu, the author of economics (*Arthashāstra*). Manu has been considered the author of *Dharmashāstra* in *Nāradasmriti* and *Skanda Purāna*.

Manusmriti consists of 12 chapters and 2694 Shlokas. The **first chapter** deals with the origin of the world. The **second** deals with various kinds of rites, celibacy and reverence for teacher. The **third chapter** deals with the rites pertaining to bath before starting *Grihastha* life. The **fourth chapter** deals with the rules of household people. The **fifth chapter** deals with the purification of objects. *Vānaprastha* and *Yatidharma* have been discussed in the **sixth chapter**. The **seventh chapter** deals with the rules of petition taxes and statecraft. The **eighth chapter** deals with the process of questing and the **ninth** deals with the rules of husband and wife enjoying life in union and separation. The **tenth chapter** dilates upon the origin of *Varnashankar*. The **eleventh** deals with the process of atonement and the **twelfth** dilates upon three kinds of worldly movements.

Manusmriti includes wide-ranging subjects within its scope, which include statecraft, *Dharmashāstra*, social laws, sociology, economics and Hindu code. Subjects falling within the periphery of statecraft include origin and nature of state, council of ministers and its number, qualification of its members, system, constitution of courts and their modus operandi, mode of punishment, theory for the increase of resources, operation of war and rules of war. Subjects included in *Dharmashāstra* are definition of *Dharmashāstra*, Vedas, *Smriti*, behaviour of people, self-knowledge. Subjects included in social laws are duties of husband and wife, rules pertaining to their right on children, arrangement of marriage, division, special part of elder brother, adopted son, succession or the part of women, cause of depriving one a share in will. Medhātithi and Govindarājakulluka are the commentators on *Manusmriti*.

Mārkandeya Purāna: Mārkandeya Purāna is the 7th Purāna in the chronological order. This Purāna consists of 9000 Shlokas and 138 chapters. It has been mentioned in Shiva Purāna that saint Mārkandeya had narrated the entire story. Some parts of the *Mārkandeya Purāna* are closely related to the Mahābhārata. It begins with the four questions that are linked with the story of the Mahābhārata. These questions remained unresolved in the Mahābhārata itself. The first question is related to Draupadi's five husbands and the last one to the death of her five sons at their tender age. Mārkandeya has not answered the questions himself rather he got them answered through birds. Besides other stories, moralising has been done on *gārahastha dharma, shrāddha*, daily work, *vrata* and festivals. Description of yoga has been made in eight chapters. In the 31st chapter, the story of Ikshvāku, Tulasi, Rāma, Pururavā, Nahusa, Yayāti, Shrikrishna and Mārkandeya has been presented. Worship of Agni, Surya and eminent Vedic gods has also been made. *Durgāsaptasati* is also a part of *Markandeya Purāna* which consists of three divisions *Prathama*, dealing with *Madhu-Kaitabha Vadha*, *Madhyamā*, dealing with *Mahishāsura Vadha*, and *Uttaracharita*, dealing with the *Vadha* of Shumbha, Nisumbha and their generals Chanda, Munda and Raktabija. This text conceives of Durgā as the fundamental force of the world.

Matrichetā: Matrichetā was a Buddhist poet belonging to the *Mahāyāna* School. He was contemporary to Kanishka. An account of his 85 verses entitled *Kanikalekha* is available in Tibatese language in which the poet has given a message to lead life according to the path paved by Buddha. His two other works include a *Stutikāvya* consisting of 400 verses and *Adhyardhāshataka*. The first text has been translated into Tibatese language. It praises Tathāgata in *Anushtupa Chhanda*.

In the second work, offerings to Buddha, has once again been made in 150 *Anushtupa Chhanda*. The language of these texts is simple and natural and the style is impressive.

Matsya Purāna: The 16th Purāna in the Purānic order, it is the most significant Purāna covering extensive and wide-ranging subjects within its ambit. It consists of 19,000 *Shlokas*. Partijer has accepted the latter part of the 2nd century as the period of composition of *Matsya Purāna*. This Purāna begins with the episode of Vishnu safeguarding Manu during annihilation transforming him into *matsya* (fish). It presents a detailed discussion of creation of the universe, *Manvantar* and *Pitrivansa*. It also deals with the story of the killing of Tarakāsura by Shiva. Lord Shankar has himself discussed the significance of Kāshi. It also presents the contents of all the *Purānas* in detail that help us arrive at a decision with regard to the periodicity of all the *Puranas*. It also deals with the dynasties of the saints like Bhrigu, Angirā, Atri, Viswāmitra, Kasyapa, Vashistha, Parāshara and Agastya. This *Purāna* also presents a detailed discussion of statecraft. The science of idol making is another important feature that is discussed at length in this *Purāna*.

Mayurabhatta: Mayur Bhatta is the author of Surya Shataka and relative of Bānabhatta. It is written in *Sāranagdhara Chhanda*. His writing has been cast on the model of Bānabhatta He has taken over Bāna's fascination for figurative and ornamental style and decorated his verse with terse and complex diction. Poetic figures too have been used in abundance. Rājashekhar noticed his poetic talent and placed him alongside the most gifted poets. It is said that *Suryashataka* was written to evade leprosy that gripped Mayura.

Mayurasandesha: Mayur Sandesha is a *sandesha kāvya* written by Udaya. He flourished in the 15th century. He has drawn inspiration from Kālidāsa's *Megheduta*. It is also divided into *Purva* and *Uttara* parts which consist of 107 and 92 *Shlokas* respectively. Except the first *Shloka* that is written in *Mālini Chhanda* in which invocation to lord Ganesh has been made, the rest of the Shlokas have been written in *Mandākrāntā Chhanda*. In this *kāvya*, the hero sends his message to his beloved who has been abducted by *Vidyādhars*. One of the relatives of the king of Mālābār was once travelling with his queen. He was confused for Shiva by Vidyādhar. The relative of the king of Mālābār laughed at the foolishness of Vidyādhar that flared up the anger of the latter who cursed him to remain apart from his wife for one month. The king begged an excuse where, upon Vidyādhar permitted him to stay at Shyānandura in Kerala. During the rainy season, the king decided to send his message to his wife through the peacock. The language of the kāvya is very persuasive and moving. The poet has thrown sufficient light on the political and geographical conditions of Kerala.

Meghaduta: Meghaduta is lyrical poem by Kālidāsa, the first romanticist; and is acclaimed all over the world as a magnificent product of imagination. It deals with the message given by a Yaksha to his beloved through cloud. Communicating message by a dejected lover to his beloved through a natural agency is the poet's imagination. *Meghaduta* is divided into two sections-*Purva* and *Uttara Megha* consisting of 63 and 52 Shlokas respectively. It provides a peculiar blend of lyrical poetry and *Khanda kāvya*. Therefore, it has been referred to as a *Khanda kāvya* based on lyrics.

The story begins with Kubera, the god of wealth, who banishes one of his servants, Yaksha for one year from his capital Alkāpuri for failing to obey his orders. He had to spend this period of banishment at the Rāmgiri mountain in the southern part of India far away from the company of his newly wedded wife Yakshini. The poor fellow waits impatiently for the completion of the period of his banishment in order to unite with his wife. He has already spent eight months and with the arrival of rainy season his separation becomes unbearable. Out of intense agony he sends his message to her beloved through the cloud. She looked like a skeleton after she is separated from him for eight long months and the bangle that he had put on her wrist falls down on the earth. On the first day of *Āsādha*, when the sky is overcast, his agony is doubled. He welcomes the cloud in a conventional manner offering *ardhya* and praising his invincible power as *'Prakriti Purusha'* of Lord Indra. The poet has given a vivid description of the geographical topography of India from Rāmgiri (Chitrakuta) to Alkāpuri and has depicted the picture of several places, mountains and rivers that the cloud passes through in course of carrying the message of the Yaksha to his beloved Yakshini. At this point *Purva Magha* concludes.

Uttara Megha presents a graphic description of Alākapuri, the palace of Yaksha, and the pathetic condition of his beloved who is lost in the memory of Yaksha forgetting even her own identity. At this point Yaksha's message to his spouse is delivered by cloud.

The travel account of Megha is equipped with a poignant description of natural scenery. *Meghaduta* is a popular example of a poem aimed at conveying a message to one's beloved. It was so popular that several poems were written taking cue form *Meghaduta*. There are as many as 50 commentaries available on *Meghaduta*. It has been translated into almost all the languages of the world. H. H. Wilson translated it into English in 1813. Charitravardhanāchārya and Haridāsa Siddhāntavāgisha are among its modern commentators.

Mimāmsā: Mimāmsā is a School of Indian philosophy propounded by Saint Jaimini. He has written *Jaimini Sutra* consisting of 2644 Sutras and 12 chapters. It is the original text of this philosophical school. *Mimāmsā* endorses Vedic rites. Jaimini flourished around 300 B.C. and has referred to 8 preceding and contemporary scholars of *Mimāmsā* which confirms that existence of the ideology of *Mimāmsā* was extant well before Jaimini. Sābar has written a *bhāshya* on *Mimāmsāsutra* that is called *Sābarabhāsya*. In course of time three different sects branched out of *Mimāmsā* which include *Bhattamata, Prabhākar* or *Gurumata* and *Murārimata* developed by Kumarila Bhatta, Prabhākara and Murāri Mishra respectively.

Kumarila flourished in 600 A.D. He wrote three *Vrittis* on *Sābarabhāshya* that include *Shloka vartikā, Tantravartikā* and *Tuptika*. His works include *Bhattakaustubha, Bhattadipikā*, and *Bhattarahasya*. His disciple was Mandana Mishra. Among other important practitioners of this school are Pārthasārathi Mishra, Mādhavāchārya and Khandadeva Mishra. Mādhavāchārya is an eminent analyst of the Veda who wrote a useful book *Nyayaratnamālā*. Khandadeva Mishra propounded of *Navya Nyāya*.

The pioneer of *Gurumata*, Prabhakara wrote two commentaries on *Sābarbhāshya* named *Brihati* and *Ladhvi*. Shālikanāth and Bhavanātha are other important exponents of this sect who wrote *Prakaranapanjikā*, *Nyāyaviveka* and *Prabhākara Vijaya* respectively. Murāri Mishra is the exponent of *Murāri mata*. Nothing is known about Murāri Mishra. His reference has been given in the works of Gangesha Upādhyāya and his son Vardhamāna Upādhyāya.

Mimāmsā signifies the evaluation of the real nature of an object. On the basis of two parts of the Vedas, *Karma Kānda* and *Gyāna Kānda*, Mimāmsā has been divided into *Purva Mimāmsā* and *Uttaramimāmsā*.

The objective of Mimāmsā is to prove the validity of the Vedas. It has accepted five kinds of testimonies, *Pratyaksha* (apparent), *Anumāna* (inference), *Shabda* (word), *Arthapatti* and *Anupalabdhi*. The validity of *Anupalabdhi* has been accepted only by the Bhatta Mimāmasaka. Like *Nyāya, Mimāmsā* has accepted *Upamāna* as an independent proof of knowledge with a minor difference from the former. It is applied when the knowledge of an object is obtained on the basis of the object seen in the past bearing similitude with it. For instance a view of *nilgāya* (a species of deer) gives the impression of a cows to a person who has seen cow in the past since they are similar in many ways.

The approach of *Mimāmsā* towards *anumāna* is similar to that of Nyāya school though Bhatta school has maintained a bit different approach on this issue. In order to establish the validity of the Veda, *Shabda pramāna* (evidence obtained through word) has been given special treatment. Two types of *Shabda pramānas* have been admitted - *Pauruseya* and *Apauruseya*. Statement made by a creditable person is considered as *Pauruseya* while statement made in the Vedas is brought within the purview of *Apauruseya*. Vedic statements have been further segregated into *siddhavākya* and *vidhāyaka vākya*. A statement that helps understand a *siddha* issue is called *siddhavākya* and that which is aimed at performing some action is called *vidhāyaka vākya*.

The school of *Mimāmsā* has laid emphasis on the futility of knowledge without authentic proof. Laying emphasis more on Vedic indictment, it has been observed that action approved by the Vedas are placed in the category of Dharma. The earlier scholars of the Mimāmsā School have confirmed that heavenly pleasure is the ultimate goal (*moksha*) of man, but in course of time pleasure is replaced by suffering and liberation lifts man from the cycle of birth and death.

Mimāmsā is a materialistic school of philosophy. It accepts the world as real, which has originated out of atoms. The world is eternal which is neither created nor destroyed. It lays more emphasis on *karma* (action) that governs the world as an independent force. It accepts three categories of action - *Kāmya Karma, Nisiddha Karma* and *Nitya Karma*. An action done for the sake of the fulfillment of one's desire such as performing yoga to secure heavenly bliss is placed in the category of *kāmya karma*. The actions that are disapproved by the Vedas are called *Nisiddhakarma*. *Nitya karmas* are those actions that are mandatory for each and every person. *Nitya karma* is essential for liberation.

Mimāmsā has accepted soul as eternal. Detachment of soul from the material world is called *Moksha*. *Chaitanya* (consciousness) is not the quality of soul (*Ātman*), it is restored to soul following attachment with body and it experiences pleasure or suffering. Accepting the supremacy of *karma*, *Mimāmsā* refuses to accept the existence of God and validates the invincibility of the Vedas.

Mitramishra: Mitra Mishra was a political essayist who composed a voluminous essay which includes political science besides all the issues falling within the purview of *Dharamshāstra*. In one of the sections of this text entitled *Rājanitiprakāsha*, political theories have been discussed. He was patronised by the king of Orachhā, Vira Singh and flourished in the 1st half of the 17th century. *Rājnitiprakāsha* has been written by the inspiration of Vira Singh. It includes all the subjects of political science such as *Prajāprashansā, Rajyābhisheka Vihitakāla, Rajyābhishekanisiddha Kāla, Durgalakshana, Durgagrahanirmāna, Rāshtra, Kosha, Danda, Mitra, Yuddha, Yuddhoparānta Vyavasthā* and *Devapujā*.

Mrichchhakatika: Mrichchhakatika is a popular drama written by Sudraka. It has been modelled on the pattern of realistic drama. It deals with the love story of Chārudatta, a Brāhmin and Vasantasenā, a prostitute in ten acts. It is considered a *prakarana* from the classical standpoint.

The plot of *Mrichchhakatika* is based on Bhāsa's drama *Chārudatta* with a marked difference in the creative approach and in the use of *Prākrita*. Sudraka has brought about a radical change in the story showing his unprecedented commitment to a new plot and theme. The plot of Chārudatta revolves around the characters of Chārudatta and Vasantasenā. Sudraka stretches the story of Chārudatta and Vasantasenā too far to give it a realistic touch.

The story moves on three different levels the love story of Chārudatta and Vasantasenā, the love story of Sarvilaka and Madanikā and the political upheaval. The main story is related to the love affair of Chārudatta and Vasantasenā and other stories revolve round it. They are intermixed with the main plot in such a way that they do not intend to hamper the movement and flow of the main story. The subsidiary story does not come in the way of the main story. The story of political unrest helps the main story to proceed properly. All characters of this sub-plot are attached to the main plot in one-way or the other. The ascendancy of Āryaka to the throne is a positive development for Chārudatta. Sudraka has successfully assimilated the three stories into a single thread to give his *prakarana* a new dimension.

In the **first act** Vasantasena manages to take shelter in the house of Chārudatta, for whom there is a soft corner in her heart, in order to evade the meeting of Shakara, brother-in-law of the king, trying to grab Vasantansenā by hook or and by crook. Vasantasenā keeps her ornaments at Chārudatta's residence. Later on Maitreya and Chārudatta drop Vasantsena to her house.

The **second act** deals with the story of Sarvilaka, who, once a respectable citizen of Pātaliputra, turns a pauper and stays at the house of Chārudatta. The gamblers are following the poor fellow for failing to give them ten *muharas* that he had lost in gambling. Fortunately he, finds shelter in the house of Vasantasena and the latter protects him by clearing off his dues.

In the **third act**, Sarvilaka steals the ornaments of Vasantasenā from the house of Chārudatta in order to set his beloved Madanikā free, a captive of Vasantasenā. Chārudatt is fed up with theft of Vasantasena's ornaments and his wife Dhuta consoles him by offering his *Ratnāvali* to hand over to Vasantosenā in return for her ornaments. Madanikā refuses to accept the ornaments offered by Sarvilaka and prepares him to return it to Vasantasenā. The latter.was listening to the gossip and was pleased by their innocence. She releases Madanikā from her captive. In the meanwhile Shakara's coach arrives at the house of Vasantasenā to take her to his palace but the latter refuses to do so. Sarvilaka on his way back home listens to the news of the captivity of Gopāladaraka by the king Pālaka and sets out for ensuring the safe release of Gopāladaraka. At this stage Maitreya goes to the house of Vasantasenā to tell her the story of the theft and asks her to accept the *Ratnāvali*. Vasantasenā accepts it asking him to tell Chārudatta to see her.

In the **fifth act**, Vasantasenā spends the whole night in the house of Chārudatta. In the **sixth and seventh acts**, Chārudatta invites Vasantasenā to the Pundakarandaka garden. Radanika, failing to pacify Chārudatta's son Rohasena who is adamant on getting a cart made of gold instead of a clay cart, brings him to Vasantasenā's house. Vasantasenā gives her entire ornament for getting a gold cart made. She mistakenly beards to the coach of Shakara instead of that carrying her to Chārudatta. On the contrary Gopāladaraka, escaping from captivity, boards the coach of Vasantasenā and the coachman confusing him with Vasantasenā, takes him to Chārudatta.

In the **eighth act** Vasantasenā receives serious jolt after looking at Shakara. She rejects the offer made by Shakara. Shakara reacts sharply to her behaviour and almost kills her by pressing her neck and spreads the rumour that Chārudatta has killed Vasantasenā. In the **ninth act** Shakara charges Chārudatta with the killing of Vanstasenā in the court. Vasantasenā's mother also accepts that her daughter had gone to see Chārudatta. Chārudatta also accepts his friendship with Vasantasenā. On the basis of the evidences gathered against Chārudatta the judge awards him death sentence.

In the **tenth act**, Chārudatta is brought to the venue for execution. At this junction one of the captives of Shakara, Sthāvaraka fortunately arrives at the spot and discloses that Shakara was the real culprit. Vasantasenā also reaches the court. Chārudatta's innocence is established and he is released. Foreseeing the impending danger Shakara runs away to a distant place. Revolution erupts in the capital. Sarvilaka kills the king and Āryaka is replaced by him to the throne. Death sentence is announced to Shakara for making false charges and Vasantasenā is wedded to Chārudatta.

The title of the drama is apposite in the sense that it reflects the growing discontent among the chief characters of the drama. Chārudatta's son is discontent for failing to get the cart made out of gold. Chārudatta is discontent with his wife and wants to marry Vasantasenā. Vasatnasenā too prefers a pauper Chārudatta instead of wealthy Shakara. The dramatist shows the worthlessness of worldly prosperity.

Mrichchhakatika holds special place in the history of *Samskrit* drama for the use of seven types of *Prakrita - Sauraseni, Avantikā, Prāchya, Magadhi, Sakari, Chandāli* and *Dhākki*.

Mrichchhakatika is a realistic drama. The dramatist succeeds in keeping touch with the ground realities of life. It is a just example of *prakarana* having ten acts.

Mudrārākshas: Mudrārākshas is a drama based on political background written by Vishākhadatta. The drama consists of 7 acts and its aim is to enable Chānakya to win the confidence of Chandragupta by defeating Rākshasa, the Prime Minister of Nand, the king of Magadha. The drama revolves around the resolve of Chānakya to restore Maurya Empire to Chandragupta by overthrowing Nanda Dynasty.

The **first act** begins with the statement of Chānakya, which serves as the prologue to the plot and presents a brief sketch of the further incidents of the drama. In the soliloquy of Chānakya, it is revealed that he has uprooted the Nanda Empire paving the way for Chandragupta ascending to the throne replacing the Nanda king. It also hints at the suspicion of Chānakya that so long as Rākshasa is unbridled, Chandragupta cannot evade the impending danger lurking behind his throne; and if Rākshasa accepts to be the Minister Chandragupta will be safe. But it was not easy to force him to accept the post. Chānakya tries a different method. For it he hatches the conspiracy to kill Parvateshwar after spreading the rumour that Rākshasa might have hand in the killing. Rākshasa had earlier made a conspiracy to kill Chandragupta by dispatching *visha-kanyā* but his bid to assassinate Chandragupta was foiled by Chānakya. He deputes Kshapanaka and Bhagurāyana to win the confidence of Rākshasa and Malayaketu and thus help their master to execute his action.

Although, it is a long soliloquy, it does not hamper the gentle movement of the drama. It helps abundantly revealing the strategy of Chānakya. In the immediate aftermath of the statement of Chānakya, a messenger informs the arrival of Shakatadās, Jivasiddhi and Chandanadās. It is also brought to the notice of Chānkaya that Rākshasa has left the city leaving his family under the protection of Chandanadās. The messenger also hands over the stamp of Rākshas having his name engraved on it to Chānakya. In order to tighten his grip over Rākshasa Chānakya forces the accountant Shakatadās to prepare a document with the stamp of Rākshas imprinted on it. He instantly announces death sentence to Shakatadās for coming in support of Rākshas and discusses his planning to Siddhānthaka to assist Shakatadās to remain loyal to Rākshasa. Chanakya compels Chandanadās to hand over the family of Rākshasa to him, which the former refuses to comply with and is imprisoned by Chānakya.

In the **second act** Rākshasas' messenger Viradhagupta reveals the secret that the conspiracy to perish Chandragupta has been foiled. Meanwhile, Shakatadās appears on the scene and Rākshasa's joy knows no bounds and awards him to protect his friend. Siddhānthaka also hands over the stamp to Rākshasa. Viradhagupta also informs Rākshasa the differences emerging between Chānakya and Chandragupta.

In the **third act**, Chānakya prohibits Chandragupta to celebrate *Kaumudi* festival for which the latter reprimands the former. Chānakya reacts sharply to Chandragupta's irrational behavior and threatened to quit the ministerial berth.

In the **fourth act**, Bhagurāyana convinces Malayaketu that Rākshas' confrontation with Chānakya has gained ground. In the face of Chānakya severing ties with the latter Rākshasa might join hands with Chandragupta. In the meanwhile, Kshapanaka tells Rākshasa about the differences emerging in the relationship between Chānakya and Chandragupta to which Rakshasa reacts positively smelling that he would be shortly availing of ministerial berth. Rākshasa and Malayaketu conspire to invade *Pātaliputra*.

In the **fifth act** Siddharthaka decides to leave for *Pātaliputra* with the document that Chānakya had obtained from Shakatadās. Kshapanaka advises him to secure the seal from Bhagurāyana that he out rightly rejects. At this juncture, Kshapanaka himself meets Bhagurāyana to secure the stamp and tells him that he has got Parvateswar, whose father was killed at the behest of Rākshasa. Malayaketu stealthily listens to the talks between Kshapanaka and Bhagurāyana and is apprehensive of the intention of Rākshasa. Till date he was convinced that Chānakya had got his father murdered but the fresh information about the killing of his father strained his relationship with Rākshasa. In the meanwhile, Siddhānthaka is caught and the document is seized from him. Apprehending the danger, he revealed the secret that he was dispatched with this letter to Chandragupta by Rākshasa. He also tells the content of the document insisting the decision of Rākshasa to grab the coveted post of the minister replacing Chānakya. Malyaketu places all the evidences before Rākshasa. The document prepared by Shakatadās is matched with his other documents to ensure whether it was written by him or not. To the sheer surprise of Rākshasa, the document matched with those of Shakatadāsa. Rākshasa is also seen putting on the ornaments of Parvateswar that he had borrowed from the market. In this way, the conspiracy between Rākshasa and Chandragupta is disclosed and Malayaketu deposes him from the post of minister. Thus Chānakya succeeds in sowing seeds of dissention between Rākshasa and Malayaketu.

In the **sixth act**, Malayaketu is captured and Chānakya overpowers his army. Rākshasa is forced to live the life of a recluse and the spies of Chānakya persued him. By the order of Chānakya,

Chandanadās is sentenced to be hanged till death. Rākshasa repents for failing to protect him. He rushes to the place where Chandanadās is scheduled to be hanged to make final bid to save his life.

In the **seventh act** Chānakya succeeds in his game plan of persuading Rākshasa to come to the rescue of Chandanadās. Rākshasa appears on the scene and sets him free. In the meanwhile, Chānakya reveals the secret before Rākshasa and the entire picture is made crystal clear to him. Chānakya compels Rākshasa to accept the post of minister but he rejects the offer. Finally he agrees on the condition that Chandanagupta's life will be saved in case he accepts the ministerial berth. The state of his father is returned to Malayaketu and Chandanadās is made *Nagarasetha*. In this way, the promise of Chānakya is fulfilled and he fastens his choti, the plait at the center of the head. The drama ends with *Bharatavākya*.

Mudrārākshas is the most successful drama of Vishākhadatta. He has avoided the accepted norms of dramaturgy. Based on the political background, the drama shows no intention to present *sringāra* and *karuna rasas*. Seriousness has been maintained throughout the length and breadth of the drama. Except the wife of Chandanadās, no female character figures in this drama. It is a drama based on events. It is the only drama that pays more emphasis on events than on *rasas*. So far as the plot is concerned, it is the most original of all the dramas written in Sanskrit. The events have been arranged in such a way that the interest of the audience is sustained throughout. Although *vira rasa* is the dominant *rasa* of this drama, nowhere in the drama the incidents of war do take place. Battle takes place on the mental level with characters using their wit and skill to defeat the designs of others. The drama is marked by order, system, balance, harmony and organic unity. Vishākhadatta's originality is seen in the division of acts. For the first time, he has divided different acts of the drama into scenes. No incident lasts for more then one day. The events also take place at three places - *Pataliputra Nagar*, the capital of Malyaketu and the military camp.

Muktaka Kāvya: Muktaka Kāvya is a form of *kāvya* in which each verse does have an independent status. The relationship of one verse with the other does not exist. *Muktaka kāvya* flowed through three varied streams - *Shringāri Muktaka, Niti Muktaka* and *Stotra Muktaka*, Samskrit literature has an enriched tradition of *Shringāra Muktaka kāvya* or *Muktaka kāvya* displaying the theme of *Shringāra*. It's origin dates back to a period before Pānini and Patanjali. The tradition of *Shringāra* Muktaka started from Kālidās in the real sense of the term. His poetic composition *Ritusamhāra* leads the poetry of this kind. Among other practitioners of this trend Bhartrihari, Amaruka, Vidhāna, Ghatkarpara, Govardhanāchārya and Jayadeva are prominent. Ghatakarpara wrote *Shringāra Tilaka* in 22 verses. Bhartrihari, in his *Shringāra Shatak*, *Vairāgya Shatak* and *Niti Shatak* has presented a moving picture of various types of past times of young women. Amaru to whom has been ascribed *Amarushataka* is hailed as the most consummate poet of this period. He has touched upon the different aspects of *Shringāra* in his *Shataka* to give the trend of *Muktaka kāvya* a new dimension. Kashmiri poet Vidhāna has presented his love story using Muktaka verses in *Chaurpanchāshikā*. Govardhānachārya's *Āryasaptashati* and Jayadeva's *Gitagovinda* are milestones in this discipline bringing the trend of *Muktaka kāvya* to a new height. *Āryasaptashati* consists of 700 *Ārya Chhandas*. Gitagovinda presents a unique blend of opulence, tender verses, alliterative charm and rhythmical grandeur in order to edify different aspects of the love of Rādhā and Krishna. It became so popular that several *kāvyas* flourished on its model to barter the popularity gained by Jayadeva. Among the imitators of Gitagovinda, Harishankar and Prabhākar's *Gitarāghava*, Shri Haryāchārya's *Jānaki Gitā* and Harinātha's *Ramavilāsa* are worth mentioning. Āchārya Visvesvara in the 18th century wrote *Romāvalishataka*. Panditrāja Jagannātha also occupies a prominent place among the contributors to *Shringāra Muktaka*. His work *Bhaminivilāsa* is replete with exceptional verses. Among the writers of *Nitiparaka Muktaka* (*Muktakas* aimed at imparting moral teachings) Chānakya, Bhartrihari and Bhallata can be mentioned. They wrote *Chānakyaniti*, *Nitishataka* and *Bhallata Shataka* respectively.

Mukundamālā: Mukunda Mālā is a devotional poem written by Kulashekhara. The objective of the poet is to show his passionate love and sincere affection for Lord Vishnu to seek his grace who permeates in every animate and inanimate objects of the world and the entire activities of the world are guided at his will. It consists of 34 hymns. Kulashekhara is supposed to be the king of *Trivankura*. He lived in the tenth century.

Mukundamālā has been accredited as the outstanding work of *Vaishnava* devotional poetry in which the poet expresses his utter helplessness and moroseness urging upon Him to come to his rescue and strives for the *bhakti* of Lord Vishnu who alone is capable of tiding over the impediments faced by mankind. The poet has taken pains to narrate the miracles performed by Lord Vishnu to keep his devotees spellbound. There is a striking pace and movement in the poem. The poet has evinced least interest in a language bristling with rough, rugged and uncouth rhythmical pattern and has craved for a diction marked by simplicity and lucidity.

It is a significant contribution as prayers directed to Lord Vishnu. Several poets have described different names of Vishnu and different weapons with which he is armed. In these *Stotras* flows a current of *Mādhurya* and *Saundarya*. Kulashekhera's *Mukundmālā* holds an honourable place in the *Stotras* dedicated to Lord Vishnu. He is recognised as the ancient king of *Chitrānkura* state. His name is associated with famous *Alvāra* saints.

Mundakopanishada: Mundakopanishada is related to the Shaunaka branch of Atharvaveda. In this Upanishada Brahman has preached *Brahma Vidyā* to his elder son Atharva. It consists of three *Mundakas* or chapters. It has been written in prose. The **first chapter** deals with the interpretation of Brahman and the Vedas. The **second chapter** deals with the nature of Brahman and His relation with the world. The **third chapter** deals with the means to obtain the knowledge of Brahman. It also introduces two kinds of knowledge, *Parā and Aparā. Parā Vidyā* is that which helps understand *Akshara* Brahman. *Aparā Vidyā* includes the Vedas and 6 *Vedangas. Akshara* Brahman is the cause of this word out of which this world originates. As the spider weaves the net and swallows it, in the same way, the world emerges from the Brahman and dissolves into Him. The relation between *Jiva* and Brahma has been established through the metaphor of two birds. Two birds (*Jiva* and Brahman) inhabit the same tree. Of the two, one enjoys the taste of its fruit while the other only silently watches it. In this metaphor, *Jiva* has been portrayed as the bird enjoying the fruit of his action while Brahma is dispassionately portrayed as the bird watching everything.

Munjala: Munjala was an eminent scholar of *Astrology* and flourished in the 9th century. He has written a popular astrological text entitled *Laghumānasa*. It consists of 8 *Prakaranas*. Munjala has made significant contribution to Indian astrology by introducing new ideas, which were alien to contemporary astrologers. He discovered new methodology by making a thorough scrutiny of stars. The language of his text is very simple and acceptable.

Murāri: Murāri is the author of the drama *Anargharāghava*. He flourished around 700 AD. No clear and definite picture of his early life emerges from the sources from which information has so far been gathered. Reference to Murāri has been given in one of the *Shlokas* of *Haravijaya Mahākāvya* written by Ratnākara who flourished around 850 A.D.

Murāri Mishra: Murāri Mishra is the pioneer of Mishra tradition within the *Mimāmsā* School of philosophy. He flourished in the 12th century. He repudiated the philosophical theses of Bhavanātha, a 11th century philosopher who supported the Guru sect of the *Mimāmsā* School. Bhavanātha's critical formulations are preserved in his book *Nyāyaviveka*. Unfortunately most of the works of Murāri Mishra are missing and those that are available are incomplete. Several philosophers including the exponent of *Navya*, Gangesha Upādhyāya and his son Vardhamāna Upādhyāya have mentioned his doctrines in their works. Fragments of two of his works including *Tripādanichlinayama* and *Ekādashadhyāyadhikaranama* are available. Of the two, the first presents an analysis of first four *sutras* of Jaimini's *Mimāmsā sutra* and the second is an interpretation of some sections of the 11th chapter of Jaimini's text. Murāri Mishra's reputation lies in presenting an authentic analysis of *Pramānyavāda*.

■■

Nāgānanda: It is a drama in five acts written by **Harsavardhana**. In this drama, the poet has described the love story of Jimutavāhana, the son of Vidyādhararāja. The story has been derived from Buddhist sources particularly from Brihatkathā and Vetālapanchavinsati. The **first act** describes king Jimutaketu leaving for forest wishing his son Jimutavāhana to be his successor. Contrary to his father's desire Jimutavāhana follows him to the forest to ensure that his father does not meet any untoward incident there. Fortunately, he has an encounter with Malayavati and is moved by her beauty. The latter also gets enamoured by the former seeing him as her husband in her dream and while she is narrating the incident of her dream to her friend, Jimutavāhana listens to it hiding behind the bushes. In the **second act**, Malayavati resolves to end her life in the wake of her brother pledging to get his sister married to a different king. But the latter finally surrenders to the wishes of his sister agreeing to wed her the boy of her liking. A twist in the story is given in the **third** and the **fourth acts** with Jimutavāhana vowing to stop the killing of innocent snakes by Garuda at the cost of his life. Jimutavāhana is moved by the pathetic story of the mother of Sankhachuda, a snake, weeping incessantly sensing the imminent death of her son. Jimutavāhan, walking along with his friend to the forest, comes across the heap of bones of snakes and the wailing mother and vows to oppose the macabre act of violence at the cost of his life.

In the **fifth act**, Jimutavāhana replaces Sankhachuda allowing Garuda (a bird of prey, divine vehicle) to devour him. The latter flies towards Malaya Mountain keeping Jimutavāhana in its beak. The shocking news of the sad plight of Jimutavāhana is brought to the notice of his family through the blood that dropped in the courtyard. His parents immediately rush to the Malaya Mountain finding him languishing in the clutches of Garuda. They drew his attention towards the mistaken identity. Garuda repents for taking the life of an innocent person. Hence it decides to commit suicide when Sankhachuda confesses his crime. Jimutavāhava consoles Garuda and the latter moved by the teachings of Jimutavāhava, promises to shun violence and live a peaceful life. Immediately, he departs to bring nectar to heal the wounds of Jimutavāhana. In the meantime, Gauri appears on the scene and gives life back to Jimutavāhana. Garuda brings and showers nectar on the bones of dead snakes that regain their life. The drama ends with the *Bharatavākya*.

Nāgārjuna: Nāgārjuna was an exponent of *Shunyavāda*, and made outstanding contribution to Buddhist philosophy. His merit lies in helping the philosophical school of *Shunyavāda* scaling new heights through his works, which was virtually negated by that time. By *Shunyavāda* or Nihilistic theory Nāgārjuna means that life is meaningless and every object of this world will ultimately dwindle into zero. Nāgārjuna revived it, vindicating its merits and bringing it to the level of the most cherished philosophical system. His works have already been translated in the Chinese and the Tibetan languages. His popularity chiefly rests on his two works *Mādhyamika Kārikā* consisting of 27 *Prakaranas* and *Vigrahavyavartini* consisting of 72 *Kārikās*. In both the works he propounded the theory of *Shunyavāda* rejecting the arguments advanced by his detractors. *Shunyavāda* is also known as *Madhyamikāvāda*. It was a pessimistic philosophy that derived its vital sap from the theory of *Parivartanavāda* (the theory of mutability) propounded in Buddhism. Some Buddhist thinkers objected to this theory and found many pitfalls in it but Nagarjuna gave appropriate answer. This theory advocates that the entire world is void and objects falling within and without it are illusions. Their existence is doubtful.

Nāgeshabhatta: Nāgeshbhatta was eminent grammarian of the 7th century. He was the court poet of Rāma Singh, the king of Shringaverapurā. His Muse has found expression in religion, philosophy and poetics, besides grammar. He wrote as an authority on these subjects and his critical formulations remain unchallenged till date, His independent works and commentaries are sufficient testimony to his critical acumen. His works on grammar are placed in the category of classics. They include *Laghusabdendushekhara*, *Brihadsabdendushekhara*, *Paribhasendushekhara*, *Laghu Manjushā*, *Sphotavāda* and *Mahābhāsyapratyākhyāna Samgraha*. His commentaries on grammar and poetics are also of equal importance, which reflect his authoritative posture. They include the commentary on Kaiyyata's commentary of *Mahābhāshya* named *Mahābhāshya Pradeep*. His commentaries on books of poetics include *Udyota*, a replica of the commentary of *Kāvyaprākāsh. Gurumarma Prakāsh* is commentary on Pandit Rāja Jagannāth's *Rasagangādhara*. He remained unassailable throughout his life. His works served as milestone in their respective fields. He was popularly known as Nāgoji Bhatta.

Naishadhiyacharita: Naishadhiyacharita is an epic written by Sri Harsa narrating the love story of Nala, the king of *Nisādha* and Damayanti, daughter of Bhimasena in 22 cantos. The story has been derived from the Mahābhārata. The **first canto** deals with the gallantry and valour of Nala and his infatuation for Damayanti. In the **second canto**, the swan, which Nala had captured from the royal pond, narrates the beauty of Damayanti before Nala and carries his message to his beloved. In the **third canto**, the swan narrates the message of Nala to Damayanti and the latter reciprocates to the offer. In the **fourth canto**, preparation of Damayanti's *svayamvara* is on. In the **fifth** *Indra* persuades Nala to convey his willingness to marry Damayanti. Nala is endowed with the power to disguise himself and he accedes to the proposal of Indra reluctantly. In the **sixth**, Damayanti reiterates her commitment to marry Nala that the latter listens to while disguising his identity. In the **seventh**, Nala praises the beauty of Damayanti from top to toe. In the **eighth**, Nala reveals his real identity narrating the messages of gods to her. In the **ninth**, he urges Damayanti to reconsider her decision and respond to their offer positively but she remains undeterred. Damayanti, on the contrary, urges Nala to attend her *svayamvara* that the latter readily accepts. In the **11th** and the **12th cantos** Saraswati gives a detailed account of the kings attending the *svayamvara*. In the **13th canto** Sarasvati introduces Nala and four other gods in a high-flown language. Damayanti seeks the assistance of gods showing her gratitude to them and the latter blessing her with the power to understand the language used by Saraswati. In this way, she manages to win the love of Nala by garlanding him. The **15th canto** is devoted to the preparation for marriage and in the **16th, Nala** and Damayanti are united in nuptial knot and Nala returns to his kingdom. In the **17th, gods** depart and Kali takes vow to dethrone Nala following the news of latter getting married to Damayanti. The **18th canto** deals with the love of Nala and Damayanti that proceeds on to the **20th canto**. In the **21st**, Nala expresses his gratitude to Vishnu, Shiva and other gods. The story comes to an abrupt end with the narration of the beauty of Damayanti in the moonlit night.

Consensus has eluded scholars on the issue whether **Naishadhiyacharita** is complete or has been left incomplete. Throughout the 22 cantos, the poet has confined himself to one aspect of the life of Nala that of love and marriage throwing the remaining portion to the backwater. Some critics have contented that the rest of the parts are either missing or the text is incomplete. Keith on the contrary has contradicted this approach observing that the poet would have hardly stretched the text to its present shape. It is the most voluminous epic ever written in Samskrit literature. The speculation is further strengthened on the ground that almost all the commentaries on it are available on 22 cantos. The earliest among the commentaries is that of Vidyādhara and is also confined to 22 cantos. The poet has praised himself and his text in four *Shlokas* after 149 *Shlokas* in the 22nd canto which is sufficient testimony to the text reaching the concluding stage.

Nalabhyudaya: Nalabhyudaya is an epic by Vāmanabhatta Bāna based on the story of the legendary king Nala of the Mahābhārata and his beautiful spouse Damayanti. The valour and heroism displayed by king Nala to secure the love of the beautiful damsel Damayanti, and the way he overcame stiff resistance from tough opponents has been beautifully portrayed in 8 cantos. The poet has retained the original story as narrated in the Mahābhārat. He has preferred a simple and sonorous style avoiding terseness. There is no effort at displaying his scholarship by the poet.

He has also authored *Pārvatiparinaya*, *Shringārabhushana*, *Vemabhupālacharita*. *Pārvatiparinaya* is a drama and is based on the story of Kalidasa's epic *Kumārasambhava*. *Vemabhupālacharita* is a prose novel in which he has successfully initiated the prose style of *Bānabhatta*, particularly his *Harshacharita*. Vāmanabhatta Bāna lived in the court of *Vemabhupāla* the king of *Tailangadesha* in whose honour the prose work was written. This book also throws sufficient light on the life of Vāmanabhatta Bāna. He lived somewhere around the first half of the 1st century.

Nalachampu: Nalachampu is the most popular *Champukāvya* ever written in Samskrit literature. The authorship is attributed to Trivikrama Bhatta. The entire text deals with the love story of the king of *Nisādha*, Nala and Damayanti, daughter of *Bhima*. It has been divided into seven *Uchhvāsas*. The poet has also followed the accepted tradition of *Champukāvya* beginning his text with the invocation to Lord Shiva. He also follows the trend of commending pious people and condemning the wicked. It is followed by the poet's objective of his *kāvya* and a detailed account of his clan.

The **first Uchhvāsa** deals with the fight between *Sukara Samrāta* and Nala. The fighting continues unabated for several years and finally the pendulum swings in favour of Nala who comes out with flying colours inflicting crushing defeat on his enemy. In the meantime, a traveller coming from south narrates the beauty of Damayanti to Nala making the latter agonized.

In the **second Uchhvāsa** Nala out of curiosity catches hold of one of the swans that tries to eat up the blooming lotus in the tank. At the instance of Nala the swan speaks the language of a human being and narrates the story of the birth of Damayanti which puts Nala to utter surprise. A voice is heard from the sky that the swan will serve as the messenger of the king to Damayanti, daughter of Bhima, the king of Kundinpura, and his queen Priyangumanjari.

The **third Uchhvāsa** presents a detailed account of the birth of Damayanti. Her mother Priyangumanjari did penance to secure Shiva's grace who in turn blessed her with a baby child.

In the **fourth Uchhvāsa,** Nala is deeply moved by the beauty of Damayanti as narrated by the swan suggesting it to fly over

Kundinpura immediately carrying his proposal of marriage to his beloved. The swan agrees to it and rushes to Kundinpura to hand over the message of Nala to Damayanti and gives a detailed account of the life of Nala when a question is raised in this connection.

In the **fifth Uchhvāsa**, the swan returns to Nala carrying the garland confirming the approval of Damayanti's love for him. Nala sets out for Kundinpura with his cavalcade to participate in the *Svayamvara* of Damayanti. Shrutashilā expresses her doubt about Nala's chances of success in the *Svayamvara*.

In the **sixth Uchhvāsa**, Damayanti's messenger *Pushkaryaksha* meets Nala in his camp handing over Damayanti's letter to him. In the **seventh Uchhvāsa** warm welcome is accorded to Nala in the court of *Vidarbha* king. Nala enters the palace by the grace of Indra and joins the fold of Damayanti.

The story of Nala and Damayanti remains a fragment in *Nalachampu*. Only half of the story has been discussed. Several new stories have been carved out in between to make the description more appealing and amusing.

Nandikeshvar: Nandikeshvar was a 12th century critic whose popularity rests on his book on the art of dancing entitled *Abhinaya Darpana*. Earlier both Bharata and Nandikeshvar were considered one and the same person. After the publication of *Abhinaya Darpana* this confusion was dispelled. In this book itself Nandikeshvar has given reference to Bharata's *Nātyashāstra*. In this way, it is proved that they were two different persons.

Abhinaya Darpana consists of 324 *Shlokas*. The three kinds of *Abhinaya* have been discussed in it - *Nātya, Natta* and *Nritya*. The six elements of *Nātya* have been referred to **Nritya, Bhava, Chita, Abhinaya, Rasa** and **Tāla**. Of these four kinds of *Abhinaya* have been mentioned - **Āngika, Vāchika, Āchār** and **Sātvika**. This book deals with at least 16 kinds of *Abhinaya* and their different kinds. 13 movements of hands have also been referred to. Dr. Manmohana Ghosa has translated it into English.

Narachanda Upādhyāya: Narchanda Upādhyāya was a 14th Century scholar of *Astrology*. Several books pertaining to Astrology have been attributed to him. Of all the books *Vedajātakavritti* and *Jyotishaprakāsh* are very significant and outstanding contributions in the field of Astrology. The latter is a significant book on *Phalita Jyotisha*. He has made Herculean effort to elevate *Jyotisha* to a high pedestal and has contributed immensely to enrich the repertory of *Jyotisha* by making numerous innovations. His writings have served his objective and have been proved to be milestones. He explored new horizon for Indian *Astrology* by his sensible and balanced writing.

Nārada Purāna: Chronologically the sixth *Purāna*. *Matsya Purāna* has indicated that a Purāna in which Nārada propagated religious ideology can be referred to as Nārada Purāna. It is divided into two sections - *Purava Khanda* and *Uttara Khanda*; the former consisting of 125 and the latter consisting of 82 chapters. The number of *Shlokas* goes up to 18,110. It is a *Vaishnava Purāna* that deals with the rituals elaborately. *Purava Khanda* pays special attention to *Vaishnava* ideology but the *Uttara Khanda* is free from this sectarian bias. The index of all the 18 *Purānas* has been presented in it. In this sense, it seems to be the latest in the order of the *Purānas*. This description might have been added to a latter date. *Vishnu Purāna* has also placed it 2nd to the 6th position among the *Purānas*. The subjects coming within its compass include - *Dharma, Nakshatra, Vyākarana, Nirukta, Jyotisha*, Construction, Method of rituals, *Varnāshrama* Dharma, *Shrāddha*, Penance and advantages of devotion and *Moksha*. The worship of Vishnu has been accepted as the only way of acquiring *Moksha* and hymns pertaining to Vishnu, Rāma, Hanumāna, Krishna, Kāli and Mahesha have been elaborately discussed.

This *Purāna* has been compiled on the basis of *Shuka-Shaunaka Samvāda*. It begins with the description of the universe that is followed by several stories. Besides *Nārdiya Purāna, Nāradiya Up-Purāna* also exists consisting of 38 chapters and 3600 Shlokas. It interprets sectarian ideology that does not contain the signs of the Purānas. Some scholars have accepted it as Nārada Purāna.

Nārada Smriti: The author of *Nārada Smriti* was Nārada. He is considered to be the author of ten *Dharmashāstras*. *Nārada Smriti* is found in two forms. One is in its abridged and another is in its larger form. Dr. Jolly has edited both the *Smritis*. There are as many as 1028 *Shlokas* in *Nārada Smriti*. In the first three sections of this book, subjects related to **Nyāya** have been described. Thereafter subjects like **Rindāna** (giving loan), **Jamā** (deposit), **Bandhaka** (mortgage), **Sahakāritā** (co-operation), **Datta Pradani** (adoption), **Abhipretasirasa** (breaking the contract of a servant), **Vetanasya Anpatal** (the not giving of salary), **Sampradāna** (not relinquishing the property after selling), **Kritanusaya** (annulment of purchase), **Dayābhāga** (partition), **Sāhasa** (robbery), **Vāteyaparuseya** (defamation) and use of derogatory words and **Dandaparuseya** (different kinds of injuries) have been discussed. There are altogether 18 *Prakaranas* in *Nārada Smriti*. In this book the subjects contained in the *Manusmriti* have been put in a precise form. It is a work that seems to have been written after *Yāgyavalkya Smriti*.

Nārāyana : Nārāyana was a 16th century scholar of Astrology. He has written an astrological text *Muharta Mārtanda* in *Sardulavikridita Chhanda*. He has also written a book on Algebra. His commentary on *Keseva Paddhati* is also very popular.

Nārāyana Bhatta : Nārāyana Bhatta was a 16th century poet. He was born in Kerala. His father Mātridatta was an eminent *Mimāmsaka*. He composed 14 complete *Champu Kāvyas* that includes – *Matsyāvatāra Prabandha, Rājasuya Prabandha, Panchāli Svayamvara, Nalayanicharita, Duta-Vākya, Hirnināsika Champu, Svāhā Svadhā Champu*, and *Kotiviraha*. He has also written a *Kāvya* entitled Nārāyaniya. Besides these, he has also authored a text on grammar *Prakarya Sarvasva* and a text on *Mimāmsa* Philosophy, *Manameyodaya*. *Matsyavatara* consists of 67 sections of verses and 12 sections of prose. It deals with the story of Manu and *Matsyāvatāra* as narrated in the *Purānas. Rajasuya Prabandha* deals with the *Rajasuya* ritual performed by Yudhisthira. *Svāhā Svadhā Champu* deals with the love story of Chandramā (Moon) and Svāhā, the wife of Agni. *Kotiviraha* deals with the imaginary story of union and separation. *Nriga Moksha* deals with the story of the king Nriga as narrated in the tenth *Skandha* of *Srimad Bhāgavata*.

Narmamālā: Narmamālā is a satire by Kshemendra. It is aimed at showing the follies and frailties latent in contemporary society and religion. Kshemendra has tried to explore new horizons in Samskrit literature by introducing satire. He has depicted grim picture of the social disorder. The poet has especially attacked the heinous designs of officials belonging to *Kāyastha* and *Niyogi* communities. He has presented a graphic description of lapses that erode the vitality and warmth of society, which are gradually shaking its foundation and causing an irreparable damage to it by tarnishing the social fabric of society. By targeting those sections he has opined that they should either mend their ways or need to be given proper training to make the society worth living. It is a strict warning to those sections to return to the mainstream of society.

Nātyashāstra: Nātyashāstra is an exhaustive text of Indian poetics and dramaturgy. It has been attributed to Achārya Bharata. It is a book that minutely and elaborately explains and analyses a variety of topics like *Rasa*, *Alankāra*, *Guna, Dosa* and *Nāyikā Bheda*. Bharat's contribution to dramaturgy as well as Sanskrit poetics is original because for the first time he dwelt upon all the main and ancillary subjects related to drama and poetry.

There is complete lack of unanimity among the scholars with regard to the period of composition of this work. Its timing has been fixed between 5th century B.C, and 1st century A.D. Two other names of Nātyashāstra are available in ancient texts – *Satasahashri* and *Dvādasasahashri*. At present, the *Satasahashri* edition is available which is spread over 36 chapters. It is a unique book that sets the ground and parameters for Samskrit aesthetic theories. Since the Vedas were out of bounds of women and the lower castes, the Nātyashāstra treatise on drama and dramaturgy, was called *Panchama* Veda, the fifth Veda, accessible to all and sundry. The fifth Veda takes its components from all the four Vedas. It incorporates the recitative from the Rigveda, the song from the Sāma Veda, enacting from the Yajur Veda and its emotional *rasas* from Atharva Veda. Besides Nātyakalā, Bharata's book takes dance, music, rhetoric (*Chhanda*), *alankāra* (figures of speech), *rasa* and construction of stage within its umbrella. The first two chapters deal with the origin of drama and stage, whereas the third chapter is restricted to two ways of worship of stage deity.

The analysis of *Rasa* has been made in the **fifth** and the **sixth chapters**. The **eighth chapter** deals with four kinds of *Abhinaya: Āangika*, *Vāchika*, *Sātvika*, and *Aharya*. The **ninth chapter** deals with organic movement specially of hands (*hastābhinaya*) and the **tenth** deals with the performance made by the movement of body. The **eleventh** and the **twelfth chapters** deal with the methodology for the construction of *chari* and *mandala*. The **thirteenth chapter** deals with *Rasa*, the **14th** and the **15th deal** with performance through the utterances (*Vāchika Abhinaya*). The **16th chapter** deals with *Chhanda*, the **17th** dwells upon languages like Prākrita and the **18th** dilates upon the lakshana of *Dasarupaka. Natya sandhiyans* have been dealt with in the **19th** and *Bhārati; Sattavati*, *Arbhati* and *Kaisiki Vritties* have been discussed in **20th chapter**. The **21st chapter** deals with *Aharyābhinaya* and the **22nd** concentrates on normal performance. *Nāyaka-Nāyika Bheda* also falls in this chapter. The **23rd chapter** relies on prostitutes and the **24th** deals with three types of characters- *Uttama, Madhyama* and *Adhama*. The **25th chapter** deals with *Chitrabhinaya* and the **26th chapter** deals with *Vikritabhinaya*. The **27th chapter** deals with the ways to achieve perfection in *Abhinaya* and obstacles coming in the way. Between the **28th** and the **32nd chapters** music has been discussed. The **34th chapter** hinges round the nature of the characters and the **35th chapter** is confined to *vidusaka* (buffoon). The **36th chapter** deals with the story of drama descending to the earth. Dr. Manamohana Ghosa has translated Nātyashāstra into English.

Three forms of Nātyashāstra are available - *Sutra, Bhāshya* and *Kārika*. Earlier it was written in Sutra form and *Bhāshya* is a latter composition. *Kārikas* are placed third in the hierarchy in which elaborate study of issues relating to drama have been made throughout the Nātyashāstra, *Anushtupa Chhanda* has been used. *Ārya Chhanda* has been used at a few places. Some *Anuvansya* Shlokas have also been included in it which are supposed to be the composition of an earlier date. The only available commentary on Nātyashāstra is Abhinava Gupta's *Abhinava Bhārati*. Reference to nine interpreters of Nātyashāstra has been given by Abhinava Gupta and Sārangadhara. They include - Udbhata, Lollata, Sri Sankuka, Bhattanāyaka, Rāhul, Bhattanārāyana, Abhinava Gupta, Kirtidhara and Mātri Guptāchārya.

Navasahasanka charita: Navasahasanka charita is the first ever epic in Samskrit based on historical facts and incidents. It has been written by Padmagupta Parimala. It deals with the marriage of Sindhurāja, the father of king Bhoja of Dhāra with the daughter of Nāgrāja Shankhaparā named Shashi Prabhā. Padmagupta has also thrown much light on his personal life through this epic. Actually he was the court poet of king Munja who had accorded high honour and prestige to Padmagupta. Munja was known for his charity and justice. Padmagupta had become almost pathetic after the death of Munja and had agreed to reconsider his decision at the behest of his (Munja's) younger brother Sindhurāj.

Padmagupta is the poet of that Vaidarbha path which is difficult to traverse. In his view moving on that path is like moving on a sword's edge. Padmagupta had however, great reverence for Bhartrimeshta who was a poet of this path. Kālidāsa, being the most mature poet of this path, was ideal for him. Like Kālidās' poetry, Padmagupta's poetry is full of the quality of *Prasād guna* and embellished with alankāras. In the description of *sringāra rasa*, the poet takes utmost precaution to see that his descriptions does not degenerate into obscenity nor his description could be so facile that it should not titillate the hearts of reader. In this respect he is a follower of the middle path. The portrayal of characters is natural and agreeable. In Padmagupta, there is unique synthesis of *Hridaya paksha* and *Kalā paksha*.

Nighantu: Nighantu is a set of Vedic words (terminology), in which an interpretation of complex words has been given. It is a compilation of difficult words coming in the Vedas. The time of its composition and its authorship is uncertain. There is a great controversy over the number of Nighantus as well. At present only one Nighantu is available on which there is a commentary by Yāska named Nirukta. Scholars are not unanimous about the composition and number of words discussed in it. In the

Nighantu there are five chapters. The **first three chapters** are called *Naighantuka Kānda* and interpretation of the words figuring in it has been made in the second and the third chapters. The number of words goes to 1341; out of which only 230 words have been interpreted. The **fourth *Kānda*** is called *Naigama Kānda*. It is divided into three sections consisting of 62, 84, and 132 *Padas* respectively. The **fifth chapter** is called *Daivata Kānda*. It is divided into 6 Kāndas that consist of 3, 13, 36, 32, 36 and 31 *Padas* respectively. The interpretation of these words have been made from the **seventh to the 12th chapters**. In the first three chapters, many *padās* have been connected. The **fourth chapter** is intended to highlight those words that are ambivalent or multifaceted. In the **fifth chapter,** there is the description of abodes of gods. There is only one explanation in Nighantu whose author is Devarāja Yajva. In the preface of Higna Nighantu he has named Kshiraswāmi; and Anantāchārya. Kshiraswāmi is the famous commentator of *Amarkosha*. There is one small book available written by the famous Tāntrika Bhāskarrai in which the author has versified some words after the style of Nighantu. This book is helpful in understanding Nighantu. In the Mahābhārata, Prajāpati Kasyapa has been considered the author of Nighantu. Yet other scholars have rejected this hypothesis and have accepted Yāska as the author of both Nirukta and Nighantu.

Nilakantha Bhatta: Nilakantha Bhatta was a 17th century eminent political thinker and analyst and interpreter of Dharmashāstra. He was the court poet of Bundela king Bhagavanta Deva. His elder brother Kamalākara Bhatta has also written a book on Dharmashāstra entitled *Nirnaya Sindhu*. He had also compiled a voluminous *Kāvya Bhagavadbhāskara* in the honour of his patron. It is divided into twelve *Mayukhas*. He has discussed various aspects of polity in his anthology *Nitimayukha*. The book deals with the nature of state, seven forms of state and the process of coronation. He has borrowed extensively from Manusmriti, Yajnavalkya Smriti, Kamandakanitisāra, Vārāhamihira, the Mahābhārata and Chānakya and quoted from them at regular intervals in his text. Impact of omens has also been discussed.

Nimbārka Ideology (Doctrine): Nimbārka was an eminent philosopher and exponent of Dvaitādvaita theory of Vaisnava philosophy. He belonged to the 12th century. His works include *Vedāntapārijāta Saurabha* (*Bhāsya* of *Brahmasutra*) *Dasasloki* and *Shrikrishnashtāvaraja.* His doctrine of the relationship between Brahman and *Jiva* is called *Dvaitādvaita* or *Bhedābheda*. He insisted on both the attachment with and the detachments from the Brahman. Like Rāmānuja, he has discussed *Chita, Achita* and the nature of God. *Jiva* is considered endowed with full Knowledge. He remains *kartā* (active) in all the states. He is also called *Bhoktā* because he enjoys through the senses. *Jiva* does not remain free. He must seek the assistance of God to attain knowledge and *Bhoga*. God is free whereas *Jiva* is in bondage and is dependent. God is free to deal with *Jiva*. But *Jiva* depends upon God in all the ways. God is Almighty and *Jiva* is the reflection of God. *Jiva* is not separate from Brahman though seems to have a distinct existence. He does not lose his identity in the state of *Moksha* and manages to retain his independent existence although enjoying proximity with God. *Jiva* enjoys the company of Brahman or God through devotion and manages to overcome his sufferings. There is no alternative choice to devotion. In Nimbārka doctrine, Krishna has been considered Brahman and all gods including Brahmā and Shiva express their gratitude to Him. The grace of Krishna can be obtained in five ways - *Santa, Dāsya, Sakhya, Vātsalya* and *Ujjvala*. Nimbārka has advised the worship of Rādhā who is the main spring behind the power of Krishna. They are virtually identical but have assumed distinct forms for the sake of beatitude. *Jiva* is a spark of God and he is *chaitanya* (conscious) and dependent on him. It is because of this phenomenon, that he is aloof from God though he is heartily connected with Him.

Nirukta: Nirukta is a commentary book on Nighantu by Yāska. It is a derivative of Vedic words. His name has been mentioned in the *Shānti Parva* of the Mahābhārata. In this sense he can be reckoned back to a much earlier date. The objective of Nirukta is to present the derivatives of Vedic words and to find out their genesis. It also explores the possibility of the exact context in which a particular word has acquired a specific meaning. Nirukta contains 12 chapters in addition to appendices. In this way, there are altogether 14 chapters, in this book. We cannot take the appendices written by any modern writer because Sāyana was fully acquainted with the ideas contained in these appendices. Un-disputably, Yāska was born before Pānini. Although Nirukta is itself a commentary but here and there its language is so difficult that even a scholar feels baffled in understanding it. Patanjali in his Mahābhāsya has given a hint at the difficult reading of Nirukta. While presenting the derivative of words, Yāska has also indicated suffixes to be added to each verb. Nirukta is also important from linguistics point of view. Seeds of several linguistics theories are contained in it. It presents an elaborate interpretation of Vedic diction. The commentator of Nirukta, Durgāchārya has pointed out in his *Vritti* that there are 14 Niruktas. Even in Yāska's Nirukta, there are names of 12 authors of Nirukta namely Agrāyana, Aupamanyava, Audumbarāyana, Aurnānābha, Katthakya, Kraustuki, Garga, Galava, Taitiki, Varsyāyani, Shakapuni and Sthaulasthivi. Amongst, them the name of Shakapuni also occurs in Brihaddevatā.

The subjects dealt with in Nirukta are *Varnāgama, Varna Viparyaya, Varnanāsa,* and *Dhātu*. Sāyanāchārya, while explaining the meaning of Nirukta, has laid down that the collating of independent words for the appreciation of meaning is Nirukta. The author of Nirukta has painstakingly explored the roots of words and the prefixes and suffixes. Yāska considers all the names as born of roots. Yaska's Nirukta anticipates many modern studies in the field of linguistics and semantics. Nirukta not only gives on exposition of Vedic gods but also by way of discussion dwells on grammar, philosophy, literature, sociology and history. Yāska has put the Vedic gods in three distinct categories, those residing on the earth (Agni) *Prithavisthāna*; who dwells on firmament, *Antariksa Sthān* (Vāyu and Indra); who dwells on heaven *Svargasthāna* (Surya). All the commentaries on Yāska's Nirukta are not available. The only commentary on Nirukta is that of Durgā Dāsa in which opinions of earlier commentators have been jotted down. Its oldest commentator was Skandaswāmi who wrote a commentary on Nirukta in Adhyāyas.

Nityānanda: Nityānand was a 17th century scholar of Astrology. He has compiled an astrological text *Siddhānta Rāja*, which is a prominent work on *Graha Ganita*.

***Nyāya School of Philosophy*:** *Nyāya* Darshan is one of the six famous schools of Indian philosophy. Maharishi Gautama propounded it. In it an object is tested by evidence. The foundation stone of this school is laid on *Nyāyasutra* written by Gautama. It is popularly known as *Akshapāda*. It consists of five chapters and each chapter is sub divided into two *Ahnikas*. It deals with 16 objects (matters) extensively-*Pramāna, Prameya, Sanyama, Prayojana, Drishtānta, Siddhānta, Avayaya, Tarka, Nirnaya, Vāda, Jalpā, Vitandā, Hetvabhāsha, Chāla, Jāti,* and *Nigrahasthāna*. Vātsyāyana has written a voluminous *Bhāshya* on *Nyāyasutra* entitled *Vātsyāyanabhāsya*. Among the prominent scholars who collaborated and aided to the enrichment of this philosophical system include - Udyotakar (*Nyāyavartikā*), Jayanta Bhatta (*Nyāyamanjari*), Udayanāchārya (*Nyāya Kusumānjali*), Gangesha Upādhyāya (*Tatvachintāmani*), Jagadisha Tarkālankara, (*Sabdashakti Prakāshikā*), Gadādhara Bhattāchārya (*Vyuttivāda*), Viswanātha Bhattāchārya (*Nyāyasiddhānata Muktāvali*,) Keshava Mishra (*Tarkabhāshā*) and Annān Bhatta (*Tarkasamgraha*).

In course of time two diverse streams of *Nyāya* school emerged - *Prāchina Nyāya* and *Navya Nyāya*. The texts aimed at refuting the allegations triggered against Gautama Sutra and its Bhāsya are placed in the category of *Prāchina Nyāya* and those finding fault in the existing system and giving new twist to it are placed in the category of *Navya Nyāya*. The *Naiyāyika* of Mithilā and Nādiā (Bengāl) have contributed significantly to the development of *Navya Nyāya* School. The prominent among those are Gangesha Upādhyāya, Jagadisha Tarkālankāra and Gadādhara Bhattāchārya. Gangesha Upādhyāya's *Tattvachintāmani* is a milestone that brought about a vital change.

The objective of *Nyāya* School is to attain *Moksha* and to reveal the identity of the supreme reality through logic. The entire *Nyāya* philosophy has been divided into four sections. The first section deals with *Pramāna*, the second concentrates on the ideologies of physical world. The third is restricted to statements pertaining to *ātman* (soul) and *Moksha* and the fourth dilates upon the existence of God.

The Nyāya School has accepted four ways to acquire knowledge- *Pratyaksha, Anumāna* (insinuation), *Upamāna* and *Shabda*. Knowledge that is obtained through sense organs is called *Pratyaksha. Pratyaksha* knowledge can be obtained through two ways - worldly and earthly. Worldly *Pratyaksha* is further divided into external and internal forms. External *Pratyaksha*, though obtained through five senses is of five kinds - *Chākshusa, Shravani, Sparshanā, Rasanā* and *Ghrānya*. Besides this, knowledge is also obtained through mind. In this way worldly *Pratyaksha* is of six kinds. Earthly or transcendental *Pratyaksha* is divided into *Sāmānya Lakshanā, Gyāna Lakshanā* and *Yogaja. Pratyaksa* has been further divided into *Savikalpa, Nirvikalpa* and *Pratyabhigya*.

Anumāna or inference is a type of knowledge in which *Pratyaksha* knowledge is obtained through *Apratyaksha* channel. It is a matter of common experience that sometimes *Pratyaksha* or apparent proves *Apratyaksha* or which is not apparent. There is logical fallacy in it. For example, by looking at the clouds in the sky one can easily insinuate rainfall. In the same way, by seeing flood in the river one can insinuate torrential rainfall. In both the examples one goes by *Anumāna* or inference or deduction. Here, effect suggests the cause.

Achievement of *Pratigyāna* through inference is called *Nigamana*. Example:

This mountain is inflammable. (*Pratigyāna*)

It is so because it contains smoke. (*Hetu*)

That which contains smoke must be inflammable. (illustrations)

This mountain is full of smoke. (*Upanaya*).

Therefore, the mountain is inflammable (*Nigamana*)

Upamāna is the third *Pramāna* of the school of *Nyāya*. Expectation of a word on the basis of the similarity with other word is called *Upamāna*.

Statement made by reverend (*Āpta*) people is called *Āptavachana*.

The present is often justified by prior knowledge of similar things. One who has seen a cow must on the basis of his prior knowledge think that a *Neelagāya* will be something like a cow.

Āpta singnifies sermon. Statement of a reverend person is brought in the category of *Shabda Pramāna* whose statement cannot be changed. *Shabda* is of two kinds - Vedic and mundane. Vedic Shabdas are free from illusion since they are uttered by God. But mundane words are not entirely perfect. They contain certain impurities. Truthfulness of only those words can be vouched which are uttered by reverend people.

The objective of *Nyāya* system is to enable *Jiva* to achieve *Moksha* in life. It has developed materialistic approach towards soul. The knowledge of soul comes through twofold channels- first, through divine sayings and second, through worldly sources.

Moksha, according to *Naiyāyikas*, is a state in which man is immune from miseries. One must give up the bondage of body and mind in order to acquire *Moksha. Moksha* is achieved through *Shravana* (or listening), *Manana* (constant contemplation) and *Nididhyāsana* (or penance) of the sermons, pertaining to self, contained in scripture. In this way, passions and evil desires are removed and a man performs every work disinterestedly and is thus freed from the cycle of birth and death. Practice of Yoga is also essential for salvation.

God has been recognised as one who creates, nourishes and annihilates the world. He participates in the process of creation with the help of atoms: *Dik*, *Kāla*, *Ākāsha*, and *mana* and *ātman*. He is the efficient cause of the world and not only its material cause. *Naiyāyikas* have given valid causes to prove the existence of God. The first proof is based on cause-effect relationship. The entire objects of the world are effects. There must be some creator of these objects. It can be proved through the example of pitcher and potter. The existence of God is also proved by the theory of *Karma*. Human beings are awarded pleasure and pain on the basis of their *Karma* and the chain-puller of the entire activities must be God. Man can neither acquire perfect knowledge nor can he evade the afflictions without the grace of God.

The logic advanced by the philosophers of *Nyāya* School is highly convincing. It does not accept the existence of the Ultimate authority for the entire universe and thus it opposes the theory of Monism. In this way, its metaphysics seems to be inferior to that of *Sāmkhya* and *Vedānta. Nyāya* philosophy is based on sound logic. It gives a systematic and coherent account of knowledge without which nothing can be known or understood. It also gives a convincing account of the creation of cosmos and puts forward the theory, that God can only be known through inference (*anumāna*). The literature of *Nyāya* philosophy is so vast and broad-based that a large part of it is still to be published. The saints and theologians who propounded the *Nyāya* philosophy were unquestionably very talented, equipped with logical acumen and power of argument. The Nyāya philosophy has two streams — one led by Gautama that is called categorist philosophy and the second led by Gangesha Upādhyāya that is called epistemological philosophy. The first stream is usually designated as old *Nyāya* and second as *Navya-Nyāya*. *Udayanāchārya* has given as many as nine evidences for the existence of god in his seminal work *Nyāyakusumānjali*, which include- *Kārya* (cause), *Āyojana* (dispensation, *Dhriti* (Possession), *Vināsha* (destruction) *Pada*, *Pratyaksha Gyāna* (apparent knowledge) *Shruti*, (Veda), *Vākya* (statement of the Veda), and *Sānkhyā* (number).

The *Nyāya* philosophy maintains that real emancipation means equipoise of mind where there is neither pain nor pleasure. Pleasure is usually connected with sense organs, when there is *Rāga* or attraction, it gives birth to bondage, liberation or emancipation. Neither pleasure exists nor pain exists. Faulty knowledge gives birth to *Dosa, Pravritti, Janma* and *Dukha*. The faulty knowledge is dispelled by the real knowledge. A seeker of truth must realise *Ātman* or soul. This is what is called Self-realization. In order to achieve its end, one should practice Yoga: *Yama, Niyama, Āsan, Prānāyām, Pratyāhār*, *Dhāranā, Dhyāna* and *Samādhi*. The ultimate aim of *Nyāya* philosophy is equipoise of mind where, there is neither pleasure nor pain and the soul is distilled and unalloyed like a transparent glass. ■■

Padmagupta Parimala: Padmagupta Parimala was the author of the popular historical epic *Navasahashankacharita*. The epic deals with the marriage of Sindhurāja (Navasahashanka), father of the king of Dhara, Bhoja with Shashiprabhā. Parimal was the court poet of Munja's elder brother Sindhurāja. It was written around 1005 A.D. It consists of 18 Cantos. In the 12th Canto the genealogy of Sindhurāja has been given which has been substantiated by the facts available through inscriptions. It is equally important as history and kāvya. His poetic talent finds a fresh outlet through the verses of his epic poetry, which seems to have been modelled on Kālidāsa's tender and flexible style of writing: avoiding ornamentation and refinement which are all set to hamper the gentle movement of the verse. He had faith in diction, which is simple, sonorous and less cumbrous.

Padma Purāna: Chronologically, Padma Purāna is the second *Purāna*. This voluminous work consists of 641 chapters and 50,000 *shlokas*. Both *Devanāgari* and *Bengāli* editions of *Padma Purāna* are available. It was published by B.N. Mandalika in 1894 from Ānandāshram. This edition consists of six-sections -*Ādi, Bhumi, Brahman, Patāla, Shrishti*, and *Uttarakhanda*. ***Shrishti Khanda**:* Shrishti Khanda is the preface to this Purāna consisting of 82 chapters in which at the behest of saints the story of *Purāna* is being narrated by Ugrashravā, the son of Lomaharshan. The story of the origin of the universe by Brahman through lotus has been discussed. *Shrishti Khanda* is divided in five *Parvas*. ***Paushkara Parva**:* Paushkara Parva deals with the creation of *Surya* and *Chandra* dynasties and *Devāsura Sangrām* (confrontation). ***Teertha Parva**:* Teertha Parva deals with several pilgrimages, mountains, islands and seven seas, and finally confirms that recitation of the name of Krishna is enough to provide salvation.

The **third *Parva*** deals with kings contributing money as donations and **the fourth** presents the genealogy of kings. The **fifth *parva*** deals with the ways and means to achieve *nirvāna*. Besides this, it also dwells upon *Samudra Manthana*, birth of Prithu, Vritrāsura conflict, incarnation of Vāmana, birth of Mārkandeya and Kārtikeya, story of Rāma and killing of Tārakāsura. The story ends with the narration of the story of Vishnu and the birth and marriage of Skanda. ***Bhumi Khanda:*** It narrates the story of Soma Sharmā who finally took birth as Prahalāda. It also deals with the story of Chyavana and the significance of the devotion to Vishnu. ***Swarga Khanda:*** It deals with the story of Shakuntalā and Dushyanta, Urvasi and Pururvā. Besides this, it dilates upon gods, *baikuntha*, ghosts, witches, *vidyādharas* and apsarās. ***Pātāla Khanda:*** It presents the story of *Nāgaloka*. The story of *Rāmāyana* has also figured in it which seems to be closer to the story as presented in *Raghuvansa* than that mentioned in the Mahābhārata. It ends with the description of all 18 Purānas and the significance of Shrimad Bhāgavata. ***Uttara Khanda:*** It is the largest section, which consists of various kinds of stories, festivals and *vratas* relating to the worship of Lord Vishnu. No exact timing for the composition of *Padma Purāna* is known.

Pancharātrā: Pancharātrā is a *Samavakar* (a kind of drama) written by Bhāsa in three acts. The story has been derived from the *Virāta Parva* of the Mahābhārata but the dramatist has molded it in a new direction making a vital change in the story as narrated in the Mahābhārata. He has enjoyed a fair amount of liberty and has brought the battle to an abrupt end.

In **the first act**, conceding defeat from the Kauravas, the Pāndavas leave for an unknown destination as per the condition and finally taking shelter in the palace of king Virāta disguising their real identity. In the meantime Duryodhana performs a Yajna in which a good number of kings are invited. When asked by Duryodhana to place his demand after the successfully completion of the Yajna, Dronachārya proposes him to hand over half of the property to the Pāndavas which, Shakuni outrightly rejects but finally agrees on the condition that he must find out the whereabouts of the Pāndavas within five nights. Drona refuses to accept this awkward demand. In the meantime, following the message received from certain sources about the killing of Kichaka, the cousin of the king of Virāta, along with his 100 brothers, Bhishma prevails upon Drona to accept the demand of Duryodhana because he was optimistic that none other than Bhima would have killed Kichaka. Bhishma's proposal to invade *Virāta Nagar* and to capture the herd of cows is also ratified by Duryodhana.

The **second act** deals with the battle between the two forces and the imprisonment of Abhimanyu. The identity of the Pāndavas is also revealed. In **the third act**, the message of the captivity of Abhimanyu is brought to the Kaurava court telling that somebody captured Abhimanyu on foot. Bhishma realised that the unknown warrior must be Bhima. At this juncture, the message of Yudhisthira is brought by a messenger, Drona reminds Duryodhana of his promise which the latter accepts and agrees to hand over half of the state to the Pāndavas. The drama ends with the *Bharatavākya*.

Pancharātrā : *Vaisnava Tantra* is called *Pancharātrā*. It has been discussed in the *Nārāyanopākhyana* section of the Mahābhārata. It has been mentioned that Nārada had imbibed the essence of this *tantra* from the saint Nārāyana. It has been accepted as a part of the Veda named Ekāyana. A great deal of literature based on *Pancharātrā* is available. As many as 215 *Pancharātrā Samhitās* have been mentioned in *Kapinjai Samhitā*. Prominent among them are *Agastya Samhitā*, *Kashyapa Samhitā, Nārdiya Samhitā* and *Vishnurahasya Samhitā*.

Several rumours are afloat with regard to the title of *Pancharātrā*. In Mahābhārata, it has been mentioned that this name was given to it due to the assimilation of the Vedas and *Sāmkhya Yoga*. *Ishwara Samhitā* has observed that these teachings were imparted in five nights by five seers - Shāndilya, Aupagāyana, Maunjāyana, Kaushika and Bhārdwāj. *Nāradapancharātrā* has opined that it was so called because of the analysis of five elements: *Param Tatva* (Supreme element), *Mukti* (liberation), *Bhukti* (worldly pleasure) Yoga and *Vishaya* (sensual pleasure). *Param Brahman* has been referred to as eternal and infinite in *Pancharātrā*, which is reflected in all the creatures of the world. He is complete, eternal and all pervasive. *Pancharātrā* has accepted both facets of Brahman: form and formless. Parabrahman has got six features - *Gyāna, Shakti, Aiswarya, Bala* (power), *Virya* and *Teja*. God manifests himself in four forms for the betterment of the world *vyuha, vibhava, archavatara* and *antaryāmi*. *Samkarsana, Aniruddha* and *Pradyumna* are three facets of God. *Sankarsana* represents *gyāna* (knowledge and power), *Pradyumna* signifies *Aishwarya* and *Virya,* and *Aniruddha* suggests *Shakti* and *Teja*. The world is the storehouse of pleasure for God generating fun and frolic. The devotee achieves *Moksha* through worship and attains communion with God. Moksha is referred to as *Brahmabhāvapati*.

Panchāsika: Panchāsika is the first organised treatise on the *Sāmkhya* philosophy. The first scholar to organise the sutras of the philosophical school of *Sāmkhya* in a proper order was the disciple of Āsuri, who himself was the disciple of Kapila, the exponent of the *Sāmkhya* School. His ideas are scattered over in several works, which are called *Panchāsika Sutra*. Chinese tradition has established him the author of *Shashthitantra* consisting of 60,000 *Shlokas*. Bhaskarāchārya has accepted Kapila as the author of *Panchāsika Tantra* in his *Bhāsya* of *Brahmasutra*.

Panchatantra: The Panchatantra is a collection of beast fables. It was written to give moral lessons through popular beast stories in which animals play a leading role. It was written way ahead of Aesop's fables. It is a major contribution to the world in the field of fable. It is said that king Amarshakti who felt frustrated at his failure to educate his three stupid and idle sons, found a *Brāhmina* named Vishnu Sharmā who taught them wisdom and made them wise through the fables of *Panchatantra*. The author has tried to resolve various problems of life through the stories of animals in a very simple language. It has been written basically in prose, although verse has also been used to vivify the text. There is no way of dating the collection beyond the fact that it was translated into Pehlevi (language of Persia) by the order of the king of Persia named Khusaro Nauservān who died in A.D.579. The tales seems to belong to the *Buddhist* tradition of the *Jātakas*. Whether Aesop is indebted to Indian tradition is a matter of dispute. The tales themselves are compressed, dramatic and humorous. The animals have all the characteristics of men. Their conduct and experiences are used to pin morals: both private and political.

There are as many as five divisions of *Panchantantra* dealing with separation of friends (*Mitrabheda*), winning of friends (*Mitralābha*), war and peace (*Samdhivigraha*), loss and gain (*Labdhapranāsha*) and hasty action (*Aparikshitakārakam*) respectively. *Panchatantra* is like a web in which several stories have been woven in an integrated form. It is not a single text but a sequence of texts.

The main story in *Mitralābha* deals with the conspiracy hatched by a wicked jackal to sever ties between Pingala lion and Sanjivaka ox who had earlier been protected by the lion and had developed friendship with him despite the opposition of its ministers. The second section deals with the story of the king of parrot, Chitragriva who successfully evades the danger posed on life and his clan with the help of his friend. The third section is concerned with the story of the crows burning the caves of the owls. The fourth section revolves round the story of a monkey and a crocodile. The fifth section communicates the message that one should not do a work without applying one's worth.

Vishnu Sharmā has thrown light on various issues ranging from morality and religion to philosophy and polity in a very simple and persuasive style. He has used simple but appealing language. The author has substantiated his ideas by jotting down the preaching from the Rāmāyana, the Mahābhārata and texts communicating moral teachings. Unlike prose, he has cultivated complex and refined structure in his verses. His style is at times ornamental, polished and chiselled reminding us of the metrical composition practised by the poets of the decadence period. Except these minor weaknesses, his poetry is superb. The *Panchatantra* is very popular amongst the common mass. It does not tell only one story but a cluster of stories. There is a unity and co-ordination in these stories, which is sufficient testimony to the skill of the author. Every story carries some moral. Various translations of *Panchatantra* are available in several languages. Like Aesop's fables, it is enjoyed and was appreciated by common reader.

The characters portrayed in the *Panchatantra* stand for various base and lofty emotions of man. For example, anger, greed, temptation, fraud, double-dealing, duplicity and betrayal in a telling and precise manner. Simplicity of narration is one of the greatest qualities of *Panchatantra*. Characters are embodiment of specific sentiment. The moral tone of these stories can be perceived at every step.

Pandita Rāja Jagannātha: Pandit Rāja Jagannāth was a 17th century critic. He is the last in the great tradition of critics on Samskrit poetics beginning from Bharata. His work *Rasagangādhara* is also the last representative work elevating Samskrit poetics to the high pedestal. He was the court poet of Shāhajahān who conferred upon him the title *Panditarāja*. He enjoyed the patronage of four kings including Jahangira, Jagat Singh, the king of Udayapura, Shāhajahān and Prān Nārāyana. He also wrote *Jagadabharana* praising the exploits and charity of Jagata Singh.

The list of his works includes: *Rasagangādhara, Chitramimāmsā Khandana, Gangālahari*, a collection of 52 *Shlokas* expressing his devotion to the Gangā, *Amritalahari*, showing devotion to Yamunā in 10 Shlokas, *Karmalahari*, invocation to Vishnu in 55 Shlokas, *Lakshmilahari*, prayer to Lakshmi in 41 *Shikharini Chhanda*, *Sudhālahari*, invocation to Surya in 30 *Shragdhara Chhanda*, *Āsafavilāsa*, narrating the life and achievements of Shāhjahān's general and relative Āsaf Khan, which is incomplete; *Prānabharana*, a prayer of Kāmarupa king Prāna Nārāyana and *Bhāmini Vilāsa*, a collection of miscellaneous verses. He has also written a book on grammar *Manorāmakuchamardana*. There is a hearsay that the Samrāt of Delhi, Shāhjahān used to offer him a pair of betel leaves to acknowledge his scholarship; shows his respect for him. Pandita Rāja was a very daring and self-esteem person. He was not in the habit of borrowing the illustrions from other works, rather he preferred to formulate the illustrations out of his own effort which he has himself accepted in one of the Shlokas-*Nirmayā nutanmudaharananurupam, kāvyasya mayatra kartum na parasya kinchita, kim sevyate sumansā mansapi gandha, kasturi*".

Pānini: Pānini is the erudite grammarian who is held in high esteem: both by Indian and Western scholars. He is the first grammarian and linguist to give an elaborate discussion on the origin of *dhātus* and inflexion. He is rightly called the originator of the philosophy of grammar. His popularity rests on his significant work *Ashtādhyāyi*. Besides *Ashtādhyāyi*, he has also written *Dhātupada, Ganapada, Unādisutra, Lingānushāsana* and *Shikshā* Sutra, which are related to Phonetics. He has also written two poetical works: *Jāmbavati-Vijaya* and *Pātālavijaya*. One more kāvya *Pārvati Parinaya* has also been attributed to him. In Shridharadāsa's *Saduktikarnāmrita*, name of Dakshiputra comes along with Subandhu, Kālidāsa, Harishchandra, Sura, Bhiaravi and Bhavabhuti. Dakshiputra is none other but Pānini. *Jāmbavativijaya* narrates the story of Krishna getting married to Jāmbavati after overpowering her father.

His *Ashtādhyāyi* is a great contribution to Samskrit grammar, which paved the way for subsequent grammarians to work along the same lines. Pānini begins with the study of the roots of words and proceeds on to discuss their manifold possibilities of meaning. Several commentators have tried to elaborate the basic principles laid down in *Ashtādhyāyi* as it is the product of a mastermind, no one could succeed in explaining the hidden meaning of this immortal work.

Kātyāyana or Vararuchi made efforts to throw light on the principles and rules laid down in the *Ashtādhyāyi* and succeeded to some extent in explaining them in detail.

Patanjali in his *Mahābhāshya* made successful effort to render the difficult portion of *Ashtādhyāyi* easily accessible and readily available to the average reader. Still Pānini's *Ashtādhyāyi* is considered the epitome of Samskrit grammar and linguistics. It was Pānini who for the first time made a full length study of the different parts of Samskrit grammar on the Vedic lines borrowing the example from the Vedas and other classical works.

Parāshar and ***Parāsharsmriti:*** Parāshar was a scholar of *Phalita Jyotisha*. His lone work is *Brihatparāsharahorā*. It is concluded from his *Brihatparāsharahorā* that he is the predecessor of

Vārāhamihira. The text has been divided into 97 Chapters, which includes various aspects pertaining to astrological symbols.

It is believed that Astrologer Parāshar is different from Parāshar Rishi, the author of Parāshar Smriti. They cannot be confused for each other. The antiquity of *Parāsharasmriti*, a text of Smrti written by Parāshar, can be evinced from the fact that as many as 39 Shlokas from Parāshar Smriti are available in *Garuda Purāna*. Its commentary by Mādhava is more authentic which was published from Mumbai Samskritamālā. The contents of *Parāsharsmriti* are as follows- teachings of religion to saints by Parāshar, division of four *Yugas*, study of the Vedas, worship of gods, compliments to guests, means of livelihood of *Kshatriya, Vaishya and Shudra, Grihastha Dharma*, purification of impurities after birth and death, punishment awarded to a wife abandoning her husband who is either pauper, foolish or victim of incurable disease, remarriage of a woman, reward to a chaste woman, purification after killing a woman, Vaishya and Shudra, purification by performing Chandrāyana after coitus with a forbidden woman, rules of consuming food, five types of bath and shunning of omen.

Pārijātaharana: Pārijātaharan is an epic written by the 16th century poet Karnapura. The story of this epic is based on *Harivansha Purāna*. Once Nārada offered a Pārijāta flower to Krishna, which the latter handed over to Rukmini, which irked Satyabhāmā, his other queen. Krishna met her grievance by promising her Pārijāta tree. He asked Indra to spare a Pārijāta tree for him, which the latter refused. Krishna along with Pradyumna, Satyaki and Satyabhāmā invaded Indra and brought the Pārijāta tree back to his kingdom.

Pārijātaharana Champu: Pārijāt-harana Champu deals with the story of taking back the Pārijāta tree from Indra by Krishna as narrated in *Haribansa Purāna*. The authorship of this Champu is attributed to the 16th century poet Shesha Krishna. This text was compiled by the poet after seeking permission from king Narottama. It consists of five *Stavakas*.

Parsvabhyudaya: Parsvabhyudaya is a kāvya aimed at communicating the message of the poet to his beloved written by a 9th century poet Jinasenāchārya. He belonged to the reign of the *Rāshtrakuta* king Amoghavarsha. It is based on Kālidās's *Meghaduta*.

Pārthasārathi Mishra: Pārthasārathi Mishra represents Bhatta branch of the *Mimāmsā* School of philosophy. He belongs to the 12th century. He has brought Bhatta ideology to new heights through his works. His works include two original texts and two commentaries- *Tantraratna, Nyāyaratnākara*, *Nyāyaratnamālā* and *Shāstra Dipikā*. The first two are commentaries on Kumārila Bhatta's *Tuptika Shlokavartikā*. *Shāstra Dipikā* is the most celebrated work of Pārthasārathi Mishra for which he has been conferred upon the title *Mimāmsa Kesari*. In this book, he has successfully rejected the doctrines of *Buddha, Jaina, Nyāya, Vaishesihka, Advaita Vedānta* and *Prabhākara*. More than dozen commentaries are extant on it, of which those of Somanātha and Appaya Dikshita entitled *Mayukhamālikā* and *Mayukhāvali* are prominent.

Patanjali : Patanjali is the author of monumental work on grammar Mahābhāshya, a commentary on Pānini's *Ashtādhyāyi*. Patanjali has done a great sarvice to Samskrit literature by writing this *Mahābhāshya*. In ancient literature, Patanjali is addressed by several names, for instance: *Gonardiya, Godikaputra, Nāganātha* and *Vahipati*. In Samskrit literature three books are usually assigned to Patanjali: *Sāmavediya Nidāna Sutra*, *Yajnasutra* and *Mahābhāshya*. There is also an inkling that he improved upon *Charaka Samhitā*, a book of Ayurveda. In Yuktidipika, a commentary on *Sāmkhyakārika* the opinion of Patanjali on *Sāmkhya* philosophy has been cited. Max Muller has acknowledged only one man as the author of *Yoga Darshana* and *Nidāna Sutra*. Bhartrihari too, in his *Vākpadiya* has accepted Patanjali as the author of *Yoga Sutra, Vyākarana Mahābhāshya* and *Charakavartikā*. Most of the modern scholars hold that the authors of yoga and grammar are one and the same and he is Patanjali. Little is known about the life history of Patanjali. According to *Patanjali Charita*, written by Rāmabhadra Dikshita, Patanjali was *Sheshāvatāra*. He hailed from Gondarda and the name of his mother was Gunikā.

Patanjali's Mahābhāshya is an elucidation of Pānini's *Ashtādhyāyi*. Its superstructure is laid on it. It has 85 *Ahnikā* or parts. According to Bhartrihari, Patanjali's *Mahābhāshya* is not only a book of grammar, but it touches the periphery of many studies. It is evident from *Mahābhāshya* that Patanjali had studied all the books of grammar written earlier and had diligently and carefully observed all the Vedic and popular uses of words before writing his book. There is no question on grammar, which is left untouched by the author of *Mahābhāshya*. In Pānini's Ashtādhyāyi there are 3995 *Sutras* but Patanjali has presented his comments only on 1689 *Sutras* and has accepted other *Sutras* as they are. Patanjali has also aptly replied to the objections raised by Kātayāyana and accepted the opinion of Pānini as valid. He has used adjectives like *Bhagavāna, Āchārya, Māngalika, Suhrida* etc.

In Mahābhāshya some original and fundamental principles of grammar have also been put forward. According to Patanjali, there is eternal relationship between word and meaning. Word has the capability to convey the meaning which is inherent in it, otherwise it is hidden in its womb. According to him, there are fourfold meanings of words—Guna, Kraya, Ākriti and Dravya. Ākriti remains constant even after change in Dravya. Patanjali has stated that gender is not determined by grammar. It is a matter of usage. It is the work of grammar to systematise and co-ordinate. It refines a word and makes it fit for proper use. Patanjali seems in favour of popular usage what may be called *Lokāvyavahara*. He raised grammar to the height of philosophy. He also dilated upon *sphotavāda* and thus conceived a word with parity of God, which he named Shabda Brahman.

Pavana Duta: Pavan Duta is a poem aimed at communicating message compiled by Vādichandra Suri. He belongs to the 17th century. It is based on Kālidāsa's *Meghaduta*. The texture of the story has been imaginatively woven by the Jain poet Vādichandra Suri. The entire 101 shlokas have been written in Madākrāntā Chhanda. *Pavanaduta* narrates the story of the king of Ujjayani, Vijaya Naresha who seeks assistance of wind (*pavana*) to communicate his message to his wife Tārā who has been abducted by a Vidyādhara named Ashanivega. *Pavana* gives the message of the king to Tārā and urges upon Vidyādhara to permit Tārā to join the fold of her husband. Vidyādhara gives his consent and thus, it becomes easy for Tārā to enjoy the fold of her husband. The poet has resorted to simple and lucid language throughout his kāvya.

Prabhākar Mishra: Prabhākar Mishra is one of the eminent exponents of the Mimāmsā school of philosophy who latter on dissented with his teacher Kumarila Bhatta and established a distinct branch of philosophy. Dr. Keith has refused to admit this fact and has held that Kumarila was the successor of Prabhākar. Prabhakara has compiled two commentaries on Sabarbhāshya entitled *Brihati* on *Nibandhana* and *Lāghvi* or *Vivarana* to establish independent hypothesis. *Nibandhana* consists of 1200 Shlokas and *Lāghvi* contains 6000 Shlokas. Prabhākara's disciple Sālikanātha Mishra has written commentaries entitled *Deepshikhā* and *Rijuvimala* on Prabhākara's works.

Prabodhachandrodaya : Prabodha Chandrodaya is an example of *Pratika* (symbolic) drama written by Shri Krishna Mishra. He belonged to the period of Kirtirvermā. In this way, Shri Krishna Mishra's timing could be around 1100 A.D. since one of the inscriptions of Kirtivermā engraved in 1098 has been unearthed. *Prabodhachandrodaya* is a philosophical drama aimed at propounding the invincibility of the theory of monism. It consists of six acts in which the dramatist has brought home the ideas that man forgets his real identity out of lust for power. In the larger interest of a better future man must give up lust for power. Unwarranted craving for power sows the seeds of ignorance in his heart and adversely affects knowledge. He manages to regain the true knowledge using his discretion or wisdom. Recourse to the worship of Vishnu and study of the *Upanishada* are necessary to have wisdom. The dramatist has succeeded in maintaining a balance between the philosophy of Monisrn and *Vaishnava* cult.

Prajapati Smriti: Prajāpati Smriti text has been attributed to Prajāpati. It deals with various aspects of Hindu code. The antiquity of Prajapati Smriti has been confirmed in the sense that various shlokas from this text have been cited in Baudhāyana *Dharmasutra* and *Mitākshara*.

Prakarana: Prakarana is a kind of *Rupaka*. It resembles drama in many ways. It is different from drama in the sense that the hero of *Prakarana* is dauntless, Brāhman by Varna, minister or Vanika. It consists of 10 acts. *Mrikshakatika* is the most popular of all *Prakaranas*. *Mrikshakatika* throws ample light on existing sociopolitical scenario, the growing disparity, chaos and anarchy gripping the entire society within its range. *Mālatimādhava* is another important contribution to this form of drama.

Besides these two, some other popular *prakaranas* include *Mallikamāruta*, *Kaumudimitrānanda*, *Prabuddha Rauhaniya* and *Mudrita Kumudachandra*. *Mallikamāruta* has been written by the 17th century poet Uddanda. It consists of 10 acts and its plot construction is similar to that of *Mālati Mādhava*. *Kaumudimitrānanda* is a less significant work of *Prakarana* lacking in fundamental elements. It has been written by Rāmachandra. *Prabuddha Rauhaniya* is aimed at communicating Jain ideology through a popular story. It has been written by the 13th century Jain Saint Rāmabhadramani. The plot of *Mudritkumudachandra* also revolves round the religious beliefs of Jainism. It deals with the debate held between *Svetāmbara Jain* saint Dayāsuri and *Digambara* saint Kumudachandra in which the latter comes out triumphantly. It has been written by Yashachandra.

Prasannarāghava: Prasannarāghava is a drama written by Jayadeva. It is based on the Rāmāyana. Jayadeva has tried to model the story of Rāmāyana on the pattern of drama. He lacks the talent of Bhavabhuti in the portrayal of the feelings and emotions of the characters. Nothing substantial about the personal life of Jayadeva has emerged from this book. He was entirely different form the author of *Geetagovinda* who was the court-poet of the 12th century king of Bengāl, Lakshmana Sena.

The entire drama has been divided into seven acts. Jayadeva is so much infatuated by the story of *Bālakānda* that it has been stretched up to four acts of his drama. In the **first act** preparation for the *svayambara* of Sitā is under way. The **second act** dilates upon the first Rāma-Sitā meeting that took place in the garden of Janaka. In the **third act**, Vishvāmitra along with Rāma and

Lakshmana makes his gracious presence at the court of Janaka. Janaka is moved by the beauty of Rāma but the vow of Sitā disheartens him. Rāma finally wins the hands of Sitā by breaking the bow of Lord Shiva. This led to a rift between Rāma and Parasurāma, an ardent devotee of Lord Shiva. In the **fourth act** Parasurāma is finally pacified. The incidents of the banishment of Rāma and death of Dasaratha are narrated through the dialogue among Gangā, Yamunā and Sarswati in the **fifth act**. The incident of the abduction of Sitā. The adventures of Hanumāna also get reflected here. The frustration of Rāma is depicted in the **sixth act**. In the **seventh** and final act Rāma and Rāvana prepare for the final showdown, which culminates into the elimination of the latter.

From the artistic point – of – view there is much to be derived from *Prasannarāghava* but it fails miserably as a drama. The dramatist has failed to give a dramatic treatment to the entire story.

Prashastapada: Prashastapada was an eminent scholar of the Vaisheshika School of philosophy. He has written an authentic book *Padārthadharma-samgraha*. He belongs to the 2nd half of the 4th century. The Chinese translation of this book was made in 648 A.D. An eminent Japanese scholar Dr. Uie has rendered the English translation of this book. Instead of making an analysis of *Vaisheshika Sutras*, this text aims at expounding the *Vaisheshika* ideology. He wrote his work taking a cue from the philosophical ideology of the school of Nyāya. Several commentaries on *Padārthadharma-samgraha* have appeared. The oldest among them is that of Vyomashikhāchārya's *Vyomāvati Bhāshya*.

Padārthadharmasamgraha is also referred to as *Prashastapada Bhāshya*. It is considered the most accomplished work of *Vaisheshika* philosophy after *Vaisheshika Surta*. The text deals with the creation and annihilation of the world, 24 *gunas*, *Parmanuvāda* and different means of *pramāna*.

Prashnopanishada: Prashnopanishada ia a text of the Pippalāda branch of Atharvaveda. Since the text is restricted to answering the questions of the saints like Sukesha, Satyavāna, Ashvalāyana, Bhārgava, Kātyāyana and Kabandhi by hermit Pippalāda, it is entitled *Prashnopanishada*. It is a prose work and questions pertaining to spirituality have been raised in it. Pippalāda has tried to find out solutions to various problems concerning spirituality. While answering these questions, he has tried to establish *Parama Brahman* as the guardian of this world and has repeatedly insisted on the worship of *Omkāra*.

The questions raised by various seers include genesis of all the creatures of the world, the force behind the enlightenment of all gods and goddesses, the root cause of the *prānas*, ways through which *prānas* enter human body, mystery about the conscious, Sub-conscious and unconscious state of man, outcome of the worship of *Omkāra* and nature *of Parama Brahma*n.

Pratigyayaugandharāyana: Pratigya Yaugadharāyana is a drama written by Bhāsa dealing with the story of the abduction of Vāsavadattā, the daughter of king of Ujjaini, Pradyota by the king of Kausambi, Udayana. It consists of **four acts**. The **first act** begins with the promise made by Yaugandharāyana, the courtier of Udayan to set Udayana free from the clutches of his enemies. Udayana was trapped in the snare of the benefactors while he was scheduled to go for hunting an elephant. He disguises himself by putting on the cloak offered by Vyāsamuni. In the **second act**, the news of internment of Udayana is brought to the notice of Pradyota who instructs his followers to bring Udayana to his court and accord the treatment of a king to him. Meanwhile, preparations for the marriage of Vāsavadattā are in full swing with the queen announcing Udayana as her perfect match. In the **third act**, Yaugandharāyana, disguising his real identity appears in the kingdom of Pradyota. In the **fourth act** Udayana who is in love with Vāsavadattā gives training to her to play on music, Udayana manages to elope with her. Meanwhile, all the messengers of Udayana including Yaugandharāyana are arrested and sent to prison. In the prison, Yaugandharāyana successfully refutes all the allegations levelled by Bharatarohaka, minister of Pradyota against Udayana and the latter.

Pleased with this he offers him a pot made of gold which the latter refuses to accept. Yaugandharāyana accepts the offer of

Bharatarohaka. Pradyota agrees to unite his daughter to Udayana in a wedding tie. The drama ends with *Bharatavākya*.

The dramatic craftsmanship of Bhāsa is seen in this drama at every step. Bhāsa has succeeded in striking a balance between the theme and the characterisation. He has skillfully maintained its organic unity. His ability as a mature dramatist is reflected in plot-construction, characterisation and dialogue, specially the characters of Udayana and Yaugandharāyana from whose promise the title of the drama has been derived.

Pratimā Nātaka: Pratimā Nātaka is a drama written by Bhāsa dealing with the story of Rāma right from his departure to forest till the death of Rāvana. It is divided into seven acts. The first act deals with the preparation for the coronation of Rāma and in the 7th act meeting of Rāma and Bharata takes place and the throne is handed over to Rāma. With *Bharatavākya*, the drama comes to an abrupt end.

The dramatist has evoked a fair amount of curiosity by giving a new twist to the traditional story of the Rāmāyana. He broke away a different path from the traditional story and succeeded in creating dramatic effect by introducing the idols of Iksvāku kings. Bharata faints after watching the idol of his dead father. It is a novel imagination of Bhāsa and has incurred amazing success by creating dramatic effect. In the same way Sitā putting on saffron dress out of humour in the first act presages the forthcoming incident. The originality of Bhāsa lies in giving a new turn to the theme of abduction of Sitā. Rāvana asks Rāma to bring golden deer to perform *Shrāddha* and manages to kidnap Sitā when Rāma is out in the forest to fetch the golden deer. The dramatist has succeeded to a great extent in cleansing the stains put on Kaikeyi's character. Kaikeyi's assertion that Dasaratha's errand of fourteen years banishment to Rāma was meant to fulfill the curse of the parents of Shravana. It was ordained. She was only an instrument in the hands of God to execute the curse. Therefore, Dasaratha himself was responsible for his separation from his dear son, which caused his death. She was not to blame. The decision of Rāma's exile was a unanimous decision. It was concurred by the saints. Rāma's exile was necessary to weed out the demons. She confessed that she had demanded fourteen years banishment to Rāma out of sheer mental anguish and slip of tongue. She uttered fourteen years in place of fourteen days. In this way, Bhāsa has succeeded in carving his characters to a new height removing the disgrace on their personality.

Pratisākhya: Pratisākhya is a part of one of the *Vedānga-Shikshā*. These texts are important in two ways. They contain seeds of Samskrit grammar and these texts consist of facts dealing with the recitations and nature of Vedic *Samhitās*. Although they are not grammar in the true sense of the term, they display certain facts associated with grammar. Samskrit grammar begins with the *Pratisākhya*. Some *Pratisākhyas* also deal with Vedic *Chhandas*. The subjects that they contain include *Uchchārana* (pronunciation), *Swara, Samdhi, Harasva* and subjects related to Samhitā. Each Veda has its own *Pratisākhya*. *Rik Pratisākhya* is the *Pratisākhya* of Rig Veda and *Vājasaneyi-Pratisākhya* is the *Pratisākhya* of Shukla Yajurveda. *Pushpasutra* is the *Pratisākhya* of Sāmaveda, and *Atharva Veda Pratisākhya* is the *Pratisākhya* of the Atharvaveda.

Priyadarshikā: Priyadarshikā is a drama written by Harshavardhana. The title is based on the heroine of the drama of the same name. It consists of four acts. The story has been derived from Gunādhya's *Brihatkathā*. The influence of Kālidāsa's *Malavikāgnimitra* cannot be ignored on the style and mode of composition of the drama. The drama deals with the love-story of king Udayana and Priyadarshikā. The **first act** deals with the violent conflict between Dridharāja, father of Priyadarshikā and the king of Kalinga. The latter's anguish is flared up at the former's failing to comply with his desire to marry his daughter with him. Dridharāja, on the contrary wants his daughter to be married to Udayana. Dridharāja suffers a crushing defeat in the ensuing battle but Kanchuki manages to send Priyadarshikā to Udayana's palace where she stays as the maidservant of queen Vāsavadattā, with a new name Aranyikā. In the **second act**, Udayana and Aranyikā meet each other in the royal orchard and the former protects the latter from the danger of the black–bees, which finally culminate into the generation of the seeds of love into their hearts. In the **third act** a drama is performed on the stage depicting the marital life of Udayana and Vāsavadattā. Udayana plays his role himself while Aranyikā is offered the role of Vāsavadattā. It no longer remains a mere dramatic performance rather the two characters behave as real characters, which infuriates Vāsavadattā who was witnessing the show. In the **fourth act**, Vāsavadattā conspires to put Aranyikā behind the bars. Vāsavadattā's wrath was not calmed down. She was mentally disturbed.

Prithavirājavijaya: Prithvirāja Vijaya is an epic written by the Kashmiri poet Jayanaka dealing with the life and achievements of the last Hindu ruler to the throne of Delhi and Ajmer, Prithvirāja. It is a fragmentary work of which only 12 cantos are available, which comes to an abrupt end with the description of the marriage of Prithvirāja. It also gives a fair amount of description of the predecessors of Prithvirāja. The victories of the Chauhājn king Prithvirāja displaying exemplary valour and heroism against his enemies in the battlefield are not available. Jayanaka, who was patronised by Prithvirāja, wrote this epic eulogising the victories of Prithvirāja achieved against dreaded enemies notable among them being that which was fought between him and Muhammad Gauri in 1191. Unfortunately Prithvirāja lost the next battle at the hand of his toughest opponent Gauri in 1193. In this way this epic must have been written around 1192. Its commentary was written by Jonarājja, whose other commentaries on *Shrikanthacharita* and *Kirājtarjuniya* have also been a great success.

Even if *Prithvirāja Vijaya* is a fragmentary work it throws ample light on the early life of Prthvirāja and his predecessors. In this way, it is a work having profound historical significance. Besides providing enormous historical facts, this epic is in no way inferior to other epics possessing enough literary grandeur. The style of Jayanaka lacks artificiality. There is no deliberate attempt at beautifying the epic using various ornamental poetic devices. Jayanaka seems to have preferred a simple and rhythmical language. The high imaginative pitch, verbal jugglery and amazing descriptive skill are rampant in this epic.

Pulastya Smriti: Pulastya Smriti text has been compiled by Pulastya. The *Shlokas* of *Pulastya Smriti* have been quoted in *Mitākshara*. This text insists on the consumption of meat by *Kshatriya* and *Vaishya* and *Madhu* by *Shudra*.

Purāna: The Purānas are of paramount importance in Indian literature. They present the history and genesis of creation. The credit to popularise Indian culture and civilisation goes to the Purānas. Besides history it accommodates Kāvya and architecture within its range. They form the backbone of Indian culture. It also accommodates, geography and polity within its ambit, to give it an extensive treatment. The language of the Purānas is sometimes figurative and hyperbolical. Still they give a glimpse of the origin and development of creation in a manner, which appeals us. The existence of the Purānas can be traced back to the Vedic age. They must have been written earlier than 6th century B.C.

Purānas are called *Panchalakshanasamanvitā*, which consists of *Sarga, Pratisarga, Vansa*, *Manvantara* and *Vansānucharita*. *Sarga* signifies creation of all kinds of objects. *Pratisarga* is opposite to *sarga*, which represents *pralaya* (annihilation, delude). The annihilation of the universe is caused in four ways *Naimittika* (purposeful) *Prākritika* (natural) *Nitya* (eternal) and *Ātyāntika* (immediate reasons). *Vansa* includes the dynasties of all the kings that flourished from Brahman. *Manavantara* includes *Manu, Devatā* (Deity) *Manuputra, Indra, Rishi* (Seer), and the incarnation of God. *Manavantaras* are 14 in number and each *Manavantara* has its own Manu. The analysis of the character trait of eminent personalities belonging to prominent dynasties forms the basis of *Vansānucharita*.

Roughly the Purānas are numbered 18 but the controversy lingers about it and have been arranged in a specific order beginning with creation and ending with annihilation of the universe. In this way the order of the Purāna preferred in *Vishnu Purāna* has been accepted. *Brahma Purāna* occupies the primal position in the order since Brahma is instrumental in the creative process. It is followed by *Padma, Vishnu, Vāyu, Bhāgavata, Nārada, Mārkandeya, Agni, Bhavishya, Brahmavaivarta, Linga, Vārāha, Skanda, Vāmana,*

Kurma, Matasya, Garuda and *Brahmānda Purāna. Garuda Purāna* narrates the situation arising out of the death of human beings whereas *Brahmānda Purāna* is confined to the treatment meted out to *Jiva* on the basis of his action. In this way, these two Purānas have been placed in the lower order.

The Tamil texts have made five categories of Purānas — i) Brahma - It includes *Brahma* and *Padma Purānas*, ii) Surya - *Brahmavaivarta Purāna*, iii) Agni – *Agni Purāna*, iv) Shiva- *Shiva, Skanda, Linga, Kurma, Vārāha, Bhavishya, Matsya, Mārkandeya* and *Brahmānda Purāna*. The rest are in the 5th catagory.

Like Purānas, Up-Purānas, which are equally significant, are 18 in number. They lay emphasis on religious beliefs of various communities. The Up Purānas include Sanatkumāra Up-Purāna, Narsimha, Nandi, Shiva, Dharma, Durvāsā, Nārdiya, Kapila, Mānava, Ushāsa, Brahmānda, Varuna, Kālikā, Vashishtha, Linga, Maheshvara, Samba, Saura, Parāshar, Māricha and Bhārgava.

The importance of the Purāna is self-evident. The Purāna provides a true description of religion supported by the Vedas in a language which is simple lucid and vivid. It was deliberately made simple when the languages of the Vedas became out of reach of the common mass. The history given in the Purānas is reiterated and supported by the carvings of the stones and coins, and the observations made by the foreigners. The style of the Purānas is inflated and exaggerated. This is why a common reader does not pin up his faith in it. But the fact remains that the Purānas give a true picture of the socio-political, religious and cultural history of India in all dimensions.

In Jainism also, Vedas, Upanishadas and Purānas have been compiled. Purānas are the texts highlighting the life of Jain saints and eminent figures. The eminent personalities have been referred as *salākāpurusha* who are 63 in number, which include 24 *Tirthankaras*, 12 *Chakravarti*, 9 *Baladeva*, 9 *Vāsudeva* and 9 *Prativāsudevas*. ■■

Rāghavapāndaviya: Rāghavapāndaviya is an epic written by Kavirāja. The stories of the Rāmayana and the Mahābhārata have been intertwined within this epic. Placing himself in the category of Subandhu and Bānabhatta, he says that no other name could be added to the list that wrote special kind of poetry called *Bhangimāmaya Shlesharachanā*. He was the court poet of Kāmadeva of Kadamba dynasty who ruled between 1182 and 1187 A.D. This epic consists of 19 Cantos. Both the stories of the Rāmāyana and the Mahābhārata have been presented concurrently. Rāma and his associates have been depicted along with Yudhisthira and his associates whereas Rāvana and his attendants have been depicted along with Duryodhana and his attendants.

The epic fulfils all the necessary pre-requisites of an epic. Rāma and Yudhisthira are the heroes and *Vira rasa* is its dominant *rasa*. The epic begins with the invocation, which is followed by the condemnation of the wicked and the praise of the pious. Both Pāndu and Dasaratha have been pitted against each other. The story of their hunting and the curse of the saint have been skillfully presented. The story of the birth of their sons has also been depicted in the like tone. Parallelism has been maintained by depicting Rāma's departure along with *Vishwāmitra* and Yudhisthira's leaving for *Varnāvata*. Similarity has been shown in the deaths of Tarakā and Hidimbā and the *svayamvara* of Sitā and Draupadi, and depriving of Rāma and Yudhisthira of their due share with the help of Mantharā in the case of Rāma and that of Shakuni in the case of Yudhisthira. Finally, the chopping off ten heads of Rāvana has been compared with the breaking of Duryodhana's thigh. Some of these comparisons obviously are far-fetched. The cutting of Jatāyu's wings by Rāvana and the humiliation of Jayadratha by Bhima and the death of Rāvana's son

Devantaka and the killing of Abhimanyu are the episodes which have been deliberately interlinked with one another and may be called just an example of dove-tailing.

Raghuvansam: Raghuvansam is an epic written by Kālidāsa. It deals with the gallantry and heroism of the kings of Surya Dyanasty in 19 Cantos. Kalidas's creative faculty reaches the highest peak in *Raghuvansa*. He has thrown his weight behind the portrayal of various facets of the kings of this dynasty. He brought the tradition of epic writing to a new pedestal bringing out a vital change in the treatment of the subject by using his wit and artistic skill. He has accorded his work the epical grandeur giving extensive coverage to his portrayal. Scholars are of the opinion that the *laksanas* (characteristics) of epic poetry were drawn out taking into account Kālidāsa's *Raghvamsam*.

The *epic begins* with the invocation to God followed by the description of general features of the personality of the kings of *Raghuvansa*. His description begins with the lively account of the activities of king Dilip. He reaches the hermitage of Vashistha along with his wife Sudakshinā in the hope that he will be blessed with the successor to his throne and he seeks the blessings of the cow *Nandini* in the hermitage.

In the **second canto** fidelity to the king towards the cow is put to the acid test. *Nandini* is trapped in the shakles of an imaginary lion and king Dilip offers his life to the lion in return for that of *Nandini*. Pleased with the generosity of the king, Nandini blesses him with a son. The king returns to his capital after taking permission from his teacher. The **third canto** deals with the birth of Raghu, his elevation to the post of heir-apparent and performance of *Ashvamedha Yajna* by Dilip. This canto concludes with Dilip along with Sudakshinā departing to forest to spend the rest of his life as ascetic. The **fourth canto** deals with the all round conquests of Raghu, and **the fifth** is devoted to the depiction of Raghu's charity. Due to excess of donation his fund runs short. At this critical moment, a celibate named Kautsa demands 14 crore gold coins from the king. In it the king invades Kuber and brings back 14 crore gold coins to pacify the grievances of the celibate. Kautsa returns with the blessings of a son to the king. The **sixth Canto** deals with the incident of Raghu participating in the *svayamvara* of Indumati. The **seventh Canto** deals with the marriage of Raghu with Indumati and Ajā's victory over envious kings. The **eighth Canto** deals with the benevolence of Ajā, death of Raghu, birth of Dasarath, death of Indumati following the falling of the garland of Nārada, the message of peace by Vashishtha and death of Ajā. The **ninth canto** eulogises the rule of Dasaratha, his marriage, his hunting, killing of Shravana unknowingly, and the curse of Shravana's father on to Dasaratha. The **tenth Canto** deals with *Putreshti* Yajna performed by Dasaratha for being blessed with sons, gods urging upon Vishnu to lessen the weight of the earth by freeing it from evil forces. The **Eleventh**, the **twelfth** and the **thirteenth Cantos** are devoted to the story of Rāma. The eleventh, and the **twelfth canto** presents the killing of Tāraka, Shurpanakhā and Rāvana; and the **thirteenth Canto** narrates the return of Victorious Rāma to *Ayodhyā* by *Pushpaka Vimāna* along with Sitā and Laxman. The **fourteenth Canto** deals with the coronation of Rāma and the banishment of Sitā; and the **fifteenth Canto** presents the killing of Lāvanāsura by Satrughana, birth of Lava and Kusha, Rāma performing *Asvamedha Yajna* and the establishment of golden idol of Sitā; Vālmiki's advice to Rāma to accept Sitā, and the latter preferring to go to the underworld (*pātāla*) and departure of Rāma to heaven. The **sixteenth Canto** deals with the rule of Kusha establishing his capital in *Kushāvati*, his phantom of Ayodhyā as *Nagaradevi* in the state of dream and his return to Ayodhyā and marriage with Kumudāvati. The **seventeenth canto** deals with the birth of Aditi and death of Kusha. The **eighteenth canto** deals with the heroism of several kings of Raghuvansa and the **nineteenth** is related to the description of the lustful king Agnivarna and his death due to tuberculosis and his widow replacing him to the throne.

Raghuvansa presents not only the story of an individual rather it incorporates the story of several kings of *Raghuvansa*. Kālidāsa has taken special interest in the depiction of the personality of Dilip, Raghu, Ajā, Rāma and Agnivarna. Of these, the characters of Raghu and Rāma have been presented with much gusto and fanfare. While the characters like Raghu and Rāma added to the prestige of *Raghuvansa*; Agnivarna, a debauch and amorous king put a stigma on this glorious dynasty.

Kālidāsahasborrowedimmenselyfromthestoryofthecontemporary Gupta kings while depicting the kings of *Raghuvansa*. There are as many as 40 commentaries available on *Raghuvansa*. Of all the commentaries, that of Mallinātha is very significant and worth mentioning.

Rājanaka Ruyyaka: Rājanaka ruyyaka was an eminent critic who flourished in the second half of the 12th century. His father Rājānaka Tilaka was also a great scholar who has written a commentary entitled *Udbhataviveka* on *Kāvya Alankār Rasa Samgraha*. Ruyyaka has quoted 5 *Shlokas* from Mankhaka's Shrikanthacharita in his text *Alankārsarvasva.*

Ruyyaka is a staunch supporter of the theory of *Dhvani*. He has presented a gist of the opinion of Bhāmaha, Udbhata, Rudrata, Vāmana, Kuntaka, Māhimbhatta and Ānandavardhana at the beginning of his monumental work *Alankārasarvasva*. It also presents a mature analysis of various kinds of *Alankāras*. Besides this, his other works include *Sahridayalilā*, *Sāhityamimāmsā*. *Nātakamimāmsā*, *Alankāranusarini*, *Alankārmanjari, Alankāravartikā*, *Shrikanthastana*, *Harishacharitavartikā, Vyaktivivek-Kāvyākhyānavichāra*. *Sāhityamimāmsā*, is a work on poetics which consists of 8 *Prakaranas*. It is divided into *Kārika*, *Vritti* and illustrations. It includes various subjects pertaining to poetics such as description of poet and aesthetician, *Vritti* and its kinds, defects of *Pada*, merits of *Kāvya, Alankāra, Rasa*, kinds of poets, and pleasure of *Kāvya* (*kāvyānand*).

Ruyyaka has contributed substantially to Samskrit poetics. He not only borrowed the ideas of his predecessors, he also gave his own critical formulations and a new approach in the analysis of various aspects of poetics. Later critics like Vidyādhara Vidyānātha and Shobhākara Mishra have borrowed immensely from the doctrinal position of Ruyyaka with regard to *Alankāra*.

Rājashekhara: Rājashekhara was an eminent dramatic critic. He has thrown ample light on his personal life in the preface to his dramas. He was born in a Brāhamin family in Mahārāshtra, with a sound literary background. His wife Avantisundari, having a Kshatriya lineage was a great scholar and poetess of *Prākrit* and *Samskrit*. Her ideologies have been referred to by Rājashekhar in his work *Kāvyamimāmsā*. He was the teacher of Mahendrapāla, the king of *Kānyakubja*, and Mahipāla. According to the inscriptions of the *Pratihāra* dynasty, Mahipāla flourished in the beginning of the 10th century. In this way, Rājashekhar can be placed in the 10th century.

Rajesekhara's works includes 4 dramas, 5 *Prabandha Kāvya* and one anthology on poetics. Besides the five *Prabandhas*, one more *Haravilāsa* has been mentioned in *Kāvyānusāsana*. *Kāvyamimāmsā* is a work on literary criticism. This work is fragment though 18 chapters are available. It is an encyclopaedia incorporating almost all topics pertaining to poetics. His four dramas are *Bāla Rāmāyana*, *Bāla Mahābhārata*, *Viddhasālabhanjikā* and *Karpuramanjari*.

A cursory glance over the dramas of Rājashekhar reveals that he was a better poet than a drāmatist. His dramas are not meant to be staged. They are for thorough reading. His narrative technique, which is a major hurdle in the way of his dramas, accords him a distinct position as a poet. *Bāla Rāmāyana* has been written in 10 acts and the episode of the *Rāmāyana* has been given a dramatic garb. It consists of 74 verses. Of these, 200 verses have been written in *Shārdulavikridita* and 86 verses have been written in *Shragdhara Chhanda*. He has unnecessarily stretched his description, which causes waywardness and monotony. The incident of Rāma's return to *Ayodhyā* in the last act covering 105 verses is redundant, and is apt to affect the beauty of the drama. Rājashekhar has shown special attraction for *Shārdulavikridita Chhanda,* and his infatuation for this Chanda has been referred to by Kshemendra in *Suvrittisraka*. He has been referred to as *'sabdakavi'* (a poet showing excellence in the use of words). His descriptive skill and the use of *Alankāras* have placed him in the category of the poets of first rank. He has made full use of his imagination in his descriptions. Use of Idioms and phrases has added new colour and flavour to his narration.

Bāla Mahābhārata deals with the story of the *Mahābhārata*. Only first two acts of this drama are available. Viddhasālabhanjikā is a mini drama (*Nātikā*) of four acts dealing with the marriage of Mrigānkavati, daughter of Samrāta Vidyādhara Malla. *Karpuramanjari* is also a miniature drama consisting of 4 acts. It is also called *Shattaka*.

Rājatarangini: Rājatarangini by Kalhana, is the most successful historical epic ever written in Samskrit. It is also a historical document, which deals with the history of kings of Kashmir beginning with Govindās in 1200 B.C. and concludes with the description of contemporary kings of the 12th century. It gives a vivid description of the socio-cultural condition of Kashmir including its geographical topography. It is divided in to eight *tarangas*. The eighth *taranga* is so big that it overweighs the other seven *tarangas*. The description of the first three *tarangas* are based on *Pauranic* text but lack historical touch. Chronological order is also missing. The **fourth *taranga*** is exclusively devoted to the *Kārākota* dynasty, which is also embedded with *Pauranic* treatment. It is a fact that the descriptions given by Kalhana do not stand in good stead, if they are examined from modern scientific point of view. The real historical account is presented from the **fifth *taranga*** onwards with the reign of Avanti Vermā. The **sixth *taranga*** covers the reign of queen Didā. The **seventh *taranga*** deals with the history of and death of Harsha. The **last *taranga*** consists of 3449 verses covering the coronation of Uchchhala till the 12th century. The description of the kings defy date in the beginning. The real description begins with 813-14 A.D. which extends to 119-20 A.D. In this way he has presented a very scientific, exhaustive and perfect description of the history of 400 years of Kashmir. The author takes much interest in describing important incidents, which took place during this span of time. Some of these descriptions are authenticated by later documents. Kalhana has covered a wide period of about 2500 years of the history of Kashmir. The poet has mostly banked upon his imagination and has given exaggerated details. In the beginning of *Rajtarangini*, there is a reference to king Bhupāla, who seems to be a *Purānic* character. He seems to be the product of the author's imagination and wistful thinking.

Rāmachandra and ***Gunachandra:*** Rāmachandra and Gunachandra were critics of *Nātyashāstra*. They have jointly composed *Nātyadarpana*. No other work of Gunachandra is available, Rāmachandra has produced several works most of which are dramas. Both were the disciples of Hemachandra and were great *Jain* scholars. References to 11 dramas of Rāmachandra are available in *Nātyadarpana*. They flourished during the reign of the 12th century kings of Gujarata: Siddharāja, Kumār Pāla and Ajaya Pāla.

Nātyadarpana is a very prominent work on *Nātyashāstra*. It has been written in *Kārika*s on which Rāmachandra has himself written *Vritti*. It is divided into four chapters (*viveka*). The **first *viveka*** deals with the elements of drama and the **second** depicts nine kinds of *Rupakas*. The **third *Viveka*** deals with the elaborate analysis of *Rasas* and dramatic performances. The **fourth *viveka*** deals with *Nāyaka-Nāyikā Bheda* and kinds of up-rupaka. This work has a historical importance in the sense that it refers to 35 dramas which are nowhere available.

Rāmacharita: Rāmacharita is a *Kāvya* based on pun. It has been written by Sandhyākaranandi. He flourished in the later half of the 11th century during the reign of Madana Pāla of Bengāl. The poet has very skillfully depicted the life of Lord Rāma and the king of Pāla dynasty, Rāma Pāla in the same verse showing his amazing authority over pun. He has written this book under the influence of Subandhu and Bāna Bhatta. This kind of writing bearing two levels of meanings was quite in vogue at that time. One such example is *Rāghavapāndaviya* written by Kavirāja presenting the story of the *Rāmāyana* and the *Mahābhārata* simultaneously in identical verses.

Rāmānujāchārya: Rāmānujāchārya was the pioneer of the Vaishnava Sect *Visitstādvaitavāda*. He was born in 1017 A.D. in Madras. His works are *Vedarnha-samgraha* (rebuttal of monoism of Shankarāchārya and Bhāskara's doctrine of *Bhedābheda*), *Vedāntasāra* (commentary on *Brahmnasutra*), *Vedāntadipa* (a detailed analysis of *Brahmansutra*), *Gitābhāshya, Shribhāshya* on *Brahmansutra* using the ideology of *Vishishtādvaitavāda*.

As opposed to Shankara who does not accept the existence of *Jiva* and *Jagata* taking them as a reflection of *Māyā* (illusion), Rāmānuja has accepted the existence of *Jiva, Jagata* and *Ishvara* (God) at one and the same time. Since *Jiva* and *Jagata* are part of God, therefore they too are real, although they manage to retain their independent status. God is both efficient as well as material cause of the world. God is *Visheshya* whereas *Jiva* and *Jagata* are *Visheshana*. *Visheshya* does have an independent existence but *Jiva* and *Jagata*, being *Visheshana*, have no independent existence and they are dependent on God. His theory is called *Visistādvaitdvāda* in the sense that it considers *Advaita Brahman* as *saguna* and *savishesha*. God is both the efficient cause (*nimitta kārana*) and the material cause (*upādāna kārana*) of this world.

Rāmapālacharita: Rāmpālacharita is an epic written by Sandhyākara Nandi. It is an excellent example of *shlesha kāvya*. Besides the story of lord Rāma, the story of the king of *Bengāl*, Rām Pāla has also been interwoven simultaneously giving his verses double sense. Sandhyākara Nandi is placed in the category of those poets who have used *shlesha* and *yamaka* to create a miraculous effect in their verse. He intends to create more effect and colouring by using the strange devices of interweaving multiple stories in the same verse leaving the readers embarrassed or bewildered causing great mental exercise to them. There is a deliberate attempt at verbal jugglery throughout the epic.

The historical facts available in this epic assume special significance since Sandhyākara Nandi was closely associated with the court. His father enjoyed a key post in the court of Rāma Pāla. In this way this epic is primary source to throw light on the history of medieval *Bengāl*. It consists of five Cantos and 220 *Āryas* and those showing least interest in the history of this period might not enjoy the epic in its totality.

Rāmāyana: The Rāmāyana is an epic by the famous sage Vālmiki. There are as may as 24000 couplets in this epic. There is a hearsay that in the beginning Vālmiki was a robber. He used to plunder the travellers and torture the passers by. One day, Nārada came across him and gave him the mantra of Rāma. Vālmiki was allergic to this name, and he wrongly pronounced it *marā* instead of Rāma. But even the continuous recitation of the word *marā,* eventually changed into Rāma, and brought about radical change in the life of Vālmiki. Vālmiki has presented a graphic description of human life in a simple language, and flexible style, which is at once sensuous and attractive. Here and there, he used figurative language to heighten the effect of his poetry.

The entire story of the Rāmāyana has been divided into seven books (*Kāndas*) *Bāla Kānda*, *Ayodhyā Kānda*, *Arnya Kānda*, *Kishkindhā Kānda*, *Sunder Kānda*, *Yuddha Kānda* and *Uttara Kānda*. Each *Kānda* is further divided into *Sargas*. The story of the Rāmāyana revolves round the towering personality of Lord Rāma, though besides the main story of Rāma, various secondary stories have been introduced in *Bāla Kānda* and *Uttara Kānda* which are supposed to have been added at a later date and do not seem to be an integrated whole. Besides the main story of Rāma and his brothers, *Bāla Kānda* deals with various stories narrated by Vishwāmitra to Rāma, such as history of the lineage of Vishwāmitra, birth of the Ganges and Pārvati, birth of Kārtikeya, story of king Sagar and his 60,000 sons, story of Bhagiratha, Diti and Aditi, account of the churning of the ocean, story of Gautama and Ahilyā, liberation of Ahilyā by Rāma, rift between Vashistha and Vishwāmitra, story of Trishanku and king Ambarisa, penance of Vishwāmitra and hindrance created by Menakā.

The heart of the epic is contained in books II to VI that can be divided in two parts. In the first part Dasratha's son Rāma along with his brother Lakshman is handed over to Rishi Vishwāmitra who seeks the assistance of the two princes to perform the *Yajnas* fearlessly which was repeatedly obstructed by the dreaded demons who were deadly against the *Yajnas* performed by the Rishis, Munies and saints. Rāma successfully overcomes the challenges of the demons by killing Tārakā, Subāhu and injuring Māricha. On his way back to Ayodhyā Vishwāmitra stays for a brief interval at Mithilā asking Rāma to attend the *Svayambara* and pacify the grievances of Janaka who was almost uncertain of getting his daughter Sitā married in the event of all the princes assembled in *svayambra* one by one failing to break the bow of

Lord Shiva as part of a condition to win his daughter. Rāma breaks the bow at the instance of his guru Vishwāmitra and wins Sitā for his wife. Rāma had to bear the brunt of Parāshurāma, a staunch admirer of Lord Shiva but was finally pacified by Rāma. Besides Sitā, all the three daughters of Janaka are wedded to the brothers of Rāma.

Rāma is named heir-apparent to the throne of *Ayodhyā* but Kaikeyi, wants to see her son Bharata to be coronated. Rāma is banished for fourteen years. Dasratha collapses. Bharata leaves for the forest to bring Rāma back but Rāma remains committed to his vow and sends Bharata back to rule. This part of the epic is purely human and natural both in its motivation and its events.

The second part of the epic begins with *Aranya Kānda* and is full of supernatural marvels. Its, characters include demons and monkeys and bears and birds. Sugriva, the commander-in-chief of the monkeys and the deposed king of *Kishkindhā*, plays a pivotal role. The friendship between the two is solemnised. Rāma promises him to bring back his wife and his kingdom which was grabbed by his elder brother Bāli Rāma killed Bāli while the two were indulged in a pitched battle. After many marvellous adventures which include killing of Māricha, Khara, Dusana and Trisirā and almost restoring peace to the forest for assured respite of the saints. Rāvana abducts Sita. Rāma, aided by bears and monkeys, including Hanumāna who crossed the sea to find out Sitā and single-handedly burnt the entire kingdom of Rāvana causing great havoc and terror; kills Rāvana and brings Sitā back.

Sitā clears herself of all suspicions of infidelity. Rāma returns to *Ayodhyā* and brings his subjects peace and prosperity.

An introduction and conclusion (Book I to VII) have been added to this story. There is also an attempt to attach it to the worship of Vishnu, book 1st explains that Rāma is an incarnation of Vishnu born at the request of the other gods for the specific purpose of wiping out the demons including Rāvana from the earth. Book VII returns to the gods, who come to Rāma and reveal to him that he is an incarnation of Vishnu. This religious frame work has given the Rāmāyana the status of a sacred text. This epic is recited throughout India and abroad particularly in Thailand, Combodia, Mālāysia and Indonesia; and is familiar to millions of the disciples of lord Rāma who take Rāma and Sitā as their models and strive to follow them in love, friendship, heroism, truth and justice.

Rasagangādhara: Pandit Rāj Jagannāth's Rasagangādhara is a scholarily work. It shows the creative and criticai talent of Panditraj. Its style is terse and pedantic. Here and there the author has tried to show his originality in the postulation of his theory. In respect of giving emphasis on the nature of poetry, its division and its object Panditraj has created a new path. In giving prime importance to *Ramniyārtha* and *Chamatakār* as the twin poetic traits he is probably the foremost Samskrit rhetorical composer, and it is probably his greatest contribution to Samskrit poetics. His style is original and thought provoking and has described poetry as something which formulates fantastic meaning (*Rāmaniyartham Pratipadakah Sabdah Kāvyam*). The book consists of *Kārika*, Vritti's and illustration, which is attributed to the author. His scholarship gets reflected in his Vritti in which he viciously interpreted the theory of *rasa* and *Vyanjana* throwing new light, which is unique. Nāgeshabhatta has written a commentary on it entitled *Marmaprakāsha*.

Rāsmanjari: Rasmanjari is a mature work on *Nāyaka-Nāyikā-bheda* written by Bhānudatta. He is an erudite scholar and a critic of *Rasa* School. *Rasmanjari* has been written in order to satiate the appetite of a man who is dying of thrust. It gives a systematic account of *Nāyikā Bheda*. He has made three broad divisions of *Nāyikās* named *Swakiyā, Parakiyā* and *Sāmānya*. Further he has made three divisions of *Swakiyā* named *mugdhā, madhyā* and *pragalbhā*. Mugdhā is again divided into two categories named *gyāta yauvanā* and *agyāta yauvanā*.

Ratnāvali: Ratnāvali is a minor drama written by Harsh. It deals with the love affair of Udayana and Ratnāvali, the daughter of Singhalesvar. It consists of four acts. The minister of Udayana, Yaugandharāyana, is moved by prophecies that the husband of Ratnāvali, would be a *chakravarti* king. In a bid to get Ratnāvali married to Udayana, he sends a message to her father. Vāsavadattā was a major hurdle so he spreads a rumour that Vāsavadattā died of burning. Singhalesvar sent Ratnāvali along a minister Vasumati but she meets a miserable shipwreck and is finally handed over to Yaugadharāyana by the businessmen that caught hold of her. He gave her the name Sāgarikā and placed her before Vāsavadattā hoping that Udayana might be attracted towards her.

This information is given in the *Vishkambhaka* of the drama. After that, the formal drama begins. The **first act** begins with the festival. Vāsavadattā invites the king to participate in the prayer of Cupid. In order to avoid the meeting of the king with Sāgarikā, Vāsavadattā asks her to hand over the materials of worship to her which she had brought for *Kanchana Mālā*. Sāgarikā stealthily observes the prayer and is infatuated towards the king at the very first glance.

In the **second act** Sāgarikā draws the portrait of Udayana on a canvas and shows it to her friend Susangatā. In the meanwhile a monkey appears on the scene to create turmoil which forces the two ladies to quit the place leaving the portrait there. After a brief interval, the king also reaches to the place and sees the portrait. With the help of Susangatā, Sāgarikā is introduced to the king. Their meeting does not persist for long and they are separated after the arrival of Vāsavadattā. Unfortunately, Vāsavadattā sees the portrait and her anger flares up. Udayana tries to pacify her but his efforts prove futile.

In the **third act**, with the help of Vidusaka, Sāgarikā along with Susangatā plans to join the company of the king disguising herself as Vāsavadattā and Susangatā in her posture. But Vāsavadattā manages to reveal the secret and catches her red handed while she is wooing Udayana. Out of anger Vāsavadattā puts Sāgarikā and Vidusaka behind the bar.

The **fourth act** begins with the description of the rumour that Sāgarikā has been made a captive by Vāsavadattā, and sent to Ujjaini. In the meanwhile, a magician comes to the court to display his tricks. When he was performing his tricks, fire broke out in the palace. Since Sāgarikā was inside the palace Vāsavadattā was apprehensive of her safety. She asked Udayana to rescue her. He immediately rushes to the spot braving fire and carries Sāgarikā to a safer place. At this moment, it is declared that the fire was created out of magic. Yaugandharāyana also comes to the scene and reveals the secret. Vasubhuti and Brabhavya also arrive there telling the story of shipwreck. Vasubhuti identifies Sāgarikā and her real identity is revealed. Vāsavadattā embraces her and allows Udayana to get married to Sāgarikā. The drama ends on a pleasant note followed by *Bharatavākya*.

Ratnāvali occupies a significant place among the minor dramas (*Nātikā*) of Samskrit. Critics like Dhananjaya and Vishvanāth have taken it as standard for framing the rules for the composition of *Nātikā*. The hero of the *Nātikā* is a king and heroine too belongs to a royal family. The hero is apprehensive of his previous wife who comes from a big dynasty. She expresses her displeasure over the conduct of the king. The hero and the heroine finally enjoy life. Ratnāvali fulfils all the requisite qualities of a successful *Nātikā*.

Rasa Nispatti: In his Nātyashāstra, Bharata has put forward a theory that the synthesis of *Bhāva, Vibhāva, Anubhāva Vyabhichāribhāva* leads to the manifestation of *rasa* (*Bhāva vibhāva anubhāva sanchāribhāva samyogāt rasanispatih)*. In this theory, the word *'samyoga'* comes which gave rise to manifold interpretations by subsequent critics like Bhattalollata, Shrishankuka, Bhatta Nāyaka and Abhinava Gupta. These critics interpret the word *'Samyoga'* to denote production, imitation, relish and manifestation. The theories, which they propounded are called *Utpattivāda, Anumitivāda* and *Bhuktivāda* respectively.

Bhattalollata puts the word *'samyoga'* for production. Shrishankuka interpreted the word *'Samyoga'* to mean imitation. Rasa is the imitation of all the ingredients. According to him, Rāma is a matter of imitation. It all depends upon the recipient how he imitates the synthesis of the different constituents of *Rasa*.

Bhatt Nāyaka was the third interpreter of Rasa theory. He interpreted the word *'samyoga'* to mean 'relish' and this relish depends upon the constituent parts of *Rasa*. According to him, *Rasa* in itself is nothing. It is a matter of enjoyment. Unless the responsive reader relishes it, it has no existence at all. The last and the fourth critic to interpret the word *'samyoga'* was Abhinava

Gupta who added a new dimension to the meaning of the word '*samyoga*'. He says that *samyoga* actually means manifestation. The pleasure is already intent in good poetry or a good piece of literature; it has to be manifested and this manifestation takes place when its four constituents, i.e. *Bhāva, Vibhāva, Anubhāva* and *Sanchāribhāva* are synthesised and crystallised so as to give a new meaning leading to the manifestation of *Rasa*.

Ratnākara: Ratnākara is the author of the epic Haravijaya. He belongs to Kashmir and was the court poet of Jayapida, the king of Kashmira. In *Rājātarangini*, he is considered to have achieved popularity during the reign of Avanti Vermā. He was alive till the 1st half of the 9th century. *Haravijaya* consists of 50 Cantos and 4321 verses. It is said that this epic was written to overshadow the popularity of Māgha. It deals with the story of the killing of Andhakāsura by Shankar. The poet uses figurative language and ornamentation to revive grandeur and beauty to the text. He has displayed his scholarship throughout the epic and has been very choosy in the use of diction reviving rhythm, music and colour to the length and breadth of the epic. The poet very proudly announces that a reading to this text may transform an *Akavi* (non-poet) into *Kavi* (poet) and a *Kavi* into *Mahākavi* (great poet).

Rāvanarjuniya: Rāvanarjuniya is an epic written by Bhattbhima or Bhaumaka. It is placed in the category of those epics in Samskrit written on grammatical pattern. It has been written taking inspiration from Bhatti Kāvya. The poet deals with the fierce fighting between Arjuna and Rāvana in 27 cantos. He belonged to Kashmir and flourished before 11th century.

Rigveda: The Rigveda is a collection of *mantras*, and is called *Mantra Samhitā*. It is the oldest of all the Veda *Samhitās*. In respect of knowledge and meaning, *Rigveda* is unique. It is available in two forms. In one form it contains *astaka, adhyāya* and *sukta*. In another form it contains *mandala, anuvāk* and *sukta*. The whole of *Rigveda* is divided into parts, which is called *astaka*. Every *astaka* contains eight *Adhyāyas*. In this way, in the whole of *Rigveda*, there are 64 *Adhyāyas*. This division seems to have been made for the convenience of reading. In another form, which contains 10 *mandalas*, and is supposed to be the most scientific and authentic, there are different kinds of *mantras* in the form of *sukta*. The divisions of these *suktas* are called '*richās*'. In order to keep the original text intact, the seers have even counted number of *mantras* in *Rigveda*. In it there are altogether 1028 *suktas* and about 11,000 *mantras*.

'*Rik*' signifies *mantras* containing prayers and 'Veda' signifies knowledge. Thus *Rigveda* suggests knowledge of the mantras containing prayer directed to gods. It is believed that the mantras were seen and realised by the rishis. The term 'rishi' is used in the sense of one who is capable of seeing. The names of some rishis are also found there, for example, Bhārdwāj, Vishwāmitra, Atri, Vāmadeva, and Vashistha etc. The mantras are intended to please gods like Indra, Usan, Soma, Agni etc. The mantras are very sublime in content. The word 'rit' often comes in the Vedas, for example: ritvij, ritambharā etc. 'Rit' means that which purifies and that is in perfect balance. Besides mantras containing prayers of gods, the *Rigveda* also contains many sublime ideas relat to the art of living.

Patanjali has referred to 21 branches of the *Rigveda* of which five are significant- Sākala, Vaskala, Ashvalāyana, Sankhāyana and Mandukāyana. Of these Sākala is the most prominent. It is considered the kernel of Vedic literature. The visionary of this branch was Sākala Rishi. The entire mantra of Kauthuma branch of Sāmaveda, except 75 mantras, has been borrowed from this branch. Most of the mantras of Krishna Yajurveda and Vājāsaneyi Samhitā have been borrowed from Sākala branch. About 1200 mantras of the Saunaka Samhitā of the Atharvaveda have been retained from it.

The *Rigveda* abounds in a variety of subjects from mundane to spiritual. It has an exceedingly, wide range which include philosophy religion, drama, ethics and poetry. The *Suktas* dealing with philosophical issues include *Purusasukta, Nāsdiyasukta, Hiranyagarbhasukta, Vāksukta* and *Shivasamkalpa Sukta. Nāsadiyasukta* presents a highly improved theory for the creation of the universe. Hiranyagarbha accepts Almighty as the regulator of entire worldly objects. Shivasamkalpa Sukta has used the analogy of *ratha* (chariot) to suggest that one should strictly confine oneself to the primary objective brushing aside other activities as the driver of the *ratha* does while handling the coach to avoid any untoward incident. Seeds of drama and epic can be found in those *suktas* of *Rigveda* written in the form of dialogue. These *suktas* are 20 in number. Of these *suktas Yama-Yami samvāda, Pururvā-Urvasi samvāda, Vishwāmitra-Nārada samvāda* are significant.

Rishiputra: Rishiputra was a great astrologer but no authentic detail about his personal life is available. He is considered to be an astrologer having a leaning to *Jainism*. Among the books written by Rishiputra only *Nimittashāstra* is available while we get reference to *Samhitā* that has prominently figured in the Bhattotpāli's commentary on *Brihatsamhitā*. He is also considered to be the Predecessor of Bārāhmihir. The impact of Rishiputra on his writing can not be ruled out.

Ritusamhāra: Ritusamhāra is an epic by Kālidāsa, consisting of six Cantos: each canto presenting a graphic description of a season. The changes witnessed in nature, caused by the impact of new season, have been vividly presented. It is considered the writing of his initial stage. The epic lacks the gravity in expression, which is evident from his major works. The poet narrates all the six seasons addressing his beloved. The description of the seasons begins with the portrayal of the scorching heat of the summer and culminates in showing the pleasant appeal of the spring. Doubts have been raised by different scholars regarding the authorship of this epic since it comes nowhere close to the major epics of Kālidāsa in style, splendour and artistic grandeur. The simplicity of style cultivated in this epic and the poet's growing apathy for conveying a moral teaching through his work which is a common phenomenon of the works of Kālidāsa has laid the critics to indulge in controversy and wistful thinking about this book. Their suspicion was further strengthened in the sense that Mallināthа has also not written any commentary on this book and no example from this book has been given by Samskrit critics in order to substantiate their ideas. A.B. Keith has tried to set at rest the speculation surrounding the composition of *Ritusamhāra* telling that Mallinātha may not have taken pains to write a commentary on it sensing that the language of the poem is simple. It would be merely a waste of time writing a commentary on it. The two shlokas of *Ritusamahāra* appearing in the book of Vatsabhatti further establish the antiquity of the epic.

Rudrabhatta: Rudrabhatta was a scholar of poetics who wrote a critical anthology *Shriangāra Tilaka* in which elaborate analysis of *Rasa* and *Nāyaka-Nāyikā-bheda* has been made. The reference to *Shringāratilaka* was seen for the first time in Hemachandra's, *Kāvyānusāsana* that flourished between 1088 and 1172 A.D. In this way, Rudrabhatta may have flourished around 10th century. Earlier Rudrata and Rudrabhatta were considered to be the same person. This was the assumption of Webar, Buhler, Ofret and Pichel. But these two have been proved to be different persons after a thorough study of *Kāvya Alankāra* and *Shringāra Tilaka*.

The difference between Rudrata and Rudrabhatta is made clear in following ways: Rudrabhatta has mentioned only nine *rasas* whereas Rudrata has introduced tenth *rasa* named Preranā. Rudrata has introduced five *Vrittis -Madhura, Praudha, Parusha, Lalita* and *Bhadra* taking inspiration from Udbhata whereas Rudrabhatta has introduced only four *Vrittis*. Their analysis of *Nāyaka-Nāyikā bheda* is also not identical. Rudrabhatta has elaborately depicted third kinds of Nāyikā called *vasya*, but Rudrata has finished this description within three *Shlokas* showing his disinclination towards it.

Rudrata has been considered a great critic and he has discussed almost all aspects of *Kāvya* in *Kāvya Alankāra*, whereas Rudrabhatta has a very limited sphere.

Shringāra Tilaka consists of three *parichchhedas* in which elaborate discussion of *Shringāra rasa* has been made. The first *parichchheda* deals with nine *rasas* and *Nāyikā bheda*. The second *parichchheda* deals with love in separation (*Vipralambha Shringāra*) and the third *parichchheda* deals with the rest of *rasas*. For the first time *Rasa* has been interpreted from the standpoint of *Kāvya*.

Rudrata: Rudrata was an eminent critic belonging to the first half of the 9th century. His popularity rests on his monumental work *Kāvya*

Alankāra. It is a voluminous work consisting of 16 chapters, which touches upon all the topics of poetics. Rudrata has presented a more balanced and embellished description of the poetic figures than Bhāmaha, Dandin and Udbhata. This establishes that Rudrata was their successor. On the other hand 10th century critic, Rājashekhar, Pratiharendurājā, Dhanika and Abhinava Gupta have borrowed substantially from him which further indicates that he was their predecessor. In this way Rudrata's period can be fixed around the 1st half of the ninth century.

Rudrata has made a detailed analysis of *Kāvya lakshana*, kinds of *Kāvya*, *shabda shakti*, *Vritti*, poetic blemishes, poetic figures, *rasa* and *Nāyaka-Nāyikā bheda,* and has come out with numerous new facts which were foreign to his predecessors. For the first time, Rudrata has made a scientific division of different poetic figures such as *Vāstava, Aupamya, Atisaya* and *Shlesha* and assimilated all *Alankāras* within the ambit of these four divisions. Rudrata was the most adherent admirer of *Rasa* after Bharata. He has introduced a new *rasa Preranā* and has proved the worthlessness of *Kāvya* without *rasa*.

Rukmini Harana Mahākāvya: Rukmini Harana Mahākāvya is one of the most accomplished epics of the 20th century written by Kāshinātha Sharmā Dwivedi. It is based on the story of Rukmini Harana as narrated in the *Shrimadbhāgavata* dealing with the marriage of Shri Krishna and Rukmini. The epic begins with the account of the king Bhismaka of Kundinpura which is followed by the birth of Rukmini, Nārada's visit to Kundinapura, Shishupāla paying a visit to Kundinpura, Rukmini dispatching a messenger to Krishna, Krishna leaving for Kundinpura and abduction of Rukmini by Krishna.

This epic consists of 21 Cantos and has been modelled on the traditional pattern of epic writing. The poet has exhibited special inclination towards the depiction of the ocean, morning (dawn) and the six seasons.

Rukmini Parinaya Champu: This Champu Kāvya, *Rukmini Parinaya Champu*, has been attributed to Amalānanda who flourished in the latter half of the 14th century. This *Champu* deals with the story of the marriage of Rukmini with Krishna in a polished, refined and finished manner. The language is embellished with all kinds of artistic devices. The story of this Champu has been borrowed from *Harivansa Purāna* and *Srimad Bhāgavata*.

Roopagoshwāmi: Roopagoswāmi was a great saint and critic of Gaudiya cult. He was the disciple of Chaitanya Mahāprabhu. He devoted himself towards Vaishnava sect and has written several books on it. He and his brother Sanātana Goswami were popular exponents of Vaishnava sect. His prominent works are *Hansaduta, Uddhava Sandesh, Vidagdha Mādhava, Lalitā Mādhava, Danakelikaumudi, Bhakti rasa amrita sindhu, Ujjvalanilamani* and *Nātakchandrikā*. Of these works, the first two are *Kāvyas*, the next two are dramas and the last three are works on poetics.

No clear picture of the period of Roopagoswāmi is available. Chaitanya Mahāprabhu flourished in the last decade of the 15th Century. In this way Roopa Goswāmi must have flourished in the first half of the 16th century.

Roopa Goswāmi's popularity rests chiefly on his monumental works *Ujjvalanilamani* and *Bhaktirasamritasindhu*. *Ujjvalanilamani* presents an elaborate analysis of *Nāyaka-Nāyikā bheda*. He has discussed two types of *Nāyakas: Pati* and *Up-pati*. These two have been further divided into 96 kinds. In the same way two types of *Nāyikās* (heroines) – *Swakiyā* and *Parakiyā* have been mentioned.

Bhaktirasamrtasindhu has been divided into four *vibhāgas* (sections). *Purva Vibhāga* deals with the nature of *Bhakti* (devotion) and its *lakshana* and *Dakshina Vibhāga* deals with different *bhāvas* of *Bhaktirasa* including *Vibhāva, Anubhāva, Sthāyi, Sātvika* and *Sanchāri*. *Paschima Vibhāga* deals with *bhakti rasa,* and *Uttara Vibhāga* concentrates on *rasas* like *Hāsya, Adbhuta, Vira, Karuna, Raudra, Vibhatsya* and *Bhayānaka*. ■■

Sabar Swāmi: Sabar Swāmi was a prominent scholar of *Mimāmsā* School of philosophy. His lone work is *Mimāmsā Bhāshya*. He has referred to Pānini and Kātyāyana in his *Bhāshya*. In this sense, he seems to be the successor of these two. He is supposed to have flourished around 100 B.C. Sabar Swāmi's *Mimāmsā Bhāshya* helped *Mimāmsā* School achieve excellence in the latter period.

Sāgar Nandi: Sāgar Nandi was an eminent dramatic critic who flourished in the middle of the 11th century. His popularity rests on his text *Nātaka Lakshanāratna Kosha* related to *Nātyashāstra*. It is based on Bharata's *Nātyashāstra*. He has thrown sufficient light on various aspects of *Nātyashāstra* such as *Rupaka, Avasthāpanchaka, Arthaprākrit*, act, *Up-kshepaka, Sandhi, Vritti, Lakshanā*, poetic figure, *Rasa*, *Nāyikā bheda*, features of hero, *Rupaka, Up-rupaka* and their divisions. He came ahead with several new ideas through his works showing his animosity towards the existing theory. He vehemently opposed Abhinavagupta's hypothesis declaring the existing king as the hero of a drama.

Sāhitya Darpana: Sahitya Darpana is a text on Samskrit poetics by Āchārya Vishwanāth dealing with all the ten parts of *Kāvya Shāstra* (poetics). Vishwanāth is an acknowledged scholar of Samskrit poetics. Sāhitya Darpana is a monumental work of *Alankār Shāstra*. In this work Vishwanāth has tried to establish the enevitbility of *Rasa* and has subordinated *Alankār* to its fulfilment. It consists of 10 *Parichchhedas* and deals with *drishya* as well as *shravya kāvyas*. The **first *Parichchheda*** deals with the nature of *kāvya* (poetry) and its different forms. The **second** deals with *vākya, pada* and *sabdashakti*.The **third *Parichchheda*** presents and elaborate account of *rasas*, which include the nature of *rasa*, parts, nine *rasas* and *Nāyaka-Nāyikā bheda*. The **fourth *Parichchheda*** deals with *Dhvani* and *gunibhuta Vyāngani.* The

fifth is restricted to *Vyanjana*. The **Sixth *Parichchheda*** deals with the kinds of *shrayakāvya* such as *Mahākāvya*, *Khandakāvya, Rupaka* and *Up-rupaka* and its kinds. The **seventh *Parichchheda*** deals with 70 poetic blemishes and the **eighth** dwells upon the analysis of *Gunas*. The **ninth *Parichchheda*** deals wirh *Vrittis* like *Vaidarbhi*, *Gaudi, Laid* and *Panchāli* and the **tenth *parichchheda*** presents a detailed account of *Sabda Alankār, Arth Alankār* and *Mishra Alankār*. By and large, he has discussed seventy *alankārs* but it would be noticed that some of the *alankārs* are not original ones but the offshoots of some other *alakārs*. Besides this, seven *Rasavat Alankārs* have also been mentioned, and *Nishchaya* and two new types of alliteration have been mentioned: *Srutyānuprāsh* and *Antyānuprāsh*. At least four commentaries on *Sāhityadarpana* are available. He has defined epic as one, which in divided into Cantos (*Sarga*) with gods playing the leading role. People belonging to renowned dynasties can also be exalted to the position of the hero of an epic. Āchārya Vishwanāth is a *rasavādi* critic. According to him any utterance stipped in *Rasa* is *Kāvya*. Since *Rasa* is the primary source of enjoyment any utterance bereft of *Rasa* will be drab and insipid and trite. Actually this kind of idea has been expressed earlier also by several *Rasavādi* critics. Āchārya Vishwanāth reiterates the same point with added emphasis.

Shaiva Tantra: Shaiva Tantra is a tantra related to the worship of Shiva. It was bifurcated into four Sects following ideological differences. These sects are Pāshupata Sect, Shaivasiddhānta Sect, Virashaiva Sect and Pratibhigya Sect.

Lakulisa has propounded *Pāshupata* Sect. A handful of literature of this Sect is available. *Pāshupata Sutra* is the original text of this Sect, which is written by Maheshvara. Mādhavāchārya has interpreted the philosophical ideology of this Sect in his work *Sarv-darshan-samgraha*. The spiritual ideology of this Sect has been discussed as *Yogamātā* in Rājashekhara Sutra's *Shadadarshan Samuchchya*. This Sect was basically confined to Gujarāt and Rajputānā region.

Shaivasiddhānta Sect is spread over Tamil region. The admirers of this Sect have compiled stotras in Tamil showing their devotion to Lord Shiva. It has acquired the status of the Vedas. At least 84 saints are attached to this Sect. Of these four are very significant. They are Appār, Sant Gyānasambandha, Sundarmurti, and Mānikkavāchaka. These four saints have set up four independent schools, which include *Mārgāchārya, Kriyā, Yoga* and *Gyāna*. They flourished between the 7th and the 8th century. Some of their works are also available in Samskrit. If *Āgama* is called *Shaiva Siddhānta*, then *Shaivāgamas* are overall 208 in number. It is said that 28 *tantras* originated from the five mouths of Shiva. Sadyojyoti (8th century) Naradatta Shivāchārya (11th century) and Ramākantha (11th century) are the prominent torchbearers of this Sect. Sadyojyoti wrote *Nareshvaraparikshā* and Haradatta Shivāchārya wrote *Tātparya Samgraha*.

The followers of *Vira Shaiva* Sect are called *Lingāyata* or *Jangam*. They do not pin faith in the division of four *Varnas*. They garland the *Lingāyata* idol of Shankar in their neck. This Sect was established by Vāsava, a minster of the Kalachuri king Bijjala. He flourished in the 12th century. *Siddhānta Shikhāmani* is the standard work of this Sect. This Sect was popular in Karnātaka. Vāsava was guided by reformative zeal. His objective was to tone down the differences amongst various Sects of Hindu religion. He vehemently opposed caste system. He disseminated his ideas to bridge the gap and cement the relationship among different Sects. His objective was to bring people to a single platform irrespective of their caste, creed and religion. In order to achieve his objective he deliberately preached sermons aimed at mitigating racial differences and ethnic violence. He was a prophet with the reformative zeal.

Pratibhigya Sects was popular in Kashmir. It is called *Tarka Darshan* because it lays emphasis on three elements *pasu, pati* and *pāsa*. The spiritual aspect of this Sect was discussed by Abhinavagupta in hls *Tantraloka*. It is said that Lord Shiva has propagated his ideology to disseminate *Advaita* ideas dissenting *Dvaita* cult led by *Shaivāgamas*. The 9th century philosopher Vasugupta was the founder of this Sect, which spread over Kāshmir. He made an elaborate analysis of *Shiva Sutra* in *Spanda Kārikā,* which is considered the primary source of this Sect. Later on, his disciples Kallata and Shāmānanda propagated *Spandasiddhānta* and *Pratibhigya* Sects through their works *Spanda-sarvasava* and *Shivadrishti* respectively. Other important practitioners of this Sect are Utpal Āchārya and Kshemarāja who wrote *Ishvara-pratyabhigya Kārikā* and *Shivasutra Vimarshini* respectively.

Sāma Veda: Sāma Veda is of the Veda Samhitā giving top priority to the element of song recited by the rishi named Udgata. Krishna has claimed to be Sāma Veda among the Vedas. It was designed to lay down the codes for Yajnamaya or a *ritvik*. At the time of Yajnas '*homas*' were offered in the name of God, and in order to invoke gods, *Mantras* were recited in the form of prayers, which were usually lyrical. The prayers were recited in a singsong form, which were called *Sāma*.

Sāma Veda has been divided into two sections- *Ārchika* and *Gāna*. *Ārchika* is futher divided into *Purvāchika* and *Uttarāchika*. They jointly consist of 1810 mantras of which 261 mantras have been repeated. In this way, the number of mantras is reduced to 1549. Except 75 mantras, rest has been borrowed from the Rig Veda Samhitā. In this way, Sāma Veda is the smallest of all the Vedas. *Purvāchika* and *Uttarāchika* have been divided into *Dashati*, and *Dashati* is further divided into mantras. The entire *Purvāchika* consists of 585 mantras. *Uttarāchika* is divided into 9 *Prapāthakas*. First five are divided into 2 *Ardhakas* and the rest four are divided into 3 *Ardhakas*. It consists of 1810 mantras. The original mantras of Sāma Veda are referred to as Yoni. According to subjects there are four divisions entitled: *Āgneya Parva* related to fire; *Ārnayaka Parva*, related to forest, *Pavamāna Parva* related to moon; and *Aindra Parva* related to Indra. There are seven subdivisions of these divisions such as *Dasavatra, Samavatsara, Ekak, Ahin, Satra, Prayāschita,* and *Chhudra*. About 1000 branches of Sāma Veda have been mentioned in certain *Purāna*s But only three branches are available: *Kauthumiya, Rāmayāniya* and *Jaiminiya*. Kauthuma branch is very popular and is basically confined to Gujarāt. Rāmāyaniya branch is popular in Mahārāshtra. There is no basic difference betwwen Kauthumiya and Rāmāniya branch. Jaiminiya branch is related to Jaiminiya Samhitā.

The Sāma Veda is the source of *Sangeet*. Seven rhythms have been used in singing the songs of Sāma Veda. Thus one can find the importance of *sangeeta* even in those ancient days, which is indicative of rich Indian cultural heritage.

The song pattern of Sāma Veda has been divided into four sections: *Grām geya gāna, Aranyaka gāna, Aha gāna,* and *Urdhva gāna*. According to Chhāndogya Upanishada, Sāmagāna had seven parts- *Hinkara, Ādi, Upadrava, Prastāva, Udgitha, Pratihāra* and *Nidāna*.

Savitā or Surya is considered to be the chief deity of Sāma Veda. Prayers have been offered to Indra and Agni also but they do not play a prominent role. It lays emphasis more on worship. Agni, Surya and Soma have been shown as gods to worship.

Samayamātrikā: Samaya Mātrikā is a satire written by Kshemendra, which aims at protecting the rich from the snare of the prostitutes in order to live a better life. It was wiritten during the reign of the 11th century Kāshmiri king Anantadeva. It is divided into 8 *parichchhedas*.

Shankarāchārya: Shankarāchārya is the propounder of the monoistic theory of Advaita Vedānta, which substantially enriched Indian Philosophy and achieved universal acclaim. Originally, the theory of Vedānt was put forward by Gaudpāda, his guru. Shankar wrote an exhaustive commentary on *Brahamsutra* and other various treatises like Upanishadas and the Gitā in which he develop the philosphy of his master.

Shankarāchārya was a prodigy. There is a shloka which says: "At the age of eight, he read all the four Vedas; at the age of 12, he marshalled all the scriptural treatises, at the age of 16, he wrote commentaries on various religious books and at the age of 22 renounced the world and became a *samyāsi*." The chief aim of Shankarāchārya was to propagate the philosophy of Vedānta and to restore its lost glory by giving a major thrust to the movment aimed at revamping Indian philosophical credo. In order to achieve his objective he had to outwit Buddhist scholars. Vedānta literally means at the close of the Vedas, as it is the conclusion of the Vedas. Although the theory of Vedānta was propounded much earlier, and it is abundently found in the Upanishadas the credit to give it a systematic foundation goes to Shankarāchārya. Shankarāchārya was a strong supporter of *Māyāvāda*. His philosophy precisely is that God alone is true and the phenomenal world is an illusion. He observed it in an aphoristic term, "*Brahma satyam jagan mithyā*." This means that the world looks real out of ignorance or *Māyā*. The world is not real. It is illusory. God is real. Shankarāchārya proves it by citing an illustration of serpent and rope. The rope appears to be serpent because of ignorance. When the confusion of ignorance is dispelled, the truth or the reality comes before us in its true form. Similarly, the world appears to be real because we are unable to see the reality. The moment we understand that God alone is the ultimate truth, the world turns out to be unreal, false and illusory. Another example that Shankarāchārya cited is relatively suggestive. So long we are in dream, everything appears to be real, but after waking the things seen in the dream appear to be unreal.

Shankarāchārya had a short life. He died at the age of 32. The authorship of some books is disputed. He raised the banner of monoism or monotheism afloat. He did a great service to Hinduism by incorporating the basic principles of Buddhism into Hinduism. As the hearsay goes, he had shāstrārtha with Mandana Mishra, a scholar from Mithilā in Bihār and the latter gave in before him. Subsequently the pandit's wife came forward and challenged him by asking some questions about Kāmakalā.

He spread Vedānta ideology to the length and breadth of India. In order to give firm footing to Vedānta ideology and to avert the impending danger posed by non-Vedānta Sects, he established *Mathas* in four directions of India. Jyotishmatha was established near Badrikāshrama in the north, Shringeri matha at Rāmeshwarama in South, Gowardhana Matha at Jagnnātha Puri in the east and Shāradāmatha at Dwārika in the west. He appointed the head of the matha and fixed their areas of operations with the sole intention to authorize them to propagate Vedic philosophy. He also laid down the rules to be practiced by the head of the mathas. He should be pious, overpowering the senses and should be an authority on the Vedas.

About 200 works have been attributed to Shankarāchārya. These works can be divided into three categories – **Bhāshya**, **Stotra** and **Prakarana**. His **Bhāshya** include *Shārirakā Bhāshya* on 13 Upanisadas, *Vishnu Sahasranāmā Bhāshya* and *Gāyatri Bhāshya*. **Stotra** works include *Ganeshastotra, Shivastotra, Shivaparādha-kshamāpana-stotra, Shivapanchaksāra, Umamaheshwara stotra, Daksināmurti stotra, Dwādasalinga stotra, Saundarya Lahari, Devibhujanga stotra, Tripurasundari stotra, Annapurnāstaka* and *Minākshistotra* etc. **Prakarana** granthas are plenty in number: *Upadeshapanchaka, Tatvabodha, Nirvānamanjari* and *Svātma-prakāshikā* etc.

Sāmkhya Philosophy: Maharshi Kapila propounded the Sāmkhya Philosophy. Kapila was a seer of Upanishada era. The Sāmkhya philosophy is older than the Nyāya and the Vaisesika philosophy. The seeds of this philosophy may be found in the Upanishadas like Katha, Chhāndogya, Shwetāshwara and Maitrāyani. The Sāmkhya philosophy supports Dualism. The world was created out of two primordial elements - *Prakriti* and *Purusha*. *Prakriti* is active while *Purusha* is inactive. The Sāmkhya philosophy is based on the Satkārya Veda. Satkārya Veda precisely means that the effect lies dormant in the cause. If effect does not lie in the cause, then no effort can take it out from the cause. That effect lies in an unmanifested condition in the cause. Effect is nothing but manisfestation of the *gunas* lying in an unmanifested manner in the cause. The *Nyāya* and the *Vaisheshika* philosophy do not agree with this view. They hold that the cause and the effect are two separate entities. The effect is different from the cause. The earthen pot is different from the clay out of which it is made. One can pour water in the earthen pot but one cannot do so in clay. The *Sāmkhya* philosophy maintains that *Prakriti* in its normal state is the name of equilibrium of *sat, raj* and *tam*. When there is disturbance amongs these gunas, creation comes into existence. (This way, he is forerunner to Darwin's Theory of Evolution.) This happens when *Prakriti* and *Purusha* are united, and they give birth to *mahāttatva* or intellect or *buddhi*. From intellect is born *ahamkāra* or ego. *Ahamkāra* is double-edged. From *ahamkāra* dominated by *satva* are born eleven *indriyas* or sense organs.

From *ahamkāra* dominated by ignorance or *tamas* are born five *sukshma tanmātras* (cells) and *sthula pancha mahābhutas*.

The *Sāmkhya* Philosophy is realistic in its approach. Kapila wrote *Tatva Samhitā* running into 22 *sutras*. Thereafter, Kapila elaborated his Philosophy in his book *Sāmkhyasutra,* which runs into 534 *sutras*. Āsuri was an ardent disciple of Kapila and Panchāsikha was the pupil of Āsuri. Unfortunately, their writings are not available. Ishwar Krishna was another Āchārya of this school who wrote *Sāmkhya Kārikā*. This book was so famous that Pravaranātha translated it into Chinese language, which is still available. The translation in Chinese is entitled *Hiranyasaptati* or *Suvarnasaptati*. Later Vigyāna Bhiksu wrote a commentary on this philosophy entitled *Sāmkhya* Pravachana Bhāshya.

Lord Buddha derived the ideas of existence of misery, the futility of Vedic *karmakānda*, the negation of the existence of God and the mutability of wordly object from the *Sāmkhya* Philosophy. The believers in the *Sāmkhya* Philosophy were the first men who were *ahimsāvādi*. The Jains and the Buddhists borrowed the philosophy of *ahimsā* from the *Sāmkhya* Philosophy. The speciality of the *Sāmkhya* Philosophy that it tries to explain the mystery of creation by taking recourse to two fold basic elements, *Prakriti* and *Purusha* is still relied upon by many modern scientists.

***Samrātacharita**:* Samrātacharita is an epic written by the 20th century poet Harinandana Bhatta. It was written in 1993. It deals with the life of English king George V. It runs into 2500 *shlokas*. The epic begins with the description of the city of London, which has been compared with Amarāvati. The second and the third chapters are devoted to the reign of queen Victoria. The fifth chapter deals with the voyage to India made by George V. The sixth and the seventh chapters deal with the request made by the king of Kāshi to George V to pay a visit to Vārānasi. The eighth chapter presents bewitching picture of the court of Delhi.

***Samvarta Smriti**:* Samvarta Smriti is a text of moral and legal code written by Samvarata. About 227 *shlokas* of *Samvarta Smriti* are available in the books of Jivanānda and Ānand Sharmā. It has also been referred to in *Mitākshara* and *Smritisāra*.

Sandesha Kāvya: Plenty of Sandesha Kāvya has been written in Samskrit. It is also called *Dutakāvya*. The plot of *Sandesha kāvya* is basicaly confined to sending message to one's ladylove or to one's lover through a messenger. These *Sandesha kāvyas* originated from the *Rāmāyana* in which the message of Rāma was delivered to Sitā by Hanumāna. Kālidāsa's *Meghduta* is unquestionably the best work as *Sandeshakāvya*. *Sandesha kāvyas* are divided into two parts *Purva* and *Uttara*. The *purva bhāga* deals with the hero or heroine mourning over the separation from their loved ones. It is followed by introduction of the messenger to deliver the message to the counterpart. The *Uttara bhāga* (part) deals with the destination and the pathetic condition of the beloved.

In course of time, novel ideas were incorporated in *Sandesha kāvya* and religious, devotional and philosophical topics were included in it. Jain poets have contributed signifcantly to the development of *Sandesha kāvya*. Jinasena's *Parshvābhyudaya*, Vikrams's *Nemiduta*, Sundaragani's, *Shilāduta* and Vimalakirti's *Chandraduta* are major contributions of Jain Poets.

A healthy tradition of *Sandesha kāvya* is seen from the 12th century onwards. The 12th centurey poet Dhoi's *Pawanaduta* is a memorable work. The 13th century poet Avadhuta Rāmayogi's *Siddhaduta,* the 15th century poet Vishnudāsa's *Manoduta* and Rāmasharmā's *Manoduta*, the 16th century poet Madhava Kavindra Bhattāchārya's *Uddhava Duta* and the 17th century poet Rupa Goswāmi *Uddhava Sandesha* are excellent examples of *Sandesha kāvya*. Among the 17th century *Sandesha kāvya's* Vāchaspati's *Pikaduta*, Vādirāja's *Pawanaduta*, Lambodara Vaidya's *Gopiduta* and Trilochana's *Tulsiduta* can be given top priority. Rudravāchaspati's *Bhramaraduta* and Nityānand Shāstri's *Hanumataduta* are the *Sandesha kāvyas* inspired by the story of Rāma. Rāmāvatāra Sharmā's *Mudgaladuta* is a notable example of 20th century *Sandesha kāvya*.

Sangeeta *Shāstra* : The history of Indian music dates back to the Vedic period. There has been a pretty rich tradition of music in India, which acquired the status of an independent form of art. The elements of music are available in the Sāma Veda. One of the

Up-Vedas, Gandharva or Sangeeta *Shāstra* is attached to Sāma Veda. Even in Rig Veda several kinds of musical instruments have been referred to such as *Dundubhi, Karkari, Choni, Vinā* and *Vanā*. Various terms related to music come in the Rig Veda also. Words like *Gāmageyagāna, Stova* and *Stoma* are sufficient testimony to the rich tradition of music during the Vedic period. Methods of singing and rules for the use of different notes have been mentioned in the Sāma Veda. The seven notes of music have been developed from the Vedic notes *Udātta, Anudātta* and *Svarita*. *Nisāda* and *Gāndhāra* originated from *Udātta; Rishabha* and *Dhaivata* from *Anudātta;* and *Sadaj, Madhyamā* and *Panchamā* originated from *Svarita*. In *Charanavyuha* of Shanakara about 1000 Sects of music have been referred to of which only three *Kauthuma, Rāmāyaniya* and *Jaiminiya* are found. *Udātta* is called *Tāra*, *Anudātta* is called *Uchcha* and *Swarita* is called *Madhya*. *Rikpratisākhya* has mentioned the ways through which seven notes developed from *Tāra, Uchcha* and *Madhya*. Seven divisions of Vedic music have been mentioned as *Prastāva, Hunkāra, Udgitha, Pratihāra*, *Upadrava, Vidhāna* and *Pranava*.

An enriched form of music is available in the Post-Vedic period. In the *Purāna*, the *Rāma*yana and the *Mahābhārata,* vital chages in the rules and systems of musical composition can be witnessed. It opened a new vista to musical compositions both vocal and instrumental. *Harivansa Purāna* has also mentioned several musical intruments besides highlighting the antiquity of *Gāndhāra Rāga*. *Mārkandeya Purāna* and *Vāyu Purāna* also present various facts pertaining to music. During the *Rāmā*yana and the *Mahābhārata* period music no longer remained confined to the classes, it came down to the masses. Rāvana was himself a great musician. His text on music *Rāvaniyama* is a glaring proof of it. In the Mahābhāratā period music acquired new dimensions. Krishna, the arch model of this period was himself a great player on the flute.

In *Astādhyāyi, Arthashāstra* and in the works of Kālidāsa references to music are available profusely. Gupta period is considered the golden period for the development of art. Samudra Gupta was himself a great admirer of art. In one of his coins he has been depicted playing Veenā.

Bharata's *Nātyashāstra* is the most accomplished work on music. In the 28th, the 29th and the 30th chapters of *Nātyashāstra* there is a detailed discussion of various forms of music available during that period. It has also been admitted in *Nātyashāstra* that before Bharata, Nārada initiated this trend of music. Nārad contributed a good book entitled *Sangeeta Makaranda*. Bharata has referred to several contemporary musicians such as Nāradra, Kohala, Kashyapa, Shārdula and Dattilā. The 6th century scholar Mātanga wrote a book on music entitled *Brihaddeshiya*. Abhinava Gupta has accepted the 9th century scholar Utpal Āchārya as the most accomplished scholar of music. Sārangadeva has referred to Kambala, Ashvātara, and Ānjaneya as the eminent musicians in the post-Bharata era. In the same way, Abhinava Gupta has referred to Bhattamātra Gupta, Lātmuni and Vidhatrāchārya in his books. Reference to Vishvavasu, Umāpati and Pārshvadeva has been given in *Sangeeta Ratnākara*. Pārshvadeva and Somanātha wrote *Sangeeta Sāmayasāra* and *Rāgavivodha* respectively. The 11th century scholar Nānyadeva has mentioned ragas like Dakshinātya, Saurāshtri, Gurjari, Bengāli, and Sāndhavi in his book Saraswati Pradeyālankār.

Sārangadeva made the most significant contribution to the up gradation of music. His *Sangeetaratnākara* is the most celebrated work on music. He was associated with the court of the king of Devagiri. His book is an encyclopaedia on music. Rāmaratya wrote a monumental book *Swarasudhānidhi* in 1610 A.D. Mānasingh is considered as one laying the foundation of Dhrupada style, which achieved maturity in the 18th century schoar Bhavadatta's *Anupamasangeeta Ratnākara*. Stupendous achievements were made during the reign of Akbar. Swāmi Haridāsa and Tānasena were the two great musicians of this period. Akbara's contemporary Pundarika Vitthala wrote four books on music: *Sadarāga Chandrodaya, Ragāmālā, Rāgamanjari* and *Nirnaya Dāmodara*, and Anobāla wrote *Sangeeta Darpana* and *Sangeetapārijāta* during the reign of Jahangira. These works provide a blend of northern and southern musical systems. The 17th century scholar

Bhāvabhatta wrote three monumental works on music: *Anupavilāsa*, *Anupankusha* and *Anupasangeetaratnākara*. In Venkatamukhi's, book *Chaturdandaprakāshikā*, 71 *Thātas* and 45 *rāgas* have been discussed. The king of Mewār, Rānā Kumbhanadeva's wrote *Vādyaratnakosha,* which is another important contribution to music. The 18th century scholar Shrikāntha enriched the repertory of music through his book *Rasakaumudi*. In 1843, Pd. Krishnānada Vyāsa wrote a monumental work *Rāgakalpadruma*. Among prominent musicians of south, King Tulaja, Tyāgaraja, Muttu Swāmi Dikshita and Shyāma Shāstri can be mentioned. King Tulaja wrote a book entitled *Sangeetasamrāta*. Vishnu Nārāyana Bhātakhande also wrote a significant book on music in 1910 entitled *Lakshyasangeeta*. He is considered the most celebrated scholar of Hindustani Sangeeta.

Sānkhayāyana Brāhmana: Sānkhayāyana Brāhmana is related to Rig Veda and is also called Kaushikiti. It consists of 30 chapters and 226 khandas. It deals with those subjects, which occur in Aitareya Brāhmana. This text has given special importance to Rudra. Several synonyms of Shiva have been discussed such as Rudra, Mahādeva, Ishāna, Bhāva, Pashupati, Ugra and Asani. It also deals with several *Vratas* related to Shiva. It also points out the importance attached to *gotra*. Special attention has been given to Shākvari Chhanda, which helps Indra overcome the challenge of Vritrāsura.

Samskrit Dictionary: Dictionaries have been produced in Samskrit since the Vedic period. During the primitive period Koshas and grammars were placed under the same category. Most of the dictionaries written during that period have perished. In *Amarkosha*, reference to *Bhāguri Kosha* is available. The name of Bhāguri dictionary was *Trikānda*, which has been confirmed by Purusottamadeva's *Bhāsāvratti* and Srisitidhara's *Bhāsāvrattitikā*. Reference to Apishali dictionary has been given in Bhānuji Dikshita's *Amarakosha*. The dictionaries of Shākatāyana and Vyāddhi have also been mentioned in several texts of that period.

The first dictionary of Vedic words is *Nighantu*. Yāska has written a commentary on *Nighantu* entitled *Nirukta*. Several dictionaries on

Vedic terminologies have been written in modern age; prominent among them are Vishvabandhu Shāstri's *Vedic Shabdārtha Pārijāta*, *Vedic Padānukramakosha* and *Brahmanodhara Kosha*, Shrichamupati's *Vedārtha Shabdakosha*, Madhusudana Sharmā's *Vedic Kosha*, Hansarāja's, *Vedic Kosha*, Kevalānanda Saraswati's, *Aitareya Brāhmana Aranyaka Kosha*, Gayānanda Sambhusādhale's *Upanishada Vākya Mahākosha*, Lakshmana Shāstri's *Dharmakosha*. Grassman has also written a popular dictionary '*Lexicon to the Rig-Veda*'.

Amarkosha is the most popular dictionary of Samskrit written by Amarasingh. It is also called *Nāmalingānushāsana*. It has been written between the 4th and the 5th century. At least, 50 commentaries on Amarakosha have been produced; prominent among them are Prabhā, Maheswari, Sudhā, Rāmāshrayi and Nāmachandrikā. *Amarkosha* is divided into three kāndas. It basically presents a Synonym of Samskrit words. In the post - *Amarakosha* period, dictionaries followed three broad ways - Nānārtha Kosha, Samānārthaka Shabda Kosha and Paryāyavāchi Kosha. Shāsvata wrote *Anekarthasamuchchya* in 800 *Anustupa Chhandas*. Purushottama. Deva wrote two dictionaries- *Trikānda Kosha* and *Hārāvali* in the 7th century. The 10th century scholar Halāyudha wrote *Abhidhāna ratnamālā,* which is also called Halāyudha Kosha. The impact of Amarkosha can be easily seen on it. Yādava Prakāsha wrote a voluminous and authentic dictionary *Vaijayanti* between 1055 and 1337 A. D. Hemachandra also wrote a dictionary *Abhidhānachintāmani*. It is a compilation of synonyms. The 12th century scholar Maheshvara wrote two dictionaries *Viswaprakāsha* and *Shabdabheda prakāsha*. Mankhaka wrote a dictionary *Anekārtha* in the 12th century. Ajayapāla wrote a dictionary *Nānārthasamgraha* between the 12th and the 13th century. Dhananjaya wrote *Nāmamālā* in the 12th century and Keshava Swāmi wrote *Nānārthārnava Sankshepa* and *Shabdakalpadruma*. Medinikara wrote Nānārtha Shabda Kosha in the 14th century.

Shabdakalpadruma and *Vachaspatyama* are great achievements of the modern age. Rādhākānta Deva wrote *Sabdakalpadruma* between 1828 and 1858 A.D. It gives a derivative of each word according to *Ashtādhyāyi*. It has been written in seven *khandas* and is supposed to be an encyclopedic dictionary of Indology.

Vāchaspatyama is a voluminous dictionary written by Tārānātha Bhattāchārya in 1873 A.D. It presents a detailed analysis of words/ terms taken from literature, grammar, jyotisha, tantra, philosophy, music, poetics, history and medical sciences.

Monier Williams *Samskrit English Dictionary*, Benafey's *Samskrit English Dictionary* and dictionaries by Wilson and McDonald are very popular. But the best one is compiled by Vāman Shivarāma Āpte. The uniqueness and the beauty of the dictionary lies in the fact that he has quoted lines from different books to illustrate the word used with different meanings. He has written many authentic dictionaries: *Samskrit Angareji Kosha* in three volumes and *Samskrit Hindi Kosha.*

W.B. Yeats' *Samskrit-English Dictionary* published in 1846 and Rath and Bothalinga's *Samskrit-German Dictionary* in seven volumes are wonderful achievements. Rāmāvatāra Sharmā's *Vangamayārnava* is a great work written in 1967A.D.

Samskrit Drama: Elements of drama can be traced back in the *sutras* of the Rig Veda particularly those designed in dialogue form. In the dialogue between Pururvā-Urvasi, Yam-Yami, Indra-Indrāni the dynamics of drama can be discerned. Four elements of drama: dance, music, acting and dialogue can be easily found in the Vedic literature. Fair amount of dramatic elements can be seen in the *Rāmāyana* and the *Mahābhārata*. In Harivansa *Purāna*, a part of the *Mahābhārata*, the story of *Rāma* has been presented in a dramatic form. Reference to *Nātyasutra* appearing in Pānini's *Ashtādhyāyi* further establishes that the drama by then had developed to such a proportion that *nātyasutra* was required to give proper concept of a drama. Two dramas *Kansabaddha* and *Bālibaddha* have been mentioned in the Mahābhāshya. Kulishavāsa, whose chief aim was to entertain the audience has been mentioned in Vatsyāyana's *Kāmasutra* and Chānakya's *Arthashāstra*.

Scholars have yet not reached at a consensus on the issue of the origin of drama. Dr. Gye has observed that the origin of drama can be traced back to virapuja. German scholar Pichel has traced the origin of drama to putalkanritya (puppet dance). The loophole of this theory stands vindicated.

Bharata's theory seems to be more reasonable in this respect. He insisted that sensing the moroseness of mundane people, the deities approached lord Brahmā to compile another Veda which could be appreciated by all and sundry. Brahmā agreed to their proposal and created the fifth Veda borrowing theme from the Rig Veda, music from Sāma, mimicry from Yajur Veda and Rasa from Atharva Veda. It became Nātyashāstra. At the behest of Brahma, Bharata taught the basics of Nātyashāstra to his hundred sons.

A healthy tradition of drama began in Samskrit from 1st century onwards. In the preface to *Malavikāgnimitra*, Kālidāsa has referred to dramatists like Kaviputra, Bhāsa and Saumilla of which only Bhāsa's dramas are available. Ganapati Shāstri published his dramas in 1912 A.D. His period has been fixed around 4th century B.C. His drama are Dutavākya, Karnabhāra, Dutaghatotkacha, Urubhanga, Madhyamavyāyoga, Pancharātra, Abhisheka, Bālacharita, Avimāraka, Pratirna, Pratigya Yaugandharāyana, Svapnavāsavadattā and Daridra Chārudatta. Of the 13 drama, the stories of 6 have been borrowed from the *Mahābhārata*, 2 from the *Rāma*yana and of the rest 5 have been borrowed from other stories.

Samskrit drama was elevated to the new heights at the hands of Kālidāsa. Three drama, Malavikagnimitra, Vikramorvasiya and Abhigyānashākuntala are attributed to him. Kalidas's dramatic craftsmanship touches its highest watermark in this last drama.

Sudraka's *Mrichchhakatika* is placed in the category of realistic drama. It is based on Bhāsa's drama *Chārudatta*.

Of the three drama of Ashvaghosha, two are incomplete. Sāriputra, a prakarana has been written in 9 acts dealing with the teachings of Lord Buddha. The three dramas of Harshavardhana include two shorter plays (nātikā)- *Priyadarshikā* and *Ratnāvali*. The third one is a rupaka named *Nāgānanda*. *Venisamhāra* of Bhatta Nārāyana is a drama based on *Vira Rasa*. It consists of 6 acts and adheres to the classical rules and regulations. It derives the story from the *Mahābhārata* dealing with Bhima besmearing the hairs of Draupadi with the blood of Duryodhana.

Vishākhadatta's *Mudrārākshasa* is a monumental work on political manoeuvers and diplomacy. Bhavabhuti also occupies a significent place among the prominent writers of Samskrit drama. His dramas include *Mālatimādhava, Mahāviracharita* and *Uttara Rāmacharita*.

A major shift is noticed in the dramas of post-Bhavabhuti period. The dramatists of this period are least concerned with innovating dramatic techniques in their dramas. They, on the contrary seem inclined to show off their scholarship and command over language. They have deliberately resorted to witty remarks, exaggerated expressions and terse style.

Shaktibhadra, Dāmodara Mishra and Rājshekhara are important dramatists of this period. Shaktibhadra's *Āshcharyachudāmani* deals with the story of the *Rāmayana* from Surpanakha's episode up to the acid test of Sitā. Damodara Mishra wrote *Hanumān nātaka*. Rajsekhara's dramas are *Viddhashāla bhanjikā*, *Bāla Rāmāyana* and Bāla *Mahābhārata*. Buddhist scholar Dinganāga has dealt with the story of *Uttara Rāmacharita* in 6 acts under the influence of Bhavabhuti. In the beginning of the 11th century Krishna Mishra wrote his symbolic drama *Prabodh Chandrodaya*. Its dominating rasa is *shānta rasa*. He is considered the propounder of symbolic drama in Samskrit. Several dramas were written on the pattern of *Prabodha Chandrodaya*. Prominent among those symbolic dramas are Yashapal's *Mohāparājaya* (13th century), Venkatanātha's, *Sankalpa Suryodaya* (14th century) and Karnapura's *Chaitanya Chandrodaya* (16th century). Jayadeva (1250 A.D.) wrote a drama *Prasanna Rāghava*, which is also saturated with the features of the drama of the decadent period. Several *prahasanas* and *bhānas* have also been written in Samskrit. Among those Mahendra Vikrama Verma's *Mattavilāsa prahasana* (6th century) is significant. *Shankhadhara Lātakametaka* is also a fine example of *prahasana*.

Samskrit Epic : Samskrit Epic has originated from the *Rāmāyana* and the *Mahābhārata*. The succeeding epic poets bringing about necessary changes in the themes have inherited the stories appearing in these two epics. Of the two epics, the *Rāmāyana* and the *Mahābhārata*, the former is better in respect of epic qualities. In the *Mahābhārata*, historical elements overweigh poetical elements. The plots in the succeeding epics have been taken from the *Mahābhārata* and the style and narrative technique from the *Rāmāyana*.

The epics of Kālidāsa, Ashvaghosa and Kumaradāsa are placed under the section ornamental epic. Bhāravi's *Kirātarjuniya*, Ratnakara's *Haravijaya*, Shiva Swāmi's *Kapphin Abhyudaya* and Mankhaka's *Shrikāntha charita* are included under the category of classical epics. Bhatti's *Bhattikāvya*, Hemachandra's, *Kumarapālacharita*, Dhanajaya's, *Dwisandhāna Kāvya*, Sandhyākara Nandi's, *Rāmacharita*, Vidyāmādhava's, *Pārvati-Rukminiya* and Haridatta Suri's *Rāghava Naishadhiya* are placed in the category of epics aimed at creating miracle with the use of artificial style. Among the epics based on the Puranic style are Jinasena's *Ādi Purāna*, Gunabhadra's *Uttara Purāna*, Jatāsinghnadi's, *Varangacharita*, Kshemendra's *Rāmāyanamanjari*, *Mahābhāratamanjari* and *Dasāvatāracharita*, Hemachandra's *Trishashtisalākā purusha charita*, Amara Chanda Suri's *Bālabhārata*, Venkatanātha's, *Yadavābhyudaya*, Jayadratha's, *Haracharita chintāmani*, Krishnadāsa Kaviraja's *Govindalilāmrita*, Nịlakantha Dikshit's *Shivalilārnava*, Yasodhara's *Yasodharacharita*, Amarachanda's *Panānanda*, Harishchandra's *Dharmasharmābhyudaya*, Abhayadevasuri's *Jayantavijaya* and Vāgbhatta's *Neminirmāna*.

Among the historical epics, Ashvaghosa's *Buddhacharita*, Padmagupta's *Navashahashanka charita*, Vilhana's *Vikramānakadevacharita*, Kalhana's, *Rajtarangini*, Hemachandra's, *Kumārapālacharita*, Amarsingh's *Sukritasankirtana*, Bālachandasuri's, *Vasantavilāsa* and Jayachandrasuri's *Hammir Mahākāvya* are included. Somadeva's *Kathāsaritsāgar*, Viranandi's *Chandraprabhā charita*, Someshvara's *Surathotsava*, Bhāvadevasuri's, *Parshvanātha charita* and Munibhadrasuri's *Shāntinātha charita* are considered epics aimed at creating thrill.

Several epics were written in the pre-Kālidāsa era. Although they are not available, still references to these epics have been given in several books. An epic *Devarshicharita* by Chargya has been mentioned in the *Shāntiparva* of the *Mahābhārata*. Pānini is said to have written two epics *Jāmbavantivijaya* and *Patālavijaya*. Two epics have been attributed to the grammarian Vyādhi entitled *Bālacharita* and *Pradip bhuta*. Reference to Vararuchi's kāvya, *Swarārohana* has been given in Patanjali's *Mahābhāshya*. Patanjali has himself written an epic *Mahānanda*.

All the epics written in Samskrit have been placed under three distinct categories - Paurānika, period of elevation and period of decadence. The *Rāmāyana* and the *Mahābhārata* are placed under the category of the Pauranika epics. The epics of Kālidāsa represent the epics belonging to the period of elevation. The post Kālidāsa era is called the period of decadence.

A significant development was made in the 20th century. Several epics were written with change in plot, diction and structural harmony. The plots of the 20th century epics virtually revolve round patriotic themes. The epic poets also highlighted the personality of eminent figures contributing substantially to nation building activities. They borrowed immensely from ancient Indian mythologies. Annācharana's *Rāma Abhyudaya* and *Mahāprasthāna*, Batukanātha Sharmā's, *Sitā Svayambara*, Guruprasāda Bhattāchārya's, *Shrirasa*, Shivakumār Shāstri's *Yatindrajivana Charita*, Nāgarāja's, *Sitāsvayamvara* and Bhāgavatāchārya's *Bharatapārijāta* are based on mythological stories. Vishnudatta's *Saulochaniya*, Meghavrata Swāmi's *Dayānandadigvijaya*, Umāpati Sharmā's, *Pārijātaharana*, Shrirāma Sanehi's *Jānakicraranāmrita,* Dwijendra Nātha's, *Swarājyavijaya*, Harinandana Bhatta's, *Samrātacharita* and Vishnukānta Jhā's *Rāstrapatirajendra Vāmshaprashasti* are modelled on patriotic themes.

***Samskrit Fictional Literature**:* Fictional literature originated in India for the first time and it spread over other countries of the world in course of time. Samskrit fictional literature can be divided into beast tale (animal tale) and folk tale. Stories based on animals also occur in the Vedic literature. Fables are also found in the *Mahābhārata* and *Jātaka Kathā*. Buddhist scholar Vasubandhu has also used fables to evoke humour in the stories aimed at propagating message in his book *Gāthā Samgrah*.

Panchatantra is a major contribution to the fable literature of the world. It has been translated into at least 40 major languages of the world. The king of Persia had got the stories of *Panchatantra* translated into Persian after dimplomatic understanding between India and Persia. A Hakim named Burjoi translated *Panchatantra* in Pahalvi or ancient Persian language in 533 A.D. A Serian translation of *Panchatantra* was made in 560 A.D. under the title *Kālilaga and Damānaga*. From the Serian edition, it was translated into Arabian as *Kalilaha and Damanaha* by Abdullah Bin Almukaffa in 750 A.D. From Arbian, it was translated into Latin, Greek, German, French, Spanish and English. The stories of Aesop and the Arebian Nights were written under the influence of *Panachatantra*. These stores were more popular during the middle ages. The German scholar Hertel published the original text of *Panchatantra*. It consists of five parts viz, *Mitralābha, Mitrabhāga, Sandhi-Vigraha, Labdha-Prasansa* and *Aparikshitakārakam*. It has been written by Vishnu Sharmā in order to impart moral teachings to the king's sons.

Several moral stories were compiled in Samskrit such as the 14th century scholar Nārāyana Pandita's work *Hitopadesha*. Another important folk story in Samskrit is *Brihatkathā*. The original text is missing, but its three translations in Samskrit are available. These works are Buddha Swāmi's *Brihatkathā Samgrah*, Kshemendra's, *Brihat kathā manjari*, and Somadeva's *Kathāsarit Sāgar*. Naravāhanadatta is the hero of the stories figuring in *Brihatkathā*. He manages to marry his beloved Madanamanjushā and secures the kingdom of Vidyādharas. Dandi, Subandhu, Bānabhatta and Trvikrambhatta have accepted the importance of *Brihatkathā*.

Vetalapanchavinshati, Sinhāsanadvātrinshikā and *Shukasaptati* are placed under the category of popular folk-tales. *Vetalapanchavinshati* is the collection of 25 stories written by Shivadāsa. *Sinhāsanadvātrinishikā* presents the story of 32 putalis. *Shukasaptati* deals with the story of a parrot imparting suggestions to his mistress flirting with a person other than her husband. Jain poets have also written very interesting tales in verse in Samskrit. These stories have become popular due to their plain style. Of these works, *Prabandhachintāmani* and *Prabandha Kosha* are very popular. *Prabandhachintāmani* was written by Merutung Āchārya in 1305 A.D. It consists of five *Prakāshas* or *Khandas*. The **first** Prakāsha deals with the story of Vikramārk, Shatavāhana, Munja, and Mularāja. The **second** Prakāsha deals with Bhoja, the king of Dhārā. The **third** Prakāsha deals with the stories of Siddharāya and Jayasingh. The **fourth** presents the stories of Kumārpāla, Virādhavala and his charitable minister Vastupāla and Tejapāla; and the **fifth** deals with Lakshamanasena, Jayachandra, Vārāhmihir, Bhartrihari and Vaidya Vāgbhatta. *Prabandha Kosha* has been written by Rājashekhara. It deals with the story of 24 elites. These 24 personalities consist of 10 Jaina scholars, 4 Samskrit poets, 7 primitive and medieval kings and 3 Jaina household people. It has been written in 1405 A.D. Vallalasena's *Bhojaprabandha* is a famous composition. Anand's *Mādhavanala Kathā* and Vidyapati's *Purusha Parikshā* are other notable contributions to Samskrit folk literature.

***Samskrit Literature**:* Samskrit by common consent is placed under the category of the greatest literature of the world. It has a very rich mint of literature. Samskrit writers have left no field of knowledge untouched such as Dharmashāstra, ethics, philosophy, medical science, astrology, mathematics, Sāmudrika Shāstra, rites, rituals, devotion, sexology, poetics, grammar, music, dramatugy, kāvya (poetry) drama and fictional literature.

The literature available in Samskrit has been divided into two Sections-Vedic and secular (non-Sectarian). Secular literature originates from the *Rāmāyana,* which is accepted as the first *kāvya* ever written. Secular literature is redically different from Vedic literature. A clean cut demarcation line between the two can be drawn on the basis of treatment of subject, language and narrative technique and structure of *chhanda*. The *Rāmāyana* and the *Mahābhārata* are not only the primary epics paving the way for succeeding epics, they also assimilate within their embryo Indian cultural values, politiy, religion, philosophy, economics, law and many other branches of knowledge. (See Samskrit epic)

Samskrit *stotras* are rich both in quality and quantity and on both the scores there is no peer. Several philosophers and devotees have wirtten *stotras* to express their profound feeling for their gods and goddesses.

Prose works also form the backbone of Samskrit literature. They are available in the form of stories, moral stories and flok tales. Two forms of prose have been brought to the limelight: simple prose used for general talks and ornamental prose used for composing secular literature.

Fictional literature is available in two forms in Samskrit- Moral stories and folk tales. Bharata, Bhāmaha, Dandi, Rudrata, Udbhata, Abhinavagupta, Vāmana, Sankuka, Dhananjaya, Dhanika, Kuntaka, Kshemendra, Ānandavardhana, Māhimbhatta, Mammata, Panditrāja Jagannātha and Vishwanāth have contributed immensely to the development of Samskrit prose work.

Samskrit Prose *:* Most of the texts in Samskrit are available in Verse. Even works on Poetics, Mathematics, Jyotisha and Āyurveda have been written in Verse. Despite this fact, prose literature is aboundantly available in Samskrit. In Vedas too, prose extracts have been mentioned. The most primitive form of *gadya* (prose) is available in *Krishna Yajur Veda*. The sixth part of *Atharva Veda* is available in prose. The rich tradition of Vedic prose has been successfully handed down through the *Brāhmanas*, the *Aranyakas* and the *Upanishadas*. In the course of time, prose was accepted as a pure medium for philosophical compositions including books on grammar, science, astrology and commentaries. The simple as well as artificial prose is found in fictional works, *Akhyāyikas*, *Champu kāvyas* and works on criticism.

The prose available in Vedic literature is very simple whereas in regional literature a polished, refined and chiselled prose has been employed. The *Purānas* present a blend of simple and ornamental prose. *Shrimadbhāgavata* and *Vishnu Purāna* are appropriate examples of this kind of prose. Samskrit prose abounds in compound words. Terse style is the soul of Samskrit prose, which has accorded it a distinct flavour and colour.

Patanjali, Sabara Swāmi, Shankarāchārya and Jayantabhatta have successfully exploited simple and refined prose to deal with complex and cumbrous philosophical issues. Patanjali has written *Mahā Bhāshya* in a dialogue form, exchanged between ordinary people. Sabara Swāmi has written a *Bhāshya* on *Mimāmsā sutra* in a simple and plain language avoiding obscurity and verbosity. The prose of Shankarāchārya's *Vedānta Bhāshya* is mature and lucid. Jayanta Bhatta has dealt with the most intricate subject of *Nyāya* in a simple and lucid style in *Nyāyamanjari*.

Akhyāyikās and prose *kāvyas* have contributed significantly to the development of Samskrit prose. In the inscriptions also particularly those written during the Gupta period considerable effort has been made to bring prose work to high position.

Before Subandhu, Dandi and Bāna, a healthy tradition of prose writers is seen. Harishchandra, Vararuchi, Raumillasaumilla and Pālita had done a commendable job to guide Samskrit prose to a new direction. Samskrit prose witnessed its hey day in the works of Subandhu, Dandin and Bānabhatta. Several prose works were written taking inspiration from Bānabhatta. These works include Dhanapāla's, *Tilakamanjari*, Bādibhasingh's *Gadyachintāmani*, Sodhala's *Udayasunadari kathā*, Agasta's, *Krishnacharita* and Vāmanabhattabāna's *Vemabhupālacharita*. Beside this, Pt. Hrishikesha Bhattāchārya's, *Prabandhamanjari* and Pt. Ambikādatta Vyāsa's, *Shivarājavijaya* are excellent pieces of prose.

Several prose works have come to light on historical, sociological and political issues in the 20th century. Journals and magazines like Gāndiva, Bhārati and Ratnākara have brought Samskrit prose to a high pedestal. Narasimhanchārya wrote a novel *Saudāmini*.

Rāmādhina Mishra in company with another Mishra wrote history of Samskrit literature in Samskrit displaying mastery over prose. They wrote *Samskrit Sāhitya Itihāsa*, *Samskrit Sāhitya Vimarsa*, and *Samskrit Bhāshāvigyāna*.

Shaktibhadra: Shaktibhadra is the author of the drama Āshcharya Chudāmani. He was the disciple of Shankarāchārya. In this drama, the story of Rāma has been given a dramatic form. It is considered the most successful of all dramas based on the story of Rāma. In this drama, he has given special treatment to *Āshcharya rasa*. Besides this, he has written other dramas like *Vinavāsavadatt*, and *Unmādavāsavadattā*.

Sārangadhara Samhitā: Sārangadhara Samhitā is a popular work of Āyurveda written by Sārangadhara. It was written somewhere around the 12th century. It is divided into three *khandas*. The **first** *khanda* deals with the appropriate time to take medicine and test of *Nādi*. The **second** *khanda* deals with *swās*, *guatha*, *churna*, *avaleha*, *āsava* and burning of metals. It also deals with the method for the preparation of medicines. The **third** *khanda* deals with *snehapand* methods, Veda method and Vāmana method.

Saraswati Kanthabharana: Saraswati Kanthabharana is a noted work on Indian poetics written by Bhoja somewhere around 10th century. It consists of 643 *Kārikās*. It is not an independent work rather a collection of ideas held by several scholars. At least, 1500 slokas from the texts of Bhoja's predecessors have been accommodated in it, which help maintain a sequence of writers contributing their works to the enrichment of Samskrit literature.

The entire text has been divided into five *Parichchhedas*. The **first** *Parichchheda* deals with the objective of *kāvya (kāvya prayojana), kāvya Lakshana, kāvya bheda* and *Vākyārtha Dosha*. Bhoja has mentioned 48 *gunas* and 48 poetic blemishes. The **second** *Parichchheda* deals with 24 *Shabdālankārs* and the **third** *parichchheda* deals with 24 *arthālankārs*. The **fourth** *Parichchheda* is restricted to 24 *Ubhayālankārs*. The **fifth** *Parichchheda* deals with *rasa*, four *Vrittis* and *Nāyaka Nāyikā bheda*. It also deals with 65 *bhedas* (forms) of *Chitrālankārs*.

Commentaries of Jagadhara and Ratnessa (*Ratnadarpana*) are available on *Saraswati kanthabharana*. Bhoja's merit lies in throwing new light on *Nāyikā bheda* and *Shringāra rasa* and his work is of special significance in this respect.

Shatapatha Brāhmana : Shatapatha Brāhman is a Brāhman text of Yajur Veda. It is called Shatapatha because it consists of 100 chapters. Scholars are divided in opinion regarding the period of its composition. Tilaka in his work Arctic Home of the Vedas, has fixed the period of its composition around 25000 B.C. It is the most extensive and comprehensive of all Brāhmana texts. Its peculiarity lies in referring those Yajnas, which are nowhere mentioned in other Brāhman texts. It consists of several stories such as the story of Rāma, Pururvā, Urvasi and the Āshwini Kumārs. These stories have historical significance. It consists of 12000 Richās. At least three, *Bhāshyas* on it have been written by Hari Swāmi, Sāyana and Kavindra respectively.

Saundarānanda: Saundarānanda is an epic in 18 cantos written by Ashvaghosha. It deals with the teachings imparted by Buddha to his pupils to make their lives worth living. It deals with a conflict between sexual desire and religious leaning in a very interesting manner. It is studded with rich poetic qualities leaving *Buddhacharita* far behind.

The epic deals with the love-story of Nanda, the stepbrother of Buddha and his wife Sundari. The **first** canto deals with the genealogy of the *Shākyas*, birth of Siddhārtha and the beauty of Nanda and Sundari. The **second** canto is devoted to the exaltation of king Suddhodhana. The **third** canto deals with ways of Buddha achieving *nirvāna*. The **fourth** canto deals with the sexual pleasure and amorous feelings of Nanda and his wife Sundari. In the meantime, a female attendent informs Nanda that Buddha has returned from the palace without receiving alms. Nanda is ashamed of his behaviour and immediately rushes in the direction of Buddha to seek his forgiveness. In the **fifth** canto, Buddha pardons Nanda and initiates him into *Buddhism* by giving him invaluable teachings. The **sixth** canto deals with the pangs of separation of Sundari. In the **seventh** canto Nanda prepares to be back to his wife recalling her sweet memories. In the **eighth** canto, he seeks the assistance of a Buddhist monk to find out the apparent cause of his suffering and the latter suggests him to give up the company of women who are the major hurdle in his penance. In the **tenth** canto, Buddha consoles Nanda telling him to follow the commands of Dharma. Buddha finally accompanies him to sky to have a glimpse of the Apsarās asking him whether his wife is as beautiful as the Apsarās. Nanda replied in the nagative urging upon Buddha to suggest the ways to win the Apsarās.

Buddha suggests him to perform penance. In the **eleventh** canto, a monk ridicules Nanda for performing penance to win the favour of the Apsarās. In the **twelfth** canto, Nanda requests Buddha to tell him the ways to achieve nirvāna. The **thirteenth** canto deals with Buddha's teachings to Nanda. The **fourteenth** canto deals with the ways to overcome the senses and the **fifteenth** suggests the process of mental purification. The **sixteenth** canto deals with four noble truths and the seventeenth canto is devoted to enlightenment securing *ātma tatva*. The **eighteenth** canto deals with the penance of Nanda, his victory over Māra and awakening of true knowledge in him dispelling ignorance.

Saundarānand is out and out a peotic composition unlike *Buddhacharita* in which Ashvaghosha dwells upon the teachings of Buddha. In this way, the poetic element is subordinated to the religious element in *Buddhacharita* but in *Saundarānanda*, the poetic element gets the upperhand.

Sāyana: Sāyana was a minister of the 14th century kings of Vijayanagara: Harihara and Bukkā. He has written *Bhāshya* on the Vedas and the Brāhmanas at the bnehest of King Bukkā. It has been mentioned in *Taittariya Samhitā* that Bukkā urged upon his spiritual teacher Madhavāchārya to compile a *Bhāshya* on the Veda but the latter expressed his reluctance to compile *Bhāshya* due to excess burden that he was bearing at that time. He suggested him to seek the assistance of his younger brother Sāyana to accomplish this arduous task.

Sāyana has followed a particular order in the composition of this *Bhāshya*. At first, he wrote Bhāshya on Taittariya Samhitā and its Brāhmana texts. He observed that at the time of the Yajna, of the four *Ritvijas*, *Adhavaryu* plays a prominent role therefore he began his Bhāshya on Yajur Veda, which is the Veda of *Adhvaryu*. *Taittariya Samhitā* is followed by *Taittariya Brāhmana* and *Taittariya Aranyaka*. Rig Veda was placed next to Yajur Veda. Therefore, its *Bhāshya* was written after *Taittariya Samhitā*. The *Bhāshya* on Rig Veda is followed by the *Bhāshya* on Sāma Veda and Atharva Veda. The *Bhāshya* on *Shataptatha Brāhmana* was written towards the end. Sāyana took 24 years (1420-1444) to complete his *Bhāshyas*. Considering the bulk of *Bhāshya* attributed to Sayanāchārya, some scholars have expressed doubts whether these *Bhāshya* were actually written by Sāyana himself or by a group of scholars. How could it be possible for Sāyana to steal time for the writing of the *Bhāshya* in the wake of performing ministerial responsibities? This fact is substantiated by the writings on an inscription mentioning that scholars like Nārāyana Vājpeyee, Narahari Somayogi and Pandhāri Dikshit were given donations for the compilation of *Bhāshya* on the four Vedas. Another group of scholars has accepted Sāyana as the author of these *Bhāshyas*.

Sāyana Bhāshya is an exemplary contribution to the study of the Vedas. He wrote the *Bhāshya* using conventional method taking inspiration from the *Bhāshyas* written earlier. He looked back to *Vedāngas*, the *Purānas*, history, smriti and the *Mahābhārata* to give his *Bhāshya* distincet flavour and strurctural unity.

Shilā Duta: Shilāduta is a poem intended to communicate a message based on Kālidāsa's *Meghaduta*. Jain poet Charitrasundargani has written it. This poetry is the outcome of fulfilling the problem raised in the last *shloka* of the *Meghaduta*. It consists of 131 *shlokas* and is divided into *Purva* and *Uttara* parts like the *Meghaduta*. The hero Shilabhadra returns to his house seeking permission from his teacher after having been initiated in the Jain order. His wife compels him to deal with the household affair narrating her deteriorating condition. Shilabhadra, on the other hand, rejects her offer asking her to initiate into the Jaina ideology. His wife accepts his proposal and joins the order of the Jainism.

Shishupāla Baddha: Shishupāla Baddha is an epic written by Māgha. It deals with the story of the killing of Shishupāla by Krishna during the Rājasuya Yajna performed by Yudhisthira. The **first** canto begins with Nārada predicting the death of Shishupāla. The **second** canto deals with the altercation amongst Krishna, Balarāma and Uddhava on the issue of the killing of Shishupāla. The **third** canto deals with Krishna leaving for Indraprastha along with his army to participate in Rājasuya Yajna. The **fourth** and the **fifth** cantos present a graphic description of Raivātaka Mountain.

The **sixth** canto is devoted to the description of six seasons and their characteristics.

From the **seventh** to the **eleventh** canto natural descriptions are rampant. The **twelfth** canto deals with Krishna resuming his Journey. The **thirteenth** canto deals with the wordy argument between Krishna and Yudhisthira. The **fourteenth** canto deals with the preparations leading to the beginning of Rajasuya yajna and prayer of Yudhisthira and Krishna. The prayer to Krishna is performed by Bhishma. In the **fifteenth** act Shishupāla gets angry with Bhishma and Yudhisthira over offering prayer to Krishna. Bhisma threatens him, which leads to a rift between the Pāndavas and the kings showing their fidelity to Shishupāla. The background for the ensuing battle is prepared with the impasse remaining unresolved. In the **sixteenth** canto Shishupāla's messenger delivers a message to Krishna bearing double entendre in which praise as well as blame on Krishna is latent. Satyaki gives an appropriate reply to the messenger. The **seventeenth** canto deals with the preparation made by the two armies for the upcoming showdown. The **eighteenth** canto presents a terrific picture of the battle, which continues till the **19th** canto. The **twentieth** canto deals with the fierce fighting between Krishna and Shishupāla culminating into the killing of Shishupāla.

The plot of this epic lacks structure, unity and grandeur. Instead of depicting various aspects of life, it is restricted to a slice of life and thus it cannot be considered an epic. Actually, the plot of *Shishupāla Baddha* is apt to be treated as a *Khandakāvya*. From the third to the thirteenth canto the connection of the main story with the subsidiary incidents has not been properly shown. The poet seems quite at ease in the delineation of city, Mountain, moonlit night, sunshine and battle leading to disruption. Only a handful of characters appear in this epic. In this way, *Shishupāla Baddha* fails to meet the basic requirements of an epic.

Sitā Swayamvara : Sitā Swayamvara is an epic written by Nāgarāja in 1940 A.D. It is divided into 16 contos. The plot is based on the story of *Rāmayana*. Its style is ornate but the poet was conscious of simplicity to give rhythmical movement, and colour to the epic.

His other works are *Stotra muktā phala*, *Bhārtiya desbhakta charita* and *Shabarivilāsa*.

Shivalilāranava: Written by the 17th century poet Nilakantha Shivalilārnava is an epic. It deals with the story of Lord Shiva in 22 cantos. He has written one more epic entitled *Gangā Avatarana*.

Shiva Purāna: Shiva Purāna is a text of *Purāna* dealing with the life and exploits of Lord Shiva. There are several Samhitās in Shiva *Purān: Vidyaesvara Samhitā, Rudra Samhitā, Sata Rudra Samhitā, Kotirudra Samhitā, Umā Samhitā, Kailās Samhitā*, and *Vāyaviya Samhitā*.

There is a reference to *Shiva Purāna* in Al-Biruni's works. This also confirms the fact that Shiva *Purāna* was compiled before 1030 A.D. In **Kailas Samhitā** theory of *Pratibhijna Darshan* has been discussed which also contains two *sutras* from *Shiva Sutra*. Vasugupta, who belongs to 850 A.D has written Shiva Sutra. In this way, *Shiva Purāna* is supposed to be a composition of 10th century probably after *Vayu Purāna*. In *Shiva Purāna Tāntrika* system has been elaborately discussed. It also deals with various stories related to Lord Shiva, system of worship and rituals. **Rudra Samhitā** deals with story of the daughter of Daksha Prajāpati in 43 chapters, which includes the incident of Sati disguising herself into *Sitā* to examine whether Rāma is an ordinary man or God while he was wandering in forest searching Sitā. *Pārvati khanda* is devoted to the story of Pārvati, which includes her birth and penance to win Shiva's blessings to accept her as spouse. The impact of *tantra* can be seen on **Vāyaviya Samhitā**. It also propagates the theory of *Shaiva tantra* and the method of worshiping him. *Purāna Pancha Lakshana* doesnot figure in *Shiva Purāna*.

Shiva Purāna also deals with Shiva's penance and the curse turning Kāmadeva into ashes, Shiva's test followed by their marriage, birth of Kārtikeya, his leadership of gods and killing of Tārakasura, worship of linga and its significance, story of Ganesha and his marriage, Kārtikeya shifting to Krauncha mountain and various other stories including that of Prahalāda, Narsimha and clash between Arjuna and Shiva.

Skanda Purāna: Skanda Purāna is the Thirteenth *Purāna* in chronological order. It is supposed to have been written between the 7th and the 9th century. It is the most extensive of all *Purāna*s containing 81000 slokas. It is named after the son of Shiva, Kārtikeya, the military general of the gods. Kārtikeya has himself propageted the philosophy of *Shaiva tatva*.

Skanda Purāna is divided into 6 *Samhitās* and 7 *Khandas*. Among all its Samhitās, **Suta Samhitā** assumes special significance in the sense that it deals with the worship of Shiva. Both Vedic and *tāntrika* worships have been elaborately discussed here. Madhvāchārya's *Tātparyadeepikā* is the most authentic commentary on it. *Suta Samhitā* is further divided into four *khandas*. The first khanda Shiva *mahātmya* deals with the dignity of Lord Shiva in 13 chapters. The second *khanda Gyānayoga* deals with rigorous yoga. *Muktikhanda*, in three chapters deals with the ways and means to achieve salvation. *Yajna baibhava khanda* is divided into *Purva* and *Uttara khandas*. **Purva khanda** dwells upon the theory of monoism (*Advaita Vedānta*) with the worship of Shiva. **Uttara khanda** consists of two Gitās entitled *Brahma Gitā* and *Sutta Gitā*.

Its *Maheshvara khanda* deals with the amorous sport of Shiva and Pārvati. *Vaishnava khanda* deals with the temple of Lord Jagannāth and the method of worship. It also deals with the emergence of *Shivalinga* and its significance. *Brahmakhanda* deals with the importance of *Dharmāchārya* and the method of worship of Mahākāla of Ujjaina. *Kāshi khanda* deals with the might of all deities of Kāshi and *Shivalinga*. It also presents the geography of Kāshi. *Revākhanda* deals with the origin of the River Narmadā and the pilgrimages situated on its bank and the story of Satya Nārāyana. *Avantikhanda* deals with the *Shivalinga* situated at Avanti or Ujjaina with special reference to Mahākāleshwara. *Tāptikhanda* incorporates the pilgrimages situated on the bank of the river Tāpti. *Prabhāsh khanda* is devoted to the description of *Prabhāsh teertha*. It presents a geographical description of Dwārikā.

***Smriti* (Dharma Shāstra):** Smritis are texts aimed at laying down certain rules for the smooth and proper functioning of society. Initially the term Smriti was used in a broader sense incorporating *Vedānga*, *Dharma Shāstra*, History, *Purāna*, *Artha Shāstra* and ethics within its area. In course of time, its area narrowed to *Dharma Shāstra* only. In the beginning, the Smriti texts were handful in number, but later on their number increased to 18. Gautama has referred to only Manu as the writer of Smriti. Baudhāyana has mentiond 7 Smriti writers besides him. They are Aupajesina, Kātya, Kashyapa, Gautama, Prajāpati, Maudagalya and Hārita. Manu has referred to six, such as, Atri, Bhrigu, Vashistha, Vaikhānasa, and Shaunaka.

At present 18 Smritis are known, they are Manu, Yāgyavalkya, Atri, Vishnu, Hārita, Usānas, Angirā, Soma, Kātyāyana, Vrihaspati, Parāshara, Vyāsa, Daksha, Gautama, Vashistha, Nārada, Bhrigu and Angirā. *Mānava Dharma Shāstra* that Manu compiled is the oldest Smriti while the text that he wrote is entirely different from *Mānava Dharma Shāstra*.

The tradition of Smriti is given in the Shānti Parva of the *Mahābhārata* in which a text of ethics written by Brahmā has been mentioned. It deals with *Dharma, Arth, Kāma* and *Moksha* in 1 lakh chapters. Shiva abridged the text in 10,000 chapters, which was further brought down to 5,000 chapters by Indra under the title *Bahudantakathā Shāstra*.

In the *Smritis* special emphasis is laid on the issues including rights and the concomitant duties of the kings and his subjects, social codes and conduct, *Varnāshrama Dharma,* policy, good conduct and rules concerning administration. They give an organised form to social laws. Punishment was awarded on the basis of the provisions made in the Smriti texts.

Shobhākara Mishra: Shobhākara Mishra was a schoar of poetics. His period has been fixed between 1250 and 1350 A.D. He has composed a text on *Alankār*, entitled *Alankār sāra ratnākara,* which deals with 133 *Alankārs*. He has discussed 41 new poetic figures and has come out with a new approach to Metaphor, *Smarana*, *Bhrāntimāna*, *Sandeha* and *Apahnuti*.

Shri Harsha: Shri Harsha is the author of the epic *Naisādhacharita*. He has given sufficient information about his personal life in it. He was the son of Shrihira and Mamallādevi. His father was the court poet of Vijayachanda, the king of Kāshi. Shri Harsha was the court poet of Vijayachanda's son Jayachanda. Both the father and the son ruled between 1156 and 1193. According to a popular hearesay, the eminent *Naiyayika* and the author of *Nyāyakusumanjali*, Udayanāchārya humiliated Shri Harsha's father in a wrangle and Shri Hira committed suicide out of shame. Shri Harsha decided to avenge the death of his father. He offered penance to please Tripurasundari. The goddess was pleased with his devotion and blessed him with scholarship. Shri Harsha appeared in the court making statement punctuated by scholarship leaving Udayanāchārya spellbound. He accepted his defeat and Shri Harsha was elevated to the post of the court poet of Jayachanda.

Besides *Naisādhacharita*, his other works are *Vijayaprashasti* describing the heroism and gallantry of Jayachanda's father Vijayachanda. *Khandana khand khādya*, a philosophical work aimed at refuting the ideology of the *Nyāya* philosophy and vindicating the philosophy of the *Vedānta* School, *Chhindaprashasti, Shiva Shaktisiddhi* and *Navasāhasānka charita champu.*

Shri Harsha occupies a significant position among the poets of the post Kālidāsa period. His epic is a peculiar blend of exaggerated expression, scholarship and ornamentation. His objective was not to please the common reader rather it was aimed at providing amusement to scholars. His indepth philosophical knowledge is reflected at several places in *Naisādhacharita.* The seventeenth chapter is entirely devoted to the philosophical speculations in which he has successfully repudiated the Chārvāka doctrine. Shri Harsha assimilates the basic features of different philosophical schools in his works. Taking a cue from *Vaisheshika* philosophy, he compared the minds of Nala and Damayanti with two atoms, which was in conformity with the *Vaisheshika* School.

The popularity of Shri Harsha is chiefly confined to *Naisādhacharita* in which he elevated the ornamental and artifical style of the decadence period to a high pedestal.

Srimad Bhagavata Mahapurāna: Srimad Bhagavata Mahapurāna is one of biggest of all the *Purānas*. It is an encyclopaedia of Indian wisdom. Along with the Brahmasutra, the Gitā and the Upanishada it contains *Prasthānachatustaya*, four pillars disseminating essence of Indian culture and philosophy. It is the basic text of devotion, which imparts the message of selfless service.

The story of Srimad Bhāgvata is told by Veda Vyāsa. Shukadeva first narrated it to Parikshit. It is in the form of dialogne between Shuta and Shaunaka. The story relates to God Krishna and Rādhā, his beloved, the miracles created by lord Krishna as an incarnation of lord *Vishnu*. It also narrates the stories of numerous kings, saints and other important personalities. The graphic narration of the tales and the metaphysical analysis of dharma, love, soul, God and salvation vivify the book. Parikshit is fear-striken because he is doomed to die by snakebite after seven days. The story of the Bhāgvata is intended to remove from his mind the fear of death and make him realise *Amartava*. In the ninth *skanda*, the story of *Rāma* has also been incorporated. In the beginning of the Srimad Bhāgvata there is a shloka, which speaks of the significance of the text. The shloka insists that it is almost ripe fruit that emeged from the Veda (*Nigama*) which is as good as *Kalpataru*. Since it emanates from the mouth of Shukadeva (Shuka is also referred to parrot, the sweetness of a fruit is enhanced following the bite of a parrot) its sweetness is further intensified. Therefore, the *Rasikas* (lover of poetry) are suggested to go through it repeatedly because it is the storehouse of *Rasa (Nigama Kalpatarur galitam phalam, shukamukhād amritam dravasamyutam, Pivatu Bhagavatam rasamalayam, muhurahorasika bhuvibhauka).*

It consists of 12 *skandhas*, 335 chapters and 18000 *shlokas*. Of all the forms of *Bhakti: Vaidhi bhakti, Navadhā Bhakti, Nirguna Bhakti* and *Prema Lakshanā Bhakti*, the last one is considered the most significant means to achieve the grace of Krishna. It rejects the importance of knowledge as a source of communion with God.

The objective of this theory is to provide a synoptic view of the ideas contained in all philosophical schools that finally culminates in devotion. It gives special importance to *pancharātra* doctrine, which insists that devotee can achieve perfection through *Kriyā yoga*. It also propagates the significance of Shiva who is referred to as supreme *Bhāgvata* and *Vaishnava*.

The chief objective of the Srimadbhāgavata is to establish the authority of formless Brahman (*Nirguna Brahman*). It has assimilated *Vedānta* philosophy with *Bhakti* to work out an entirely new ideology.

The Bhāgvat lays stress on the point that Krishna is God incarnate. It accepts Krishna as Brahman. He pulls the chain from behind the curtain and the whole cosmos moves accordingly. Krishna is described as the source of all powers and at the centre of everything that exists on the earth. Apart from the literal meaning of the Bhāgavata, there is also latent symbolic meaning, which suggests that the *Gopies* are *Jivas* and Krishna is God. In the very beginning of the Bhāgvata, Shukadeva invokes Parameshvara, the creator of the universe, which means that the Bhāgavat is not meant only for the worship of Krishna, its philosophy is pervasive and can be followed without regard to religious sect, creed and faction. Behind the simple story of the life of Krishna and his miraculous deeds, there is in it the latent essence of the secret of the communion with God, for which as Shukadeva says one has to shake off all wordly allurments and egotism.

The *Venugeeta* and *Gopigeeta* in the Srimad Bhāgavata are very significant. In *Gopigeeta*, the miraculous effect of flute played by Krishna has been shown. When Krishna played on the flute, the ripples of waves were standstill under the magical effect of the song. The *Gopies* would rush to the spot in whatever condition they were. *Rasapanchādhyāyi* is the heart of the Bhāgavata. It describes *rāsalilā* and other divine and spiritual activities.

Several commentaries have been written on Srimadbhāgavata. Prominent among them are Sridhara Swāmi's *Bhāvārtha Prakāshikā*, Sudarshan Suri's *Shukapakshiya*, Virarāghva's *Bhāgavata Chandrikā*, Vallabhāchārya's *Subodhini Tikā*, Shukadevāchārya's *Siddhānta Pradeep*, Sanātana Goswāmi's *Brihatvaishnavatoshini*, Jiva Goswāmi's, *Karmasandarbha* and Vishvanātha Chakravarti's *Sārthadarshini*.

Shri Shankuka: Shri Shankuka was a prominent scholar of poetics. He achieved excellence as the interpretor of *Nātyashāstra*. He propounded the theory of *Anumiti Vāda* by opposing Bhattalollata's *Utpatti Vāda*. No independent work of Shri Shankuka is available. His shlokas have been mentioned in *Abhinavabhārati* and *Kāvyaprakāsha*. He is also supposed to have written a *kāvya*, *Bhāvanābhyudaya* and reference to this effect is available in Kalhana's *Rājatarangini*.

Shri Shankuka's *Anumiti Veda* is based on the philosophy of *Nyāya* in which Rasa has been analysed on the basis of *Chitraturaga Nyāya*. A horse pointed in a picture is for the time being taken as the real horse. In the like manner Shakuntalā and Dushyant acting on the stage are for the time being taken as real characters and the spectators derive *rasa*. If they were to be taken as mimicry, the spectators can neither relish nor get *rasa*. Shankuka uses the word *vāsanā* in twofold senses. In its adjectival use it means perfume; in its use as a verb it means to spray perfume. It is a matter of common experience that when oil is perfumed with a certain scent, it gets perfumed by that scent and gets the flavour of that scent. Similarly, when an actor plays the role of a particular character he loses his original identity and takes on the identity of the character he is performing on the stage. The spectators enjoy the scene because the characters are perfumed with the characters played on the stage. This is the secret of aesthetic enjoyment. He observes that the real experience of *Rasa* is enjoyed by the *Sāmājika* (spectator).

Shringāraprakāsha: Shringāra Prakāsha is a stupendous work on poetics written by Bhoja. It is a voluminous work consisting of 36 *prakāshas* covering 2500 pages. It deals with all the subjects related to poetics and drama. Bhoja has given primary importance to *Shringāra Prakāsha* permeating all the *rasas* into it. Chapters 11 to 36 are devoted to bring out the importance of *Rasa*. V. Rāghavana has presented an abridged version of the book in English.

Stotrakāvya: There has been a rich tradition of Stotra kāvya in Samskrit. A glimpse of *Stotras* (devotional poems) can be obtained from the Vedas in which several mantras have been uttered to show the devotion to the Almighty. These *stotras* are aimed at showing the helplessness of the devotee and invincible power of the deity. The devotees seek the grace and blessings of the deity to get through the impediment surrendering him completely to his feet. In the *Rāmāyana*, the *Mahābhārata* and the *Purānas stotras* are scattered all over. In the *Lankā kānda* of the *Rāmāyana* with **Ādityahridaya** *Stotra* Agastya Muni welcomes Shri Rāma. In the *Mahābhārata* Bhishma has narrated **Vishnusahasranāma** to Yudhisthira. **Durgāstotra** has been introduced in Markandeya *Purāna*.

Initially, stotra kāvya were not written independently. They formed the part of religious texts. Later on, their independent status was recognised. Besides Hindu devotees, Jaina and Buddha devotees also complied *stotras*.

Shivamahimnastotra by Pushpadanta, composed in the 8th century, is considered the most significant composition of stotra literature. It has been written in *sikharni chhanda* and each *shloka* presents a story dealing with the omnipotence of Shiva. At present only its 40 *shlokas* are available. Out of which 31 *shlokas* are engraved on the walls of the temple of Amareswara Mahādeva at Mālawā. Mayurbhatta and Bānabhatta have also written *Surya Shataka* and *Chandishataka* respectively in *Shragdhara Chhanda*.

Shankarāchārya has written more than 200 stotras. These stotras present a unique blend of devotion and philosophy. Shlokas like *Shiva aparādha kshamāpana*, *Mohamudgara, Charpatamanjarika, Dashashloki* and *Ātmashataka* are some of the significant shlokas compiled by him. Perhaps the most significant stotra is *Saundaryalahari* in which Shankarāchārya has depicted the eternal beauty of goddess Durgā.

Lakshmana Āchārya's *Chandi kucha panchāshika*, Kulasekharas *Mukundamālā* and Yamunāchārya's, *Alambandarastotra* and Lilāshuka's *Krishna karnāmrita* also occupy important place. Venkatadhvari wrote a stotra on goddess Lakshmi in the 17th century running into 1000 shlokas. Someshvara has written *Rāmashataka* in *Sragdhara Chhanda* in 100 shlokas. Another poet, also named Shankarāchārya has composed a stotra *kāvya* on Lord Vishnu named *Vishnupadadikesantavarana* in 51 *Sragdhara Chhandas*. Madhusudana Sarasvati's *Ānandamandākini,* composed in the 16th century describes the beauty and grace of Lord Vishnu in 102 verses. Mādhava Bhatta's *Dānalilā* is based on the amorous sports among Krishna, Rādhā and *gopikās*. It consists of 48 verses. Appaya Dikshit wrote *Varadarāja stava* eulogising God Varadarāja of Kānchi in 106 Slokas.

Kāshmiri poets have enriched the *stotra* literature with *stotras* on Bhagawān Shiva. Utpaladeva's *Shivastotrāvali*, Jagdddhara Bhatta's *Stuti Kusumānjali*, Nārāyan Panditāchārya's *Shiva Stuti* and Gokulanātha's *Shivashataka* are of great importance.

Jain poets have also contributed immensely with *Bhaktamāra* by Manatunga, *Kalyānamandira* by Divākara, *Chaturvinshika* by Samantabhadra, *Ekibhāvāstotra* by Shri Vādirāja, *Suktimuktāvali* by Somaprabhāchārya and *Jinashataka* by Jambu Guru.

The poets and scholars belonging to Mahāyāna Sect of Buddhism have written *stotra kāvyas* in abundance. Nāgārjuna has composed *Chatuhstava*, Vajradatta wrote *Lokeshvara shataka,* Sarvagya wrote *Āryataragdharā* in 37 *shlokas* in the 8th century and Kavi Bhārati wrote *Bhakti Shataka* in the 13th century showing their devotion to Lord Buddha. Hemachandra's *Anyāyogevyavachchhedika* is also a popular *stotra kāvya.*

Besides these stotras *Devi pushpānjali* by an anonymous poet and *Shiva tāndava stotra* by Rāvan are very significant and popular.

Subandhu: Subandhu is the authour of Vāsavadattā, a prose tale, and significant contributor to the enriched tradition of Gadyakāvya (prose literature) in Samskrit. Subandhu has not given any concrete infromation about his personal life in his work. He is supposed to be an inhabitant of Kashmir as he has given emphasis on metaphorical expressions, a general habit of Kāshmir poets. Bāna has himself mentioned *Vāsavadattā* in his prose work *Harshacharita* which further establishes that Subandhu was the predecessor of Bāna.

Subandhu has banked upon an imaginative story in *Vāsavadattā*. He is considered to have laid the foundation of ornamemtal prose style bristling with puns. His intellctual faculty is always at work leaving no room for feelings and emotions. He seems to be playing on words and his interest is confined to the selection of apt and effective words to add to the beauty of his expression.

Shudraka: Sudraka is considered one of the best Samskrit dramatists. He has written an epoch making play *Mrichchhakatika*, which deals with the ground realities of life. It is an excellent amalgam of realistic and romantic themes.

In the preface to *Mrichchhakatika*, Shudraka has been referred to as a very powerful, efficient and peace-loving king who handed over his kingdom to his son and died at the ripe age of over 100 years. This fact has been mentioned in other texts also. *Skanda Purāna* has observed that Shudraka ruled over his kingdom 27 years before Vikramaditya. Shudraka has been referred to as a king in *Vetalapanchavinsati*, *Kathasarit Sāgar* and *Kādambari*. In Harshacharita, he has been referred to as the enemy of Chandraketu, the king of Chakora.

Shuka Sandesha: Shuka Sandesha written by Laxmidāsa is a poetic work intended to communicate a message. He flourished in the 15th century. It is modelled on the pattern of *Meghadua*. It deals with the story of a lover and his beloved living at Gunakapuri. The lover communicates the message to his beloved in a state of dream. While they were sleeping the lover felt his beloved is dragged far off from him to Rāmasetu near Rāmesvarama and so he sends his message to her through a parrot. It consists of two parts. The first part deals with the account of the way from Rāmesvarama to Gunakapuri. In the second part the message has been communicated. The poet has used *Mandākrantā chhanda* throughout the Kāvya. This kāvya is of paramount importance on account of its bearing on the history and society of Kerala.

Shukasaptati: Shuka Saptati is a popular fiction. It is a collection of very captivating stories. In this book, a story has been spoken out through a parrot to his lady-mistress who has affairs with others in the absence of her husband. The stories are aimed at finding a corrective to her infidelity towards her husband. The parrot dissuades her by telling the story. The book is available in two forms - one in its comprehensive form and the other in its compressed form. The Comprehensive form has been attributed to Chintāmani Bhatta whose time was 17th century. The author of its compressed form is a Jain Scholar. In the 14th century it was translated into a crude Persian language. *Shukasaptati* has been translated into several languages. It was introduced to the western world through its Persian translation. Dr. Smith has translated both the forms of this book into German Language.

Shukra: Shukra was an eminent political analyst and the author of *Shukraniti*. Shukra has been referred to as the propounder of one of the streams of Indian polity. Kautilya too has introduced him as a great political thinker. Shukraniti deals with the nature of state, Divine theory, the duty of king, theory for the appointment of king, succession, preferance to the elder, bodily strength, character and consent of the subjects, theory of coronation, need of the council of ministers, their number and qualification, theory of the appointment of royal officers, theory of their deposition, source of income of the king, law and order, armed forces, limbs of army, war, kinds of war, *Daivika yuddha, Asura yuddha, Mānava yuddha, Shāstra yudda, Bahu yuddha, Dharma yuddh* and rules of *Dharma yuddha*.

Sukti Sangraha: ***Subhāshita Sangraha***: Sukti or Subhāshita Sangraha is a collection of verses aimed at comminicating moral teachings. It is not attributed to a single poet. Works of several poets are included in these collections of verses. What is striking about these texts is that they have mostly included those works, which are not available. In this way, these *Suktisangrahas* have done a great service by bringing to light several texts including:

i. *Subhāshita Ratna Kosha* - It has been written after 11th century. It consists of works of those poets that flourished before 1300 A.D. The author of this text is anonymous.

ii. *Subhāshitāvali* - It is a volumionus text prepared by Vallabhadeva of Kāshmir. It consists of 3527 verses. It contains the quotations from approximately 360 poets. It was compiled around the 15th century.

iii. *Saduktikam amrita* - This collection was prepared by Shridharadāsa in 1205 A.D. It consists of works of several anonymous writers of Bengāl. It is divided into five *pravāhas* - *Amara, Sringāra, Chatu, Upadesa* and *Uchchhvācha*. Each *prāvaha* is divided into *vichis*, which are 476. Each *vichi* consists of 5 *shlokas*. The number of *shlokas* is 2380. Out of 485 poets mentioned in this text, 50 poets are popular and the rest are unknown.

iv. *Suktimuktāvali* - This collection was prepared by Jalhana, the minister of Southern Indian king Krishna. He belonged to 13th century.

v. *Sārangdhara paddhati* - It was prepared in 1362 A.D. by Sārangadhara, the son of Dāmodara. It consists of 4689 shlokas, which are divided into 163 subjects.

vi. *Padyāvali* - It is a collection of 386 verses of 125 poets.

vii. *Sukti ratna hāra* - It was compiled by Suryakalingarāya in the 14th century.

viii. *Padyaveni* - It is a collection of works of 144 poets belonging to the medieval ages prepared by Venidatta. It also includes the works of several poetesses.

ix. *Padyarachanā* - This collection of 756 verses has been prepared by Lakshmana Bhatta. It was prepared in the first half of the 17th century.

x. *Padya amrita tarangini* - This collection was prepared by Haribhāskara in the latter half of the 17th century.

xi. *Suktisaundarya* - It was prepared by Sundaradeva in the second half of the 17th century.

xii. *Kavindra Vachana Samuchchya* - A collection of 525 verses edited by F.W. Thomas on the basis of the manuscripts available.

Sushruta Samhitā: Sushruta Samhitā is a popular text of Āyurveda written by Kāshirāja Dhanvantari. The text is addressed to Sushruta. The book has been written to overcome the problem of operation faced by Sushruta. The present form of *Sushruta Samhitā* is the outcome of the effort made by Nāgārjuna. He was the friend of the king of *Satavāhana* dynasty. *Sushruta Samhitā* consists of 120 chapters of which 46 are devoted to *Sutrasthāna*, 16 to *Nidāna*, 10 to *Sharira*, 40 to *Chikitsāsthāna*, 8 to *kalpsthāna* and 66 to *Uttaratantra*.

The purpose of this book is to provide proper training for surgical operations. It also deals with the method of autopsy, management of hospital, adequate surgical tools and plastic surgery. Sushruta has prohibited the attendance of woman by patient's bedside. Gayādāsa has written a commentary on it.

Swapna Vāsavadattā: Swapna Vāsavadattā is the most successful drama written by Bhāsa dealing with the story of Udayana, Padmini and Vāsavadattā. (See Samskrit Drama and Bhāsa)

Swarājyavijaya: The epic Swarājyavijaya (1960) is based on patriotic theme. It begins with highlighting the enriched cultural heritage of India, which is followed by the foreign aggression, birth of the Congress, and achievements of great freedom fighters like Tilaka, Subhāsh, Patel and Gāndhi and the exploits of revolutionaries. It is a significant contribution to the 20th century Samskrit literature aimed at reviving patriotic feeling and at the same time inculcating positive ideas in the heart of the youth urging them to imitate the life-style of the great heroes of the past and to work for the betterment of the country. ■■

Taittariya Aranyaka: Taittariya Aranyaka, a part of Rig Veda, consists of 10 *Parichchheda,* which is also called *Aran*. Its *Parichchheda*s have been divided into *anuvāks*. The first *Parichchheda* deals with the worship of *Agni*. Self-meditation and *pancha mahā yagya* have been discussed in the second *Parichchheda*. The third and the fourth *Parichchheda* deal with mantras meant for various purposes.

Taittariya Brāhmana: Taittariya Brāhmana is the Brāhamana text of the *Krishna Yajurveda*. It does not have an independent status rather it is a part of *Taittariya Samhitā*. Its chapters are called *kānada*. The rules of *Yagya*, which do not figure in the *Taittariya Samhitā* have been mentioned in this *Brāhmana,* and the methodology of the *Yagya* propounded in the *Samhitās* has been elaborately discussed. The first *kānda* deals with *Yagya*s like *Agnadhāna, Vājapeya, Sāma, Nakshatra shresthi* and *Rājasuya.* The second deals with *Agnihoma, Upahoma* and *Sotramani.* Several hymns of Rig Veda have been included in it. In addition to them, some new hymns have been also added to it. The third chapter gives a detailed discussion of *Nakshatra shresti Yagya* and accepts Sāma Veda as the most prominent of all the Vedas. It has also explained the origin of *Vaishya* from *Rik*, of *Kshatriya* from *Yajusa* and of *Brāhmana* from Sāma Veda. The provision for performing *Ashvamedha Yagya* has been made for *Kshatriya* only. *Shudras* have been termed as impure for *Yagya*. The stories of the *Purānas* and the incarnation of *Vārāha* are narrated here.

Taittariya Pratisākhya: Taittariya Pratisākhya is in the form of *Sutras* and divided into two sections. Each section contains 12 chapters. The first chapter deals with the origin of *Varnas* (letters) and the second chapter deals with *Anusvāra, Anunāsika* and *Svarati bheda*. Several commentaries have been written on it of which Somāchārya's *Tribhāshya ratna* and Gopālayajva's *Vaidakābharana* are prominent.

Taittariya Samhitā: Taittariya Samhitā consists of 7 *kāndas,* which are further divided into 44 *prapāthakas* and 631 *anuvākas*. It presents a detailed account of *Yagya*s including *Paurodāsa, Vājpeya* and *Rājsuya*.

Taittariya Upanishada: Taittariya Upanishada is a part of *Taittariya Aranyaka* falling under the Taittariya branch of Krishna Yajurveda. The seventh, the eighth and the ninth chapters of *Taittariya Aranyaka* are called *Taittariya Upanishada*. The three chapters are called *Ikshāvalli, Brahmānandāvalli* and *Bhriguvalli*. The entire section has been written in prose. The chapter entitled *Ikshāvalli* is intended to frame rules for the recitation of the hymns of the Vedas and the invaluable teachings imparted by the teachers to their disciples after the completion of their teachings. *Brahmānandvalli* deals with the ways and means to achieve Brahman. It also discusses *Brahmavidyā*. This section also discusses *Panchakoshas*: *Annamaya, Prānamaya, Manomaya, Vigyānmaya* and *Ānandamaya koshas*. Brahman resides inside the cavity of heart, and *pancha koshas* are the routes leading to Brahman. Brahman resides in the *Ānandamaya kosha* and the Jiva enjoys a sense of eternal bliss after reaching the final stage. *Bhriguvalli* emphasises penance (*Tapa*) as a means to secure the company of Brahman. Emphasis has also been laid on highlighting the significance of the services rendered to the guest. Brahman is eternal pleasure and the entire living beings originate from pleasure itself.

Tantra: Tantra is significant part of Shaiva Philosophy. Tantra, which signifies expansion, is *shāstra* that helps the expansion of knowledge. In a wider perspective works belonging to *shāstra, siddhānta, anusthāna* and *viggyāna* have been included in the orbit of *Tantra*. Shankarāchārya used the word *Tantra* for *Sāmkhya. Tantra* is included in *Āgama Shāstra. Āgama* is generally concerned with *Moksha* through *Karma* and *Upāsanā*.

The word tantra has been derived out of the root 'tan' meaning Knowledge. The terminology used in Tantra Shāstra must be understood in the right perspective. *Tantra Shāstra* lays emphasis on *panchamakāras: Mānsa, Mudrā, Matasya, Maithuna*, and *Madya.* But these terms do not carry crude meaning. These five terms have been used in a Symbolic Sense. The term '*madya'* is used in the sense of nectar existing in *Sahasrār chakra*. The term 'mānsa' is used in the sense of meat, which is procured by killing the beasts of *Pāpa* and *Punya* through the sword of knowledge. '*Matasya'* is used in the sense of ebb and flow passing through '*erā'* and '*pinglā'* nerves. '*Mudrā'* means abandonment of bad company and yogic postures also. Similarly the term '*maithuna'* signifies fusion: the fusion of *Mulādhāra* chakra with Sahasrāra. The Sacrifice of *pashu* means the sacrifice of one's egotism and the *Vikārs* of senses like *Kāma* (physical satisfaction), *Krodha* (anger), *Ahamkāra* (pride), *Matsara*, etc. The tantra shāstra is considered very secret and recondite.

Kaul School of tantra is based on practical utility of Tantra. Matsyendra Nāth is usually associated with *Yogini kaul*. His disciples lived in kāmarupa in Assam. Gorakha Nāth and many others believed in *Hatha Yoga.* As time passed, the *Tantra* literature was interpreted afresh.

The teachings of Tantra were originally given by Lord Shankara to Pārvati for the welfare of the people of *kaliyuga*. Works in Tantra fall in two distinct divisions *Vedānukula* (agreeing with the Vadas) and *Vedabāhya* (out side the Vedas). The theories discussed in *pancharātra* and *Shaivāgama* have derived the sources from the Vedas. *Shāktāgama* accords not with the Vedas. The Literature of *Tantra* is vast and varied, but most of the books have not been published yet.

Teerthayātrā Prabandha Champu: Teerthayātrā Prabandha Champu, by Samarapungava Dikshita who belonged to the second half of the 16th century, is divided into 9 *uchchhwās* and deals with several pilgrimages of north and south India. The name of the author is nowhere mentioned. The poet has presented a copious picture of nature at several places in his *kāvya*. The poet seems to have excelled in presenting the geographical topography of India.

Trivikrama Bhatta: Trivikrama Bhatta is the author of the *Champu kāvya Nala champu*. It is the oldest *champu kāvya* ever written in Samskrit. Certain facts, appearing in the beginning of *Nala champu* help arrive at a decision with regard to its composition. References to poets like Gunādhya and Bāna have been made in the beginning of *Nala champu*. One shloka of the sixth *ucchvāsa* has been mentioned in Bhoja's *Sarashvati-kantha-bharana*. Besides this, in the inscription of the *Rāshtrakuta* king Indra III excavated from the village Bāgumber of Gujarāta, the name of its author has been mentioned as Trivikrmabhatta. Trvikrama Bhatta was the court poet of Indra III. The donations given by Indra III on the occasion of his coronation ceremony have been mentioned in his inscriptions and Trvikrama Bhatta is supposed to have written those inscriptions. There is peculiar coincidence between figurative style of the *shlokas* of the inscriptions of Indra III and that of *Nala champu*. One more book *Madālasā champu* has also been attributed to him though there is a marked difference between the writings of these two *champu kāvyas*. The figurative style of *Nala champu* is nowhere evident in the *Madālasā champu*. *Nala champu* has been divided into *Uchchhavāsas* and *Madālasā champu* is divided into *Ullāsas*. The author has given an account of his family clan in *Nala champu* but in *Madālasā champu*, no such evidence is noticed. The inscription of Nausari in which Trvrikrama Bhatta has eulogised his patron is an example of excellent piece of art and is very close to the mode of expression one gets in *Nala champu*.

Nala champu deals with the story of the marriage of king Nala and Damayanti. It does not present the whole sequence of incidents Nala had to undergo in course of his life and the story ends suddenly in the seventh *uchchhvāsa* with Nala communicating the message of gods to Damayanti. The influence of *Naisadha chartia*, a preceding work dealing with the same story cannot be ignored. The skill of Trivikrama Bhatta lies in his narrative technique. He is too much conscious of displaying his authority in this particular department that he virtually forced the story element to the background. His poetry is marked by figurative language.

■■

Ubhaya Kushala: Ubhaya Kushala was an eminent Astrologer who excelled in *Phalita Jyotisha*. His period has been fixed around 1737 AD. His works include *Vivāha-Patāla* and *Chamatkāra Chintāmani*.

Udayanāchārya: Udayanāchārya, an eminent scholar of the Nyāya School, compiled works to give fitting reply to the objections raised by others and thwarted them successfully with cogent arguments and substantiating his ideology in his works: *Lakshanāvali; Nyāya-Vārtikā-Tātaparyatikā-Parishuddhi; Nyāya Kusumānjali*; and *Ātmatatva Viveka*. He has also written a commentary, *Kiranāvali* on a work of Vaisheshika philosophy: *Prashasta-pada-bhāsya*.

Udaya-Sundari-Kathā: Udaya Sundari Kathā is a *champu kāvya* by Soddala written at the advice of Vatsarāja, the *Chālukya* king. The poet's intense desire to use terse style, compound words and elliptical expressions is evident throughout the text. It is laboured, and quite indifferent to feelings and emotions.

Udabhata: Udabhata, an eminent rhetorician, authored a celebrated work: *Kāvyālankāra-sāra-samgraha*. According to Kalahana's *Rāja-tarangani* he was the court poet of Jayapira, the king of Kashmir. Two other books: *Bhāmaha Vivarana* and *Kumāra-sambhava kāvya*, have been attributed to him. It is different from Kālidāsa's work of the same name.

Uddhava Duta: Uddhava Duta by Mādhava is a poem written in the 17th century to communicate a message. It consists of 141 *Shlokas* composed in *Madākrāntā chhanda*, the concluding one is in *Anushtupa chhanda*. With Uddhava as the messenger of Krishna the poet gets the opportunity to describe the pain and agony of Rādhā and the Gopikās. He hands over the apparel of Krishna to console them.

Uddhava Sandesha: Uddhava Sandesha by Roop Goswāmi is another poem based on the theme of Uddhava as a messenger of Krishna trying to teach *gyān* to Rādhā and Gopikās and in return gets ample lessons in *bhakti* and complete surrender. It contains 131 *shlokas* in *Madākrāntā chhanda*.

Udyotakara: Udyotakara is a 6th century philosopher whose fame rests on *Nyāya vartikā*, a commentary on *Vātsyāyana Bhāsya*. He has launched a tirade of scathing attack in defense of *Nyāya* philosophy, and has successfully justified its validity by highlighting its merits.

Upanishadas: Upanishadas are the concluding section of Vedas, and contain the essence of Indian philosophy. The *Upanashidic* period is considered the hay day of Indian ideology when emotionally and intellectually surcharged Vedic rishis were stimulated to meditative contemplation.

The word *Upanishada* has been coined by adding '*up*' and '*ni*' prefix to '*sad' dhātu*. 'Up' signifies proximity, 'ni' is for certainty and 'sad' means 'to sit'. Thus *Upanishada* suggests sitting near the teacher to secure knowledge. It is aimed at imparting teaching, which might enable one to have communion with Brahman. Shankarāchārya has written *Bhāsya* on all the ten important *Upanishadas* out of 108 available and 1041 claimed. They are *Isha, Kena, Katha, Prashna, Mundaka, Māndukya, Aitareya, Taittariya, Chhāndogya* and *Brihadāranyaka*. Other than Shankarāchārya, Rāmānuja and Mādhava have also written commentaries to reveal and explain the ideas contained in them.

It is the subject matter of the *Upanishadas* to reveal the knowledge of Brahman. It has been presented in conversational language through story and poetry. The issues, which have been extensively discussed in the *Upanishadas* include Metaphysics, Ethics, Creation of Cosmos, Brahman, *Jeeva, Jagata, Moksha*, religious consciousness, sin, sorrow, karma, life after death, *Sāmkhya, Yoga*, and Psychology. Each Veda has its independent *Upanishada*.

Dārā Shikoha got the Upanishadas translated in the 17th century in Persian as '*Sirre Akbar*' or '*Mahārahasya*' which was translated into Hindi as Upanishada Bhāsya. In 1975, French traveller Duren translated them into French and Latin. Rājā Rām Mohan Roy published English translation of some *Upanishadas* along with the original text in 1816 and 1819. Maxmuller published English translations of 12 *Upanishadas* during 1879-84 as Sacred Books of the East Series. Dressden translated them into German in 1882. F. Mishell and Bohtlingk translated ten *Upanishadas* into German and R. Hume produced the translations of 13 prominent *Upanishadas* in 1921. Dr. S. Rādhākrishnan published English translations of selected *Upanishadas* along with the original text as 'Principal *Upanishadas*'. (Also see *Upanishada* philosophy below.)

Upanishada Brāhmana: Upanishada Brāhmana is *Sāmvediya Brāhmana* and is also called *Chhāndogya Brāhmina*. It consists of 257 Mantras and covers a wide range including marriage, embryology, sacred-thread ceremony, *deva-bali-homa*, *nava-graha-pravesha*. Sāyana and Guna Vishnu have written *bhāsyas* on it.

Upanishada Philosophy: Upanishadas form the foundation of Indian philosophy on which the lasting mansion of eternal religion is shining. They were compiled neither at one time nor by one person.

They provide a solution to the eternal problems related to God and soul, as its primary objective is to provide solution to the perplexing problem of exploring the truth: ethical-cum-spiritual truth. *Upanishadas* are the first attempt of its kind to unveil the mystery of the universe. Issues like the ultimate authority, nature of the world and the problems affecting the universe, the final goal of an individual, one's ideal, relationship between *karma* and liberation, and rebirth have been dealt with. The question: whether soul ends with the dissolution of the body or it exists even after death, have been discussed elaborately.

The objective of life is vividly discussed in the *Shwetāshwar Upanishada*. It begins with the question: where do we come from? Which way we finally lead to?

Kathopanishada and others maintain that soul is immortal and imperishable. *Chhāndogya* holds that so long the soul remains in the body it is chained with good or bad objects. Once, it is disentangled from the body it is free from bondage. *Brihadāranyaka* takes soul as Brahman. According to *Kenopanishada* it falls well within the reach of both known and unknown objects; and according to *Mundakopanishada* Brahman is both the efficient (*Nimitta*) and the instrumental (*Upādāna*) causes of the universe.

Upanishadas have emphasised two forms of the Brahman: *Saguna* and *Nirguna*. *Nirguna* Brahman is *Parā, Paramātmā* and *Saguna* Brahman is *Aparā*. All worldly objects are the part of the power emanating from Brahman emerge from Brahman and dissolves into Him. Brahman is real. Brahman is effulgent light and pure knowledge, and the storehouse of *rasas*. *Jiva* rejoices the company of Brahman. He is all pleasure and enlightenment. But *Upanishadas* have expressed inability to reveal the identity of Brahman and hence, have called Him '*neti-neti*' for Brahman has no end. As the spider spins out its web from its own body and finally eats it up, in the same way, Brahman creates the universe out of Himself and devours it. With the analogy of *Ratha, Sārathi*, *Ashva, Lagāma* (reign) and *Ātmā*; the body, intellect, sense organs, mind and the master of *ratha* all these facts are suggested; and the superiority of *Ātmā* over everything else is established.

Urubhanga: Urubhanga is a drama by Bhāsa that deals with an incident from the Mahābhārata when Bhima breaks the thigh of Duryodhan. Against the traditional norm the drama it contains only one act but the unity of time and place is maintained. Bhāsa has shown his sympathy towards the characterisation of Duryodhan; particularly towards his bravery and generosity. Bhāsa was bold enough to show the death of his hero on the stage, again against the classical norms. *Vira* and *karuna rasa* flow out of the fiery speeches of Bhima and Duryodhan and from the wailing of Dhritrāshtra and Gāndhāri after the death of the beloved son.

Uttara Purāna: Uttara Purāna, composed by Gunabhadra, is attributed to *Jains*. Gunabhadra was a disciple of Jinsena. The *Uttara Purāna* is taken as the other half of another *Purāna* of *Jains*, named *Ādi Purāna*. There is an anecdote that Jinsena died after completing the 44th Chapter of *Ādi Purāna* and the rest of the work was completed by Gunabhadra and is called *Uttara Purāna*. It deals with the life of 23 Tirthankars from the 2nd Ajita Sena to the 24th Tirthankar Mahāvira. It is considered as an encyclopedia of the *Jain Purānas*. In addition to the essence of all the Purānas it contains the Index of 32 'successive *Purānas*. It presents the life of 63 people: 24 Tirthankaras, 12 kings, 1 Vasudeva 1Shuklabala, 1 Vishnudivisā and others.

Uttara Rāmacharita: Uttara Rāmacharita, in seven acts, is the most successful play by Bhavabhuti. It presents a detailed account of the life of Rāma from after his coronation. It is imbued with the dramatic skill of Bhavabhuti and is a monumental work.

1st Act: Coronation of Rāma, Sitā is banished on account of rumours. **2nd Act:** Birth of Luva and Kusha to Sitā at the hermitage of Vālmiki; Rāma kills Shudraka. **3rd Act:** Sitā and Rāma faint at different places while thinking of the spouse. **4th Act:** Janaka and Kaushalyā reach the hermitage of Vālmiki to meet Sitā. Lakshaman's son Chandraketu appears with the horse of Ashvamedha, and Luva Kusha taking it as a challenge, abduct the horse. **5th Act:** Luva defeats the army of Chandraketu, and final show down between them. **6th Act:** Rāma returns to the venue, stops the battle, as he feels the reflection of Sitā on the face of Luva. Vashistha, Vālmiki, Janaka and Kaushalyā join Rāma. **7th Act:** Rāma loses his poise at the sight of Sitā drowning in the sacred river Ganges; Lakshamana consoles him, Sitā appears, and the drama ends with family re-union.

The story is taken from Vālmiki *Rāmāyana* but has been presented with fresh flavour and tint. The pathetic ending is changed to happy union. The creation of '*Chhāyā* Sitā' (shadow Sitā) is a novelty. Drama within a drama is a significant contribution and milestone. Yet it suffers from structural incongruity. The principle of three unities had to be ignored because the story begins before the birth of Luva and Kusha and ends when they have grown almost young. The scene of action too, shifts from Ayodhyā to hermitage. There is no buffoon in the play. Despite some technical shortcomings Bhavabhuti succeeds in carrying out the message, and enchanting the readers and spectators. ■■

Vāchaspati Mishra: An eminent philosopher, Vāchaspati Mishra flourished in the 1st half of the 8th century contributed significantly to the enrichment of *Nyāya* School of philosophy. His *Nyāyavartikā Tātparya Tikā* is a popular book on *Nyāya* philosophy. It was aimed at repudiating the doctrines of Buddhist Naiyayika Dharmakirti. Dharmakirti had refuted the philosophical ideology of the *Brāhmana Naiyayikas* and proved the superiority of Buddhist *Nyāya* over the former. Vāchaspati Mishra made fruitful effort to bring the glory of *Nyāya* back on the track throwing the hypothesis by Dharmakirti to the backwater.

He has written *Sāmkyatatva-kaumudi* on *Sāmkhyakārikā*, and *Tatva-vaisāradi* on *Yoga-darshana*. He has also written *Bhāmati tikā*, a commentary on *Shankara-bhāsya,* which is considered his most successful work. His scholarship and in depth study of Indian philosophical system is successfully reflected in his works.

Bhāmati Tikā has been named after his wife, Bhāmati. Vāchaspati Mishra maintained austerity throughout his life and shunned carnal pleasure. There is hearsay that Vāchaspati Mishra was married to Bhāmati 36 years back. He was so engrossed in writing commentary on Shankara's *Bhāsya* on *Brahman Sutra* that he did not recognise his wife even after a lapse of 36 years. One day when the candlelight extinguished. His wife Bhāmati rushed to light it. Vāchaspati Mishra questioned his wife as to who she was? Bhāmati replied that she was his wife. Vāchaspati Mishra was full of remorse for not having recognised her. Then and there, he promised to immortalise her. He decided to name his commentary on Shankara's *Bhāsya* after her.

Vāg Bhatta: Vāg Bhatta was a 5th century scholar. He wrote an epic named *Neminirmāna* dealing with the story of Jain Tirthankara

Neminātha in 13 cantos. Bhattāraka Gyānabhusana has written a commentary *Panjikā* on it.

Vāg Bhatta: Vāg Bhatta was a 5th century scholar of *Āyureda*. He wrote a monumental work *Ashtānga-samgraha*. His teacher Avalokiteshvara was a Buddhist. He was also a follower of Buddhism. *Ashtānga-samgraha* presents a unique blend of prose and verse. It deals with all the 8 parts of *Āyurveda*. He has largely borrowed from Charaka and Sushruta. Of all the ancient texts on *Āyurveda*, maximum commentaries were written on *Ashtānga-samgraha*.

Vāg Bhattal I: Vāg Bhatta I was an eminent critic belonging to the first half of the 12th century. He wrote a text entitled *Vāgbhattālankāra*. *Vāgbhattālankāra* has been written in five *parichchhedas*. It presents a brief account of the various theories of poetics in 260 verses. The **first** *parichchheda* deals with the nature and cause of *kāvya*. The **second** *parichchheda* deals with different kinds of *kāvya* and the **third** *parichchheda* deals with the nine *rasas* and *Nāyaka-Nāyikā bheda*. He has given illustrations both from *Prākrita* and Samskrit texts.

Vāg Bhatta II: Vāga Bhatta II was an eminent critic of the 14th century. A popular work *Kāvyānushāsana* has been attributed to him. He was one of the forerunners of Jainism. He also wrote a couple of *Kāvyas* including *Chandānushāsana* and *Risabha-deva-charita*.

Kāvyānushāsana has been written in sutras on which he has himself written a *Vritti*. It is divided into five chapters. The **first** chapter deals with the objective, cause and kinds of *kāvya*. The **second** chapter deals with 16 defects of *pada*, 14 *Vākyas* and defects of meaning. The **third** chapter deals with 63 *arthālankāras* and the **fourth** with 6 *Shabdalankārs*. The **fifth** chapter deals with nine *rasas*, *Nāyaka-Nāyikā-Bheda* and the defects of *Rasa*.

Vaiyāghrapāda: Vaiyāgrapāda was a grammarian of the pre-Pānini era. According to an illustration appearing in *Kārikā*, it seems that his grammar runs into 10 chapters.

Vājasaneyi Pratisākhya: *Vājasneyi Pratisākhya* of *Shuklayajureda* was written by Kātyāyana. He is different form Kātyāyana, the author of *Vartikā*. It consist of 8 chapters and its objective is to present a detailed analysis of definition, *swara*, and *samskāra*. He was considered to be the predecessor of Pānini as the latter has borrowed immensely from *Vājasaneyi Pratisākhya*. This also shows the gravity and excellence of this text.

Vakroktijivita: Vakrokti-jivita is a critical treatise written by Kuntaka, the exponent of the theory of *vakrokti* (satirical comment). It is the leading text of this school in which Kuntaka has tried to establish *Vakrokti* as the kernel of poetry. It has been divided into four *Unmesha*. It is further divided into *kārikā*, *Vritti* and illustration. Kuntaka has himself written *kārikā* and *Vritti* whereas illustrations have been quoted from the works of other poets. It consists of 165 *kārikā*s. The **first** *Unmesha* deals with the motive of *Kāvya*, *kāvya lakshana, vakrokti*, its nature and its six kinds. This section also presents a detailed analysis of *gunas* like *Oja, Prasāda, Mādhurya, Lāvanya* and *Abhijātya*. The **second** *Unmesha* deals with *sadāvidhāvakritā*. The **third** Unmesha deals with *Vākyavakratā* and the **fourth** deals with *Prakarana* and *Prabandha Vakratā*.

Kuntaka was a fierce detractor of Ānandavardhana. He along with Māhimbhatta and Dhananjaya caused an irreparable damage to the theory of *Dhvani* and merged different kinds of *Dhvani* within *Vakrokti* denying its independent existence.

Vākyapadiya: Vākya-padiya is a very mature book on the philosophy of grammar. It was written by Bhartrihari, and has three sections: *Āgama* or *Brahman kānda*, *Vākya kānda* and *Pada kānda*. At present only its first section is available. It has been written in *Shlokas* and consists of 1964 *Shlokas*. Certain fundamental questions related to linguistics, semantics and grammar have been raised in *Vākyapadiya* and the author has suggested a viable solution. The objective of the poet is to establish the significance of grammar. Actually its objective is rounded up in the first two sections, some unrelated subjects dealt in first two *kānda*s have been discussed in the third *kānda*. Its third section works only as an appendix.

In the first section called *Brahman Kānda*, there is the description of *Shabda Brahman*. In the first section there is also the description of *sphota*, which means eternal vibration. Several commentaries have been written on *Vākyapadiya*. Bhartrihari has himself written explanatory note on it. Amongst its commentary only those by Brishabhadeva and Dhanpāl are available. Pushparāja (11th century) has written something on its second section. Helrāja (11th century) has written commentary on all its three sections. But at present only the commentary on third section is available which is named *Prakirna Prakāsha*.

The first section of *Vākyapadiya* consists of 156 *Shlokas*. Its second section contains 493 and third section contains 325 *Shlokas*. The three sections of the book deal with three distinct subjects.

In the first section named *Brahmankānd*, *Shabda Brahman* is described. Bhartrihari has taken *Shabda* as *Brahman*. As *Brahman* or God is infinite, without beginning or end, so word has no beginning or end. In the second section, which is named *Vākyakānda*, the author discusses the formation of sentence and *pada* and the ramification of meanings and their relative importance. He considers *pada* as a definite unit of meaning and its relative importance is shown when it is used in a sentence in a particular context. The third section, which is named *padakānd* is *prikirnaka*. In this section the author discusses subjects like *linga, vibhakti, sankhyā, dravya*, *vritti, subanta* and *jati*.

Vallalasena: Vallala Sena, the son of Lakshmana Sena, the king of Mithilā, was an eminent scholar of Astrology. He compiled a voluminous work *Adbhuta-sāgara* in 1168 A.D. It consists of 8000 *Shlokas*. He has himself made a thorough assessment of the planets (*grahas*) before passing his final verdict on their nature and impact on human beings. He has used prose at regular intervals. He has presented a scientific analysis of *grahas* that had a lasting effect and opened up new vistas for further exploration in this regard. He also explored the possibility of various ups and downs in the life of an individual as a consequence of the movement of *grahas* and their relationship with other *grahas*.

Vālmiki : By universal consent Vālmiki is considered as one of the greatest epic poets of Samskrit literature, Ādi Kavi, the first poet. There is a hearsay that in the beginning of his life Vālmiki was a a plunderer who in the later phase of his life by compelling circumstances and on the advice of Nārada became a *Bhakt* and pioneering Samskrit epic poet. The anecdote to this effect has been mentioned in the *Bālakānda* of the Rāmayana. While walking on the bank of the river Tamasā, Vālmiki saw a *krowach* bird and his beloved she-*krowach* in passionate mood on the branch of a tree. An archer suddenly killed the she-*krowach* with his arrow leaving the male wailing over the dead body of his spouse. This moved Vālmiki deeply and out of pity and compassion, poetry overflowed from his mouth. He wrote a couplet to decry the cruel archer. The anguish of Vālmiki flowed through the couplet and this utterance is the beginning of poetry:

Mā nishāda pratishthām tvam gamah shāshwati shamāh;
Yat krowach mithunādekam vadhih kām mohitām.

Vālmikiya *Rāmāyana,* is the beginning, foundation and landmark on which Samskrit epic poetry developed and stands. He is considered to be a contemporary of Rāma, who is the *nāyaka* of the *Mahākāvya*; because there is evidence to show that when Sitā was banished by Rāma from the palace she found a shelter in Vālmiki's *āshrama* where she gave birth to Luva and Kusha. Vālmiki's Rāma as depicted in his *Rāmāyana* is not *Brahman*. He is just an embodiment of high human Values. He is a king full of flesh and blood and is not endowed with divine bliss as latter poets ventured to establish; particularly Tulsidāsa, whose Rāma is the incarnation of Vishnu, infinite, omnipresent and omniscient. Vālmiki's Rāma has all the follies from which a man suffers. Vālmiki never wanted to make him a symbol of godhood. Vālmiki has taken the character of Rāma and Sitā as role models and has inculcated those qualities, which elevate their personality to a great height. Rāma is a man of indomitable will and extra-ordinary courage who forces his way out of danger showing exemplary mental equipoise.

Vālmiki's vision as a seasoned political thinker has been successfully crafted in the *Rāmāyana*. He insists that the king must serve as the guardian of society. As father showers his blessings on his sons in equal proportion, in the same manner the king must bestow affection upon his pupil irrespective of their cast, creed and religion. The king must give top priority to the welfare of the state and his pupil.

Vālmiki has presented the ideal character of *Purushottama* Rāma through the *Rāmayana*. The imaginative faculty, style and characterisation are at its highest pitch and Vālmiki has handled it in an unprecedented manner. He has portrayed colourful picture of natural scenery throughout his work. He resorts to various kinds of poetic figures to refurbish his description.

Vālmiki's *Rāmāyana* is not only a poetic work rather it is a living record narrating the exploits, gallantry and achievements of our predecessors. He is equally competent in the delineation of Nature and evoking aesthetic pleasure. He has successfully exploited poetic figures particularly, similes to bring home his ideas in a very apt and suggestive manner. His command over words and diction is incomparable.

Vāmana: Vāmana was the exponent of the school of Riti (style). He wrote *kāvya-alankāra-sutra Vritti* in which he took style as the main pivot of poetry (*kāvya*). References of Vāmana are available in the works of Rājasekhara and Abhinavagupta. It consists of 319 sutras and is divided into 5 *adhikaranas*. Vāmana has himself written *Sutra* and *Vritti* on it. He has given extensive treatment to *guna* (merit), style blemishes and poetic figures. He made a major contribution by showing difference between *gunas* (merits) and poetic figures. He claimed that *gunas* are the permanent features of poetry and *alankārs* are *anitya* (eternal). He accepted *Upamā* (simile) as the chief poetic figure, and the importance of *rasa* in poety.

Vāmana Purāna: Vāmana is the Fourteenth *Purāna* in the sequence of Purānas. It deals with the incarnation of Vishnu in the form of Vāmana. *Matasya Purāna* has maintained that Vāmana *Purāna* is that *Purāna* which deals with Vishnu measuring the entire Universe in three *degas* (steps). It consists of 10000 *Shlokas* and 92 chapters. It is divided into two parts: *Purva* and *Uttara*. It also consists of four *samhitās: Maheshwari samhitā*, *Bhagavati Samhitā*, *Sauri Samhitā* and *Ganeshvari Samhitā*. Besides this, it also presents the significance of Shiva, Umā-Shiva marriage, birth of Ganesha and Kartikeya.

Vārāha Purāna: Vārāha Purāna is the 12th *Purāna* in order. It deals with the *Vārāha* incarnation of Lord Vishnu. It is a *Vaishnava Purāna*. In order to redeem the affliction of the earth, Vishnu had to take recourse to this form. It consists of 24000 *Shlokas* and 217 chapters. It presents a brighter account of creation and dynasties of kings. It has paid proper attention to Shiva and Durgā also. It also deals with the story of *Nachiketā* and reveals the mystery of heaven and hell; lays special emphasis on various rites related to Vishnu, particularly *Dwadashi*; and presents an elaborate analysis of the theory of *Vishishtādvaitavāda* propounded by Rāmānujāchārya.

Vārāhamihira: Vārāhamihira was an eminent scholar of astrology. He occupies a respectable place among Indian astrologers. He has written a monumental work *Brihajjātaka*. His other works include *Pancha-siddhānt Tikā, Brihat samhitā, Laghujātaka, Vivāha patala, yogayātrā* and *Samāsa-samhitā*. He flourished in the first decade of the 6th century. He received formal training of *Jyotisha* from his father Adityaḍāsa. He is reckoned among the *Navaratnas* in the court of king Vikramaditya.

He made three categories to *Jyotisha* - *Tantra*, *horā* and *samhitā*. *Siddhānta*, *Jyotisha* and opinion regarding mathematics are included within *Tantra*. Horoscopes are included in *Hora*. *Samhitā* is called *phalita Jyotisha. Brihatsamhitā* is the most acceptable work on *phalita Jyotisha*. He has tried to put *Jyotisha* to the practical surface bringing it close to human life. Western scholars have also acknowledged his unparalleled talent. In this book he has presented a study relating to the influence of *nakshatras* on the fate of man while making a study of the impact of movement of the Sun and the moon and their relationship with other planets.

Vashistha dharmasutra: Vashistha Dharmasutra belongs to *Rig Veda*. References borrowed from other Vedas are also available in it. The original text has been subject to frequent changes and modifications. At present, it has 30 chapters. *Shlokas* form Manusmriti and Gautama Dharmasutra have been quoted in it. There is a peculiar similarity between the 19th chapter of *Gautama dharmasutra* and the 22nd chapter of *Vashistha dharmasutra*, although it has not yet been proved which one was written first and which came later.

Among the wide ranging subjects covered in this text, the most prominent are six types of marriages, entitlement to the king of the 1/6 of the amount from his subject as tax, rights and duties of four *varnas*, *Brāhmana* permitted to perform the Job of a *Kshatriya* or a *Vaishya*, the duty of *grihastha* and *sanyasins*, conduct of *snātaka*, rules of adoption, the duty of the king and the significance of *purohita*, repentance for the actions happening knowingly or unknowingly, repentance for the celibate for adultery and drinking, feature of pranāyāma, praise of woman and Vedic mantras consorted with charity.

Vasubandhu: The most prominent exponent of the *vaibhāsika* sect of Buddhism, Visubandhu propagated the theory of *Sarvāstivāda*. His monumental work *Abhidharma-kosha* is the most significant work on *Vaibhāsika* sect. It is divided into 8 *parichchhedas*. Besides this, his other works include *Parmārtha Saptati*, *Tarka Shāstra*, a text of Buddha *Nyāya* divided into three *parichchhedas*. It deals with *Panchāvayava, Jati* and *Nigraha Sthāna, Vādavidhi*, a commentary of *Abhidharmakosha*, *Sad-dharma-pundarika*, *Mahāparinirvāna-stuti*, *Vajrachedikā Pragyā-pārmitā* and *Vigyāpti-matri-siddhi*.

Dr. Purse has translated the original text *Abhidharma-kosha* into Chinese. It is said that towards the last phase of his life he accepted *Yogāchāra* doctrine under the influence of his brother Asanga, himself an eminent Buddhist philosopher.

Vatsabhatti: No work of Vatsabhatti is available. In the name of text, only **Mandasaura Inscription** is available which was engraved during the reign of Kumāra Gupta. It was written around

529 A.D. This inscription called *Mandasaura Prashasti* consists of 44 *Shlokas*. It deals with a Sun temple constructed by the weavers in 437 A.D. and was reconstructed in 473 A.D. The inscription begins with the prayer of Lord Shiva, which is followed by a moving and graphic description of *Mandasaura*. The poet has raised aloft the contemporary king Narapatibandhu Vermā belonging to the 5th century. It is an excellent piece of art from the classical point of view and the impact of Kālidāsa on it cannot be ruled out.

Vatsarāja: Vatsrāja was a dramatist and minister of the king of Kalinger, Paramārdi Deva. He flourished between 1163 and 1203 A.D. He has written six dramas. *Karpuracharita* deals with the fantastic experience of the gambler Karpura. It is a *bhāna* having one act. *Kirātarjuniya* is based on the epic of Bhāravi of the same name. It is a *Vyāyoga* containing only one act. *Hāsya-chudāmani* is a comedy consisting of one act. *Rukmini-harana* dilates upon the heroics of Krishna who rushes to the urgent call of Rukmini to save her. *Tripuradāha* is a *Dim* (a kind of drama), consisting of four acts. It deals with the destruction of the capital of Tripurāsura by lord Shankara. *Samudra-manthana* is *samabhākara* (another type of drama) consisting of 3 acts. It deals with the story of churning of the ocean by gods and demons and finally culminates into the marriage of Vishnu with Lakshmi.

Vatsarāja uses simple and plain diction. He has successfully contrived the structure of his drama and has presented the mythological stories taken from various scriptures in a very fabulous and poignant style.

Vātsyāyana: Vātsyāyana was an eminent philosopher and commentator on *Nyāyasutra*. Even before Vātsyāyana some explanatory books on *Nātya Shāstra* were written which have been mentioned by Vātsyāyana in his *Bhāsya*. But Vātsyāyana's *Bhāsya* is the most authentic and accomplished one of *Nyāyasutra*. In Samskrit there are several Vātsyāyanas. It seems that the commentator of *Nyāyasutra* is different from the author of *Kāma Shāstra*. In Hema Chandra's *Abhidhāna-chintāmani*, there is a reference to several persons as Vātsyāyana. Chānakya is one of them. At the end of the first *sutra* of Vātsyāyana *Bhāsya* there is one Shloka from *Arthashāstra* written by Chānkya as Kautilya. This is why some scholars deduct that Chānakya is the Commentator of both *Nayāyasutra* and *Kāma Sutra*. Udyotakara has written a voluminous *bhāsya* on Vātsyāyana *Bhāsya*.

Vātsyāyana Kāma Sutra: Kāma Sutra by Vātsyāyana is the most significant and authentic work on the concept of physical union, which is universally acknowledged as a unique work of its kind and has thus achieved popularity world over. Both Kautilya and Vātsyāyana have been addressed as single person in the dictionaries like Hemachandra's *Vaijyanti.* Most of the scholars have earmarked that he flourished in the 3rd century. Controversy persists whether the commentator of *Nayāsutra* and the author of *Kāmsutra* are the same Vātsyāyana.

It has been mentioned that this *Shāstra* was at first propagated by *Brahman,* which was divided by Nandi in 1000 chapters. Svetaketu provided the abridged form of Nandi *Kāma Shāstra*.

Kāma sutra has been divided into three parts: *Adhikarana, Adhyāya* and *Prakarana*. There are 7 *Adhikaranas*, 36 *Adhyāyas* and 1250 *sutras* (*Shlokas*) in it.

The **first** *Adhikarana* consists of 5 chapters and 5 *Prakaranas*. It is a prologue to *Kāma sutra* and provides general description of the subject. The **second** *Adhikarana* is called *Samprayogikā*, which means *Sambhoga* or cohabitation. It consists of 10 chapters and 17 *Prakaranas*. It deals with several kinds of sexual intercourses between man and woman. The **third** *Adhikarana* deals with girls fit enough for marriage. The **fourth** *Adhikarana* deals with two types of wives, *ekachārini* and *sapatni*. The author of *Kāma sutra* has looked upon marriage as sacrosanct and permanent union between the husband and the wife. Here one also gets a discussion on the duties and obligations of husbands towards their wives and vice versa. The **fifth** *Adhikarana* is related to the love with a lady other than one's own wife and man other than one's own husband. It is also discussed under what circumstances love grows and diminishes. The **sixth** *Adhikarana* is divided into six *Adhyāyas* and 12 *Prakaranas*. It is restricted to the character of prostitute, and means of cohabit with them. It throws ample light on the gestures of prostitutes. The author of *Kāma sutra* has condemned prostitution in unequivocal terms. The **seventh** *Adhikarana* deals with the methods to overpower *Nāyakas* and *Nāyikās* by means of *tantra, mantra, yantra* and medicines. It also deals with the devices to entice women and to enhance one's physical lusture.

In Kāmasutra, copulation is divided into three categories: for the birth of progeny; for the preservation of race and born out of pure love and welfare of the counterpart and for celebration. Vātsyāyana has dealt at length with the importance of *dharma* and *artha*, which he considers the important wheels of life. The author has also devised the ways and means to make marital life happy and eschew mutual bickering, heart burning, malice, attack and counter attack.

Kāma sutra has a broad based programme. It examines and analyses *Kāma* from different angles and proves its importance in life. Vātsyāyana postulates several principles with regard to the variety of woman and the different ways to satisfy physical appetite.

Several texts were written in Samskrit on the model of *Kāma sutra,* which include *Ratirahasya*, *Nāgara-sarvasva* and Pancha-shāyaka written by Kokā Pandita, Bhik Supadma Shri and Jyotirisvara respectively.

Vāyu Purāna: Vāyu Purāna is the fourth *Purāna* in order. It consists of 12000 *Shlokas* and 112 chapters. It is divided into four *khandas-prakarana*, *anusanga, upoddhāta* and *upsamhār.* Like other *Purānas*, it also deals with the creation and lineages of several kings. The aim of *Vāyu Purāna* is to highlight the significance of the worship of Shiva. Other gods have also been included within its compass. The story of Vishnu and his various incarnations have also been depicted. From the 104th to 112th chapters facts related to the Vaishanava worship have been included, which are considered interpolation and have been added to the text at a later date. It also presents various acts of Lord Krishna along with Rādhā. In the last eight chapters (105-112) significance of Gayā has been brought out.

Vedas and its Bhāsya: Each Veda (Samhitā) has several *Bhāsyas*. Prominent among the writers of *Bhāsyas* are Skāndasvāmi, Nārāyana, Udgitha, Mādhava Bhatta, Venkata Mādhava, Dhanuskyajvā, Ānandatirtha, Ātmānanda, and Sāyana. They have written *bhāsyas* on *Rig* Veda.

Skāndaswāmi flourished in 625 A.D. His *Rig Bhāsya* is very exhaustive in size, which mentions gods and saints of each *sukta* and has given references from *Anukramani* texts, *Nighantu* and *Nirukta* to substantiate his stand.

Nārāyana belongs to the 7th century. From one of the *Shlokas* occurring in his *Rig Veda bhāsya*, it is clear that Skandsvāmi, Nārāyana and Udgitha have jointly written *bhāsyas* on *Rig* Veda. The reference to Udgitha is available in the *bhāsyas* of Sāyana and Ātmānanda. Mādhava Bhatta is one of the four *bhāsya*-writers on *Rig* Veda whose *bhāsya* bear the same name. Venkata Mādhava has written a *bhāsya* on the entire *Rig Veda Samhitā.*

Dhanuskyajvā came well before 1300 B.C. He has written *bhāsyas* on three Vedas. Ānandatirtha is another name of eminent dualistic philosopher Madhvāchārya. He has written a *bhāsya* on some mantras of the *Rig* Veda, in the form of Verse. Ātmānanda was the predecessor of Sāyana.

Sāyana was the minister of Harihara and Bukkā, the kings of Vijayanagara. He flourished in the 14th century. He has written *bhāsyas* and began with the *bhāsya* on Yajuraveda. It was followed by that of *Rig* Veda, the Sāmaveda and the Atharvaveda. Sāyana *bhāsya* occupies a significant place in revealing the mystery shrouding Vedic language and literature. This is the only authentic source through which Vedas can be studied rather easily.

Mādhava, Bharatasvāmi, and Guna Vishnu can be mentioned as the important *bhāsya* writers of Sāmavada. Mādhava has written a *bhāsya* on the Sāmaveda entitled Vivarana. He belongs to the 7th century. Bharatasvāmi flourished in the 14th century. Besides compiling a *bhāsya* on Sāmaveda, he has also written a *bhāsya* on Sām, a *Brāhmana Grantha*. Guna Vishnu has written a *bhāsya* entitled *Sāma-mantra-vyākhyāna*. He flourished in the first half of the 13th century.

The 11th century scholar Uvvata wrote a *bhāsya* on Shukla-Yajur Veda. Anantāchārya and Ānandabodha have written *bhāsya*s on *Kanva Samhitā* of the Shukla Yajur Veda. The 16th century scholar Anantācharya has written a *bhāsya* on the second half of the *Kanvasamhitā*.

***Veda* (Introduction)**: The Vedas are the most prominent texts of the world, which assimilate the soul of knowledge within their axis. The foundation of the huge mansion of Indian religion, literature, civilisation, and philosophy stands on the Vedas. Vedas signify knowledge. The Vedic knowledge emanates from the rishis and has been expressed through mantras. According to the Indian tradition, the Vedas are not human creations rather they are divine creations. They reflect the experiences gained by the rishis in course of their penance. *Brāhmana*s are also part of Vedic literature. One of the meanings of *Brāhmana* is Yagya. Thus *Brāhmana* texts are those, which present an account of various activities related to Yagya. They are divided into three parts *Brāhmana*, Aranyaka and Upanishada.

On the basis of *Samhitās* the Vedas are four in number: Rig, Yajur, Sāma and Atharva. *Samhitās* are collection of mantras for the benefit of different *Ritvijas* (seers) during the yagya. These four *Samhitā*s fulfill the basic requirements of four types of seers playing vital role in the yagya. Four Ritvijas are *Hotās, Udgātā, Adhvaryu*, and *Brahmā*. *Hotā* used to invoke the gods while reciting the mantras of the *Rig* Veda. *Hotā* means caller, one who calls someone, *Udgātā* means singer. He is related to the Sāma Veda. He used to pray the gods during the Yagya. The purpose of *Adhvaryu* was to accomplish the works related to yagya in proper manner. He is considered the pivotal figure in the completion of Yagya. He used to recite the hymns of Yajur Veda. *Brahmā* was considered the supreme commander at the time of performing a Yagya and the entire ritual was performed under his guidelines. The objective was to protect the Yagya from external obstructions, to remove the latches in the recitation of mantras and to remove the errors occurring during the Yagya. Initially, he was not associated with an independent Veda. He was considered to have acquired a mastery over all the Vedas. In course of time Atharva Veda became its prime Veda.

***Veda* (Period):** There is complete lack of unanimity of opinion among the scholar about the period of composition of the Vedas. Indian tradition has considered it as the version of God and thus cannot be confined within the rigid demarcation of time. They are timeless (*ārsa*).

Max Muller, an eminent German scholar collected and collated various facts and evidences and finally came to the conclusion that the Vedas were written around 1200 B.C. He has placed the entire Vedic literature into four periods; each period lasting for 200 years. These four periods are: *Sutra* period, *Mantra* period, *Brāhamana* period and *Chhanda* period. But Max Muller's classification of each period in 200 years is hardly tenable. Even western scholars have objected to it. While Whitney protested this trend, Schroeder tried to prove the antiquity of the Vedas maintaining that they were written between 1500 B.C. and 2000 B.C. Yakobi has fixed 4000 B.C. as the period of composition of the Vedas on the basis of the astrological calculations.

These are the periods when *Laukika* Samskrit was fully in vogue and Vedic Samskrit was not in use. There must be a difference of thousands of years when Vedic Samskrit lost its ground and *Laukika* Samskrit developed. Everything points to a much earlier period difficult even to imagine.

The facts must be different. Vedas and great rishis were in existence before the period of Rāma and Krishna. Their period can be calculated only on the basis of the four Yugas: *Satayuga, Dwāpar, Tretā* and *Kaliyuga*. Any conclusion without considering them will be erroneous, and not acceptable to Indians. Since, those periods cannot be fixed correctly so it's a futile effort to try to fix a time frame for the composition of Vedas. They have been in existence since very primitive period.

Vedānga: Vedānga are the integral parts of Vedas. *Vedānga* means the organs of Vedas. They are separate only from *Samhitās* and not from Vedas. It is wrong to take them as texts aimed at revealing the meaning contained in the Veda *Samhitas*. They have their independent existence and worth too. In broad divisions they are six in number: **Shikshā, Kalpa, Vyākarana, Nirukta, Chhanda** and **Jyotisha.** The *Vedāngas* have been written with a distinct purpose; and there are many books in each category. They serve variety of purposes which include correct recitation of Vedic mantras, performance of Vedic rituals in proper manner, etymology of the words contained in Vedic literature, deriving the knowledge of the Vedic *Chhandas*, ascertaining the specific period for the performance of Yagya and making the meaning of Vedic texts clear. **Shikshā** is aimed at understanding the way to recite the Vedic *svars*: *Udātta, anudātta* and *Svaritta* in a proper manner and to suggest a methodology for this purpose. The purpose of the Vedas is to perform rituals and yagyas. **Kalpas** were as sutras to the extended Vedic rituals. Each Veda has a separate **Kalpa**. It has been divided into four categories - *Shrauta sutra*, *Grihya sutra*, *Dharma sutra* and *Sulva Sutra*. Each Veda possesses all the four sutras. *Srauta sutra* deals with various kinds of Yagyas including Dasha-purna-māsa. *Grihya surta* consists of those rituals, which are performed through the household fire such as yagya, marriage and *upnayan*. *Dharma sutra* deals with the duties of four *varnas* and four *āshrams* (stages of life which a man undergoes in the course of his life). *Sulva sutra* deals with the process of the construction of Vedikā. The seeds of geometry are contained in the *sulva sutra*. The aim of **Vyākarana** (grammar) is to understand the nature and *pratyaya* (prefix) of the words in order to find out their real meaning. **Chhandas** are aimed at obtaining the real knowledge of Vedic verses. Vedic *chhandas* do not have syllables (mātrās) like *laghu* (unaccented) and *guru* or *deergha* (accented syllable). Instead of counting the mātra of the letters and only letters are directly counted. The Vedic *chhandas* include *Gāyatri* (8+8+8), *Usnika* (8+8+12), *Anushtupa* (four *charanas* consisting of 8 letters), *Brihati* (8+8+12+8) *Pankti* (five *padas* consisting of 8 letters), *Tristupa* (four *padas* consisting of 11 letters) and *Jagati* (four *padas* consisting of 12). **Jyotisha** aims at finding out the appropriate time to perform Yagya. It has been mentioned in the Taittiriya Aranyaka that a *Brāhmana* should invoke fire during spring season, *Kshatriya* in summer and *Vaisya* in winter. Some yagyas are to be performed at dusk, some at day break and some are performed in a particular month and *paksha*. *Jyotisha* is considered the eye of the Veda. For want of *Jyotisha* Vedic rituals cannot be performed fully well. Therefore, only those possessing sufficient knowledge of *Jyotisha* are entitled to perform Yagya. **Nirukta** is the derivation of words. It primarily deals with the rules to know the derivatives of Vedic words. *Nirukta* is a *bhāsya* of Vedic dictionary called *Nighantu* in which derivative of all words have been given. In *Pānini-shikshā*, the relationship of the Vedāngas with the Vedas has been established by insisting that *Chhandas* are the legs of four Vedas, *Kalpas* are hands, *Jyotisha* eye, *Nirukta* its ears, *Shikshā* its nose and *vyākarana* (grammar) mouth.

Vedānga Jyotisha: Vedānga Jyotisha is the most primitive work of Indian *Jyotisha*. It is supposed to have been written in 5000 B.C. and consists of 44 *Shlokas*. It deals with the rules for the preparation of *panchānga*. It has been written by many or an anonymous author.

Vedānta: Vedānta is the last section of the Vedas but not the end of Vedas as the word may give such meaning. Because *Vedānta* refers to the last section therefore, *Vedānta* signifies *Upanishadas*. But Vedānta means 'the book that is to be read after finishing Vedas.' As the *Upanishadas* are many in number and they contain contradictory views so, in order to resolve these contradictions Vādarāyana Vyās wrote *Brahmansutra*. That *Brahma Sutra* is synonym to *Vedānta* and it is also called *Vedānta Darshan*. The spiritual ideas scattered over here and there in the Vedas have been collected by Vādarāyana Vyāsa and given the form of *Vedānta sutra*, which is called *Brahman sutra*, which consists of four chapters and 550 *Shlokas*. It provides a synthesis of all sentences available in the Vedas related to *Brahmạn*. The **first** chapter is called *Samanvyādhyāya*. Four sutras of the first chapter of the first *pāda* are called *Chatuh-sutri* and are very significant. The **second** chapter is called *Avirodhādhyāya*. In this chapter all disputes of logic and *smriti* have been toned down. The **third** chapter is called *Sādhanādhyāya,* which deals with several *sādhanās* related to *Vedānta* and the **fourth** chapter deals with their outcome or result and is called *Phalādhyāya*. Several scholars have proposed independent theories by writing *bhāsya* on the Vedānta. Some of these are: Shankara, Bhāshkara, Rāmānuja, Mādhva, Nimbārka, Grikantha, Shripati, Ballabhāchārya, Vighnanāshikshu, and Baladeva. The sutras are so cryptic that it cannot be understood without deep study. This is one reason that the philosophers of later generation interpreted them according to their own philosophical cult.

Vedānta literature is very rich. Achārya Shankara has written *bhāysa* on the *Brahmansutra*. Mandana Mishra, a contemporary to Shankara, has written a text on *Vedānta Brahman-Siddhi*. Vāchaspati Mishra has written a *bhāsya*, *Bhāmti Tikā* on Shankara *Brahmansutra Bhāsya*. Sureshvarāchārya has written *Vartikā* on *Upanishada Bhāsya*. His disciple Sarvagyatvamurti has written an interpretation of *Brahmansutra* in verse named *Sankshepa-sāriraka*. Nrisinha Sharmā and Madhusudana Sarasvati have written *Tatvabodhini* and *Sāra Samgrah* respectively. Sri Harsha has written an outstanding work *Khandana-khanda-khādya*. The 13th century scholar Chitsukhāchārya has written an illuminating work *Tatva-dipikā* on it. Mādhvāchārya has also written a book *Panchadasi*. Madhusudana Sarasvati's work *Advaita-siddhi* is the best ever book written on *Vedānta* philosophy. Dharmarājadhvarindra and Sadānanda have written *Vedānta Paribhāsa* and *Vedānta-sāra* respectively, which are very popular works on *Vedānta* Philosophy.

Vedic Gods: There are three categories of Vedic gods according to their abodes: heavenly gods (*dyutasthāna*), gods of Universe (*antarikshasthāna*) and earthly gods (*prithvisthāna*). Varuna, Pusāna, Surya, Vishnu, Shiva and Ushā are considered heavenly gods. Indra, Rudra and Māruta are placed in the category of gods of universe and among earthly gods Agni, Brihaspati and Soma can be included. Vedic gods are merely reflections of Natural entities like Surya, (the Sun); Ushā, (Morning); Varuna, (Water); Agni, (Fire) and Māruta, (Air). The external form of Vedic gods is imaginary but their inherent power is attached to natural objects. No reference to idol worship is available in the *Rig* Veda, though in the sutra texts idol has been mentioned. All gods have been depicted as benevolent, long-lived and capable of granting prosperity to their disciples, except Rudra who is likely to cause panic. Vedic gods are epitomes of excellent moral values. The relationship between gods and *yajamānas* (disciples) is that of the benefactor and the receiver. As many as 30 gods have been mentioned in the *Rig* Veda and at some places, they have been referred to as Triguna. Indra, Agni and Soma were the main deities of the *Rig* Veda and Shiva and Vishnu were relegated to secondary position. At the initial stage of the *Rig* Veda polytheism was popular, but with the passage of time it was replaced by monotheism. One of the features of Vedic gods is that whoever is invoked, is considered the most powerful, others become secondary under him. It is henotheism.

Among all the Vedic gods **Varuna** is the most charitable. He is considered the god of water. Varuna signifies one who covers everything (*Āvaranakartā*). He radiates in the blue sky through, which he covers the entire world. In the *Rig* Veda he is placed next to Indra, in so far as the number of mantras to be attributed to him is concerned. Every worldly object is guided by the rules framed by him. In course of time his power declined and he was merely reduced to the status of a minor god. The Greek god Helios can be equivalent and synonym to Surya, yet Surya is more powerful and potent. He is considered the guardian of the entire world who silently monitors the activities of worldly creatures. He is also referred to as Ushāspati. He is bent upon extending the duration of day and blessing people with long life. **Vishnu** has been depicted as a minor god in the Vedas. He has been referred to as *Trivikrama* since he travels in all the three *lokas* (worlds). He is called Vishnu because he is perceived (*vyāpta*) in everybody. He achieved excellence in the Paurānic Period. There are less mantras offering prayers to Vishnu than to Surya, **Savitā** and Pusāna. **Ushā** is a significant god of the *Rig* Vidic period. With the arrival of Ushā, darkness is removed. The light of Surya delights her. **Indra** is the most powerful god of the universe. Almost 1/4th *suktas* of the *Rig* Veda have been dedicated to him. He is the most powerful god. He keeps a *Vajra* in his hand and overpowers all gods by his strength. He has been referred to as one who ensures victory to Arya and has also been referred to as *Puranadara* (breaker of the forts).

The prayer to **Rudra** has been offered only in three *suktas* of the *Rig* Veda. He is a minor god and is placed next to Agni, Varuna and Indra. In the *Rudrādhyāya* of Yajur Veda, he has been referred to as one having 1000 eyes and blue neck. In the *Rig* Veda, Rudra has also been addressed as Shiva. In one of the *Shlokas* of the *Rig* Veda, he has been referred to as *Trayambaka* (three eyed). **Māruta** has been accepted as the offspring of Rudra. He has been referred to, independently in 33 *suktas* and in 7 *suktas* along with Indra. He is supposed to have been invoked for overcoming the diseases, evading dangers and for bringing rainwater. **Agni** is the most powerful god of the earth. He is supposed to be the connecting link between God and man. The offerings made by man, is dispatched to gods through Agni. He is placed next to Indra, as he has been referred to in about 200 *suktas* in the *Rig* Veda. The worship of **Soma** has been described in 120 *suktas* in the *Rig* Veda.

Vedic Sāhitya: Vedic Sāhitya, popularly called Vedic Wāngamaya, is broadly divided in two categories: **Shruti** and **Smriti**. Vedic literature includes *Samhitās*, *Brāhmana*, *Aranyaka*, *Upanishadas*, and Vedānga. There are four *Samhitās:* Rig Veda, Sāma Veda, Ajura Veda and Atharva Veda whom we treat as the complete Vedas while Vedas are almost infinite in number, and are '*aparājeya*' (indefatigable).

Brāhmana texts deal with the rituals and ways to perform yagya. Aranyakas are devoted to those who have surrendered themselves at the feet of God. *Brāhmana*, *Aranyaka* and *Upanishada* are related to *Karmakānda*, *Upāsanakānda* and *Gyānakānda*.

The *Rig* Veda is the rock bottom of all Vedic literature. Of the five branches of the *Rig* Veda: *Sākala, Vaskala, Āsvalāyana, Sāmkhāyana* and *Māndukya*, only *Sākala* branch exists.

Brāhmana Granthas (texts) have been written in prose. Each Veda has a separate *Brāhmana*. It is basically concerned with rituals (*karmakānda*). *Aranyakas* consist of several philosophical ideas.

Upanishadas are the concluding parts of the Vedas. The objective of the Upanishada is to secure the knowledge of Brahman.

Venisamhāra: Venisamhāra is a drama written by Bhatta Nārāyana. It is dominated by *Vira rasa*. Its plot has been derived from the story of the *Mahābhārata* narrating the vow of Draupadi not to braid unless she avenges the humiliating treatment meted out to her by Duhshāsan.

It has been written in six acts. The **first** act begins with Krishna leaving for a peace mission to avert the ongoing strife between the *Pandavas* and the *Kauravas*. This news dashes the hopes of Bhima and Draupadi, awaiting the battle eagerly to avenge the humiliation suffered at the court of Duryodhana. Bhima consoles Draupadi telling her that he would soon tear away the thighs of Duryodhana, and wash her hair with his blood. The pleasure soon returns to the face of Draupadi, as the talks between Krishna and the *Kauravas* fail to yield a positive outcome and Yudihisthira gave a go ahead for the battle to settle the differences.

The **second** act deals with the apprehensions of Duryodhana's wife caused by an omen which she has been subject to and tries her level best to avert the impending danger likely to take place in the immediate aftermath of the omen. Towards the end of the act a treacherous incident of the killing of Abhimanyu takes place and Arjuna pledges to avenge the murder by killing Jayadratha by dawn.

The **third** act deals with the death of Dronāchārya and the clash between Aswathāma and Karna for the stewardship of the *Kaurva* army. In the meantime, Bhima grabs Duhshāsana and Duryaodhana, Karna and Aswathama come to his rescue but the efforts prove in vain, and Bhima manages to kill Duhshāsana. The clash between Aswathāma and Karma blows out of proportion and the former failing to get the stewardship promises not to use weapons till Karna is alive.

The **fourth** act deals with the wailing of Duryodhana consequent upon the death of Duhshāsana. In the **fifth** act Dhritarāshtra and Gāndhāri compel Duryodhana to agree to come to terms and stop fighting but he rejects their proposal. He immediately rushes to battlefield in the wake of the killing of Karna. Bhima and Arjuna also arrive and Bhima makes sarcastic remarks to Gāndhāri, which Duryodhana opposes severely leading to the clash between the two. In the meantime, Aswastthāma expresses his wrath against Karna, which makes Duryodhana angry.

In the **sixth** act a new twist has been given to the story. Yudhisthira is apprehensive of the future of Bhima who had pledged to kill Duryodhana by dawn otherwise he would himself commit suicide. Duryodhana is nowhere visible. In the meanwhile, a messenger brings the message of clash between Duryodhana and Bhima and the latter is almost certain to inflict a crushing defeat upon the former. Draupadi's joys know no bound. She is almost certain to wash her hair in Duryodhana's blood.

At this point the drama takes a sudden shift. One of the servants of Duryodhana disguising himself into an ascetic reaches there with the information that Bhima was killed in the battle, and Arjuna is almost on the brink of humiliating debacle. This heart-rending scene leaves Yudhisthrira and Draupadi spellbound with the latter's desires dashing down to the ground. In the meantime some one appears on the scene looking at the enemy (Duryodhana) before him. Yudhisthira catches hold of his weapon. He tries to tighten his grip over Duryodhana with the intention to kill him. Actually the newcomer was Bhima and Yudhisthira loses his hold only when Bhima introduces him. Bhima is released and he ties the hair of Draupadi with the blood of Duryodhana. The story ends with *Bharata Vākya*.

Venkatadhvari: Venkatadhvari was a staunch admirer of Rāmanuja sect. He wrote three popular *champu kāvyas*: *Vishvagunādarsha Champu, Hastigiri Champu* and *Uttararamacharita Champu. Vishvagunādarsha Champu* consists of 254 *khandas* and 597 *Shlokas*. In this *Champu* the poet deals with two imaginary *Gandharvas* Krishānu and Vishvavasu committed to have a glimpse of the entire world. The entire *Champu* has been written in the form of dialogue. *Uttara Rāmacharita Champu* deals with the story of *Uttara kānda* of the *Rāmāyana*. He has also written a *kāvya Laxmisahāsranāma*.

Venkata Nāth's Hansa-sandesha: An eminent scholar of Rāmanuja sect, Venkata Nāth belongs to the 14th century. He is considered a great interpreter of *Vedānta*. He has written *kāvya*s like *Hansa-sandesha, Kumāra-sambhava,* and *Yādavābhyudaya* (an epic in 21 cantos). He has also written a drama *Samkalpa Suryodaya*.

The story of *Hansa-sandesha* has been derived from the *Rāmāyana*. It deals with the message dispatched by Rāma through the swan to Sitā, kept forcefully by Rāvana in *Ashoka Vatikā*. The story precedes the fierce battle of Rāma with Rāvana. The poet has presented the story of the *Rāmāyana* in brief in *Madākrāntā Chhanda*. This *kāvya* has been divided into two *āsvāsas* consisting of 111 *Shlokas*.

Vetāla Panchavinshati: Vetāla Panchavinshati is a favourite book among the common mass of India. The book is designed to moralise. The suspense and curiosity of readers are sustained throughout. There is continuity in the narration of the stories and one story is artistically linked up to the other story till the chain terminates. The beauty of the book lies, not so much in the tales as in the manner of telling. It is fraught with prose, and *Shlokas* have also been used at regular interval. It is a collection of 25 mythical stories which narrate the story of king Vikrama and the Vidyādhar Vetāla. These hilarious stories have been compiled by Shivadāsa. Vetāl hangs on the soldiers of king Vikrama and narrates some stories and at the end of each story puts some questions with the condition that if the king avoids to give the answer his head would be broken into hundred parts, and if he answers correctly the Vetāla would return to the tree. King Vikrama answers them correctly and Vetāla returns to the branch of the tree. He tells 24 stories and every time Vikrama brings him down from the tree and marches towards the burning ghāt. The Vetāla is pleased with the wisdom and bravery of the king and reveals the secret plans of the monk. On the suggestion of Vetāla, Vikrama kills him and gets all the supernatural powers, the *kāpālika* was trying to get.

Viddha-shālabhanjikā: Viddha-shālabhanjikā is a *natikā* (minor drama) by Rājashekhara. It is based on *Mālavikāgnimitra,*

Ratnāvali and *Svapna Vāsavadattā*. It deals with the love story of prince Vidyādhara Malla and two princesses Mrigānkavati and Kuvalayā Mālā.

The **First act** begins with the story of king of Latā accepting her daughter Mrigānkavati as son named Mrigānkavat Varmana and dispatching her to the court of Vidyādhara Malla. One day, Vidyadhara tells his buffoon that in a state of dream he wanted to catch hold of a beautiful girl who manages to escape leaving the garland of pearls. The minister of Vidyādhara is aware of the secret of Mrigānkavat Varmana that he is a girl, and one who marries her will be a *chakravarti samrāta*. Therefore he deliberately keeps her close to the king so that, the latter gets infatuated towards her. Mrigānkavat Varmana saw the king placing the garland of pearls in the neck of his beloved Viddha shālabhanjika.

In the **second act**, efforts are on to get Mrigānkavat Varmana married to Kuvalayā Mālā. One day, king Vidyadhara sees Mrigānkavat varmana in his original form and falls in love with her. In the **third act**, the king arranges a meeting with Mrigānkavat Varmana and offers her his proposal. In the **fourth act** the queen comes to know that Mrigānkavat Varmana is a lady. She receives a severl jolt and was compelled to get Kuvalayā Mālā married to the king.

Vidyādhara: Vidyādhara was an eminent critic. In his critical treatise, *Ekāvali*, he has made an analysis of all the ten parts of *kāvya*. The illustration of this book is his own composition. It has been written to glorify Narsingh, the king of *Utakala*. It has three component parts *Kārikā*, *Vritti* and illustrations. All these three have been attributed to Vidyādhara. It consists of 8 *unmesha*. The **first** *unmesha* deals with the nature of poetry. The **second** deals with *Vritti*, the **third** and the **fourth** with *Dhvani* and *Guni-bhuta-vyangya* respectively. The **fifth** *unmesha* deals with *guna* and style, the **sixth** with defects, the **seventh** with *Shabdālankāra* and the **eighth** throws light on *Arthālankāra*. *Ekāvali* is deeply influenced by *Dhvanyāloka*, *Kāvyaprakāsha* and *Alankāra-sarvasava*. Vidyādhara has also written a text on sexology entitled *Keli-rahasya*.

Vigyāna Bhikshu: Vigyāna Bikshu is the last renowned scholar of the philosophical school of *Sāmkhya*. He belongs to the 16th century. He has written *bhāsyas* on *Sāmkhya*, *Yoga* and *Vedānta*. He has also written a commentary on *Sāmkhya Sutra* named *Sāmkhya pravachana Bhāsya*. He has written *Yoga-vartikā* on Vyāsa *bhāsya* and *Vigyāna-amrita-bhāsya* on *Brahman Sutra*. In his two other works *Sāmkhya-sāra* and *Yoga-sāra*, he has presented an abridged form of the principles of various theories.

Vijjikā: Vijjikā is an eminent poetess of Samskrit. No work of her has yet been identified. In the collection of *suktis*, however, some of her verses are available. Several critics have quoted the *Shlokas* of Vijjikā in their works. Mukula Bhatta in *Abhidhā-vritta-mātrikā* and Mammata in *Kāvya-prakāsha* have quoted her *Shlokas*.

Vikramorvasiya: Vikramorvasiya is a *trotaka* (a kind of *Upa-rupaka*) written by Kālidāsa in five acts. Its characters represent both human and divine categories. It deals with the love story of Pururvā and Urvashi. On his way back to *Indraloka* from *Kailāsha*, Pururvā comes to know about the abduction of Urvashi by a monster Keshi when she was coming out of palace of Kubera. Pururvā frees her from the clutches of the monster and is attracted by the beauty of Urvashi. In the meantime, Pururvā receives a letter from Urvashi showing her love for him. At this juncture, Bharat stages a drama enacting the *svayamvara* of Lakshmi. Urvashi plays the role of Lakshmi. Unfortunately, she recites the name of Pururvā instead of Purusottam. Bharata is infuriated and he curses her that she will be deprived of the pleasure of heaven. Indra tells her to remain on the earth till Pururvā beholds his son. Urvashi's friends hand over Urvashi to Pururvā. One day, while Pururvā and Urvashi were enjoying their company at the Gandhmādana Mountain, Pururvā glances at a Vidyādhari, which infuriates Urvashi. Out of frustration she goes to Gandhamādana garden of Kārtikeya and is converted into a plant. Actually, women were prohibited from entering that place. In case a woman dared go there, she was to be converted into a plant. Pururvā loses his mental equilibrium as Urvashi was missing. In the meantime, the oracle is made that he must have *sangamaniya* jewel with him while embracing the plant. In this way, he may regain the company of Urvashi. Pururvā embraces Urvashi with the jewel and she returns to life. They return to their kingdom. One day, a tribal lady appears to the court with a boy declaring him as the son of Urvashi. Once the identity of the boy is deciphered Urvashi is freed from the curse and she immediately goes to heaven. Pururvā becomes insane in the absence of Urvashi and decides to go to the forest leaving the throne to his son. At this juncture, Nārada approaches telling Pururvā that by the grace of Indra, he will be joining the company of Urvashi for long. Kālidāsa has used a famous story for the play.

The curse of Bharata, and Urvashi changing into a plant are the innovations of the dramatist. They have given added charm to this drama.

Vishākhadatta: Vishākha Datta was an eminent poet and dramatist. Besides his monumental drama *Mudrā-rākshasa*, he wrote another play *Devichandragupta.* The reference to this drama is found in *Nātya-darpana* and *Shringāra-prakāsha*. It deals with the love-story of Dhruvaswāmini and Chandragupta and the cowardly treatment of his elder brother Rāma Gupta. *Mudrā-rākshasa* is a realistic drama dealing with the political upheaval involving Chandragupta, Chānakya and Rākshasa, the minister of Malayaketu. In the preface to this play, he has presented a brief account of his life but it is not sufficient enough to arrive at a concrete conclusion about his early life.

There is no unanimity of opinion among the scholars regarding the period of Viskhādatta. Sri Kantha Shāstri has accepted him as the contemporary of Chandratgupta II. In the *Bharata Vākya* of Mudraraksasa reference to Chandragupta has been given; but Carpelius considers him the contemporary of Samudragutpa.

Vishnu-dharmottara Purāna: Vishnu-dharmottara-purāna is placed among 18 *Up-Purāna*s. It is an encyclopaedia of Indian art, which deals with Sculpture, Painting, Architecture and Criticism. A thorough interpretation of Nātya-*Shāstra* and criticism is in it in as many as, 1000 *Shlokas*. The text begins with the dialogue between Vajra and Mārkandeya. Mārkandeya has ruled that only that idol of god is worth worshipping, which has followed the instructions given in *chitra-sutra*, a section in this *Purāna* dealing with various kinds of arts including architecture, painting and sculpture.

Vishnu Purāna: Vishnu Purāna is the third *Purāna* in order. It eulogises Vishnu as the sole deity. It is divided into six sections and 126 chapters. It consists of 6000 *Shlokas*. Parāshara has narrated the story to Maitreya.

The **first** section deals with the story of Dhruva and Prahalāda, besides the graphic description of the universe. The **second** section is confined to the geographical description dealing with seven island, oceans and *Sumeru* Mountain. The **third** section deals with the rights and duties to be performed in a hermitage.

The **fourth** section is packed with historical evidences presenting the dynastic history of the kings of *Suryavansa* and *Chandravansa*; besides dealing with the *Pāndavas, Kauravas*, Rāma and Krishna. It also presents an account of the coming dynasties like *Magadh, Shishunāga, Nanda, Maurya* and *Sunga*. The **fifth** section deals with the story of Lord Krishna as narrated in the *Bhāgavata*. The sixth section deals with four Yugas: *Krita, (Sat) Tretā*, *Dvāpara* and *Kaliyuga*.

It is supposed to have been written before the Christian era. According to *Nāradiya Purāna*, it consists of 24000 *Shlokas*. Three commentaries on this *Purāna* are available. They include a commentary of Shridhara Svāmi, *Vishnuchittiya* by Vishnuchitta, and *Vaisnava-kuta Chandrikā* by Ratnagarbha Bhattāchārya.

Viswanātha: Viswanātha was an eminent citric, poet and dramatist of the 14th century whose popularity rests chiefly on his critical treatise *Sāhitya Darpana*. He was born in a prominent *Brāhmana* family of *Utkala*. His father Chandrashekhara had written books like *Pushpamālā* and *Bhāshārnava,* references to which are available in the *Sāhitya Darpana*. The period of Viswanātha has been fixed between 1300 and 1350 AD. He has also composed an epic: *Rāghava Vilāsa*, a *Prākrit Kāvya*: *Kuvalayas-charita* and dramas including: *Prabhāvati Parinaya* and *Chandrakalā* and a commentary on *Kāvya-prakāsha* entitled *kāvya-prakāsha Darpana*.

Sāhitya Darpana is the most celebrated of all his books. It consists of 10 chapters. It contains all the subjects falling within the domain of Samskrit poetics including *Nātya Shāstra*. A detailed discussion of the nature, kinds and purpose of *Kāvya*, *Shabda-shakti*, *Rasa*, *Dhavni*, *Riti*, *Guna, Dosha*, *Alnkāra, Drishya* and *shravya Kāvya* and *Nāyaka-Nāyikā Bheda* has been made which is sufficient testimony to his scholarship. Vishwanātha has accepted *Rasa* as the essence and soul of poetry, and has analysed it in an indeperndent way. To him *Rasa* is not a part of Dhvani. Thus, he was a Rasavādi Āchārya and has defined *kāvya* as one steeped in *Rasa* (*Vākayam Rasātmakam Kāvyam*). Viswanātha says that ornate poetry may enchant us for the time being but it cannot give us permanent pleasure. Pleasure emanating from Verbal effect is short lived. Therefore, all devices that make poetry readable are ancillary to one cherished goal: to relish *rasa*. He has extended the scope of *Alanakāra*. He has multiplied the number of *Alankāras* by adding many new *Alankāras*. Panditrāj Jagnnātha in his *Rasagangādhara* had raised some controversial points with regard to Alankāras and Viswanātha provided the answers in his *Sāhitya Darpana*.

Vishweshwara Pandita: A renowned scholar and aesthetician, Vishweshwara Pandita has written a matchless work *Alankāra-kaustubha*. He flourished at the beginning of the 18th century. He has written on grammar, criticism and logic with the same force and vigour. His works are: *Vyākarana-siddhānta-sudhā-nidhi, Tarka-kautuhala, Didhita-pravesha, Alankāra-kaustubha, Alankāra-muktāvali, Alankārapradip, Rasa-chandrikā* and *Kavindra-kanthā-bharana*. Of these works, the first is a grammatical text, next two are based on the philosophy of *Nyāya* and the rest are devoted to poetics. *Alankāra-kaustubha* is his masterpiece in which he has given a systematic and coherent analysis of 61 poetic figures.

Vyākarana: Vyākarana is called the mouth of the Vedas. It occupies the third place among the Vedāngas. It has been highly praised in the Vedas. There is a popular mantra in the *Rig Veda,* which describes *Vyākarana* as a bull with four horns: *Nāma, Ākhyata, Upsarga* and *Nipāta* and three legs forming three kālas (tenses) present, past and future. *Sup* and *Tinga* are two hands and seven *vibhakties* are his seven hands. This bull is fastened at three places *Ura* (heart), *Kantha* (neck, throat) and *Sira* (head) (*Rig Veda* 4/28/6). Another mantra in the *Rig Veda*, says that a man not acquainted with *Vyākarana* does not see even though he sees and does not hear even though he hears. *Vyākarana* discloses its secret to a true inquisitive in the same manner in which a woman undresses herself before her husband (*Rig Veda* 10/71/4). Patanjali has laid down 13 objectives and purposes of the use of grammar. This issue has been discussed in detail in the very beginning of *Mahā-bhāsya*. Achārya Vararuchi has pointed out five objectives of the use of grammar. The following are five purposes of the use of grammar: to protect the reading of the Vedas (*rakshā*); to innovate new *padas* (*Uha*); to read the Veda along with the different organs of Āgama; to marshal all the *shātras* in short time with minimum of labour (*laghu*) and to help remove confusion while understanding Vedic terminology (*Asandeha*).

Grammar originates from the *Rig Veda*. Derivatives of several words have been given in the *Rig Veda*. Grammar developed as an independent branch of knowledge in India and all the branches of linguistics were incorporated into it. In *Brāhmana* texts *krita, kurvat* and *karishyata* have been used according to *linga*, (Gender) *vachana* (Number) and *kāla* (Tense). *Aranyakas* and *Upanishadas* have also dealt with *vara, usmān, dhātu*, *pratipadika, nāma, ākhyāta, pratyaya* and *vibhakti*. *Gopatha Brāhmana* also deals with several grammatical terms and rules.

According to the Indian tradition Brahmā gave the first grammar. Brihaspati further elaborated it. It is mentioned in the *Mahā-bhāsya* that Brihaspati had propagated *pratipada*. In the pre-Pānini era, a healthy tradition of grammar was already in existence. At least 13 grammarians in the pre-Pānini era have made a mark with their outstanding contributions. They include Indra, Vāyu, Bharadwāj, Bhāguri, Charāyana, Kashakritsna, Vaiyāgrapāda, Mādhyāndini, Raudhi, Shaunaka, Gautama and Vyādi. Ten other grammarians have been referred to in Pānini's *Ashtādhyāyi*. They are: Apishali, Kāshyapa, Gārgya, Gālava, Chakra Varmana, Shāklya, Sakatāyana, Senaka, Sphotāyana, Bhārdwāja. In this way, before the advent of Pānini, Samskrit grammar had assumed special significance with as many as 23 grammarians laying down the foundation of independent school of grammar enabling Samskrit grammar to open new horizons. Among these grammar schools the following schools were famous: Aindra; Bhāguriya; Karmānda; Senkiya; Kāshyapiya; Chakra-varmaniya; Āpishali and Vyāsiya school. Pānini is indebted to these grammarians in manifold ways.

For the sake of convenience the history of Samskrit grammar can be divided into five periods - (i) Pre-Pānini period, from beginning up to Pānini; (ii) *Muni-traya* period, from Panini to Patanjali, (iii) The period of interpretation, from kasika to 1000 A.D. (iv) Prakriya period-1000-1700 A.D.(v) The fifth period begins with 1700 onwards.

Pānini, Kātyāyana and Patanjli are the *Muni-traya*. They are the pioneers of Samskrit *Vyākarana;* and they have been rightly called three *munies* (Muni-traya) of Samskrit grammar. They wrote *Sutra, Vartikā* and *Bhāsya* respectively. Actually, Pānini overshadowed them. As a result only Pānini is quoted almost everywhere.

The *Sutras* by Pānini were difficult to comprehend and required elucidation. So Vartikās were written. Some of the Vartikās are in prose while others are in rhythmical poetry. New trends of grammar emerged in course of commenting upon the works of Pānini and Patanjali.

Among the writers of *Vritti*s on *Ashtādhyāyi* the joint venture of Jayāditya and Vāmana *Vritti-kāsikā* is outstanding, the former writing 8 chapters and the latter 3 chapters.

Vimala Sarasvati took efforts to make Pānini's grammar convenient with *Rupa-mālā* that came in 1350 A.D. This text was completed on the pattern of *Kaumudi* and sutras were arranged according to the subjects.

Besides Pānini, independent tradition of grammar also branched out which led to the foundation of numerous schools, which are still in practice. These sects (*sampradaya*), are: Chandra; Jainendra; Shākatāyana; Haim; Karantra; Sarasvati; Bopadeva; Kramādiswara; Jaumara and Saupadya school.

The 6th century Buddhist scholar wrote *Chandra* grammar. It became very popular in Sri Lankā. The 13th century Buddhist scholar Kāshyapa enriched Chandra grammar through his text *Balava-bodha*.

The grammar of Jaina sect is called Jainendra grammar. Mahavira wrote it. It is the outcome of the questions raised by Mahavira before Indra. It is called Jainendra because it seems to be an outcome of the joint effort of Jina (Mahavira) and Indra. It consists of 1000 sutras out of which 300 have been collected from other sources. Somadeva has written a commentary on it.

In the 9th century Svetāmabara Jain scholar Shākatāyana who wrote *Shabdanushāsana* founded Shākatāyan School. It consists of 8 chapters and 4500 sutras.

The last watermark of development of Samskrit grammar is available in the philosophy of grammar. The grammarians have accorded the status of *Brahman* to *Shabda* (word) i.e. *Shabda-Brahman*. The significant contribution to the philosophy of grammar is *sphota-darshana*.

Vālmiki is accredited with the honour of giving the first grammar of *Prākrita*. His work is called *Prākrita sutra* or *Vālmiki sutra*. The 14th century scholar Trivirakrama Pandita wrote a commentary on it entitled *Prākrita-sutra Vritti*.

Vyakti-viveka: Vyakti-Viveka is a seminal book on Indian poetics written by Māhimbhatta. It was written to controvert *Dhvani* theory propounded by Anandavardhana in *Dhvanyāloka*. In its very prologue, its author has expressed his intention. *Vyakti-viveka* has been divided into three sections.

Veda Vyās: The name of Veda Vyāsa is very famous as the author of many philosophical and literary treatises. He is considered the author of the *Mahābhārata*, *Brahman-Sutra*, *Bhāgavata* and many *Purānas*. He is that greatest editor. who edited and arranged the Vedas. The process and the tradition that he created is so perfect that it is still followed. According to ancient belief, Veda Vyās is born in every Dwāpara era. In *Vishnu purāna*, 28 Vyās are mentioned. Krishna Dwaipāyana Vyāsa is the 28th Vyāsa. ■■

Yāgyavalkya *Smriti*: The Yāgyavalkya Smriti text has been written by Yāgyavalkya. He has been addressed in *Brihdāranyaka Upanishada*, as a great philosopher. The relationship between Yāgyavalkya *Upanishada* and *Shukla* Yajurveda has also been established. Kātyāyana in his *Vartikā* of *Ashtādhyāyi* has acknowledged him as the author of Yāgyavalkya *Smriti*. In Yāgyavalkya *Smriti* also Yāgyavalkya has been accepted as the author of *Aranyakas*. Although scholars have shown their disinclination on the issue of identical authorship of both *Brāhmanas* and *Aranyakas*, the commentator of Yāgyavalkya, Vigyānesvara in his book *Mitākshara* has asserted that the abridged form of *Dharma shāstra* may have been produced by certain disciple of Yāgyavalkya.

Yāgyavalkya *Smriti* consists of three *kāndas*. The **first** *kānda* deals with the analysis of 20 dharma and 14 Knowledge, constitution of the council, all *sȧmskārs* (rites) from the time of conceiving till the marriage, duty of a *brahmachāri* (celibate) and the prohibited objects and requirements from a girl who comes of age, eight kinds of marriages, inter-caste marriage, rights and duties of four *varnas*, *Vedic yagya*, *Shrāddha* and its period, method of *Shrāddha*, State religion, qualities of a king, minister, *Purohita* and rule of law. The **second** *kānda* is devoted to the description of the members of court, judge, his works, charges to secure securities, kinds of court, rate of interest, oath, partition, share of woman in partition, joint ownership of father and sons, succession of an issueless father, right of husband over the property of wife, defamation and adultery. The **third** *kānda* includes offering of water to dead ones, rules of purification after birth and death, three types of works according to *sat, raj* and *tam*.

Yajur Veda: Yajur Veda is related to *Adhvaryus* whose objective is to accomplish *yagya*. It consists of prayers intended for *Adhvaryus*. Various layers of meanings have been attached to the term '*Yajus*'. Some scholars maintain that *yajus* signifies a collection of hymns written in prose and chanted at the time of performing *yagya*. Excess of prose hymns have probably given it the name *yajus*. It occupies an independent position among all the Vedas on account of its emphasis on *karma*. This Veda is directly related to *Yagya-anusthāna*. Yajur Veda has got a very extensive literature. Patanjali has streamlined approximately 100 branches of Yajur Veda. It has two branches- *Krishna* Yajurveda and *Shukla* Yajurveda. *Shuklayajurveda* is more significant. The mantras of *Shuklayajurveda* are called *Vājasaneyi samhitā*, which consists of 40 chapters and the last 15 chapters are termed as *khila*, have been accepted as later work. They have been written keeping in view the different kinds of *Yagya*s. The first two chapters deal with mantras relating to *darsha* and *purnamāsa*. The 31st chapter deals with *Pururvā Sukta*. *Shiva-samkalpa* has been discussed in the 32nd and the 33rd chapters. According to Charanavyuha, Krishna, Yajurveda consists of 85 branches of which only four exist: *Taittariya, Maitrayāni, Katha* and *Kathopanishada samhitā*.

Yaksha-milana-kāvya: Yaksha Milana Kāvya is a *sandesha kāvya* written by Parmesvara Jhā. It is also called *Yaksha Samāgama*. His period dates back between 1913 and 1981. The title of Mahā-mahopādhyāya was conferred upon him. *Yaksha-samāgama* deals with the story contained in the *uttara* section of *Meghaduta*. The poet has presented a bewitching picture of Yaksha and his beloved. Yaksha enquires about the well being of his beloved. He narrates several kinds of stories to her. He awakes from slumber in the morning after listening to the songs of Bhattas, and the panic-ridden Yaksha appears before Kubera. Kubera is pleased with him and gives him a very coveted and responsible job. Both Yaksha and his wife lead a very pleasant life for several years. This *sandesha kāvya* consists of 35 *shlokas*. It has been written in *Mandākrāntā Chhanda*.

Yasastilaka Champu: Yasha Tilaka is a *Champu Kāvya* written by Somadeva Suri, the court poet of Krishna III, the *Rāshtrakuta* king.

The Jaina Saint Sudatta wrote this *Champu Kāvya* in 959 A.D. *Yasastilaka Champu* deals with the initiation of king Māridatta into Jainism. The story of Yashodharā was narrated to Māridatta, a cruel king who was initiated into religious order by Abhaya Ruchi, the disciple of Jaina Saint Sudatta. The story of Yashodharā has also been depicted in *Jaina Purānas*. The poet has taken the story from ancient texts and has given it a new twist by introducing numerous changes within its framework. This *Champu* accommodates the story of Yashodharā and that of Māridatta. It has been raised to the position of a religious text. The text consists of 8 *Ashvāsas* or chapters. The first five chapters deal with the story and the rest three chapters are aimed at propagating the teachings of Jainism displaying nirvāna as its prime objective and *shānta rasa* is its dominant *rasa*. The tinge of *shringāra rasa* cannot be overlooked. The poet has used an enriched prose style and smaller sentences as per the demand of the time. Its verses embrace almost all the qualities of an ideal poetry. The *Champu* begins with the poet streamlining his approach with regard to *Kāvya* accepting the significance of preceding poets. He has quoted from the works of several poets in the fourth chapter. One more work *Niti-vākya-amrita* has also been attributed to Somadeva.

Yatirājavijaya Champu: Yati-rāja-vijaya *Champu* has been attributed to Ahobala Suri. He flourished in the 2nd half of the 14th century. *Yatirājavijaya Champu* has been divided into 17 *Ullāsas* but the last one is incomplete. Depicting the strong tradition of the scholars of the *Vishishtādvaita* sect, the poet has dealt with the life of Rāmānujāchārya. Its style is simple and compressed and pun has been used at several places.

Yoga School of Philosophy: Yoga Philosophy, is a school of Indian philosophy propounded by Patanjali. It lays emphasis on restrain or inner self (*mana, buddhi* and *ahamkāra*) through meditation. The term Yoga has been originated from *'Yusa'*, which signifies trance or intense meditation. *Yoga Sutra* is its original text compiled by Patanjali. Scholars are of the opinion that the author of *Mahā-bhāsya* and the pioneer of Yoga school were one and the same person. Although various yogic processes are very old and its reference has also been given in *Samhitās, Brāhmanas* and

Upanishadas. Yāgyavalkya *Smriti* has stated that *Hiranyagarbha* was the pioneer of Yoga and Patanjali had only propagated it.

Patanjali *Yoga Sutra* is divided in four *Vibhāgas* or *Pāda*: *Samādhi Pāda; Sādhanā Pāda; Vibhuti Pāda* and *Kaivalya Pāda*. The **first** deals with the nature of Yoga, aim and features, measures to restrain mental equipoise and the analysis of several kinds of Yoga. The **second** deals with the *Kriyā Yoga*, suffering, outcome of action and measures to eradicate suffering. The **third** deals with the internal stages of Yoga and the supernatural powers acquired through Yogic practices. The **fourth** deals with the analysis of *Moksha* or Liberation, soul and the other world. That is the reason that Yoga is a complete philosophy and is not limited to only *āsanas*, physical exercises.

Yoga observes and maintains that the restraint of bodily and mental dispositions is a prerequisite to understand the real identity of soul or *ātmān*. Restrain signifies victory over body, mind, senses, intellect and ego (*ahamkāra*). Once this feat is achieved, separation of soul from external organs can be vouchsafed. Liberation from suffering or *Mukti* can be achieved through *ātmagyāna*, self-knowledge and the knowledge of the self.

Yoga has eight divisions: *Yama, Niyam, Āsanas, Dhyāna, Dhāranā, Pranāyāma, Pratyāhāra* and *Samādhi*. The first five are called external means and the rest are called internal means. Five Yamas must be observed: *Ahimsā* (non-violence); *Satya* (truth); *Asteya* (not stealing); *Aparigraha* (detachment) and *Brahmacharya* (celibacy). Niyama includes: *shaucha* (external and internal purity); *santosha* (contentment) *tapa* (penance); and *Ishwar parnidhāna* (Meditation on God and surrendering completely to Him). Āsanas are aimed at reviving strength, concentration and discipline. The *āsanas* are of several kinds: *padmāsana, virāsana, bhadrāsana, siddhāsana, sirshāsana, garudāsana, mayurāsana* and *shavāsana*. The body remains free from diseases through *āsanas* and it develops the ability to perform meditation. All objects of body are kept in control eschewing perversion.

Restrain, control and balancing of breath is called **prānāyāma**. It has got three parts: *puraka* (inhaling), *kumbhaka* (stopping breath inside) and *rechaka* (exhaling). By performing *prānāyāma*, the body remains healthy. To have control over the senses and to remove their contact with external objects is called **pratyāhāra**. To concentrate one's mind on the desired object is called **dhāranā**. The medition of **dhyeya** (objective) is called *dhyāna*. A Yogi can achieve the desired object through *dhyāna*. The culmination of *Yogāsana* is **samādhi**. At this stage, Yogi dissolves himself into his objective (*dhyeya*). Yogi can acquire several supernatural powers. They are eight in number, such as (i) *Animā* (to reduce oneself to an atom), (ii) *Mahimā* (to enlarge oneself to a mountain), (iii) *Laghimā* (to lighten one's weight), (iv) *Garimā* (to increase one's weight), (v) *Prāpti* (to obtain the desired object), (vi) *Prakāmya* (the will-power of *Yagi* remaining unhindered), (vii) *Vashitva* (to obtain the power to exercise control over all *Jiva*), and (viii) *Yātrā Kāma-vashayitva* (the fulfillment of *samkalpa* or commitment to Yoga). A *Yogi* is strictly prohibited from running after supernatural powers. *Ātma-Darshan* (Vision of the self) should be the final goal of a *Yogi*.

The ancient scholars held that meditation is essential for concentration but succeeding scholars had reposed more faith in God laying emphasis on attaining God. God is considered above all defects and weaknesses. He is eternal, omnipresent, omnipotent and omniscient. Yoga school has given abundant proof for the existence of God. Existence of God has been proved by *smriti* and *shāstras* and joining the company of God is the ultimate objective of man.

Except showing deep and potent faith in the existence of God, Yoga stands on equal footing with *Sāmkhya*.

Yudhishthira: Yudhishthira is an epic written by Vasudeva. He has also compiled epics like *Trapura-dahana* and *Saurikodaya*. It is a *Kāvya* consisting of *yamakas*. The poet has used simple puns in place of composite and complex one. This epic has been divided into 8 *ucchvāsas*. It presents the story of the *Mahābhārata* in a short compass. A commentary of Rājanaka Ratna Kantha has been published on it.

Yudhishthira Mimānsaka: Yudhishthira Mimānsaka was an eminent grammarian of modern times. He was born in Rajasthan is 1909. He has made a detailed study of grammar, *Nirukta, Nyāya* and *Mimāmsā*. He has edited ten eminent works including: *Nirukta samuchchya, Bhāg-vritti sankalanam, Kaskritshna vyākarnama* and *Unādikosha*. He also edited a Samskrit magazine entitled *Veda Vāni*. ■■

More shades of Hinduism

(HB)

Postage Rs. 25/- per book. Rs. 10/- extra for each additional book

---

Available at all leading bookstores or
log on to our online bookstore www.pustakmahal.com

More shades of Hinduism

Postage Rs. 25/- per book. Rs. 10/- extra for each additional book

---

Available at all leading bookstores or
log on to our online bookstore www.pustakmahal.com